The Social Psychology of Nonverbal Communication

The Social Psychology of Nonverbal Communication

Edited by

Aleksandra Kostić
Professor of Social Psychology, University of Niš, Serbia

and

Derek Chadee
Professor of Social Psychology, University of the West Indies, St. Augustine, Trinidad, West Indies

First published 2015 by
PALGRAVE MACMILLAN

Palgrave Macmillan in the UK is an imprint of Macmillan Publishers Limited,
registered in England, company number 785998, of Houndmills, Basingstoke,
Hampshire RG21 6XS.

Palgrave Macmillan in the US is a division of St Martin's Press LLC,
175 Fifth Avenue, New York, NY 10010.

Palgrave Macmillan is the global academic imprint of the above companies
and has companies and representatives throughout the world.

Palgrave® and Macmillan® are registered trademarks in the United States,
the United Kingdom, Europe and other countries.

ISBN 978–1–137–34585–1

This book is printed on paper suitable for recycling and made from fully
managed and sustained forest sources. Logging, pulping and manufacturing
processes are expected to conform to the environmental regulations of the
country of origin.

A catalogue record for this book is available from the British Library.

A catalog record for this book is available from the Library of Congress.

Typeset by MPS Limited, Chennai, India.

To my parents: Eileen and Johnson Chadee; Dolly Ablack (grandmother) – DC
To my children: Marko, Filip, and Una – AK

Contents

List of Figures and Tables

Figures

Tables

Acknowledgments

We thank the following persons and institutions for making this volume move from an idea to a realization. First we say thanks to all of our diligent contributors: Ross Buck, Tony Docan-Morgan, Mark G. Frank, Denise Frauendorfer, David B. Givens, Darrin J. Griffin, Sarah D. Gunnery, Judith A. Hall, Jessica Harvey, Arvid Kappas, Eva Krumhuber, Dennis Küster, Valerie Manusov, Andreas Maroulis, Albert Mehrabian, Mike Miller, Milkica Nešić, Vladimir Nešić, Fernando Poyatos, Marianne Schmid Mast, and Elena Svetieva. Special thanks to Raecho Bachew, Kalifa Damani, Steve Dwarika, and Nikita Ng Ying, and Nylessia Nicome for administrative assistance, literature searches and research assistance.

This book is an output of the ANSA McAL Psychological Research Centre of The University of the West Indies. We thank The University of the West Indies and the ANSA McAL Psychological Research Centre, and The Faculty of Philosophy, Department of Psychology, University of Niš (Serbia) for their support. We express our gratitude to the staff at Palgrave Publishers and in particular Elizabeth Forrest, Niocla Jones and Geetha Williams from MPS Limited. Of all those who provided technical and other kinds of support resulting in this publication, we would like to indicate our deepest appreciation. Of those we may have inadvertently not mentioned, we say thank you for all the encouragement and assistance you rendered.

Notes on Contributors

Ross Buck is Professor of Communication and Psychology at the University of Connecticut. His research is concentrated on social development of motivation and emotion, and emotional communication as the basis of the social order. He is the author of *Human Motivation and Emotion* (1976, 1988, 2002), *The Communication of Emotion* (1984, 2000), and *Emotion: A Biosocial Synthesis* (2014). His research has engaged concepts such as social biofeedback fostering, emotional education and emotional competence, among others.

Derek Chadee is Professor of Social Psychology, Chair, Department of Behavioural Sciences and Director, ANSA McAL Psychological Research Centre, The University of the West Indies, St. Augustine Campus. His current research interests include the social psychology of fear of crime and general fear, antecedents of emotions, copy-cat behaviour, media, HIV, AIDS and jury decision making. He is also a Fulbright Scholar undertaking research on fear of crime in two American universities. He continues to maintain a cross-cultural research agenda.

Tony Docan-Morgan is Associate Professor in the Department of Communication Studies at the University of Wisconsin-La Crosse. Morgan is a Ph.D. graduate of the University of Washington, whose research examines how communication is used to engender change in interpersonal relationships. He developed RelationalTurningPoints.org, a website dedicated to enriching relationships between educators and students. His preoccupation with interpersonal communication has led him to teach courses in effective communication, public speaking, communication studies, and nonverbal communication, as well as "Lying and Deception in Human Interaction," and "Theories of Communication".

Mark G. Frank is Professor of Communication at the State University of New York, at Buffalo, as well as the Director of the Communication Science Center. He is an alumnus of the School of Psychology at the University of New South Wales in Sydney, Australia, and the Communication Department at Rutgers University. A former National Institute of Mental Health postdoctoral fellow in the Psychiatry Department at the University of California, San Francisco, he received his Ph.D. in social and personality psychology from Cornell University.

His research on nonverbal communication, deception, the expression of emotion, and the role of emotion in violence, has led him to work extensively with law enforcement and military authorities, and he has also assisted in the development of automated systems for reading nonverbal communication.

Denise Frauendorfer is currently a postdoctoral fellow at the University of Neuchâtel in Switzerland. She obtained her Ph.D. in 2013 from the same university, and is now engaging in the study nonverbal behavior and first impressions in work settings.

David B. Givens is currently Director of the Center for Nonverbal Studies in Spokane, Washington, lecturer in the School of Professional Studies at Gonzaga University, and author of the online Nonverbal Dictionary, a reference tool which is used around the world. Givens acquired his Ph.D. in anthropology by studying "body language" at the University of Washington in Seattle, Washington, USA, and has since accumulated vast expertise in nonverbal communication, anthropology, and the brain. From 1985 to 1997, he served as Anthropologist in Residence at the American Anthropological Association in Washington, D.C. Givens also has experience of teaching anthropology at the University of Washington.

Darrin J. Griffin (Ph.D. – Buffalo, State University of New York) is Assistant Professor in the Department of Communication Studies at the University of Alabama. His research in deceptive communication integrates the study of linguistics as well as nonverbal behavior, and is designed with the goal of providing practical knowledge of the type utilized by those working in applied settings.

Sarah D. Gunnery became a postdoctoral scholar at Tufts University after she received her Ph.D. in Psychology from Northeastern University. Her research concentrates on the expression and perception of spontaneous and posed facial expressions. This includes investigation of the compensatory function of posed facial expression resulting from a loss of spontaneous facial expressivity in certain populations, such as those with Parkinson's disease.

Judith A. Hall is University Distinguished Professor of Psychology at Northeastern University in Boston, M.A. For over 30 years, her research has been contributing to the discipline of social psychology via her research interest in group and individual differences, including the role of gender in nonverbal communication. She has co-authored, inter alia, *Sensitivity to nonverbal communication: The PONS test* (R. Rosenthal, J. A. Hall, M. R. DiMatteo, P. L. Archer, and D. Archer, 1979). More recently, she co-edited *Nonverbal Communication in Human Interaction* (8th edition, M. L. Knapp, J. A. Hall, and T. G. Horgan, 2014).

Jessica Harvey is Assistant Professor in the Communication Department at Saint Vincent College. She acquired her Ph.D. from the University of Washington. Her research explores parent-child verbal and nonverbal communication as this relates to young people's media use. Her teaching focuses on children and media, mass media, media effects, research methods, and public relations.

Arvid Kappas is Professor of Psychology at Jacobs University, Bremen. Since obtaining his Ph.D. at Dartmouth College, NH, USA, Kappas has acquired international experience, having lived and worked in Switzerland, Canada, the UK, and in Germany, and visiting as Professor in Austria and Italy. His research examines the influence of factors such as social context and cognitive processes on the interaction of components of the emotion system, including what is felt, the expressions shown, and body reactions. Kappas has been Associate Editor of the journals *Emotion* and *Biological Psychology* and also serves on the editorial boards of several journals including *Cognition and Emotion* and the *Journal of Nonverbal Behavior*. In 2011, he co-edited *Face-to-face Interaction over the Internet* (Kappas & Kramer, 2011).

Aleksandra Kostić is Professor of Social Psychology, University of Niš, Serbia. Her research interests include nonverbal communication, emotional experience, ethnic identity, and culture-based similarities and differences.

Eva Krumhuber is an Assistant Professor at University College London, United Kingdom, and has been a member of the editorial board of the *Journal of Nonverbal Behavior* since 2010. Krumhuber's research focuses on the analysis and re-synthesis of facial expressions in human and artificial characters. She has also contributed to the design specifications of artificial systems and investigated processes that lead to the attribution and denial of human-like traits and emotions in humans and virtual agents, while working on the EU FP7-ICT project "eCUTE".

Dennis Küster is currently a Postdoctoral Fellow at Jacobs University, Bremen, Germany. His research focuses on the psychophysiology of online communication, as well as the role of implicit social contexts for psychophysiological and facial responding, and the role of online social contexts in self presentation. He has published works on psychophysiological methods, and is currently involved in a large-scale interdisciplinary research investigation of the role of empathy in learning with robotic tutors.

Valerie Manusov is Professor at University of Washington. Mansunov's research focuses primarily on the ways people interpret nonverbal cues and how such interpretations reflect culture, relationship quality, and personal characteristics. In addition to contributing to the naissance of the Nonverbal Communication Division of the National Communication Association, she has edited the *Sourcebook of Nonverbal Measures: Going beyond Words*, and has co-edited *The Sage Handbook of Nonverbal Communication*.

Andreas Maroulis has a B.A. and M.A. in Communication from the State University of New York, at Buffalo. His research focuses on nonverbal communication, behavior, and automated systems for recognition and judging emotions, particularly in the area of product usage, preferences, and deception. He currently works in the automated computer vision industry in Europe.

Albert Mehrabian is currently Professor Emeritus of Psychology at the University of California, Los Angeles. Mehrabian's experience with engineering and the natural sciences has supplied his psychological research with a distinctively scientific approach, which has contributed immensely to the development of various psychological tools as well as theoretical models aimed at measuring and describing complex psychological phenomena.

Mike Miller is an Assistant Professor in Residence of Communication at the University of Connecticut. His work, which centers on emotions, friendship, and physical touch, has been recently published in *Personal Relationships* and *Nonverbal Behavior*. While his main area of research concerns observable human communication, his efforts to explain innate, biological, and pan-cultural displays related to touch and nonverbal communication have also directed his research towards animal behavior and brain functioning.

Milkica Nešić is currently Full Professor of Physiology at the Department of Physiology, Medical Faculty, University of Niš. After acquiring her first degree in Medicine in 1979, Nešić acquired her Master's degree, looking at the role of interhemispheric asymmetry in discrimination of different tone qualities. She also specializes in Neuropsychiatry and has been instrumental in the organization of courses related to neuroscience and the physiological basis of psychological processes, as well as behavioral and cognitive neuroscience, for both medicine and psychology students at the University of Niš. Nešić is a member of both the Serbian Association of Physiologists and the Serbian Association of Anthropologists, and has published over 100 scientific papers and handbooks in the field of neurophysiology and neuropsychology.

Vladimir Nešić is a Full Professor of Social Psychology, and member of EASP (European Association of Social Psychology), currently employed at the Department of Psychology, Faculty of Philosophy, University of Niš, where he took up tenure in 1973. An alumnus of both the University of Belgrade and the University of Niš, his diverse research interests have included the influence of job satisfaction on mental health, and individual differences in accuracy of person perception. He has also published over 100 scientific papers, and two books on the psychology of music. His work has led him to visit several Departments of Psychology in Germany.

Fernando Poyatos is an accomplished author and leading international scholar in the field of nonverbal communication. In 1993, he became the first Canadian citizen to be admitted to the prestigious Spanish Royal Academy of Language. He has also lectured extensively at universities throughout Europe, and has chaired and organized two international symposiums in Greece. During his 32-year tenure at the University of New Brunswick, Poyatos lectured in the departments of Spanish, anthropology, psychology and sociology, and also served as chairperson of the UNB department of Spanish and Latin American Cultures from 1992 until his retirement in June 1998.

Marianne Schmid Mast is a Professor of Psychology at the Department of Work and Organizational Psychology at the University of Neuchâtel, Switzerland and an Associate Editor of the *Journal of Nonverbal Behavior*. Through her use of immersive virtual environment technology, as well as computer-based automatic sensing and analyzing of nonverbal behavior in social interactions, her research investigates, inter alia, the effects of first impressions on interpersonal interaction, interpersonal sensitivity in the formation of impressions, interaction, communication and perception among persons in power hierarchies, the effects of physician communication on patient outcomes, and the effects of first impressions and nonverbal behavior in job interviews.

Elena Svetieva is a postdoctoral research fellow at the School of Business and Economics, Católica-Lisbon. With a background in communication and psychology, her research focuses on processes of emotion expression and expression regulation in organizational and interpersonal contexts. Current projects focus on the antecedents and consequences of expression suppression, both in everyday life and specific events such as social exclusion.

Introduction

The interest of scientists in studying different aspects of nonverbal behavior does not subside. There are still lists of arguable, neglected, open questions that should be given reliable answers based on strong empirical evidence guided by theory. Despite potential differences in theoretical and methodological approaches, as well as in the fields which they are interested in, scientists see the value of systematic research in this field. They also see both theoretical and practical implications in this research, believing that gaining knowledge of nonverbal mechanisms can improve the ability to understand others, and at the same time raise awareness of our own communicative capacities.

The purpose of the book is to bring together a number of nonverbal behavior researchers to discuss current themes and research. The book is meant for senior undergraduates, graduates, academics and nonverbal communication researchers, as well as for everyone else who wants to interpret and understand better nonverbal behavior and the states of their interlocutors. The texts in this book show the results of contemporary research and theorization of the nature, functions, and modalities of nonverbal behavior in different areas of life.

In "Nonverbal Neurology: How the Brain Encodes and Decodes Wordless Signs, Signals, and Cues," David B. Givens explores human nervous-system circuits that encode and decode nonverbal cues. Givens begins with a look backward at the 500-million-year evolution of *Homo sapiens'* "nonverbal brain." The focus then turns to the communicative movements of specific body parts, starting with the lips and continuing downward through the neck and throat, shoulders, hands, and feet. Exploration begins with the neurology of each body-movement cue (outgoing or efferent) – followed by a neurological examination of the movement's perception (incoming or afferent). Key players on the

1

encoding side include special visceral nerves and subcortical reflexes like tactile withdrawal. Central players on the decoding side, meanwhile, include specialized cortical recognition areas (such as those for facial recognition) and mirror neurons.

Milkica Nešić and Vladimir Nešić provide an important overview of the neurobiological basis of different aspects of nonverbal communication, such as the perception of face identity and facial expressions, as well as gestural communication. Different aspects of face perception, including the neuroanatomical and the neurophysiological basis of face identity and expressions perception, and the time-course of face perception, are reviewed. Nešić and Nešić have a special emphasis on in the roles of neurotransmitters, hormones, and pheromones on face perception, as well as on the dependence of facial perception on social context. Gestural communication is reviewed from the perspective of its relation to verbal communication (or the link between action and language), and the possible neurophysiological explanations are considered.

In "Measuring Gestures," David B. Givens broadens the concept of measurement to include an account of the neural dimensions that are involved in our head-nod, head-shake, and shoulder-shrug cues. Doing this enables him to explain why head, neck, and shoulder muscles have been recruited in our evolution as *Homo* – rather than other muscles of the body – for the expression of feelings of agreement, disagreement, submissiveness, and uncertainty. Charting the neural centers and pathways that underlie our nods, shakes, and shrugs – that is, taking their measure in the nervous system – reveals that evolution has clearly favored special-visceral over somatic nerves for emotional cues. This evolutionary postulate explains why, as Charles Darwin concluded years ago, so many of humankind's emotional gestures are in widespread, if not universal, usage throughout the world.

The phrase "it's not what you say, but how you say it" refers to the importance of the nonverbal elements of voice – that is, everything contained in utterances outside of the spoken word. Mark G. Frank, Darrin J. Griffin, Elena Svetieva, and Andreas Maroulis' chapter outlines the various ways in which these nonverbal, or "paralinguistic" elements of voice affect social behavior. The chapter first examines the mechanics of speech production, and details some of the more popular and useful paralinguistic measures of the voice, such as fundamental frequency (pitch), amplitude (loudness), timbre (quality), resonance (via formants), speech rate, response length, speech latency, pauses, and speech errors. It ties these measures into previous studies to show

how they have utility in understanding social behavior. The chapter then delves specifically into how socially useful information is derived from the voice, including research showing that people can recognize in others various enduring traits, such as personal identity, age, ethnicity, social status, and personality. It also shows that people can recognize in others various transient states such as emotional reactions, and looks at its universality, as well as higher cognitive load, along with the methodological and cross-cultural issues associated with this work. Finally, the chapter examines how subtle voice clues are used to facilitate interactions, through signaling one comprehends the other, managing turn-taking, or possibly even provoking the reactions of others. It concludes that advances in technology will likely identify new clues that will further help us understand the importance of voice in social behavior.

The Duchenne smile has for some time been described as the expression of true and genuine happiness that is only produced in conjunction with congruent underlying feelings of positive emotion. In their chapter Sarah D. Gunnery and Judith A. Hall assess the findings from recent research that suggest the Duchenne smile can be produced deliberately in the absence of felt happiness, indicating that the Duchenne smile, like most other nonverbal behaviors, can be used as a tool to accurately communicate thoughts and feelings. The chapter "The Expression and Perception of the Duchenne Smile" reviews research on how and when people communicate emotion with the Duchenne smile, and how people utilize the Duchenne smile as a cue when making judgments about what others are feeling and when making attributes about others' personalities. This chapter specifically emphasizes research on the expression and perception of the deliberate Duchenne smile and comments on how previous research may need to be reframed in light of these newer findings on the Duchenne smile.

Aleksandra Kostic and Derek Chadee's chapter emphasizes the importance of emotional recognition. They note that research into the accuracy of perceiving facial emotional expressions has a hundred-year history and researchers have found inconsistency in their attempts to determine whether observers are capable of accurately decoding facial expressions of emotion. Discussing some of the major issues of emotional recognition, they focus on fear recognition. Fear is an emotion that has been the subject of numerous studies, more often than any other primary emotion. Strong empirical confirmation of the universality of the facial expressions of primary emotions, including the expression of fear, as well as high agreement in their recognition, has diverted the attention of contemporary researchers towards questions on which there had been no concord and which have been neglected and disputed, providing no reliable answers. The authors finally discuss recent research on general fear and the recognition of emotions.

Manusov, Docan-Morgan, and Harvey provide evidence in this chapter that nonverbal behaviors have the potential to be transformative. That is, they may act as triggers for a change in a relationship, perception, behavior, or affect. In particular, they argue that when a nonverbal behavior occurs or is noticed for the first time, these behavioral "firsts" can have big implications, positive or negative, for people in relationships. Among other things, the authors find that touch, eye behavior, and personal space are the cues reported most commonly as triggers for change and which help bring about the start of a romantic relationship, perception of how much or little another cares, relational problems, instant break-ups, and indicators of another's untrustworthiness.

The classic primary affects (e.g., happiness, sadness, fear, anger, surprise, and disgust) are the emotions most closely associated with facial expressions, and they have been emphasized in nonverbal communication research, often to the exclusion of the consideration of other important primary motivational-emotional states (primes). Ross Buck and Mike Miller, in their chapter, argue that a major variable in the natural selection of displays of emotion is the spatial distance in the ecology of an organism at which a given prime is typically displayed. This analysis allows for the explication of the nonverbal display and communication of an expanded range of specific and discrete emotions, consistent with emerging research in affective neuroscience concerning the brain's organization of emotions. Displays of primary affects function best at moderate personal distances, at which the face is easily seen. At more intimate distances, a variety of emotions including love, lust, gratitude, anger, and sympathy can be reliably communicated through displays involving pheromones and touch. At longer social and public distances, social and moral emotions including pride/arrogance/ triumph, guilt/shame/humiliation, envy/jealousy/resentment, and pity/ scorn/contempt are communicated through larger and more substantial body postures and gestures associated with ancient dominance and submission displays. Finally, the GREAT emotions (gratitude, respect, elevation, appreciation, and trust) are signaled at a dyadic level via mutually contingent responsiveness and interpersonal synchrony.

The analysis of the GREAT emotions is particularly relevant to a classic and comprehensive approach to interpersonal communication which has to date not emphasized its emotional aspects: the interpersonal adaptation theory (IAT: Burgoon, Stern, & Dillman, 1995). IAT makes interaction predictions for reciprocity or divergence based on differing driving forces that vary by external and internal conditions, and it is particularly well suited to considering individuals' emotional responses related to the mutual signaling of gratitude, respect, elevation, appreciation, and trust.

The chapter by Albert Mehrabian utilizes data from Pleasure-Arousal-Dominance (PAD) Emotion and Temperament models to generate a number of hypotheses to understand the nonverbal behavior impact of political candidates. For example, individuals with more pleasant (arousable, dominant) temperaments are seen as (a) more likely to be attracted to promises that their favorable votes would produce pleasant (arousing, controllable) social and economic conditions and (b) as most susceptible to negative messages that threatened unpleasant (unarousing, controlling) conditions. Dominance is also expected to appeal more to men than to women, whereas messages of high arousal (i.e., complexity, variety, novelty) are expected to appeal more to women than to men. Effects of anxiety (stress, distress, fear, bewilderment), as an emotional state or as a characteristic emotional predisposition, on political judgments are also considered. Findings show negative correlations between anxiety (as a state) or anxiety (as a trait), and cognitive differentiation. Findings suggest that anxiety is conducive to increased influence of emotions on political judgments, simplification of decision rules and political beliefs, and greater conformity to accurately or inaccurately depicted beliefs of the majority.

The effects of stress on voter emotionality and susceptibility to emotional contagion are discussed. The importance of positive campaigns for wooing uninvolved voters is noted.

Denise Frauendorfer and Marianne Schmid Mast, in their chapter, review the role of applicant and recruiter nonverbal behavior in job interviews. Based on the Brunswikian lens model approach, they provide an overview of applicant-expressed nonverbal and recruiter assessment of the applicant's traits and states. They show how the recruiter's nonverbal behavior influences the applicant's perception and performance during the job interview and how nonverbal behavior can impact recruiter selection bias. Finally, they discuss the validity of recruiter inferences based on applicant nonverbal behavior during the job interview, closing the chapter with a synthesis of different perspectives on nonverbal behavior in the job interview, and provide an outlook for future research.

Fernando Poyatos' focus is on the expression of nonverbal behavior in literature. Students of interaction in the past have often tended to neglect many of its nonverbal aspects, in terms of the things that happen in the course of it (while simply ignoring what "did not happen"), as merely "incidental," "contextual," or "marginal." This paper, besides trying to correct this unfortunate reality, shows how researchers (whether in experimental or observational analysis) would benefit greatly from the virtually inexhaustible wealth of illustrative data offered by creative literature, particularly the novel. Therefore, in marrying psychology and literature (although within editorial requirements), a number of methodological avenues are briefly outlined for the study of both interactions in general and conversations which at least acknowledge: personal and extrapersonal components of encounters, both face-to-face and with whatever surrounds us; our sensory perception and how physiopsychological synesthesial associations also operate as components; in addition, the sensible and intelligible components that function independently or in double or multiple clusters; the qualifiers of interactive activities and non-activities; how interaction components are associated to preceding, simultaneous or succeeding ones; and a model for an interdisciplinary study of conversation.

Küster, Krumhuber, and Kappas discuss recent developments relating to nonverbal behavior on the Internet. Focusing on interactions with and via artificial agents and avatars, their chapter outlines general aspects of the function, application, and design of artificial systems with an emphasis of psychological aspects of interacting with them. To this end, the chapter summarizes current research on the appearance and perceived human-likeness of artificial systems in the controversial debate about the uncanny valley, as well as the use of virtual avatars for self-presentation, in contexts such as online dating or Facebook. The chapter concludes with a discussion of implications for psychologically-oriented research in this area by presenting data from a set of pilot studies aiming at mediated self-presentation in communication between humans over the Internet.

This volume provides a diversity of relevant articles from a range of perspectives within the literature of nonverbal behavior, capturing some of the central controversies and debates that are of interest to researchers and students.

Reference

Burgoon, J., Stern, L. A., & Dillman, L. (1995). *Interpersonal adaptation: Dyadic interaction patterns.* Cambridge: Cambridge University Press.

Part I
Theoretical

1

Nonverbal Neurology: How the Brain Encodes and Decodes Wordless Signs, Signals, and Cues

David B. Givens

The brain, spinal chord, and peripheral nerves are seldom mentioned in research on human nonverbal communication. Though they play key roles in body-motion expressivity, the neurons, neural pathways, and brain modules that control movements are often discounted, or entirely left out of the picture. In this chapter, the nervous system plays a leading role in explaining how our facial expressions, hand gestures, and bodily postures are produced and deciphered. We begin with an overview of the nonverbal brain's evolution, from ca. 500 million years ago to the present day.

Evolution of the nonverbal brain

The "nonverbal brain" (Givens, 2013) consists of those circuits, centers, and modules of the central nervous system which are involved in sending, receiving, and processing speechless signs. In right-handed individuals, modules of the right-brain cerebral hemisphere are considered to be more nonverbal, holistic, visuospatial, and intuitive than those of the more verbal, analytic, sequential, and rational left-brain hemisphere (Givens, 2013). Despite its size and abilities, our brain continues to house ancient neural layers, nuclei, and circuits that evolved millions of years earlier in vertebrate forebears – from the jawless fishes to more recent human ancestors (genus Homo) – for communication before the advent of speech (Givens, 2013). The nonverbal brain consists of six interrelated divisions which merged in an evolutionary process from ca. 500 million to two million years ago:

(1) The oldest neural division – the Aquatic Brain & Spinal Cord (Givens, 2013) – was present ca. 500 million years ago in the jawless fishes. It

includes the spinal cord's interneuron pools and motor neuron pathways (a) for tactile withdrawal, and (b) for the rhythmic, oscillatory movements of swimming (and much later, for walking and running, and for the bipedal rhythms of dance).

(2) In the subsequent Amphibian Brain, which originated ca. 380 million years ago, the hindbrain's pontine reticular excitatory system became more elaborate (Kandel et al., 1991). The pontine tegmentum's link to the spinal cord's anterior-horn motor neurons and muscle spindles raised the body by exciting antigravity extensor muscles (enabling us to stand tall today, and to perform other versions of the vertebrate high-stand display). Further, the vestibulospinal pathway elaborated – from receptors in the inner ear via the vestibular nerve (cranial VIII), and via cerebellar fibers to the vestibular nucleus in the upper medulla – running the length of the spinal cord, for body posture (i.e., for basic stance) in relation to gravity. Further still, the tectospinal tract evolved, consisting of the superior (and inferior) colliculus and its links, via the brain stem, running (a) to cervical cord interneurons, then (b) to anterior-horn motor neurons, then (c) to spinal nerves, and finally reaching (d) muscle spindles for postural reflexes in response to sights and sounds (responses such as the startle reflex). Finally, the rubrospinal tract further evolved, with circuits running from the red nucleus of the midbrain (a) to thoracic cord interneurons, then (b) to anterior-horn motor neurons, and (c) to muscles and muscle spindles for the postural tone of our limbs' flexor muscles.

(3) Subsequently in the Reptilian Brain, coming online ca. 280 million years ago, several new body movements were added. The vestibuloreticulospinal system evolved to control axial and girdle muscles for posture relative to positions of the head. The basal ganglia-ansa lenticularis pathway reverberated links between the amygdala and basal ganglia via the ansa lenticularis and lenticulate fasciculus to the midbrain tegmentum, red nucleus, and reticular system to spinal-cord interneurons required for today's ATNR (asymmetrical tonic neck reflex) and the high-stand display.

(4) With the Mammalian Brain, originating ca. 150 million years ago, nonverbal communication became distinctively emotional. The amygdalo-hypothalamic tract became more elaborate. The central amygdala's link to the hypothalamus, via the stria terminalis, provided wiring for defensive postures (such as the broadside display). Hypothalamus-spinal cord pathways adapted as well. The hypothalamus's dorsomedial and ventromedial nuclei fed (a) indirectly via the brain stem's reticular system, and (b) directly through fiberlinks

to lower brain-stem and spinal-cord circuits to cord motor neurons for emotion cues such as anger. The septo-hypothalamo-midbrain continuum evolved. The medial forebrain bundle (from the olfactory forebrain and limbic system's septal nuclei), via the hypothalamus's lateral nuclei to midbrain-tegmentum brain-stem motor centers, mediated emotions such as fear. The cingulate gyrus facial circuit evolved. Links run from the anterior cingulate cortex (a) to the hippocampus, (b) to the amygdala, (c) to the hypothalamus, and (d) through the brain stem, and finally (e) to the vagus (cranial X) and facial (cranial VII) nerves which, respectively, control the larynx and facial muscles required for vocalizing (as in screaming) and moving the lips (as in smiling, frowning, and lip-compression).

(5) In the Primate Brain, which originated ca. 65 million years ago, manual dexterity and hand gestures, along with facial expressions and their recognition, were added to our nonverbal repertoire. The neocortex's corticospinal tract further evolved. The posterior parietal cortex linked to supplementary motor, premotor, and primary motor cortices (with basal-ganglia feedback loops) via the corticospinal tract, to cervical and thoracic anterior-horn spinal interneurons, and to motor neurons in control of arm, hand, and finger muscles for the skilled movements of mime cues and the precision grip. Modules of the inferior temporal neocortex evolved to provide visual input (a) to the occipital neocortex's parvocellular interblob system (V1 to V2 and V4), permitting recognition of complex shapes, and (b) to the inferior temporal cortex, permitting heightened responses to hand gestures and the ability to recognize faces and facial expressions.

(6) Finally in the Human Brain, which developed ca. four million-to-200,000 years ago in members related to the genus Homo, the corticobulbar tract further evolved. Corticobulbar pathways to the facial nerve (cranial VII) permitted intentional facial expressions such as the voluntary smile. Broca's cranial pathways grew from Broca's-area neocircuits via corticobulbar pathways to multiple cranial nerves, permitting human speech. And Broca's spinal pathways also evolved. Broca's-area neocircuits passing through corticospinal pathways to cervical and thoracic spinal nerves permitted manual sign language and linguistic-like mime cues.

Evolution of mirror neurons

The nonverbal brain's evolution has been pieced together over time since the fifth century B.C. in Greece. Ever so gradually, a detailed picture of the human nervous system has emerged. Each time I open my copy of *Gray's Anatomy* (Williams, 1995), I marvel at the extensive neural knowledge our species has amassed through the centuries since Hippocrates. And yet, in the 2,092 pages of my 1995 British edition of *Gray's*, there is not a single mention of "mirror neurons."

The shoulder-shrug

Since 1977, I have followed research on the shoulder-shrug display, first described by Darwin in 1872. While on the encoding (efferent) side, its distinctive body movements can be explained by appeal to circuits of the Aquatic Brain's tactile-withdrawal reflex, on the decoding (afferent) side its neurology has remained something of a mystery. The perennial question is, how do we so readily understand the gesture's meaning? Do we apprehend it by watching – which is to say, via experiential learning – or do we somehow infer what it means through "intuition"? Experience most certainly plays a role, but now it appears that an innate form of intuition based on mirror neurons is involved as well.

Mirror neurons

In the early 1990s, mirror neurons were discovered in the premotor cerebral cortex of macaque monkeys. Vittorio Gallese, Giacomo Rizzolatti, and colleagues at the University of Parma in Italy identified neurons that activate when monkeys perform certain hand movements – such as picking up fruit – and also fire when monkeys watch other primates perform the same hand movements. In *The Imitative Mind*, Andrew Meltzoff (2002) invoked mirror neurons to explain how human newborns, from 42 minutes to 72 hours old (mean = 32 hours), can imitate adult head movements, hand gestures, and facial movements (such as tongue protrusion, lip protrusion, mouth opening, eye blinking, cheek and brow movements, and components of emotional expressions). Mirror neurons have been located in Brodmann's area 44 (Broca's area) and other regions of the human brain.

Regarding the shoulder-shrug and other possibly innate nonverbal signs (such as compressed lips and the Adam's-apple-jump, described below), mirror neurons provide brain circuitry that helps us intuit, decode, and understand their meanings. When we see a grasping-hand gesture, for instance, or hear an angry voice tone, mirror neurons set up a motor template – a prototype or blueprint in our own brain – that allows us to mimic the particular gesture or vocal tone. Additionally, through links to the Mammalian Brain's limbic system, mirror neurons enable us to decode emotional nuances of the hand gestures we see and the tones of voice we hear. What has emerged from mirror-neuron research is that we are seemingly wired to interpret the nonverbal actions of others as if we ourselves had enacted them.

To explore in greater detail the nervous system's role in encoding and decoding innately predisposed nonverbal signs, we focus below on five body parts: lips, neck, shoulders, hands, and feet. From head to toe, and throughout the world, these features are richly expressive.

Lip cues

Efferent cues (outgoing)

Lips are the muscular, fleshy, hairless folds that surround the human mouth opening. They may be moved to express an emotion, show a mood, pronounce a word, whistle, suck through a straw, and kiss. Their connection to the Mammalian Brain's limbic system, and to the enteric (visceral) nervous system, renders them among the most emotionally expressive of all body parts.

Lip muscles. The principal lip muscle, orbicularis oris, is a sphincter consisting (a) of pars marginalis (beneath the margin of the lips themselves), and (b) pars peripheralis (around the lips' periphery from the nostril bulbs to the chin). (P. marginalis is uniquely developed in humans for speech.) Contraction of orbicularis oris tenses the lips and reduces their eversion. Lips may be moved directly by orbicularis oris and by labial tractor muscles in the upper and lower lips. Lips may also be moved indirectly by nine (or more) additional facial muscles (e.g., by zygomaticus major in laughing) through attachments to a fibromuscular mass in the cheeks called the modiolus. That so many facial muscles interlink via the modiolus makes our lips extremely expressive of attitudes, opinions, and moods.

Expressions. Among the lips' principal facial expressions are the smile (happiness, affiliation, contentment), the grimace (fear); the canine snarl (disgust, disliking), the lip-pout (sadness, submission, uncertainty), the lip-purse (disagreement), the sneer (contempt), and lip-compression (anger, frustration, uncertainty). That these expressions are emotional is because the facial muscles that shape them are controlled by special visceral efferent nerves.

Special visceral nerves. A special visceral nerve is a nerve that links to a facial, jaw, neck, shoulder, or throat muscle that once played a role in eating or breathing. Special visceral nerves are cranial nerves whose original role in digestion and respiration long ago renders them emotionally responsive today (see "Neural blueprint for emotion", below).

Special visceral nerves mediate those "gut reactive" signs of emotion we unconsciously send through facial expressions, throat-clears, sideward head-tilts, disgusted looks, and shoulder-shrugs. Nonverbally, these nerves are indeed "special," because the muscle contractions they mediate are less easily (i.e., voluntarily) controlled than those of the skeletal muscles (such as the biceps, which is innervated by unemotional somatic nerves).

Neural blueprint for emotion. Before the Mammalian Brain, life in nonverbal world was automatic, preconscious, and predictable. Motor centers in the Reptilian Brain reacted to vision, sound, touch, chemical, gravity, and motion sensory cues with preset body movements and preprogrammed postures. With the arrival of night-active mammals, ca. 180 million years ago, smell replaced sight as the dominant sense, and a newer, more flexible way of responding – based on emotion and emotional memory – arose from the olfactory sense. In the Jurassic period, the Mammalian Brain invested heavily in aroma circuits to succeed at night as reptiles slept. These odor pathways gradually formed the neural blueprint for what was later to become our limbic brain. Smell carries directly to limbic areas of the Mammalian Brain via nerves running from the olfactory bulbs to the septum, amygdala, and hippocampus. In the Aquatic Brain, olfaction was critical for detecting food, foes, and mates from a distance in murky waters. Like an emotional feeling, aroma has a volatile or "thin-skinned" quality because sensory cells lie on the exposed exterior of the olfactory epithelium (i.e., on the bodily surface itself). Like a whiff of smelling salts, a sudden feeling may jolt the mind. The force of a mood is reminiscent of a smell's intensity (e.g., soft and gentle, pungent, or overpowering), and similarly permeates and fades. The design of emotion cues, in tandem with the forebrain's olfactory prehistory, suggests that the sense of smell is the neurological model for our emotions.

Pharyngeal arches. From an evolutionary standpoint, special visceral nerves are associated with the pharyngeal arches of ancient vertebrates. Nerves controlling the primitive pharyngeal arches are linked to branchiomeric muscles that once constricted and dilated "gill" pouches of the ancient alimentary canal. Paleocircuits of special visceral nerves originally mediated the muscles for opening (dilating) or closing (constricting) parts of the primitive gill apparatus involved in eating and breathing. Anatomically, a pharyngeal arch is a column of tissue in the throat (or pharynx) of the human embryo that separates the primitive visceral pouches or gill slits. Originally this issue was used by Silurian-Period jawless fishes as part of their feeding and breathing apparatus.

Today, many human facial expressions derive from muscles and nerves of the pharyngeal arches. Originally, these arches were programmed to constrict in response to potentially harmful chemical signs detected in water. Today their special visceral nerves mediate displays of emotion by causing branchiomeric muscles to dilate or constrict.

Embryology. Pharyngeal arches are visible as swellings in the throat of the human fetus. Radical changes take place as these tissues grow into our maturing neck and face, but the underlying principles of movement established in the jawless fishes remains much the same. Unpleasant cues cause cranial nerves to constrict our mouth, eye, nose, and throat openings, while more pleasant sensations dilate our facial orifices to incoming cues. According to Chevalier-Skolnikoff (1973), "In mammals the primitive neck muscles gave rise to two muscle layers: a superficial longitudinal layer, the platysma, and a deeper transverse layer, the sphincter colli profundus, which have come to extend well into the facial region" (p. 59). That colli profundus is a sphincter – i.e., a muscle that constricts or widens a bodily opening – strengthens the contention that unpleasant emotions and stimuli lead cranial nerves to constrict eye, nose, throat, and mouth openings, while more pleasant sensations widen facial orifices to incoming cues. Seawater was pumped in and out of the early vertebrate pharynx through a series of gill slits at the fish's head end. Each pharyngeal arch contained (a) a visceral nerve and (b) a somatic muscle to open or close the gill opening (should, e.g., positive or negative signs, respectively, be sensed). In human beings, the nerves and muscles used to close the mouth derive from the first pharyngeal arch, while those which constrict the throat derive from the third and fourth arches. From the second pharyngeal arch, the facial nerve (cranial VII) contracts (a) orbital muscles to narrow the eyes, (b) corrugator and associated muscle groups to lower the eyebrows, and (c) orbicularis oris muscles to seal the lips, should we detect, for instance, a noxious or disgusting smell – or should we feel disgust, disliking, or displeasure with a fellow human being. A widespread and arguably universal facial expression that conveys such negative feelings is lip-compression.

Lip-compression. Lip-compression is a usually negative cue produced by pressing the lips together into a thin line. A sudden lip-compression may signal the onset of anger, discomfort, disliking, grief, sadness, or uncertainty. Barely noticeable lip-clenching may signal unvoiced opposition or disagreement. Like other lip cues, in-rolling is controlled by special visceral nerves. At rest, the lips make gentle contact, and the teeth are slightly separated. In a compressed-lips display, the prime mover is orbicularis oris (both the pars peripheralis and marginalis components contract); the teeth may or may not occlude.

In rage, according to Darwin (1872/1998), "The mouth is generally closed with firmness" (p. 236). Apes express anger by staring, clenching the jaws, and compressing the lips (Chevalier-Skolnikoff, 1973). In chimpanzees, a compressed-lips face "typically accompanies aggression" (Goodall, 1986, p. 123). According to de Waal, "In an aggressive mood, the [bonobo chimpanzee's] lips are compressed in a tense face with frowning eyebrows and piercing eyes" (de Waal & Lanting, 1997, p. 33). In the Highlands of Papua New Guinea, when tribal men were asked to show what they would do when angry and were about to attack, "They pressed their lips together" (Ekman, 1998, p. 238).

Rolling the lips in is a socially aversive cue in young children (McGrew, 1972). In children, as well, smiles in threatening situations are combined with tightening and compressing the lips (Stern & Bender, 1974). In babies, lip-compression and brow-lowering (combined in the pucker face) appear when mothers persist in playing or feeding beyond an infant's tolerance (Givens, 1978).

> You glance toward Mom at the other end of the table. You notice that her eyes are focused on Dad, and her lips are pressed tightly together. You brace yourself. You are about to get it. That look always means "you're in hot water now!" (Richmond et al., 1991, p. 75)

In conclusion, lip-compression is a gestural fossil, an ancient primate display with deep mammalian roots. The expression is emotionally responsive today as it reflects visceral sensations aroused by aggression, anger, and other usually negative emotions. In effect, we tighten our lips to seal off our mouth opening in a form of nonverbal lock-down.

Afferent cues (incoming)

Facial expressions such as lip-compression are decoded through an elaborate network of nervous-system pathways. Light reflected from facial features casts tiny images on the eye's nerve-sensitive retina. From here, electrochemical impulses cable through the optic nerve to a visual area at the back of the neocortex called V1. V1 neurons respond (a) to linear details, and (b) to wavelengths of color. A second visual area, V2 (in front of V1), enhances our image of linear and color aspects of the face. Additional processing takes place in V3 (recognition of form and movement), V4 (additional color recognition), and V5 (movement) (Restak, 1994, pp. 27–8). Apart from conscious awareness, these modular areas of neocortex unify and give meaning to our vision of the face and its diverse expressions.

Our higher-primate (anthropoid) ancestors (ca. 35–40 million years ago) had an enlarged visual cortex at the back of the head, on the occipital lobe, with which to process color vision and depth. Today, the anthropoid's is the most complex visual cortex on earth, with anatomically separate areas for (a) analyzing form, (b) coordinating hand-and-eye movements, and (c) recognizing faces. A few nerve cells in the lower temporal lobe are so narrowly specialized that they respond only to faces.

The lower (or inferior) temporal cortex receives information fed forward through a series of sensory and association areas, beginning with the retina's relay in the occipital lobe at the back of our skull. Regarding the temporal cortex itself, it has become a remarkably specialized part of the nonverbal brain. Some of its cells respond only to frontal or profile views of the face, while others fire only when facial expressions appear (Kandel et al., 1991, p. 459). Facial familiarity registers in the superior temporal polysensory area (Young & Yamane, 1992, p. 1327).

Our perception of faces is likely rooted in the fusiform face area (FFA), located in Brodmann's area 37 of the neocortex's temporal lobe. This proactive brain area is highly sensitive to facial templates. So actively does it seek out facial schema that we often see "faces" in cloud formations, shrouds (e.g., the Shroud of Turin), sandwiches, and screen doors – and periodically in our nearest celestial neighbor, the moon. Working alongside the specialized neural circuitry that gives rise to the Primate Brain's heightened alertness to facial features and their expressive cues are mirror neurons. Mirror-neuron properties for creating and perceiving facial expressions are found in the inferior parietal lobe (which mediates the body movements involved in human tool usage as well as our perception of emotions in facial expressions), the frontal operculum (involved in cognitive and perceptual motor processing), and the premotor cortex (involved in spatial and sensory guidance of our own body movements, and in understanding the body movements of others) (Haxby & Gobbini, 2011, p. 101). According to van der Gaag et al. (2007),

> Facial expressions contain both motor and emotional components. The inferior frontal gyrus (IFG) and posterior parietal cortex have been considered to compose a mirror neuron system (MNS) for the motor components of facial expressions, while the amygdala and insula may represent an "additional" MNS for emotional states. (van der Gaag et al., 2007, p. 179)

According to Haxby and Gobbini (2011),

> The activity in these areas suggests that understanding the emotional meaning of expressions involves evoking the emotion itself – a simulation or mirroring of another's emotion that is analogous to the putative role of the hMNS [human mirror neuron system] in simulating or mirroring the motor actions of another. (p. 102)

Earlier, Niedenthal (2007) found substantial empirical support for the idea "that recognizing a facial expression of emotion in another person and experiencing that emotion oneself involve overlapping neural circuits" (p. 1004).

Disgust. As an emotion, disgust shows most clearly in the lower face (Ekman et al., 1971). Disgust is a mammalian elaboration of the pharyngeal gag reflex. Theoretically, disgust originated as a response to bad tastes, and later evolved as a "moral" emotion (as reflected, for example, in college students who judged the raised upper lip as a sign of aversion to body boundary violations, inappropriate sex, poor hygiene, and death (Rozin et al., 1994). Additional facial signs of disgust include a wrinkled nose, raised nostrils, and lowered inner corners of the eyebrows (Ekman, 1998, p. 256). From the standpoint of mirror neurons, perhaps the best understood emotion – including the perception of its telltale raised-upper-lip expression (via contraction of levator labii alaeque nasii) – is disgust. In an fMRI study, Wicker et al., (2003) imaged the brains of participants who smelled a disgusting odor, and in separate trials with the same subjects, imaged participants who viewed videotapes of others' faces expressing disgust. Both trials activated the same brain areas of the anterior insula and the anterior cingulate cortex. "Thus," they conclude, "observing an emotion activates the neural representation of that emotion. This finding provides a unifying mechanism for understanding the behaviors of others" (Wicker et al., 2003, p. 655).

Neck cues

From the face we continue downward through the human neck to focus on two nonverbal cues, one visual (the Adam's-apple-jump), the other auditory (tone of voice). Both signs are modulated by special visceral nerves, and both are decoded with the help of mirror neurons.

Efferent cues (outgoing)

Adam's-apple-jump. The Adam's-apple-jump is a conspicuous up-and-down motion of the Adam's apple. The latter is a projection at the front of the throat called the laryngeal prominence, where the largest (or thyroid) cartilage of the Adam's apple shows prominently (as a bump) in men and less noticeably in women. The projection's movement in the throat is visible while gulping or swallowing, as in nervousness, apprehension, or fear.

The Adam's-apple-jump may be read as an unconscious sign of emotional anxiety, embarrassment, or stress (Givens, 2013). At a business meeting, for instance, a listener's Adam's apple may inadvertently jump should he or she dislike or disagree with a speaker's suggestion, perspective, or point of view. According to Grant (1969, p. 528), swallowing "associates well with flight and submission." Guyton (1996) notes that stimulating the emotionally sensitive amygdala can cause involuntary body movements "associated with olfaction and eating, such as licking, chewing, and swallowing" (pp. 758–59). Acting through the vagus nerve (cranial X), emotional tension from the Mammalian Brain's limbic system causes unconscious muscular contractions of the sternothyroid, thyrohyoid, and associated inferior pharyngeal constrictor muscles of the Adam's apple. Movement is evident as the muscles contract to swallow, throat-clear, or vocalize an objection. The Adam's apple is emotionally responsive because its muscles are mediated by the vagus, one of five cranial special visceral nerves.

Tone of voice. Directly behind and attached to the Adam's-apple cartilage is the larynx (or "voice box"). Also innervated by the vagus, tiny muscles of the larynx enable us to vocalize, and to add emotional flourishes to our words. Anger, disgust, and other nonlinguistic feelings may be attached to spoken words for affect. Unlike the facial movements outlined above, tone-of-voice cues are heard, not seen, since their sounds are produced by muscle-activated movements of tiny body parts hidden within the voice box.

Like the Adam's-apple-jump, tone-of-voice cues (including vocal tension, throat tightness, and the ubiquitous throat-clear) are responsive to emotional stimuli from the Mammalian Brain's limbic system, carried by special visceral nerves originally designed for respiration and feeding. Today, visceral feelings of anxiety or nervousness may be revealed as throat, larynx, and pharynx muscles unconsciously tighten as if to seal off the alimentary canal from harm.

Afferent cues (incoming)

Tone of voice is processed by the Human Brain's right cerebral hemisphere. "The right brain," Siegel (2012) writes, "both perceives and sends messages through facial expressions and tone of voice" (p. 177). Since the left auditory nerve cables to the brain's right-hand side, music, prosody, and emotional tone-of-voice qualities are more likely to be perceived through the left ear (Siegel, 2012, p. 179).

Nonverbal cues in general are more strongly interpreted by modules of the right-side neocortex (especially in right-handed individuals) than they are by left-sided modules. Anatomically, this is reflected (a) in the greater volume of white matter (i.e., of myelinated axons that link nerve-cell bodies) in the right neocortical hemisphere, and (b) in the greater volume of gray matter (i.e., of nerve-cell bodies or neurons) in the left. The right brain's superior fiber linkages enable its neurons to better communicate with feelings, memories, and senses, thus giving this side its deeper-reaching holistic, nonverbal, and "big picture" skills. The left brain's superior neuronal volume, meanwhile, allows for better communication among the neocortical neurons themselves, which gives this side a greater analytic and intellectually narrower "focus" (Gur et al., 1980).

Mirror neurons play a role in decoding both voice-tone and Adam's-apple-jump cues. In the latter instance, a study by Ushioda et al. (2012) found that subjects' mirror neurons responded both to the sound and to the sight (i.e., seeing profile views of laryngeal elevation) of swallowing. The sight of body movements involved in swallowing stimulated mirror neurons in the visual association area of cerebral cortex (Brodmann's area 18), while the sound of swallowing stimulated mirror neurons in auditory areas of cortex (Brodmann's areas 6 and 40) (Ushioda et al., 2012). It has been suggested that the sound of music (and presumably also that of the melodic qualities of voice tone) "can invoke motor representations of emotions by recruiting the insula, a neural relay between the limbic and motor systems" (Molnar-Szakacs & Overy, 2006, p. 238). Molnar-Szakacs and Overy (2006) propose that both communicative body movements and music may be interpreted by mirror neurons in the brain's fronto-parietal region.

Shoulder cues

Shoulders are paired, jointed organs which connect arms to the torso. They are the prominently rounded – as well as angular – parts of the external anatomy which give the human torso its squared-off silhouette. As very visible body parts, shoulders are often singled out for display with clothing cues (Givens, 1977). The flexibility of human shoulders – and the fact that they are moved by emotionally sensitive branchiomeric muscles – renders them expressive as signs. The bones of our shoulder girdle consist of a pair of flattened blades (scapulas), each connected to a bracing collar bone (clavicle). The sides of the bony girdle sit upon our rib cage like shoulder pads. Unattached to any bones but the clavicles, scapulas glide up and down, move back and forth, and rotate about our back and spine. Only the clavicles' attachments to the breastbone stabilize their motion.

Efferent cues (outgoing)

Muscles. Six muscles move and connect the shoulder girdle to our main skeleton. Anterior are subclavius, pectoralis minor, and serratus anterior; posterior are levator scapulae, rhomboid, and trapezius. The accessory nerve (cranial XI, a special visceral efferent nerve) links to the upper trapezius muscle and innervates it to lift the shoulders. As a branchiomeric muscle, the upper trapezius is emotionally responsive. Since the accessory nerve also feeds into the larynx, shoulder-shrugs and vocal whines may be given at the same time. The shoulder-shrug has been observed in Australia, China, England, France, India, Italy, Malaysia, Micronesia, Native North America, Saudi Arabia, and South Africa (Darwin, 1872/1998). "When a man wishes to show that he cannot do something, or prevent something being done," Darwin wrote, "he often raises with a quick movement both shoulders" (p. 264). Pulling in the shoulders is a response to spatial invasion (Sommer, 1969). The shrug is listed in two checklists of possibly universal nonverbal signs: (a) as "A fairly sudden raising of both shoulders" (Brannigan & Humphries, 1972, p. 60), and (b) "Raising both shoulders" (Grant, 1969, p. 533). Shrugging the shoulders has been interpreted as a submissive sign in children (McGrew, 1972). Morris (1994) defines "shoulders shrug" as a worldwide sign that means "I do not know" (p. 200). From Columbia in South America, to East Africa and North America, the shrug cue means "don't know" (Kendon, 2004, p. 336).

Reflexive origin & embryology. The shoulder-shrug display incorporates defensive crouch movements from the Aquatic Brain and Spinal Cord's protective, tactile-withdrawal reflex. In mammals, the most primitive protective response is a flexion withdrawal, which "takes the head and neck away from the stimulus" (Salzen, 1979, p. 130). The crouch posture is "a protective pattern characteristic of the early embryonic flexion response" (Salzen, 1979, p. 136). By eight weeks of age, the human fetus already "knows" to withdraw its head and neck when its mouth is touched. Defensive, coordinated flexing and withdrawing movements have been seen in immature fish larvae, in marine snails, and in human embryos at eight weeks of age. In four-legged animals whose brains have been surgically disconnected from the spinal cord, almost any tactile stimulus will cause flexor muscles to contract and withdraw a limb from whatever touched it (Guyton, 1996).

Feelings & emotions. Socioemotional stimuli for the shrug-display involve the forebrain's amygdala (LeDoux, 1996) and basal ganglia (or "reptilian core"; MacLean, 1990). Submissive feelings find expression in coordinated muscle contractions designed to bend, flex, and rotate parts of our axial and appendicular skeleton to "shrink" the body and show a harmless, lower profile. Unlike the assertive high-stand, the diverse motions of the shrug complex were designed for defense rather than offense – for self-protection in the physical world, as well as for emotional self-defense and preservation in an interpersonal world mediated by social signs, signals, and cues.

Afferent cues (incoming)

Unlike the facial, Adam's-apple, and tone-of-voice cues examined above, I am unaware of studies that find links between mirror neurons and the shoulder-shrug. I agree with a provocative comment by Freedberg, however, that such links are likely "in principle." "In principle, " he writes, "it should be possible to do so [to map mirror-neuron areas that decode and respond emotionally to particular gestures], even in the case of shoulder movements such as this one [pictured in Jean-Michel Basquiat's untitled oilslick-on-paper illustration (1982), depicting a shrug in response to fear]" (Freedberg, 2009, p. 23). Again, what has emerged from mirror-neuron research is that we are seemingly wired to interpret the nonverbal actions of others as if we ourselves had enacted them. In principle, then, the shoulder-shrug is likely decoded, in part, by mirror neurons.

Hand cues

From shoulders we move downward to hands. Hands are the terminal end organs below the forearms, used to reach, grasp, and gesture. Their combined verbal and nonverbal IQs make hands our most expressive body parts. Hands have more to say even than faces, for not only do fingers show emotion, depict ideas, and point to butterflies on the wing – they can also read Braille, speak in sign languages (Corina & Knapp, 2006), and write poetry. Human hands are such incredibly gifted communicators that they always bear watching. Important hand cues include hand-behind-head, point, self-touch, steeple, palm-down, and palm-up. The neurology of the latter two signs is explored below.

Efferent cues (outgoing)

Palm-down. The palm-down cue is an insistent speaking or listening gesture made with the fingers extended and the hand(s) rotated to a downward (or pronated) position. It is a gesture in which the hands and forearms assume the prone position used in a floor pushup. Palm-down cues have been observed as anger signs in infants and children (Blurton Jones, 1967; Givens, 1978). Push and flat gestures appear in Grant's (1969) and Brannigan and Humphries' (1972) checklists of possibly universal signs. Palm-down signs are diagnostic of a dramatic or dominant nonverbal style (Norton, 1983). Palms down is a worldwide speaking gesture used to "hold down" an idea or "calm down" the mood of an audience (Morris, 1994, pp. 194–95). Palms front, made with hyperextended wrists and pronated palms, shows "I disagree" or "I hold you back" (Morris, 1994, p. 195).

To make a verbal statement emotionally stronger, we rotate our palms downward, as if preparing the body to press-up to an aggressive, gravity-defying, postural high-stand. The amygdala (acting through reptilian areas of basal ganglia (MacLean, 1990; Grillner, 1996)) mediates our palm-down gestures. That we show dominance by pronating, extending, and figuratively stomping with our forelimbs reflects the amygdala's evolutionary kinship with the basal ganglia. While the former directs our emotional stance, the latter governs our physical stance in relation to gravity. Thus, slapping a desktop for emphasis is not unlike a sumo wrestler's ceremonial stomp in the ring. Both are postural displays that demonstrate stability, strength, and standing on the earthly plain.

Palm-up. The palm-up cue is a speaking or listening gesture made with the fingers extended and the hand(s) rotated to an upward (or supinated) position. It is a gesture made with the opened palm raised to an appealing, imploring, or "begging" position. Uplifted palms suggest a vulnerable or nonaggressive pose that appeals to listeners as allies rather than as rivals or foes. Throughout the world, palm-up cues reflect moods of congeniality, humility, and uncertainty. Accompanied by "palm shows," our ideas, opinions, and remarks seem patronizing or conciliatory rather than authoritative or aggressive. Held out to an opponent across a conference table, the palm-up cue may, like an olive branch, enlist support as an emblem of peace.

The first scientific study of palm-up gestures was conducted by Darwin (1872/1998), who saw them as signs derived from the larger shoulder-shrug display. The open-palm-up hand-shrug has been interpreted as a sign of helpless uncertainty and confusion (Ekman & Friesen, 1968). In chimpanzees, palm-up signs are used to beg for food, to invite bodily contact, and to seek support during a conflict: "We call the gesture with the extended arm and open palm 'holding out a hand'. It is the most common hand gesture in the colony" (de Waal, 1982, pp. 34–36).

Palm-up cues are used to ask "who," "what," "when," "why," "where," and "how" questions in diverse sign languages of the deaf from Papua New Guinea to Colombia and New York (Givens, 1986).

Afferent (incoming)

Although researchers have determined that object-directed hand movements (such as reaching for a piece of fruit, tossing a coin, and turning a key) engage mirror neurons in viewers, there has been uncertainty as to whether the purely communicative hand gestures (such as point, halt-hand, and thumbs-down) also engage these neurons. A functional magnetic resonance imaging study by Montgomery and colleagues found that both object-directed and communicative hand motions lead to the firing of mirror neurons in the inferior parietal lobule (IPL) and frontal operculum areas of viewers' brains (Montgomery et al., 2007). In a review article, Keysers and Fadiga (2008) found general agreement among researchers that both transitive (object-directed) and intransitive (e.g., communicative) hand gestures caused mirror neurons to fire. Iacoboni (2009), meanwhile, has found that while grasping an object may trigger mirror neurons in an observer, the act of merely pantomiming a hand gesture (without an object) may not. "In two baseline conditions," he writes, "the firing of the cells was measured for observation of grasping and of grasp pantomime. As expected, mirror neurons fired for grasping but not for observation of the pantomime" (p. 660). A mime cue (Givens, 2013) is a position or movement of the hands used to depict the shape, motion, or location of a person, place or thing. A mime cue used while speaking is a gesture in which the hands and fingers mimic physical, spatial, and temporal relationships among objects, activities, and events. Because they reveal conceptual thought, mime cues may be our most intellectual gestures. Unlike palm-down and palm-up cues, which convey mainly emotion, mime cues also express narrative thinking, relationships among objects, and the association of ideas. In this regard, mime cues resemble the spoken words they so often accompany.

To mimic an act such as changing a lightbulb, mime cues use the same brain modules to move the same muscles as the physical activity itself. Thus, neurologically, swinging a bat is nearly the same as gesturing the act of batting without using the bat itself. Computer imaging studies show that mentally rehearsing an activity involves the same brain areas, as well (Sirigu et al., 1996, p. 1564). Mime cues engage many areas of neocortex, as well as evolved sub-regions of the basal ganglia and cerebellum. Miming in temporal order and tracing shapes in space involve a highly evolved area of the Human Brain's parietal lobe. The right posterior parietal helps us perform and perceive complex gestures, and recognize complex objects placed in our hand, unaided by vision (Ghez, 1991, p. 623). Eccles (1989) has written, "The right parietal lobe is specially concerned in the handling of spatial data and in a non-verbalized form of relationship between the body and space" (p. 197). As it integrates arriving visual, spatial, auditory, and tactile information, our parietal cortex receives emotional input from the cingulate gyrus of the Mammalian Brain. The parietal lobe then directs our body movements for gesture through fiber links to premotor areas of the brain's frontal cortex and lateral cerebellum (Ghez, 1991, p. 623). Mime cues are produced by nerve impulses traveling down the lateral corticospinal tract. This evolutionarily recent pathway channels the fine-motor control of our finger and wrist muscles required by the mime gesture.

Foot cues

We arrive now at our final destination, the feet. Feet are the terminal end organs below the legs, used for such bipedal activities as standing, walking, and dancing. Unlike hands, feet make direct contact with the earth and ground. Like hands, feet are neurologically gifted; both body parts are well connected to areas of the spinal cord and brain. Notable nonverbal signs involving the feet include boots, dance, goose-step, high heels, men's shoes, women's shoes, and walking (Devine, 1985). Efferent and afferent nervous-system circuits for walking are explored below.

Efferent cues (outgoing)

Walking. Primary muscles of walking are the quadriceps, hamstrings, calf muscles, and hip adductors. Gluteal and abdominal muscles play roles, as well. The nervous-system circuits innervating these muscle groups come from cervical, thoracic, lumbar, and sacral spinal nerves. Above the spinal cord, the Human Brain's cerebellum contributes to balance. Additionally, the Reptilian Brain's basal ganglia play a role, as do the Primate Brain's cortical motor-control centers. Particular walking styles encode information about a walker's age, physical health, state of mind, and gender, as well as about the walker's emotions, feelings, and moods. As improvisational students learn, we can perform versions of a "happy walk," "sad walk," "angry walk," "mincing walk," and so on.

Arm-swing. In tandem with walking itself is the arm-swing. The arm-swing is a body movement in which the upper limbs swing back and forth rhythmically with the walking feet. As a counterweight, the arm-swing helps balance our upright body while walking, jogging, and running. In dances such as the Locomotion, the Swim, and the Twist, vigorous arm-swinging gyrations express inner feelings and moods in time to music's rock 'n' roll beat. In a happy walk the arms may swing high, while in a sad walk the arms hang downward and barely move.

Spinal circuits from the Reptilian Brain's basal ganglia govern the rhythmic, alternating movements of arm-swinging. These ancient circuits evolved, in tandem with those of the legs, for locomotion. The act of swinging the arms while walking – and of pumping them while running – is an evolutionary holdover from earlier days, when the arms, used as forelimbs, participated with the feet in quadrupedal locomotion. In the Human Brain, supraspinal circuits for arm-swinging have been identified in the cerebral motor cortex, with possible influences from the cerebellum, basal ganglia, and afferent sensory feedback (Barthelemy & Nielsen, 2010).

Afferent cues (incoming)

Our neurological perception of walking is mediated by mirror neurons. The human gait registers in cells of the brain's superior temporal sulcus (STS) that respond selectively to "biological motion" – to distinctive bodily movements of animals in activities such as running, crawling, and leaping. "Point-light" research reveals that we decode bodily actions from a relatively small number of physical prompts. Our ability to decode animate actions, such as walking, from minimal point-light cues is likely due to mirror neurons.

Pioneered by Swedish researcher Gunnar Johansson in the 1970s, point-light methodology has enabled study of biological motion in human activities such as walking, throwing, and dancing. Researchers attach as few as 12 small "light spots" to the body, one each attached to the head, shoulders (at their widest points), elbows, hands, pelvic girdle (at the midpoint), knees, and feet. As the body moves, the lighted points – and only the lighted points – are filmed. From animated movements of the attached spots alone (all other bodily features are invisible), viewers are able to identify a point-light subject's gender (Mather & Murdoch, 1994), physical activity (such as climbing stairs; Johansson, 1973), and even emotions (Brownlow et al., 1997). In a study of how subjects perceived point-light renditions of humans performing jumping-jack and kicking movements, Ulloa and Pineda (2007) concluded that the point-light motions engaged mirror neurons in viewers' supplementary motor-cortex areas (SMAs). SMA circuits, which originated in the Primate Brain (Brodmann's area 6 in the Human Brain), project directly to the spinal cord, and are involved in the control of movement.

Conclusion

This aim in this chapter was to explore human nervous-system circuits that encode and decode nonverbal cues. The focus was on communicative movements of specific body parts, beginning with the head and continuing downward through the neck, shoulders, hands, and feet. Exploration began with the neurology of each body-movement cue (efferent), followed by a neurological examination of the movement's perception (afferent). Key players on the encoding side included special visceral nerves and subcortical reflexes (such as tactile withdrawal). The central players on the decoding side included specialized cortical "recognition areas" (such as those for facial recognition) and mirror neurons.

References

Barthelemy, D., & Nielsen, J. B. (2010). Corticospinal contribution to arm muscle activity during human walking. *Journal of Physiology, 588*, 967–79.

Blurton Jones, N. G. (1967). An ethological study of some aspects of social behaviour of children in nursery school. In D. Morris (Ed.), *Primate Ethology* (pp. 347–68). Chicago: Aldine.

Brannigan, C., & Humphries, D. (1972). Human non-verbal behaviour: A means of communication. In N. G. Blurton Jones (Ed.), *Ethological Studies of Child Behaviour* (pp. 37–64). Cambridge: University Press.

Brownlow, S., Dixon, A. R., Egbert, C. A., & Radcliffe, R. D. (1997). Perception of movement and dancer characteristics from point-light displays of dance. *The Psychological Record, 47*(3), 411–21.

Chevalier-Skolnikoff, S. (1973). Facial expression of emotion in nonhuman primates. In P. Ekman (Ed.), *Darwin and facial expression* (pp. 11–89). New York: Academic Press.

Corina, D. P., & Knapp, H. (2006). Sign language processing and the mirror neuron system. *Cortex, 42*(4), 529–39.

Darwin, C. (1998). *The expression of the emotions in man and animals* (3rd edn). New York: Oxford University Press. (original work published 1872.)

de Waal, F. (1982). *Chimpanzee politics*. London: Jonathan Cape.

de Waal, F., & Lanting, F. (1997). *Bonobo: The forgotten ape*. Berkeley: University of California Press.

Devine, J. (1985). The versatility of human locomotion. *American Anthropologist, 87*, 550–70.

Eccles, J. (1989). *Evolution of the brain: Creation of the self.* London: Routledge.

Ekman, P. (1998). Commentaries. In C. Darwin (Ed.), *The expression of the emotions in man and animals* (3rd edn). New York: Oxford University Press.

Ekman, P., & Friesen, W. V. (1968). Nonverbal behavior in psychotherapy research. In J. Shlien (Ed.), *Research in psychotherapy* (pp. 179–216). Washington, DC: American Psychological Association.

Ekman, P., Friesen, W. V. & Tomkins, S. S. (1971). Facial affect scoring technique: A first validity study. *Semiotica, 3,* 37–58.

Freedberg, D. (2009). Movement, embodiment, emotion. In T. Dufrenne, & A. Taylor (Eds), *Cannibalismes disciplinaires, quand l'Histoire de l'Art et l'Anthropologie se rencontrent* (pp. 37–61). Paris: INHA/Musee du Quai Branly.

Ghez, C. (1991). Voluntary movement. In E. R. Kandel, J. H. Schwartz & T. M. Jessell (Eds), *Principles of neural science* (3rd edn, pp. 609–25). Norwalk, Connecticut: Appleton & Lange.

Givens, D. B. (1977). Shoulder shrugging: A densely communicative expressive behavior. *Semiotica, 19*(1/2), 13–28.

Givens, D. B. (1978). Social expressivity during the first year of life *Sign Language Studies, 20,* 251–274.

Givens, D. B. (1986). The big and the small: Toward a paleontology of gesture *Sign Language Studies, 51,* 145–67.

Givens, D. B. (2013). The nonverbal dictionary of gestures, signs & body language cues. Spokane, Washington: Center for Nonverbal Studies Press. Retrieved from www.center-for-nonverbal-studies.org/6101.html

Goodall, J. (1986). The chimpanzees of Gombe: Patterns of behavior. Cambridge: Belknap Press of Harvard University.

Grant, E. (1969). Human facial expressions. *Man, 4,* 525–36.

Grillner, S. (1996). Neural networks for vertebrate locomotion. *Scientific American, 274,* 64–69.

Gur, R. C., Packer, I. K., Hungerbuhler, J. P., Reivich, M., Obrist, W. D., Amarnek, W. S., & Sackeim, H. A. (1980). Differences in the distribution of gray and white matter in human cerebral hemispheres. *Science, 207,* 1226–28.

Guyton, A. C. (1996). *Textbook of medical physiology* (9th edn). Philadelphia: W. B. Saunders.

Haxby, James V. and M. Ida Gabbini (2011). Distributed neural systems for face perception (Ch. 6). In A. J. Calder, G. Rhodes, M. Johnson, J. Haxby (Eds), *The Oxford Handbook of Face Perception* (pp. 93–110). New York: Oxford University Press.

Iacoboni, M. (2009). Imitation, empathy, and mirror neurons. *Annual Review of Psychology, 60,* 653–70.

Johansson, G. (1973). Visual perception of biological motion and a model for its analysis. *Perceptual Psychophysiology,14*(2), 201–11.

Kandel, E. R., Schwartz, J. H. & Jessell, T. M. (Eds) (1991). *Principles of neural science* (3rd ed.). Norwalk, Connecticut: Appleton & Lange.

Kendon, A. (2004). *Gesture: Visible actions as utterance.* Cambridge: Cambridge University Press.

Keysers, C., & Fadiga, L. (2008). The mirror neuron system: New frontiers *Social Neuroscience, 3*(3–4), 193–98.

LeDoux, J. (1996). *The emotional brain: The mysterious underpinnings of emotional life.* New York: Simon & Schuster.

MacLean, P. D. (1990). *The triune brain in evolution.* New York: Plenum Press.

Mather, G., & Murdoch, L. (1994). Gender discrimination in biological motion displays based on dynamic cues. *Proceedings of the Royal Society of London: Series B, 258,* 273–79.

McGrew, W. C. (1972). Aspects of social development in nursery school children with emphasis on introduction to the group. In N. G. Blurton Jones (Ed.), *Ethological Studies of Child Behaviour* (pp. 129–56). Cambridge: University Press.

Meltzoff, A. N. (2002). Elements of a developmental theory of imitation. In Meltzoff, A. N. & Prinz, W. (Eds), *The imitative mind: Development, evolution, and brain bases.* Cambridge: Cambridge University Press (pp. 19–41).

Molnar-Szakacs, I., & Overy, K. (2006). Music and mirror neurons: From motion to 'e'motion. *Social Cognitive and Affective Neuroscience,. 1,*(3), 235–41.

Montgomery, K. J., Isenberg, N., & Haxby, J. V. (2007). Communicative hand gestures and object-directed hand movements activated the mirror neuron system. *Social Cognitive and Affective Neuroscience, 2*(2), 114–22.

Morris, D. (1994). *Bodytalk: The meaning of human gestures.* New York: Crown Publishers.

Niedenthal, P. M. (2007). Embodying emotion. *Science, 316,* 1002–005.

Norton, R. (1983). *Communicator style: Theory, applications, and measures.* Beverly Hills: Sage Publications.

Restak, R. (1994). *Receptors.* New York: Bantam.

Richmond, V. P., McCroskey, J. C. & Payne, S. K. (1991). *Nonverbal behavior in interpersonal relations* (2nd ed.). Englewood Cliffs, New Jersey: Prentice Hall.

Rozin P., Lowery, L. & Ebert, R. (1994). Varieties of disgust faces and the structure of disgust. *Journal of Personality and Social Psycholology, 66*(5), 870–81.

Salzen, E. A. (1979). The ontogeny of fear in animals. In W. Sluckin (Ed.), *Fear in Animals and Man* (pp. 125–63). New York: Van Nostrand Reinhold Co.

Siegel, D. J. (2012). The developing mind: How relationships and the brain interact to shape who we are (2nd ed.). New York: Guilford Press.

Sirigu, A., Duhamel, J. R., Cohen, L., Pillon, B., Dubois, B., & Agid, Y. (1996). The mental representation of hand movements after parietal cortex damage. *Science, 273,* 1564–568.

Sommer, R. (1969). Personal space: The behavioral basis of design. Englewood Cliffs, New Jersey: Prentice-Hall.

Stern, D. & Bender, E. (1974). An ethological study of children approaching a strange adult. In R. C. Friedman, R. N. Richart, & R. L. Vande Wiele (Eds), *Sex differences in behavior* (233–58). New York: John Wiley and Sons.

Ulloa, E. R., & Pineda, J. A. (2007). Recognition of point-light biological motion: Mu rhythms and mirror neuron activity. *Behavioural Brain Research, 183*(2), 188–94.

Ushioda, T., Watanabe, Y., Sanjo, Y., Yamane, G. Y., Abe, S., Tsuji, Y., & Ishiyama, A. (2012). Visual and uditory stimuli associated with swallowing activate mirror neurons: A magnetoencephalography study. *Dysphagia 27*(4), 504–13.

van der Gaag, C., Minderaa, R. B., & Keysers, C. (2007). Facial expressions: What the mirror neuron system can and cannot tell us. *Social Neuroscience, 2*(3–4), 179–222.

Wicker, B., Keysers, C., Plailly, J., Gallese, V., & Rizzolatti, G. (2003). Both of us disgusted in my insula: The common neural basis of seeing and feeling disgust. *Neuron, 40*(3), 655–64.

Williams, P. L. (1995). Gray's anatomy: The anatomical basis of medicine and surgery. London: Churchill Livingstone.

Young, M. P., & Yamane, S. (1992). Sparse Population Coding of Faces in the Inferotemporal Cortex. *Science 256*, 1327–31.

2
Neuroscience of Nonverbal Communication

Milkica Nešić and Vladimir Nešić

Nonverbal communication is essential for human social interaction, either through static physical cues, such as phenotypic traits, facial and body appearance, or dynamic cues, such as faces and bodies in motion. Communication may be via touching, i.e., haptic communication, or at the spatial distance, i.e., proxemic communication. Communication among animals is most commonly mediated by olfactory signals. In many primates, sense of smell is significantly reduced compared to the smell of other vertebrates, while the visual modality is critical for social communication. About a quarter of the cortex is devoted to human visual perception and analysis. Visual modality provides a large amount of information about the identity of other individuals, their social status, emotional state and intended actions. The importance of face processing for survival is reflected in the extraordinary memory abilities of facial features and expressions in humans and other primates, as well as expressed powers of observation of subtle differences between faces.

Usually, communication is achieved through several types of non-verbal cues or in combination with verbal cues. Successful communication implies integration of different modalities of nonverbal and verbal communication in unique percept (de Gelder & Bertelson, 2003). Verbal (word content) and nonverbal (e.g., facial expressions, gestures, tone of voice) messages can be congruent or incongruent. If the verbal message contradicts the nonverbal expression, the nonverbal information is usually perceived as being more authentic, since it is less controllable. Nonverbal information, termed as a "leaky" cue (Ekman & Friesen, 1969), reveals the "true feelings" or intentions of the speaker. The pattern of breathing, the frequency of swallowing, the amount of sweating, as well as autonomic nervous system (ANS) changes registered in the face, such as blushing, blanching, and pupil dilation, can be

31

very reliable clues to deceit (Ekman, 1992). A "nonverbal dominance" in emotion communication, i.e., implicit effects of nonverbal cues on emotion judgements, is evidenced in situations when attention is not explicitly drawn toward nonverbal cues (Jacob et al., 2013) or even when attention is directed away from nonverbal signals and focused on verbal cues (Jacob et al., 2014).

Numerous studies have used different methods and approaches, such as Positron Emission Tomography (PET), regional Cerebral Blood Flow (rCBF), functional Magnetic Resonance Imaging (fMRI), Transcranial Magnetic Stimulation (TSM), lesion, and single-cell recording studies, to explore neurobiological bases of nonverbal communication. FMRI is based on comparatively slow hemodynamic brain responses to stimuli, and methods such as event-related brain potential (ERP) or magnetoencephalographic (MEG) measures are more useful in obtaining information about the time course of emotional processing. Studies aiming to identify the neural substrates of emotional processing have mainly used emotional faces as experimental stimuli and found that the same brain areas activated during the processing of facial emotion are involved in the processing of emotional information in general. The analysis of emotional events is undertaken by a complex interconnected network of brain structures.

This chapter will discuss the neurobiological basis of different aspects of nonverbal communication, such as the perception of face identity and facial expressions, as well as gestural communication. Different aspects of face perception, including the neuroanatomical and the neurophysiological basis of face identity and expressions perception, and time course of face perception, will be reviewed. Particular attention will be paid to the roles of neurotransmitters, hormones, and pheromones on face perception, as well as to the dependence of facial perception on social context. Gestural communication is reviewed from the aspect of its relation to verbal communication (or the link between action and language), and possible neurophysiological explanations are considered.

Face perception

The purpose of this section is to summarize relevant data about face perception, through successive levels of processing, from the retina to different cortical areas, such as the occipito-temporal cortex and the posterior parietal cortex, and other cortical areas. Different models of identity perception and perception of facial expressions, or static and dynamic aspects of the face, are considered.

Identity perception and perception of facial expressions

The function of the occipito-temporal lobe in recognition of familiar faces was documented in the last decade of nineteenth century, when the selective defect, prosopagnosia (from the Greek words "prosopon" = "face," "agnosia" = "not knowing"), or agnosia of faces, was described as a consequence of occipito-temporal lobe damage, in adults. Typically, the problem these patients have is recognition of new faces, even if they are able to recognize new objects. Therefore, these individuals recognize people according to other characteristics, such as their favorite clothes or voice. This fact indicates that prosopagnosia is a specific visual deficit for faces.

Ungerleider and Mishkin (1982) proposed the existence of two processing streams: occipito-temporal or ventral stream, and occipito-parietal or dorsal stream. The parvocellular and the magnocellular pathways can be distinguished, from the retina, through the lateral geniculate nucleus of the thalamus, and up to the visual cortical regions of the primary visual cortex (also known as striate cortex or V1) and extrastriate visual cortical areas (V2, V3, V4, and V5/MT) which include large regions of the temporal and parietal cortex.

The parvocellular stream, called the "What Pathway," selective for color and form, begins with ganglion cells in the retina and projects to V1, then goes through visual area V2, then through visual area V4, and ventrally toward the inferior temporal cortex, and ultimately toward brain regions, such as the fusiform face area (FFA), which are thought to be responsible for object and face recognition.

The magnocellular stream, called the "Where Pathway" or "How Pathway," is selective for properties of motion, such as speed and direction. This stream also begins with the ganglion cells in the retina and projects to V1, then goes through visual area V2, and to the dorsomedial area and visual area MT (also known as V5), and finally to the parietal cortex and to regions close to the posterior superior temporal areas.

These two parallel processing streams are functionally different; the ventral stream processes identity of faces, and the dorsal stream is engaged in social interaction-based analysis. The ventral occipito-temporal cortex of the right hemisphere is primarily responsible for the perceptual analysis of faces. Then, the information is sent to the anterior temporal region where is associated with stored information about individuals. Functional neuroimaging points out that the frontal cortex is involved in recognizing facial emotion (George et al., 1993) and it seems that the frontal cortex contributes to the analysis of emotional status, and storing faces in short-term memory. Finally, lesion studies

(Gainotti, 2007) support the view that the left temporal lobe is responsible for the connection of stored verbal information (e.g., name) with perceived face.

Perceptual analysis in the primary visual cortex continues in the higher cortical areas. In this process, more complex information about the face is extracted. The models which propose that face identity and facial expressions are processed independently are presented below.

Bruce and Young (1986) developed a model of face recognition, which emphasizes that facial expressions and identity are processed independently. Hasselmo, Rolls, and Baylis's (1989) findings of differential activation patterns for identity and expressions in the cortex of macaque monkeys are in accordance with the model postulated by Bruce and Young. Face selective neurons (FSNs) demonstrate sensitivity to global and general aspects of the face, such as the prototypical position of the eyes and the nose in the configuration of the face. Many FSNs are selective for the spatial position of the face, while other FSNs seem to specifically respond to distinctive facial expressions. Some neurons in these areas respond to specific components of the face, for example the eyes or their mutual distance, or the form of the forehead. Finally, FSNs that react when observing the entire face are partially sensitive to the gaze direction of the observed face, which is an important social signal for monkeys, as well as for humans (Farah et al., 1999). The first single-cell recordings of face processing in humans (Ojemann et al., 1992) showed significant neural activation changes of 62% and 52% in the right superior and middle temporal gyri, respectively, for identity matching and expression labelling tasks.

Haxby and colleagues (Haxby et al., 2000; 2002) proposed the functional organization of distributed system as a hierarchical model, composed from a core and an extended system. According to their proposal, static and dynamic aspects of the face have different representations in the core system and in regions of the extended system. The following three regions of the occipito-temporal visual extrastriate cortex: the inferior occipital gyri (IOG), the superior temporal sulcus (STS) and the lateral fusiform gyrus ("fusiform face area" – FFA; Kanwisher, McDermott, & Chun, 1997) compose the core system. IOG is important for the lower, initial perceptual level of analysis ("occipital face area" – OFA; Gauthier et al., 2000). FFA has a role in higher analysis for invariant aspects of faces, such as identity. The STS has a role in the perception of changeable aspects of faces such as movements of lips and understanding speech and expression (Calvert et al., 1997), and the face-sensitive region in the right posterior STS responds more strongly to dynamic, as compared to static, faces (Pitcher et al., 2011). Studies have demonstrated that the bilateral FFA is involved in the perception of emotional facial expression, in addition to its role in the perception of facial identity (Vuilleumier & Pourtois, 2007).

The key parts of the extended system for face perception are systems outside of the visual extrastriate cortex, and they have a central role in extracting various types of information from faces. The following regions are involved in analyzing the changeable aspects of the face, i.e., various facial movements and their functions: the intraparietal sulcus (for spatially directed attention), auditory cortex (for prelexical speech perception from lip movements), and the set of limbic structures including the amygdala and insula (for the perception of emotion from expression). The anterior temporal area is involved in the retrieval of personal identity, and biographical information. Both regions of the core and the extended system extract meaning from faces.

Haxby et al. (2002) proposed that the posterior superior temporal sulcus (pSTS) is important for the perception and encoding of biologic motion, including whole body motion, the hand, and the changeable aspects of faces, such as the eyes and mouth. A particularly important aspect of communication is gaze behavior, which provides fundamental mechanisms for sharing mental states such as goals and desires, and helps to ground communicative content. Gaze direction, like facial expression, is a dynamic property of faces, and both are important functions of the pSTS (Haxby et al., 2000). The perception of averted eye-gaze faces activates intraparietal sulcus more than perception of direct eye-gaze faces (Hoffman & Haxby, 2000).

The model postulated by Haxby and colleagues is partly in accordance with the results of the lesion study by Fox, Hanif, Iaria, Duchaine, and Barton (2011), who confirmed that impairments in identity and expression recognition are dissociable. Namely, they found that damage of occipital face area (OFA) and FFA was the root cause of identity impairments. Furthermore, they found that impairments in discriminating expression can occur with damage to the right STS that affects the pSTS. They also found selective impairments in identity perception after right inferior occipito-temporal or anterior temporal lesions that affected the OFA and FFA. The small patient sample had heterogeneous lesions. The four patients with widely varying lesions had selective impairments of identity perception. Two patients with right inferior occipito-temporal cortex damage showed impaired identity perception on the morphed-face discrimination test (and intact expression perception), although one of these patients had intact FFA and OFA. The authors suggested that the important locus of damage may not be the peak regions of face selectivity in the occipito-temporal cortex (OFA/FFA), but may rather involve these regions as well as multiple connections between them and other regions of the cortex.

Some studies have directly contrasted activation in the brain during observation of static versus dynamic stimuli. Fox, Iaria, and Barton (2009) in a fMRI study showed that the face-sensitive regions were more active during the presentation of dynamic than static faces, and Schultz and Pilz (2009) found that face regions in the ventral pathway were significantly more active with dynamic stimuli. This suggests that areas that are not traditionally associated with processing motion might already integrate dynamic information in the case of faces. In addition, the recognition results for dynamic stimuli were found to be better than those for static stimuli (Bülthoff et al., 2011). Dynamic faces are the preferred stimuli for the brain, with a much more wide-spread network of activation than static stimuli. O'Toole and colleagues (2011) proposed that human judgments of identity are likely based on the collaborative computations of multiple representations of face and body, and their associated motions in the high-level visual processing network.

One of the most fascinating discoveries in neurophysiology in the last three decades, the revealing of mirror neurons in the early 1990s, changed classical concepts of nervous system functioning and influenced many concepts and models, among others the models of face perception. Mirror neurons have been recorded in the ventral premotor cortex and inferior parietal lobe in the monkey using single-unit electrode recordings (Gallese et al., 1996), and compatible activity has been recorded in these areas, as well as in the supplementary motor areas and medial temporal lobe in humans using fMRI (Rizzolatti et al., 1996) and TMS (Fadiga et al., 1995; Gazzola & Keysers, 2009). The human mirror neuron system (hMNS) has been shown to be engaged in the perception of facial expression (Van der Gaag et al., 2007).

Focusing specifically on the perception of dynamic facial expressions of different emotions, Chakrabarti and colleagues (Chakrabarti et al., 2006) suggested the existence of an intermediate module for the perception of action, which is interposed between the visual "core" system and the interaction with the expanded system which includes different structures for various emotions. The common elements of different emotional facial expressions are that they involve movements of the eyes and the lips, which are coded by a generic "mirror system." So, in a modified model, the STS, together with the inferior frontal gyrus (IFG), premotor cortex (PM), and inferior parietal lobulus (IPL), has the function of "action" perception. The activation of pre-motor areas, the human equivalent of the mirror-neuron system (MNS), might be related to motor imagery, or (unconscious) imitation of the observed expression. The mirror mechanism plays a role in action and intention understanding, imitation, speech, and emotion feeling (Fabbri-Destro & Rizzolatti, 2008).

Mirror neurons provide an inner imitation, or simulation, of the observed facial expression and they send signals through the insula to the limbic system, which provides the feeling of the observed emotion (Iacoboni, 2008).

In this part of the chapter we have summarized findings about the ventral and dorsal streams and their role in the analysis of invariant and changeable aspects of faces, and models that propose segregated visual processing pathways, which receive their inputs from early visual areas. Consistent with this idea are the presence of FSN in humans, and also the consequences of lesions to the cortex areas.

Researches on mirror neurons in humans and findings on the connection between social and emotional aspects contributed to the emergence of a new version of an integrative model of distributed neural systems for face perception and recognition. It will be presented in the next subsection. Also, the social relevance of information from the face will be considered.

Social relevance of the face

Haxby and Gobbini (2011) have updated Haxby et al.'s (2000; 2002) model of distributed human neural systems for face perception, starting from the point that appropriate social interactions are possible if a person can immediately retrieve the information about familiar individuals, i.e., person knowledge which includes the personality traits, relationships with oneself and others, and probable intentions, as well as attitudes, transient mental states, biographical information and episodic memories related to specific individuals. They paid special attention to neural systems in the extended system for familiar-face recognition and for extracting the meaning of facial gestures, in particular facial expression and eye gaze. Also, the question of understanding the emotional meaning of expressions finds answer in evoking the emotion itself, i.e., in a simulation or mirroring of another's emotion. This is analogous to the role of the hMNS in simulating or mirroring the motor actions of another. The pattern of neural activity evoked by viewing a familiar face depends on the familiarity. Haxby and Gobbini (2011) proposed three sets of brain areas in the extended system that is involved in the representation of person knowledge, in action understanding, and in emotion. The medial prefrontal cortex (MPFC) and the temporo-parietal junction (TPJ) encode those aspects of person knowledge that are related to the representation of personal traits and mental states characteristic of a familiar individual. The posterior cingulate cortex and precuneus (PCC/PC) and the anterior temporal regions may be important in retrieval of episodic memories and biographical information associated with familiar individuals. The other very important aspect is that viewing faces of familiar individuals modulates neural activity in regions usually involved in emotional responses, such as the amygdala and the insula, as well as the striatum/ reward system.

Montgomery, Seeherman, and Haxby (2009) found an enhanced response in the frontal opercular area for the perception of dynamic facial expressions associated with social meaning, in individuals who have average or high levels of empathy. Empathy is associated with differential recruitment of the hMNS during perception of social facial expressions (e.g., happiness, anger, surprise) when such activation is not explicitly required. Behaviour matching (La France, 1979) occurs when people mimic behavior patterns by adopting similar postures or showing similar body configurations. Zajonc, Adelmann, Murphy and Niedenthal (1987) found the growing resemblance of couples married for a period of 25 years and explained it as a consequence of spontaneous mimicry of facial expressions (Zajonc, 1985). Chartrand and Bargh (1999) described (nonconscious) mimicry as the chameleon effect important for smoother social interaction and interpersonal bonding. They found that empathic individuals [with a higher score on the perspective taking subscale of Davis's (1983) Interpersonal Reactivity Index] are more likely to imitate others in social interactions.

Familiar-face recognition involves visual codes for familiar individuals in core system areas in the fusiform, and possibly anterior temporal cortex. As was previously mentioned, this process occurs in cooperation with the extended system and the automatic activation of person knowledge and emotional responses.

Calder (2011) summarized the results of different researches (image-based analysis, cognitive, neuropsychology, and neuroimaging) on face perception, expression, and recognition, and proposed positions that were in contrast with Bruce and Young's (1986) and Haxby et al.'s (2000) models. He suggested that the same visual route, i.e., the ventral temporal route (and FFA) was engaged in analyzing certain aspects of facial identity and expression. Also, the integration of form and motion of facial cues occurred in the STS. Facial expression and dynamic cues of facial identity were coded by a separate route, including the STS, which was also proposed by Haxby et al. (2000). Different facial properties and multiple cues on motion (changeable facial cues) and visual form (identity, expression and other facial cues) are integrated in accordance to their relative levels of reliance.

The somatic marker hypothesis predicts that stimuli with strong affective value, such as highly familiar faces with a high degree of personal relevance and familiarity, produce somatic marker activation, indexed by skin conductance responses (SCRs) in normal subjects (Damasio et al., 1991; Bradley et al., 1992; Damasio et al., 1996). Somatic marker activation was impaired in four patients with bilateral ventromedial frontal damage, although these subjects recognized the identity of familiar faces normally (Tranel et al., 1995; Tranel, 2000). By contrast, six prosopagnosic subjects with occipito-temporal damage had significantly larger averaged SCRs to familiar faces (family members and friends, famous individuals) than to unfamiliar faces. SCRs to target faces may be evidence of non-conscious (covert) discrimination (Tranel, 2000, p. 320). In this double dissociation between conscious and non-conscious face recognition, the neural systems that process somatic-based valence (the emotional significance) of stimuli may be separated from the neural systems that process factual, non-somatic information associated with the same stimuli. Non-conscious face discrimination in subjects with occipito-temporal damage may be explained by an alternative route of neural activation. Namely, damage to the occipito-temporal region precludes activation (by faces) of ventral occipital and temporal association cortices. Activation may spread through dorsal cortices to ventromedial prefrontal cortices, and to amygdala (as autonomic control nucleus). Adolphs, Tranel, Damasio, and Damasio (1994) showed double dissociation in patients with bilateral amygdala damage. These patients were compromised in the recognition of fearful facial expressions, while identity face recognition was intact. Adolphs, Tranel, Damasio, and Damasio (1995) suggested that the amygdala serves as a link between visual representations of facial expressions, on the one hand, and representations that constitute the concept of fear, on the other. It seems that the amygdala has a role in both recognition and recall of fearful facial expressions.

The amygdala and part of the visual cortex are more active when the subject is exposed to emotion inducing images than to neutral pictures, and the upper temporal sulcus was more active on social as compared to non-social images (Vrtička et al., 2013). The amygdala has a role in assessing the possible threatening valence of a stimulus. It responds to different facial expressions, such as fear (Breiter et al., 1996), sadness, and happiness, and also have the task of categorizing unknown faces (Adolphs, 2002b; Pessoa & Adolphs, 2010). The facial expression of disgust is processed additionally by the basal ganglia and the insular cortex (Adolphs, 2002a). The other brain areas, such as prefrontal cortex (PFC), inferior frontal cortex, right medial temporal region, anterior cingulate cortex (ACC), inferior temporal cortex, and orbitofrontal cortex (OFC) are activated by different facial expressions (Posamentier & Abdi, 2003). The inferior frontal cortex may serve as an area for the integration or semantic processing of information contained in facial expressions. Attractive faces, which can be considered to be a type of reward, especially if the face has a positive facial expression such as smiling, produce enhanced activation in the medial OFC of the observer (Hornak et al., 2003; O'Doherty et al., 2003; Ochsner et al., 2004; Amodio & Frith, 2006; Jacob et al., 2012), since this area has the role in response selection and the processing of reward value. Jacob, Kreifelts, Brück, Erb et al. (2012) in an fMRI study showed that individuals with a higher degree of nonverbal dominance have an increased sensitivity not only to nonverbal but to emotional stimuli in general. "Emotional attention" centred in the amygdala may be modulated, amplified, or attenuated by the voluntary attention system in frontoparietal brain structures such as the dorsolateral prefrontal cortex (DLPFC), ventromedial prefrontal cortex, or OFC (Vuilleumier & Huang, 2009; Pourtois et al., 2012; Jacob et al., 2014). Additionally, the OFC is implicated in many cognitive activities, including decision making, and behavior control (Rolls et al., 2006; Rolls & Grabenhorst, 2008; Rolls, 2014).

Norris, Chen, Zhu, Small, and Cacioppo (2004) based their research on the assumption that social stimuli are among the most emotionally evocative stimuli for humans and found that the neural mechanisms that underlie the processing of social information are intricately connected with those implicated in emotional networks in the brain. Interactive processing of emotional and social information was found in the STS, middle occipito-temporal cortex and thalamus. These results indicate interactive effects early on during processing, potentially indicating greater attentional allocation to conspecifics in emotional contexts. The amygdala demonstrated overlap (but no interaction) between social and emotional processes, since they are primarily related to the processing of biologic stimulus or for person relevant stimulus, regardless of their social or/and emotional nature. Vrtička et al. (2013) in their fMRI 2 (valence) × 2 (social content) interaction experiment showed that the bilateral amygdala, more the right than left amygdala, were engaged in the interactive integration of both valence and social content. Several cortical regions, including the right fusiform gyrus, the right anterior superior temporal gyrus, and the medial OFC, intimately connected with the amygdala, were also engaged in relevance detection in humans.

Perceptual representations of emotionally relevant stimuli are formed in the higher order sensory cortices. The amygdala, OFC, and ventral striatum are engaged in classification of these sensory representations according to their emotional and motivational significance, while paralimbic and higher cortical areas such as the somatosensory cortex, anterior cingulate, and MPFC generate conscious representations of emotional states. The dorsomedial prefrontal cortex and medial parietal cortex, known as the default state areas, are the system for thinking about social relationships throughout time and for considering their implications. The regions critical for social cognition, including the inferior frontal cortex, the superior temporal cortex, and the fusiform gyrus, are very important for behaviour evaluation (Iacoboni et al., 2004). They are important for strategic control of behaviour in complex social situations, and in the planning of future goals and actions (Adolphs, 2003).

In the next section, cultural influences on face perception will be considered.

Cultural aspects of face perception

Neuroscience emphasises that the brain processes the hierarchical interplay of biological, social and personal values. Cross-cultural neuropsychology is a new discipline that examines behavioral neuroscience within a cultural context. Behavioral neuroscience explores the biological bases of behaviour by drawing from the fields of neuropsychology, neurophysiology, psychopharmacology, neuroanatomy and neuroendocrinology. Cultural psychology, on the other hand, understands behaviour from the interdisciplinary perspectives of anthropology, behavioural ecology, and social and developmental psychology. Biology, culture, gender, and personality combine to shape stable patterns of nonverbal communication (Ramachandran, 2012). Researchers in cultural neuroscience have begun to examine how culture can shape processes of social perception. This multilevel approach investigates the mutual relationships of genetic, neural, and cultural forces which create dynamic mental systems.

Social information such as age, gender and race affects how we see ourselves and how others see us. In fact, one can recognize the emotions of people of all cultures quite accurately, but the emotions of members of the same culture are recognized with greater accuracy. This difference is probably due to different levels of intimacy and better understanding of our own culture (Hart et al., 2000; Phelps et al., 2000; Lieberman et al., 2005; Nešić & Nešić, 2012).

Although there is universality of facial expressions, Elfenbein and Ambady (2002) have concluded that there is a cultural specificity in emotion recognition. Chiao and colleagues (2008) revealed, in an fMRI study with American and native Japanese participants, that own-culture fearful faces, compared to faces expressing neutral affect, anger, or joy, elicited greater activity in the bilateral amygdala, relative to the fearful faces of the other culture. Freeman, Rueland, and Ambady's (2009) investigation confirmed selective responses to own-culture fearful faces. Weisbuch and Ambady (2008) explained the amygdala's selective responses to own-culture fearful faces as a reflection of the fact that these faces carry more motivational significance. It may mean that the amygdala does not represent fear itself, but have a function in changing arousal, learning, and orchestration of fight or flight response in the processes involved in situations of fear.

In summary, the reviewed studies suggest that own-culture facial emotions are recognized with greater accuracy. Also, the own-culture fearful faces elicited greater activity in the bilateral amygdala relative to the fearful faces of the other culture, probably because these faces carry more motivational significance.

Temporal information is useful to build a more comprehensive picture of the functional properties of facial perception, and in the next section we will review electrophysiological studies on the time course of face processing.

The time course of face processing

Event-related brain potential (ERP), a noninvasive measure, provides a continuous measure of processing between a stimulus and a response. A waveform depends on the type of stimulus or task and, typically, ERP is plotted with negative voltages upward (labeled as N), and positive voltages downward (P). Many ERP studies have used the face as a stimulus and investigated perceptual brain processes, and detection and analysis of emotional facial expression.

The processing of the low-level features of the face evokes a positive deflection, the P1 component, with an onset latency of between 65 and 80 ms and peaking at around 100–130 ms at occipital electrodes, mainly generated in "early" extrastriate visual areas. A face-selective component was found around 100–120 ms after stimulus onset, using MEG. Meeren, van Heijnsbergen, and de Gelder (2005) investigated how the observer evaluates the relation between facial and bodily expressions. Their behavioral and electrophysiological results showed a rapid (<120 ms) automatic evaluation where the affective information (e.g., fear) conveyed by face and body is in agreement. Viewing fearful faces and bodies in a fast detection system activates subcortical nuclei, the superior colliculus and the pulvinar, which modulates the activity of extrastriate visual areas. The extrageniculostriate pathway to the cortex that bypasses V1 may have a special role in signalling the visual saliency of the emotional stimuli. Meeren et al. (2005) proposed a neural mechanism for rapid automatic perceptual integration of high-level visual information of biological importance presented outside the focus of attention, which would enable evaluation of the relation between facial and bodily expressions before the full structural encoding of the stimulus and conscious awareness of the emotional expression. Perceptual processing of fearful expressions can be encoded before the identity of the face is fully recognized (Eimer & Holmes, 2007).

Faces consistently evoke a negative potential around 170 ms (N170), peaking between 140 and 230 ms after stimulus onset at lateral occipito-temporal sites. The presentation of parts of the face, such as eyes, elicits larger N170 than whole faces, whereas noses and lips elicit later and smaller negative ERPs (Bentin et al., 1999). Familiar faces evoke a significantly larger negative response at N400 than unfamiliar faces, which reflects the activation of semantic memory or the "personal identity nodes." Faces with positive or negative expressions are more rapidly detected than stimuli such as spiders or snakes. The most consistent capture of attention is evident for fear-relevant stimuli (Öhman et al., 2001).

Different experiments with emotional faces presented either at fixation or laterally, and with or without non-face distractor stimuli, demonstrate an increased ERP positivity compared to the neutral faces presented. These emotional expression effects, for six basic emotions, appear fronto-centrally in a period from 120 to 180 ms post-stimulus, which is remarkably early compared to broadly distributed, positive deflections beyond 250 ms post-stimulus for non-facial stimuli (Martin & Holmes, 2007).

Electrophysiological investigations showed that two components of event-related potentials (ERPs) were elicited by emotions in facial expressions: early posterior negativity (EPN) and the late positive complex (LPC) (e.g., Schupp et al., 2004; Holmes et al., 2009; Schacht & Sommer, 2009).

EPN emerges 150–300 ms after stimulus, and reflects attention allocation to the stimuli (Junghöfer et al., 2001). The results indicate that EPN is somewhat emotion-specific (Recio et al., 2011). Movements within the dynamic face cause enhanced posterior negativity due to a shift in visual attention (Trautmann et al., 2009). Similarly to Blood Oxygen Level Dependent (BOLD) activation patterns, ERPs for dynamic faces imply wider neural sources than static ones. The LPC appears at around 500 ms after stimulus and reflects elaborative processing and conscious recognition of the stimulus (Schupp et al., 2003).

The face responsive neurons found in the OFC tend to respond with longer latencies (140–200 ms) than temporal lobe face-selective neurons (80–100 ms), probably because these neurons are activated via the inputs from the temporal cortical visual areas where face-selective neurons are. Some of the OFC face-selective neurons are responsive to facial expression, gesture or movement (Rolls et al., 2006; Rolls, 2014), probably due to the fact that faces convey information that is important in social reinforcement.

To summarize briefly, ERP studies reviewed in this subsection suggest that processing of the low-level features of the face evokes potentials with short latencies, and also that perceptual processing of fearful expressions can be encoded before recognition of the face. The whole face consistently evokes a negative potential around 170 ms (N170), while familiar faces evoke a negative response at N400, reflecting the activation of semantic memory.

In the next part of this chapter we will consider hormonal influences and the modulating roles of pheromones, as well as the influences of pharmacological manipulations on face perception.

The roles of neurotransmitters, hormones and pheromones in face perception

It is important to emphasize the fact that many factors affect nonverbal communication, such as genetic, environmental, and developmental/epigenetic processes, various neuroendocrine and neurotransmitter systems, i.e., neuropeptides, steroid hormones, and biogenic amines (O'Connell & Hofmann, 2011). Newman (1999) proposed six, reciprocally connected brain regions as nodes of a "social behavior network":

the lateral septum, extended medial amygdala (i.e., medial amygdala and bed nucleus of the stria terminalis), preoptic area, anterior hypothalamus, ventromedial hypothalamus, and periaqueductal gray/central gray. These regions express sex steroid receptors and therefore they are very important for the reproduction and survival of mammals and, importantly, their responsivity to sex steroids is a highly conserved characteristic in mammals. The influences of some neurotransmitters and hormones on nonverbal communication will be considered in the next section.

The systems responsible for the processing of emotional expressions are dependent on different neurotransmitters. Serotonergic, noradrenergic and dopaminergic, and GABAergic pharmacological manipulations have been shown to influence the processing of fearful and happy emotional expressions, sad expressions, and angry expressions. The amygdala receives considerable serotonergic and noradrenergic innervations and it has a role in responding to fearful, sad, and happy expressions as unconditioned stimuli for aversive and appetitive conditioning and instrumental learning. There are high concentrations of benzodiazepine receptor sites in both amygdala and the frontal cortex. The central nucleus of the amygdala, which projects to autonomic centres in the brain stem, is densely innervated by GABA neurons, whereas the basolateral nucleus of the amygdala, projecting to the cortical regions, contains only scattered GABA neurons. GABAergic manipulations impact the role of OFC in modulating the response to interpersonal signals of conflict, such as anger. Blair (2003) proposed that the basolateral nucleus, relatively unaffected by GABAergic manipulations, is more involved in responding to fearful expressions.

Some neurobiological models propose that serotonin (5-HT) facilitates the PFC in suppressing negative emotions, generated in the amygdala. Many factors, such as 5-HT reuptake (5-HT transporter, 5-HTT), catabolism (MAO-A), and postsynaptic receptors (5-HT2A and 5-HT2C) may disrupt PFC top-down control over the amygdala. Passamonti et al. (2012) found that acute tryptophan (a precursor of serotonin) depletion altered the functional connectivity between the amygdala and right ventral anterior cingulate cortex (vACC) and ventrolateral PFC when processing angry faces, compared with neutral faces.

An intriguing field of emotion and face perception research is the genetic factors underlying the regulation of serotonin levels, and variation in the expression of serotonergic genes, e.g., the polymorphism in the serotonin transporter gene (5-HTTLPR). Short- (s-) and long- (l-) allele variants of this gene result in differential expression of the serotonin transporter (5-HTT), with the s-allele variant expressing less 5-HTT protein than the l-allele. The individuals homozygous for the s-allele display heightened amygdala activation to angry faces compared to neutral faces, houses and fixation (von dem Hagen et al., 2011).

Many studies have shown that various aspects of nonverbal communications depend on the hormones, especially oxytocin. Many manifestations of the affective bonding of a mother to her infant, such as mother-to-infant gaze (Kim et al., 2014), the affectionate touch (e.g., hugging, kissing, stroking), the touch of infant extremities, functional touch, proprioceptive touch (i.e., changing the infant's position in space), object presentation, stimulatory touch, and no touch (Atzil et al., 2011), "motherese": high-pitched and sing-song vocalizations, and expression of positive affect are the first nonverbal social contacts in the neonatal period. Maternal behavior can be in coordination with infant signals in the case of synchronous mothers, or with the excessive expression of maternal behavior in the case of intrusive mothers. It impacts behavior "from the cradle to the grave" (Bowlby, 1969). Early interactions with mother and peers are very important for adult social behaviour and the neural systems involved in social interaction, especially for high brain-derived neurotrophic factor (BDNF) levels in the hippocampus, frontal cortex and hypothalamus, and enhanced oxytocin receptor levels in nuclei of the amygdala (Branchi et al., 2013).

The biobehavioral synchrony model (Feldman, 2012) considers neurobiology across multiple relationships throughout life and the ways in which micro-social behaviours coalesce into unique affiliative bonds. It describes the transformation of early social bonds (even in the first trimester) in consistent expression. The studies suggest that a nonapeptide oxytocin, termed as a "hormone of affiliation" (Feldman, 2012; Insel, 1992), has a role in regulating many aspects of attachment-related social behaviors, such as maternal care, pair bonding, interpersonal trust, emotion recognition, and empathy.

The involvement of oxytocin is particularly important at times when the infant's need for access to the mother is the greatest. Studies suggest that while the mother's oxytocin response is positively associated with the duration of the time her gaze was directed toward her infant, it is negatively associated with the frequency with which her gaze shifted away from her infant. A significant decrease of mother-to-infant gaze during periods of infant distress is present in mothers who show low/ average oxytocin response (Kim et al., 2014).

Synchronous mothers show greater activations in the left NAcc, the correlation of left NAcc and right amygdala with emotion modulation, theory-of-mind, and empathy networks, clearer organization across time, and correlations between oxytocin with left NAcc and right amygdala activations. Contrarily, intrusive mothers show higher activations in the right amygdala, functional correlation of left NAcc and right amygdala with pro-action areas, and greater cross-time disorganization of activations of left NAcc and right amygdala. This investigation demonstrates that many factors, such as reward-related motivational mechanisms, temporal organization, and affiliation hormones, are in interplay in well-adapted parenting, whereas stress-related mechanisms and greater neural disorganization underlay anxious parenting.

The hormonal status of a woman determines her preference for the male gender. Studies have shown that women show different preferences for male faces of varying degrees of masculinity during different phases of the menstrual cycle. Women pay more attention to the phenotypic markers that indicate greater immunological competence in males during the follicular phase of the menstrual cycle, when a probability of conception is higher. Similarly, women's biases to men's scents, which are correlated with the traits dependent on testosterone, increase the likelihood of conception during a menstrual cycle. Women can choose a primary partner with low masculinity, suggesting cooperation in parental care of offspring, but the occasional sexual relationships with men with more masculine traits, which indicate strong immunocompetence, at the time of conception is more likely (Penton-Voak et al., 1999).

Gelstein et al. (2011) showed that the sniffing of negative emotion-related, odorless women's tears changed the perception of pictures of women's faces, which appeared less sexually attractive. Also, authors showed, using fMRI, that sniffing women's tears selectively reduced activity in brain substrates (the hypothalamus and left fusiform gyrus) of sexual arousal in men, which is in accordance with the results of objective measures of reduced psychophysiological arousal and lower testosterone expression. Taken as a whole, this study showed that women's tears contain a chemosignal with an emotionally relevant function.

Volumetric MRI and PET measurements suggest sexually dimorphic neuronal response to chemosignals with pheromone-like properties, indicating that neuronal response depends on sexual orientation (Savic, 2014). Common odours activate the classical olfactory regions in homosexual men (HoM), homosexual women (HoW), heterosexual men (HeM) and heterosexual women (HeW) (Berglund et al., 2006).

The 4,16-androstadien-3-one (AND) steroid, which is in higher concentrations in men than in women, activated the preoptic area and the ventromedial nuclei in women, whereas steroid estra-1,3,5(10),16-tetraen-3-ol (EST) activated an area covering the paraventricular and dorsomedial nuclei in men. Contrary to this pattern of activation, AND and EST activated the classical odour processing regions, such as the amygdala and piriform cortex, the anterior insular cortex, OFC, and the anterior cingulate cortex when men smelled AND and women smelled EST. A possible interpretation of the sex differentiated pattern of activation, given by the researchers, was that the two steroids (AND or EST) might act bimodally as pheromones and odours, depending on the sex of the responder, when one pathway dominates, whereas the other is suppressed. It could be that the anterior hypothalamus primarily processes signals from the pheromone-like component of AND and EST, whereas the olfactory brain primarily mediates the signals of their odour component. The pattern of activation changes in these groups of subjects for AND and EST. Both in HoM and HeW, but unlike HeM, the signals from AND were processed by the anterior hypothalamus with maximal cerebral activation in an area corresponding to the preoptic, ventromedial, and tuberomamillary nuclei; whereas the signals from EST were in HoM mediated by the olfactory brain. The classical odor-processing circuits (the amygdala, the piriform and insular cortex) were engaged during the presentation of AND, as well as EST, while there was an absence of preoptic activation with AND in HoW.

It may be interesting to investigate whether pheromones influence preferences for faces depending on the sexual orientation. Kranz and Ishai (2006) have already found that the perception of faces may be modulated by sexual preference. There was a stronger reaction of the thalamus and MPFC in HeM and HoW when looking at a female face, whereas the reaction in these structures was stronger in HoM and HeW when looking at a male face.

In summary, we have considered the role of different pharmacological manipulations of neurotransmitters on face perception. The influence of hormones, especially oxytocin on maternal behavior, is evidenced through gaze direction toward the infant. A correlation between oxytocin and activation of left NAcc and right amygdala in synchronous mothers was found. Also, the attractiveness of a man's face depends on the woman's phase of menstrual cycle. Chemosignals in women's tears change the man's perception of pictures of women's faces and reduce activity in brain substrates of sexual arousal. The sexually dimorphic influence of chemosignals, steroids AND and EST, was found to be dependent on sexual preferences.

Facial expressions, controlled and spontaneous, are under corical and subcortical control, as will be presented in the next section.

Facial expressions

Facial expressions have importance for both basic survival and social interaction. Even simple, basic facial responses to stimuli such as sweet and bitter tastes have communicative value. Additionally, facial responses have a more complex role in nonverbal communication. The perception and production of facial expressions are cognitive processes, and numerous subcortical and cortical areas contribute to these operations. Erickson and Schulkin (2003) argue that no specific emotion center exists over and above cognitive systems in the brain, and that emotion should not be separated from cognition.

In the next part of the chapter we briefly present measures of facial expressions, as well as subcortical and cortical control of the lower and upper face muscles movements, and left and right side face movements.

Many striate muscles, for example in the neck, back, arms, and other body parts, as well as the smooth muscles of the blood vessels and alimentary tract, contract in response to emotions. Facial movements are essential for the appropriate execution of many important functions such as mastication, swallowing, and social interaction, including speech and nonverbal communication. Lip movements support speech comprehension, whereas gaze direction informs about spatial attention. Lip muscles and the muscles that direct our gaze, together with other facial muscles communicate the emotional state to others.

Different emotions can be clearly differentiated based on the pattern of facial muscle tension. Therefore facial expressions are the most obvious emotional indicators which can be objectively described. The typical patterns of facial muscle actions change the position of various lines, wrinkles, folds, and facial landmarks in characteristic ways. These skin movements, produced by muscles or groups of muscles, may be decoded using the Facial Action Coding System (FACS; Ekman & Friesen, 1978), by a graphic representation that illustrates the sequence and the duration of expressions occurring on a subject's face over a given period of time, i.e. an affectogram (Izard & Dougherty, 1982), or with electromyography (EMG) measures, which can detect facial contractions, even when there is little or no movement of the facial skin.

Facial muscles are innervated by the facial nerves, which arrange facial features in meaningful configurations. The facial nucleus in the brainstem is innervated by direct and indirect corticobulbar pathways. Contralaterally innervated muscles – the muscles that manipulate the lips, for example – have the capacity for fine, discrete, highly controlled movements, and they are involved in learned, skilled motor behaviors much more commonly than are bilaterally innervated muscles – the frontalis and corrugator, for example – which perform only more gross movements. Whereas the lower face participates in articulating speech, the upper face participation in language is restricted to adding "punctuation" and prosody. The extrapyramidal motor system sends impulses for emotional facial movements, whereas corticobulbar projections induce, volitionally, movements of facial muscles (Rinn, 1984).

The left side of the face, controlled by the right hemisphere, is more personalized, more expressive of emotions, more uninhibited, divulges hidden personalized feelings, and displays culture-specific emotional norms. The right side of a face, controlled by the left hemisphere, reveals the more social, explicit and conscious content of personality, socially appropriate clues and more universal emotional signals (Wolff, 1933; Asthana & Mandal, 1996). Anatomical, neurological, psychological, pathological, and socio-cultural factors may influence facial asymmetry (Van Gelder & Borod, 1990; Mandal & Ambady, 2004).

Many methods, such as cortical stimulation, functional neuroimaging, and localized surgical resection, show the powerful influence of the cerebral cortices on facial movements. The primary motor cortex (M1), ventral lateral premotor cortex (LPMCv), supplementary motor cortex (M2), as well as the limbic proisocortices, i.e. rostral cingulate motor cortex (M3), and caudal cingulate motor cortex (M4), have multiple cortical facial representations. This fact suggests a potential anatomical substrate that may contribute to the clinical dissociation of volitional and emotional facial movement (Morecraft et al., 2001).

There are direct, topographically organized corticocortical connections between each facial area, which also send direct corticobulbar projections to the facial motor nucleus in the nonhuman primate. The facial representation of M1, LPMCv, and M4 preferentially give rise to contralateral axonal projections ending in the parts of the facial nucleus that innervate the lower facial musculature (Morecraft et al., 2004).

The subcortical regions, in particular the basal ganglia, and cortical regions, particularly the frontal cortex, which are reciprocally interconnected, are involved in the production of both spontaneous and controlled emotional displays. The frontal cortex is crucial for representing goals, to either show or suppress an emotional expression, while the basal ganglia receive inputs from both the amygdala and other structures processing emotional information. Therefore, damage to these structures impairs the production of emotional expressions; frontal cortical lesions cause significant impairment to the production of both spontaneous and controlled expressions, while lesions to the basal ganglia disproportionately affect the production of spontaneous expressions. Amygdala lesions reduce the display of spontaneous fearful displays to novel objects, and do not affect the production of controlled fearful or other emotional displays.

To summarize, we suggest that volitional and emotional facial movements are controlled by cortical regions, particularly the frontal cortex, and subcortical regions, in particular the basal ganglia, respectively. The basal ganglia receive inputs from both the amygdala and other structures processing emotional information. These structures are reciprocally interconnected. The amygdala influences spontaneous fearful displays to novel objects. So, there are clinical and anatomical roots for the dissociation of volitional and emotional facial movement.

The following section is focused on gestures as communicative acts. We briefly provide an overview on the gestural aspects of communication, and the relationship of gesture and speech, and gesture and thought. Many approaches suggest that gestures communicate ideas much earlier than spoken language, supporting the emergence of language.

Gestural communication: Co-speech gestures

The main feature that distinguishes humans from the great apes is the specialization of the lower limbs for upright locomotion, enabling the upper limbs for grasping and gestural communication. Bipedalism preceded the development of human language and could have been an important step towards a manual-based communication system, as proto-languages in the form of gestures (Corballis, 2002).

Gestures are present when people talk and the listener cannot see them, for example in communication by phone (Bavelas et al., 2008) and even in congenitally blind persons, who have never seen human gestures. The alternatives to speech are visual perception of hand movements. They develop in populations who cannot perceive auditory signals, for example deaf children, or if spoken language is not in the environment, such as in families where both parents are deaf and do not speak to each other or the newborn.

Gestures help speakers to express their thoughts, and also help viewers to understand what they hear. There are four main types of co-speech gesture (McNeill, 1992, 2005). The iconic gesture imagistically represents object attributes, actions, and spatial relationships, while a deictic, or pointing, gesture indexes, or connects some aspect of speech to some other idea, object, location or action. A metaphoric gesture conveys an abstract idea in a concrete form, and, finally, beat gestures are hand movements that keep the rhythm of speech. These four types of gestures are different from the fifth prominent gesture, called an emblem: meaningful hand postures, such as the "thumbs up" or "peace sign," which convey information independently of speech.

Gesture as an expressive form appears ontogenetically earlier than spoken expression (Goldin-Meadow et al., 1992). Children produce deictic (or pointing) gestures before they begin to talk, and usually by 18 months they produce iconic gestures. Throughout childhood, deictic and iconic gestures become more complex and frequent (McNeill, 1992).

Representational gestures that represent rather than replicate actions either iconically (e.g., moving two fists in the air as though beating a drum) or metaphorically (moving two open hands in the air as though weighing two sides of an argument) have a special role in comprehending relations between thought processes or mental representations of an event (McNeill, 1992). These gestures provide a unique link between action and mental representation. Also, it seems that representational gestures are a type of simulated action (Cartmill et al., 2012). These manual movements are connected with the content of the speech and facilitate speech production and enhance comprehension. According to the Lexical Retrieval Hypothesis, gesture plays an active role in lexical access, particularly for words with spatial content, and facilitates access to items in the mental lexicon (Krauss & Hadar, 1999). Gesture helps speakers to "package" spatial information into verbalisable units. According the Information Packaging Hypothesis (Alibali et al., 2000), gesture is involved in the conceptual planning of messages. It seems that representational gesture supports the organization of conceptual material for later verbalization.

Sensory-motor theories of cognition assume that representations of sensory and motor experiences constitute the bases for all levels of cognition, including communication. According to embodied cognition, the cognitive processes have roots in the body's interactions with the world (Wilson, 2002). The mind is interconnected with bodily action and interaction with other individuals (Garbarini & Adenzato, 2004).

According to this embodied cognition approach, bodily action is the basis for language, in other words, language is an embodied system since communication is possible using the body. It is known that the pantomime, which preceded language, involves the whole body, and not just the hands. Condon and Ogston (1967) found that the listener's body motions, including the trunk and the legs, are synchronous with the speaker's articulated speech. Condon and Sander (1974) showed that newborns respond to natural, rhythmic speech with bodily movements, from head to feet, in a synchronized way.

There is neurophysiological evidence for the links between gesture and language, as well as action and language in the broader sense. One possible explanation is that neural configurations initially responsible for manipulation of objects (ergotic movements) and gestures are also important for speech (Corballis, 1999).

There is an innate mechanism that links the motor and language systems. The plan for fine hand movements of sufficient complexity becomes the precursor of signs, in the same regions of the prefrontal cortex which are engaged in articulation planning throughout early normal development (Greenfield, 1991). This finding leads to speculation that before differentiation of the lower parts of the prefrontal tissue in Broca's area, there is a relatively large area of the cortex which is nearly equipotent for the control of the articulator apparatus and hands in a linguistically appropriate manner. Broca's area, in the left inferior frontal cortex that subserves language production, has other functions, too. For example, the inferior frontal cortex is involved in "the regulation of mental activity" (Thompson-Schill et al., 2005), hierarchical processing (Koechlin & Jubault, 2006), action observation, sequencing, or semantic selection (e.g., Thompson-Schill et al., 1997; Koechlin & Jubault, 2006). Taken all together, the inferior frontal cortex may be considered as a node in multiple different networks (Willems & Hagoort, 2007).

Pulvermüller and colleagues (Pulvermüller et al., 2001; Pulvermüller, 2002a, 2002b) propose that the same brain regions are engaged in language and speech and in understanding action related language. Rizzolatti and colleagues (Rizzolatti et al., 1988, 1996) explained the cellular basis of this relationship, which is already mentioned in the previous section about face perception. We will provide a more detailed summary of these proposals below.

Pulvermüller, Härle, and Hummel (2001), and Pulvermüller (2002b), were among the first to demonstrate, using high-resolution EEG during a speeded lexical decision task, that the "motor meaning" of language becomes manifest rapidly in the motor system of the human brain. They found longer latencies for words referring to the lower half of the body's actions than for words referring to actions involving face muscles. For example, the verbs semantically related to leg actions (such as "walk") and verbs semantically related to face actions (such as "talk") activated the areas in the motor cortex where these movements are controlled. This implies that the motor system is, in a somatotopic fashion (Hauk et al., 2004; Tettamanti et al., 2005), involved in understanding action-related language. Studies using fMRI (Tettamanti et al., 2005) and TSM (Pulvermüller, 2005) showed that hearing or reading words associated with the movement of particular body parts such as "lick", "kick", or "pick" are simulated in those parts of the primary motor cortex that activate respective movement in the tongue, feet, or fingers.

Rizzolatti and Arbib (1998) proposed that mirror neurons are an observation/execution matching system, a bridge from "doing" to "communicating". They make the link between actor, i.e., sender, and observer, i.e., the receiver of each message. Neurons with peculiar "resonant" properties, mirror neurons, are activated by observations of actions such as grasping, placing, manipulating, holding, and especially actions in which the experimenter's hand or mouth interacts with objects (Gallese et al., 1996; Rizzolatti et al., 1996). Fadiga, Fogassi, Gallese, and Rizzolatti (2000) postulated that the motor system not only executes actions but also internally represents them in terms of "motor ideas". Visuomotor responses of the mirror neurons may be the basis for action imitation and action understanding, inter-individual gestural communication (Rizzolatti et al., 1988, 1996), and linguistic function (Rizzolatti & Arbib, 1998), and necessary for understanding other minds (Gallese & Goldman, 1998). According to fMRI data, mirror neurons activate more intensely during the observation of gestures that are iconic and are expressed in face-to-face communication (Franks, 2010, p. 94).

Iacoboni (2008) suggests that gestures actually precede speech in language development. Mirror neurons probably have a crucial role in the evolution of language in Homo sapiens. TMS and PET studies suggest that a mirror system for gesture recognition also exists in humans and includes Broca's area (Rizzolatti & Arbib, 1998). Additionally, the IPL, another area purported to be part of the human mirror neuron system, was equally active when adults viewed, imitated and produced communicative hand gestures, emblems, and gestures, in the absence of speech. Similar activation, confirmed by fMRI (Montgomery, Isenberg, & Haxby, 2007) suggests that the human mirror neuron system may be involved in producing and comprehending hand gestures.

fMRI, TMS, and ERP studies (N400) suggest links between the language and action in the brain (Willems & Hagoort, 2007). The Perisylvian language network (left frontal and temporal areas) is recruited by purely manual languages (sign languages) in deaf signers and by spoken language in hearing subjects. Similar neural processing is evoked in the understanding of meaningful co-speech gestures and the understanding of words (Arbib & Rizzolatti, 1997; Rizzolatti & Arbib, 1998). The region with special sensitivity to human voices, termed as the "temporal voice area" (TVA), is within the anterior and middle STS (Belin et al., 2000). Beside visuomotor properties, mirror neurons respond to auditory stimuli, for example, not only when an individual kicks the ball or sees a ball being kicked, but also when an individual hears a ball being kicked, or even just says or hears the word "kick" (Iacoboni, 2008, p. 12). The same premotor and primary motor cortex is activated by the speech production and listening to speech sounds. This is in accordance with Liberman's motor theory of speech perception, which suggests that the way our brain perceives other people's speech is by simulating talking to ourselves. Arbib (2010) proposes that the ventral stream that projects to the posterior temporal cortex maps sound according to its meaning, whereas the dorsal stream maps sound onto representations based on articulation. Dorsal and ventral streams cooperate in praxis and language.

Liuzzi et al. (2008) demonstrated that the leg motor system is engaged in language processing in the adult speaker, in the reader, and to a lesser degree, in the listener. They tested corticospinal excitability during speech production and perception of continuous prose: text without leg-action words. The enhancement of motor evoked potentials (MEPs) in bilateral soleus muscles suggests that overt speech strongly engages the leg motor system, too. It implies, in the frame of the motor theory of speech, that the system of gestural communication, beside hands, includes the gestural movements of other body parts.

However, there are some cautions, since the overlap between language and action systems is not complete and, furthermore, the motor cortex is not that important for understanding the speech and action-related language. Maybe the most appropriate conclusion is that language and action are not two isolated systems in the brain, since information from the overlapping parts of the brain is used in qualitatively similar ways.

Hostetter and Alibali (2008, 2010) proposed the Gesture as Simulated Action (GSA) framework, explaining gestures as simulated actions during speaking. Although the action is not actually done, when it is realized in overt movement during speech production, the motor and premotor areas are activated adequately for the action. The idea of action simulations being involved in language comprehension and production is in accordance with the previous research (Pulvermüller, 2002a, 2002b, 2005; Pulvermüller et al., 2006).

Wartenburger et al. (2010) found that adolescents scoring high in fluid intelligence showed higher accuracy in a geometric analogy task and produced more representational gestures when explaining how they solved the task. Also, those individuals had larger cortical thickness values in regions in the left hemisphere (pars opercularis, superior frontal, and temporal cortex) than individuals with average fluid intelligence. The GSA framework, which states that gestures result from simulated perception and simulated action that underlie embodied language and mental imagery, seems like a good framework for considering above-mentioned results.

In summary, we suggest that the manual-based communication system is an important step in evolution. Co-speech gestures, and especially representational gestures, precede speech in language development. Language is an embodied system since communication is possible using the body. The mirror system for gesture recognition also exists in humans and includes Broca's area. The human mirror neuron system may be involved in producing and comprehending hand gestures. There is neurophysiological evidence that the system of gestural communication, besides hands, includes gestural movements of other body parts. With some caution, we should conclude that language and action are not two isolated systems in the brain. The inferior frontal cortex may be considered as node in multiple different networks.

Conclusion

Many cues of nonverbal communication, such as the perception of face identity and facial expressions, co-speech gestures, body language, and voice characteristics, are used for full understanding of the message. In this chapter we reviewed facial perception and expression, as well as meaningful hand movements, i.e., gestures, particularly co-speech gestures, often utilized in nonverbal communication. Gestural communication is reviewed through a broader concept of the link between action and language, and the possible neurophysiological explanations are considered. The relations between the mind and the brain and the brain and the body, and their relevance for understanding the basis of nonverbal communication are considered through the somatic marker hypothesis and the embodied cognition approach, too. Cultural aspects of nonverbal communication and the roles of humoral and neurotransmitters systems, as well as the modulatory influences of pheromones, are considered.

It remains a question whether different cues of nonverbal communication share the same neurophysiological mechanisms. The discovery of mirror neurons changed the traditional view of brain functions according the "one area one function" rule. But this does not imply equipotentiality of cortical areas, or absence of specialization in the brain. Rather, it seems that the same brain areas work in a much more "holistic" fashion and that the same cortical regions can be recruited for different cognitive processes, as well as for emotion processing. The mirror neuron system (MNS) observes actions, either facial expressions or gestures, and maps them onto motor representations. Also, the MNS has a role in simulation and understanding nonverbal communication. It may be that the IPL and the frontal operculum, where putative human MNSs are identified, are differently engaged in perception, expression and understanding different cues of nonverbal communication. The identification of nonverbal emotional signals and judging one's own or another individual's emotional state are linked to the medial frontal cortex and the OFC. Also, bilateral activation within the amygdala, FFA, TVA, and posterior temporal cortex, as well as in the midbrain and left inferior OFC/left insula, was found in the perception of nonverbally expressed emotions.

Acknowledgements

This paper was supported by Serbian Ministry of Science, project 179002.

References

Adolphs, R. (2002a). Neural systems for recognizing emotion. *Current Opinions in Neurobiology, 12,* 169–177.

Adolphs, R. (2002b). Recognizing emotion from facial expressions: Psychological and neurological mechanisms. *Behavioral and Cognitive Neuroscience Reviews, 1*(1), 21–62.

Adolphs, R. (2003). Cognitive neuroscience of human social behaviour. *Nature Reviews Neuroscience, 4,* 165–178.

Adolphs, R., Tranel, D., Damasio, H., & Damasio, A. (1994). Impaired recognition of emotion in facial expressions following bilateral damage to the human amygdala. *Nature, 372,* 669–672.

Adolphs, R., Tranel, D., Damasio, H., & Damasio, A. R. (1995). Fear and the human amygdala. *The Journal of Neuroscience, 75*(9), 5879–5891.

Alibali, M. W., Kita, S., & Young, A. J. (2000). Gesture and the process of speech production. We think, therefore we gesture. *Language and Cognitive Processes, 15*(6), 593–613.

Amodio, D. M., & Frith, C. D. (2006). Meeting of minds: The medial frontal cortex and social cognition. *Nature Reviews Neuroscience, 7,* 268–277.

Arbib, M. A. (2010). Mirror system activity for action and language is embedded in the integration of dorsal and ventral pathways. *Brain and Language, 112,* 12–24.

Arbib, M. A., & Rizzolatti, G. (1997). Neural expectations: A possible evolutionary path from manual skills to language. *Communication & Cognition, 29*, 393–424.

Asthana, H. S., & Mandal, M. K. (1996). Mirror-reversal of a face is perceived as expressing emotions more intensely. *Behavioural Neurology, 9*, 115–117.

Atzil, S., Hendler, T., Feldman, R. (2011). Specifying the neurobiological basis of human attachment: Brain, hormones, and behaviour in synchronous and intrusive mothers. *Neuropsychopharmacology, 36*, 2603–2615.

Bavelas, J., Gerwing, J., Sutton, C., & Prevost, D. (2008). Gesturing on the telephone: Independent effects of dialogue and visibility. *Journal of Memory and Language, 58*, 495–520.

Belin, P., Zatorre, R. J., Lafaille, P., Ahad, P., & Pike, B. (2000). Voice-selective areas in human auditory cortex. *Nature, 403*, 309–312.

Bentin, S., Deouell, L. Y., & Soroker, N. (1999). Selective visual streaming in face recognition: Evidence from developmental prosopagnosia. *NeuroReport, 10*, 823–827.

Berglund, H., Lindstrom, P., & Savic, I. (2006). Brain response to putative pheromones in lesbian women. *Proceedings of the National Academy of Sciences USA, 103*, 8269–8274.

Blair, R. J. R. (2003). Facial expressions, their communicatory functions and neuro-cognitive substrates. In C. D. Frith & D. M. Wolpert (Eds.), *The neuroscience of social interaction decoding, imitating, and influencing the actions of others* (pp. 241–264). New York: Oxford University Press Inc.

Bowlby, J. (1969). *Attachment*. New York: Basic Books.

Bradley, M. M., Greenwald, M. K., Petry, M. C., & Lang, P. J. (1992). Remembering pictures: Pleasure and arousal in memory. *The Journal of Experimental Psychology: Learning, Memory, and Cognition, 18*, 379–390.

Branchi, I., Curley, J. P., D'Andrea, I., Francesca, C., Champagne, F. A., & Alleva, E. (2013). Early interactions with mother and peers independently build adult social skills and shape BDNF and oxytocin receptor brain levels. *Psychoneuroendocrinology, 38*, 522–532.

Breiter, H. C., Etcoff, N. L., Whalen, P. J., Kennedy, W. A., Rauch, S. L., Buckner, R. L., … Rosen, B. R. (1996). Response and habituation of the human amygdala during visual processing of facial expression. *Neuron, 17*, 875–887.

Bruce, V., & Young, A. (1986). Understanding face recognition. *British Journal of Psychology, 77*, 305–327.

Bülthoff, H. H., Cunningham, D. W., & Wallraven, C. (2011). Dynamic aspects of face processing in humans. In S. Z. Li & A. K. Jain (Eds.), *Handbook of face recognition* (2nd ed., pp. 575–596). London: Springer-Verlag.

Calder, A. (2011). Does facial identity and facial expression recognition involve separate visual routes? In A. Calder, G. Rhodes, M. Johnson, & J. V. Haxby (Eds.), *Oxford handbook of face perception* (pp. 427–448). New York: Oxford University Press.

Calvert, G. A., Calvert, T. T. G., Campbell, R., Williams, S. C. R., McGuire, P. K., Woodruff, P. W. R., … David, A. S. (1997). Activation of auditory cortex during silent lip reading. *Science, 276*, 593–596.

Cartmill, E. A., Beilock, S., & Goldin-Meadow, S. (2012). A word in the hand: Action, gesture and mental representation in humans and non-human primates. *Philosophical Transactions of the Royal Society B: Biological Sciences, 367*, 129–143.

Chakrabarti, B., Bullmore, E., & Baron-Cohen, S. (2006). Empathizing with basic emotions: Common and discrete neural substrates. *Social Neuroscience, 1*(3–4), 364–384.

Chartrand, T. L., & Bargh, J. A. (1999). The chameleon effect: The perception-behavior link and social interaction. *Journal of Personality and Social Psychology, 76*(6), 893–910.

Chiao, J. Y., Iidaka, T., Gordon, H. L., Nogawa, J., Bar, M., Aminoff, E., ... Ambady, N. (2008). Cultural specificity in amygdala response to fear faces. *Journal of Cognitive Neuroscience, 20*, 2167–2174.

Condon, W. S., & Ogston, W. D. (1967). A segmentation of behavior. *Journal of Psychiatric Research, 5*, 221–235.

Condon, W. S., & Sander, L. W. (1974). Synchrony demonstrated between movements of neonate and adult speech. *Child Development, 45*, 456–462.

Corballis, M. C. (1999). The gestural origins of language. *American Scientist, 87*(2), 138. Retrieved from http://www.amsci.org/amsci/articles/99articles/corballis.html

Corballis, M. C. (2002). *From hand to mouth – The origins of language*. Princeton, NJ: Princeton University Press.

Damasio, A. R., Everitt, B. J., & Bishop, D. (1996). The somatic marker hypothesis and the possible functions of the prefrontal cortex [and discussion]. *Philosophical Transactions of the Royal Society B: Biological Sciences, 351*(1346), 1413–1420.

Damasio, A. R., Tranel, D., & Damasio, H. (1991). Somatic markers and the guidance of behavior: Theory and preliminary testing. In S. Levin, H. M. Eisenberg, & A. L. Benton (Eds.), *Frontal lobe function and dysfunction* (pp. 217–229). New York: Oxford University Press.

Davis, M. H. (1983). Measuring individual differences in empathy: Evidence for a multidimensional approach. *Journal of Personality and Social Psychology, 44*, 113–126.

de Gelder, B., & Bertelson, P. (2003). Multisensory integration, perception and ecological validity. *Trends in Cognitive Sciences, 7*, 460–467.

Eimer, M., & Holmes, A. (2007). Event-related brain potential correlates of emotional face processing. *Neuropsychologia, 45*(1), 15–31.

Ekman, P. (1992). *Telling lies: Clues to deceit in the marketplace, politics, and marriage* (p. 114). New York, London: W. W. Norton & Company.

Ekman, P., & Friesen, W. (1978). *Facial action coding system: A technique for the measurement of facial movement*. Palo Alto: Consulting Psychologists Press.

Ekman, P., & Friesen, W. V. (1969). Nonverbal leakage and clues to deception. *Psychiatry, 32*, 88–106.

Elfenbein, H. A., & Ambady, N. (2002). Is there an in-group advantage in emotion recognition? *Psychological Bulletin, 128*, 243–249.

Erickson, K., & Schulkin, J. (2003). Facial expressions of emotion: A cognitive neuroscience perspective. *Brain and Cognition, 52*, 52–60.

Fabbri-Destro, M., & Rizzolatti, G. (2008). Mirror neurons and mirror systems in monkeys and humans. *Physiology, 23*, 171–179.

Fadiga, L., Fogassi, L., Gallese, V., & Rizzolatti, G. (2000). Visuomotor neurons: Ambiguity of the discharge or "motor" perception? *International Journal of Psychophysiology, 35*, 165–177.

Fadiga, L., Fogassi, L., Pavesi, G., & Rizzolatti, G. (1995). Motor facilitation during action observation: A magnetic stimulation study. *Journal of Neurophysiology, 73*, 2608–2611.

Farah, M., Humphreys, G. W., & Rodman, H. R. (1999). Object and face recognition. In J. M. Zigmond, E. F. Bloom, C. S. Landis, L. J. Roberts, & R. L. Squire (Eds.), *Fundamental neuroscience* (pp. 1339–1361). San Diego: Academic press.

Feldman, R. (2012). Oxytocin and social affiliation in humans. *Hormones and Behaviour, 61*, 380–391.

Fox, C., Iaria, G., & Barton, J. (2009). Defining the face processing network: Optimization of the functional localizer in fMRI. *Human Brain Mapping, 30*(5), 1637–1651.

Fox, C. J., Hanif, H. M., Iaria, G., Duchaine, B. C., & Barton, J. J. S. (2011). Perceptual and anatomic patterns of selective deficits in facial identity and expression processing. *Neuropsychologia, 49*, 3188–3200.

Franks, D. D. (2010). *Neurosociology: The nexus between neuroscience and social psychology* (pp. 92, 94). New York: Springer Science+Business Media.

Freeman, J. B., Ruleand, N. O., & Ambady, N. (2009). The cultural neuroscience of person perception. *Progress in Brain Research, 178*, 191–201.

Gainotti, G. (2007). Different patterns of famous people recognition disorders in patients with right and left anterior temporal lesions: A systematic review. *Neuropsychologia, 45*, 1591–1607.

Gallese, V., & Goldman, A. (1998). Mirror neurons and the simulation theory of mind-reading. *Trends in Cognitive Sciences, 2*, 493–501.

Gallese, V., Fadiga, L., Fogassi, L., & Rizzolatti, G. (1996). Action recognition in the premotor cortex. *Brain, 119*, 593–609.

Garbarini, F., & Adenzato, M. (2004). At the root of embodied cognition: Cognitive science meets neurophysiology. *Brain and Cognition, 56*, 100–106. doi:10.1016/j.bandc.2004.06.003.

Gauthier, I., Tarr, M. J., Moylan, J., Skudlarski, P., Gore, J. C., & Anderson, A. W. (2000). The fusiform "face area" is part of a network that processes faces at the individual level. *Journal of Cognitive Neuroscience, 12*, 495–504.

Gazzola, V., & Keysers, C. (2009). The observation and execution of actions share motor and somatosensory voxels in all tested subjects: Single-subject analyses of unsmoothed fMRI data. *Cerebral Cortex, 19*(6), 1239–1255.

Gelstein, S., Yeshurun, Y., Rozenkrantz, L., Shushan, S., Frumin, I., Roth, Y., & Sobel, N. (2011). Human tears contain a chemosignal. *Science, 331*(6014), 226–230. doi: 10.1126/science.1198331.

George, M. S., Ketter, T. A., Gill, D. S., Haxby, J. V., Ungerleider, L. G., Herscovitch, P., & Post, R. M. (1993). Brain regions involved in recognizing facial emotion or identity: An oxygen-15 PET study. *Journal of Neuropsychiatry & Clinical Neurosciences, 5*, 384–394.

Goldin-Meadow, S., Wein, D., & Chang, C. (1992). Assessing knowledge through gesture: Using children's hands to read their minds. *Cognition and Instruction, 9*, 201–219.

Greenfield, P. M. (1991). Language, tools and brain: The ontogeny and phylogeny of hierarchically organized sequential behavior. *Behavioral and Brain Sciences, 14*, 531–595.

Hart, A. J., Whalen, P. J., hin, L. M., McInerney, S. C., Fischer, H., & Rauch, S. L. (2000). Differential response in the human amygdala to racial outgroup vs ingroup face stimuli. *NeuroReport, 11*(11), 2351–2355.

Hasselmo, M. E., Rolls, E. T., & Baylis, G. C. (1989). The role of expression and identity in the face-selective responses of neurons in the temporal visual cortex of the monkey. *Behavioural Brain Research, 32*, 203–218.

Hauk, O., Johnsrude, I., & Pulvermuller, F. (2004). Somatotopic representation of action words in human motor and premotor cortex. *Neuron, 41,* 301–307.

Haxby, J. V., & Gobbini, M. I. (2011). Distributed neural systems for face perception. In A. Calder, G. Rhodes, M. Johnson, & J. V. Haxby (Eds.), *Oxford handbook of face perception* (pp. 93–110). New York: Oxford University Press.

Haxby, J. V., Hoffman, E. A., & Gobbini, M. I. (2000). The distributed human neural system for face perception. *Trends in Cognitive Sciences, 4*(6), 223–233.

Haxby, J. V., Hoffman, E. A., & Gobbini, M. I. (2002). Human neural systems for face recognition and social communication. *Biological Psychiatry, 51*(1), 59–67.

Hoffman, E., & Haxby, J. (2000). Distinct representations of eye gaze and identity in the distributed human neural system for face perception. *Nature Neuroscience, 3,* 80–84.

Holmes, A., Bradley, B. P., Nielsen, M. K., & Mogg, K. (2009). Attentional selectivity for emotional faces: Evidence from human electrophysiology. *Psychophysiology, 46*(1), 62–68.

Hornak, J., Bramham, J., Rolls, E. T., Morris, R. G., O'Doherty, J., Bullock, P. R., & Polkey, C. E. (2003). Changes in emotion after circumscribed surgical lesions of the orbitofrontal and cingulate cortices. *Brain, 126,* 1691–1712.

Hostetter, A. B., & Alibali, M. W. (2008). Visible embodiment: Gestures as simulated action. *Psychonomic Bulletin & Review, 15,* 495–514.

Hostetter, A. B., & Alibali, M. W. (2010). Language, gesture, action! A test of the gesture as simulated action framework. *Journal of Memory and Language, 63,* 245–257.

Iacoboni, M. (2008). *Mirroring people: The new science of how we connect with others* (p. 103). New York: Farrar.

Iacoboni, M., Lieberman, M. D., Knowlton, B. J., Molnar-Szakacs, I., Moritz, M., Throop, C. J., & Fiske, A. P. (2004). Watching social interactions produces dorsomedial prefrontal and medial parietal BOLD fMRI signal increases compared to a resting baseline. *NeuroImage, 21,* 1167–1173.

Insel, T. R. (1992). Oxytocin – A neuropeptide for affiliation: Evidence from behavioral, receptor autoradiographic, and comparative studies. *Psychoneuroendocrinology, 17,* 3–35.

Izard, C., & Dougherty, L. (1982). Two complementary systems for measuring facial expressions in infants and children. In C. Izard (Ed.), *Measuring emotions in infants and children* (pp. 97–126). New York: Cambridge University Press.

Jacob, H., Brück, C., Domin, M., Lotze, M., & Wildgruber, D. (2014). I can't keep your face and voice out of my head: Neural correlates of an attentional bias toward nonverbal emotional cues. *Cerebral Cortex, 24,* 1460–1473. Advance online publication. doi:10.1093/cercor/bhs417.

Jacob, H., Kreifelts, B., Brück, C., Erb, M., Hösl, F., & Wildgruber, D. (2012). Cerebral integration of verbal and nonverbal emotional cues: Impact of individual nonverbal dominance., *NeuroImage, 61*(3), 738–747. doi: 10.1016/j.neuroimage.2012.03.085.

Jacob, H., Kreifelts, B., Brück, C., Nizielski, S., Schütz, A., & Wildgruber, D. (2013). Nonverbal signals speak up: Association between perceptual nonverbal dominance and emotional intelligence. *Cognition & Emotion, 27,* 783–799. Advance online publication. doi:10.1080/02699931.2012.739999.

Junghöfer, M., Bradley, M. M., Elbert, T. R., & Lang, P. J. (2001). Fleeting images: A new look at early emotion discrimination. *Psychophysiology, 38*(2), 175–178.

Kanwisher, N., McDermott, J., & Chun, M. M. (1997). The fusiform face area: A module in human extrastriate cortex specialized for face perception. *Journal of Neuroscience, 17,* 4302–4311.

Kim, S., Fonagy, P., Koos, O., Dorsett, K., & Strathearn, L. (2014). Maternal oxytocin response predicts mother-to-infant gaze. *Brain Research, 1580,* 133–142. Advance online publication. doi: 10.1016/j.brainres.2013.10.050.

Koechlin, E., & Jubault, T. (2006). Broca's area and the hierarchical organization of human behavior. *Neuron, 50*(6), 963–974.

Kranz, F., & Ishai, A. (2006). Face perception is modulated by sexual preference. *Current Biology, 16,* 63–68.

Krauss, R. M., & Hadar, U. (1999). The role of speech-related arm/hand gestures in word retrieval. In L. Messing & R. Campbell (Eds.), *Gesture, speech and sign* (pp. 93–116). Oxford: Oxford University Press.

La France, M. (1979). Nonverbal synchrony and rapport: Analysis by the cross-lag panel technique. *Social Psychology Quarterly, 42,* 66–70.

Lieberman, M. D., Hariri, A., Jarcho, J. M., Eisenberger, N. I., & Bookheimer, S. Y. (2005). An fMRI investigation of race-related amygdala activity in African-American and Caucasian-American individuals. *Nature Neuroscience, 8,* 720–722.

Liuzzi, G., Ellger, T., Flöel, A., Breitenstein, C., Jansen, A., & Knecht, S. (2008). Walking the talk – Speech activates the leg motor cortex. *Neuropsychologia, 46,* 2824–2830.

Mandal, M. K., & Ambady, N. (2004). Laterality of facial expressions of emotion: Universal and culture-specific influences. *Behavioural Neurology, 15*(1–2), 23–34.

Martin, E., & Holmes, A. (2007). Event-related brain potential correlates of emotional face processing. *Neuropsychologia, 45,* 15–31.

McNeill, D. (1992). *Hand and mind: What gestures reveal about thought.* Chicago, IL: University of Chicago Press.

McNeill, D. (2005). *Gesture and thought.* Chicago: University of Chicago Press.

Meeren, H. K. M., van Heijnsbergen, C. C. R. J., & de Gelder, B. (2005). Rapid perceptual integration of facial expression and emotional body language. *PNAS, 102*(45), 16518–16523.

Montgomery, K. J., Isenberg, N., & Haxby, J. V. (2007). Communicative hand gestures and object-directed hand movements activated the mirror neuron system. *Social Cognitive and Affective Neuroscience, 2,* 114–122.

Montgomery, K. J., Seeherman, K. R., & Haxby, J. V. (2009). The well-tempered social brain. *Psychological Science, 20,* 1211–1213.

Morecraft, R. J., Louie, J. L., Herrick, J. L., & Stilwell-Morecraft, K. S. (2001). Cortical innervation of the facial nucleus in the non-human primate: A new interpretation of the effects of stroke and related subtotal brain trauma on the muscles of facial expression. *Brain, 124*(Pt 1), 176–208.

Morecraft, R. J., Stilwell-Morecraft, K. S., & Rossing, W. R. (2004). The motor cortex and facial expression: New insights from neuroscience. *Neurologist, 10*(5), 235–249.

Nešić, V., & Nešić, M. (2012). The origin and the features of ethnic stereotypes – Sociopsychological and neuropsychological approach. In B. Dimitrijević (Ed.), *Other about Serbs, the Serbs about others* (pp. 131–146). Niš: Faculty of Philosophy. (In Serbian).

Newman, S. W. (1999). The medial extended amygdala in male reproductive behavior: A node in the mammalian social behavior network. *Annals of the New York Academy of Sciences, 877,* 242–257.

Norris, C. J., Chen, E. E., Zhu, D. C., Small, S. L., & Cacioppo, J. T. (2004). The interaction of social and emotional processes in the brain. *Journal of Cognitive Neuroscience, 16,* 1818–1829.

O'Connell, L. A., & Hofmann, H. A. (2011). Genes, hormones, and circuits: An integrative approach to study the evolution of social behaviour. *Frontiers in Neuroendocrinology, 32,* 320–335.

O'Doherty, J., Winston, J., Critchley, H., Perrett, D., Burt, D. M., & Dolan, R. J. (2003). Beauty in a smile: The role of medial orbitofrontal cortex in facial attractiveness. *Neuropsychologia, 41,* 147–155.

O'Toole, A. J., Phillips, P. J., Weimer, S., Roark, D. A., Ayyad, J., Barwick, R., & Dunlop, J. (2011). Recognizing people from dynamic and static faces and bodies: Dissecting identity with a fusion approach. *Vision Research, 51,* 74–83.

Ochsner, K. N., Knierim, K., Ludlow, D. H., Hanelin, J., Ramachandran, T., Glover, G., & Mackey, S. C. (2004). Reflecting upon feelings: An fMRI study of neural systems supporting the attribution of emotion to self and other. *Journal of Cognitive Neuroscience, 16,* 1746–1772.

Öhman, A., Flykt, A., & Esteves, F. (2001). Emotion drives attention: Detecting the snake in the grass. *Journal of Experimental Psychology: General, 130*(3), 466–478.

Ojemann, J. G., Ojemann, G. A., & Lettich, E. (1992). Neural activity related to faces and matching in human right nondominant temporal cortex. *Brain, 115,* 1–13.

Passamonti, L., Crockett, M. J., Apergis-Schoute, A. M., Clark, L., Rowe, J. B., Calder, A. J., & Robbins, T. W. (2012). Effects of acute tryptophan depletion on prefrontal-amygdala connectivity while viewing facial signals of aggression. *Biological Psychiatry, 71,* 36–43.

Penton-Voak, I. S., Perrett, D. I., Castles, D. L., Kobayashi, T., Burt, D. M., Murray, L. K., & Minamisawa, R. (1999). Menstrual cycle alters face preference. *Nature, 399,* 741–742.

Pessoa, L., & Adolphs, R. (2010). Emotion processing and the amygdala: From a "low road" to "many roads" of evaluating biological significance. *Nature Reviews Neuroscience, 11*(11), 773–783.

Phelps, E. A., O'Connor, K. J., Cunningham, W. A., Funayama, E. S. J., Gatenby, C., ... Banaji, M. R. (2000). Performance on indirect measures of race evaluation predicts amygdala activation. *Journal of Cognitive Neuroscience, 12*(5), 729–738.

Pitcher, D., Dilks, D. D., Saxe, R. R., Triantafyllou, C., & Kanwisher, N. (2011). Differential selectivity for dynamic versus static information in face-selective cortical regions. *NeuroImage, 56,* 2356–2363.

Posamentier, M. T., & Abdi, H. (2003). Processing faces and facial expressions. *Neuropsychological Review, 13*(3), 113–143.

Pourtois, G., Schettino, A., & Vuilleumier, P. (2012). Brain mechanisms for emotional influences on perception and attention: What is magic and what is not. *Biological Psychology, 92*(3), 492–512. doi:10.1016/j.biopsycho.2012.02.007.

Pulvermüller, F. (2002a). A brain perspective on language mechanisms: From discrete neuronal ensembles to serial order. *Progress in Neurobiology, 67,* 85–111.

Pulvermüller, F. (2002b). *The neuroscience of language.* Cambridge: CUP.

Pulvermüller, F. (2005). Brain mechanisms linking language and action. *Nature Reviews Neuroscience, 6,* 1–6.

Pulvermüller, F., Härle, M., & Hummel, F. (2001). Walking or talking? Behavioural and europhysiological correlates of action verb processing. *Brain and Language, 78,* 143–168.

Pulvermüller, F., Huss, M., Kherif, F., Moscoso del Prado Martin, F., Hauk, O., & Shtyrov, Y. (2006). Motor cortex maps articulatory features of speech sounds. *Proceedings of the National Academy of Sciences USA, 103*(20), 7865–7870.

Ramachandran, V. S. (Ed.). (2012). *Encyclopedia of human behavior* (2nd ed., pp. 731–738). Elsevier.

Recio, G., Sommer, W., & Schacht, A. (2011). Electrophysiological correlates of perceiving and evaluating static and dynamic facial emotional expressions. *Brain Research, 1376*, 66–75.

Rinn, W. E. (1984). The neuropsychology of facial expression: A review of the neurological and psychological mechanisms for producing facial expressions. *Psychological Bulletin, 95*, 52–77.

Rizzolatti, G., & Arbib, M. A. (1998). Language within our grasp. *Trends in Neuroscience, 21*, 188–194.

Rizzolatti, G., Camarda, R., Fogassi, L., Gentilucci, M., Luppino, G., & Matelli, M. (1988). Functional organization of inferior area 6 in the macaque monkey: II. Area F5 and the control of distal movements. *Experimental Brain Research, 71*, 491–507.

Rizzolatti, G., Fadiga, L., Gallese, V., & Fogassi, L. (1996). Premotor cortex and the recognition of motor actions. *Cognitive Brain Research, 3*, 131–141.

Rolls, E. T. (2014). Limbic systems for emotion and for memory, but no single limbic system. *Cortex*, http://dx.doi.org/10.1016/j.cortex.2013.12.005.

Rolls, E. T., Critchley, H. D., Browning, A. S., & Inoue, K. (2006). Face-selective and auditory neurons in the primate orbitofrontal cortex. *Experimental Brain Research, 170*, 74–87.

Rolls, E. T., & Grabenhorst, F. (2008). The orbitofrontal cortex and beyond: From affect to decision-making. *Progress in Neurobiology, 86*, 216–244.

Savic, I. (2014). Pheromone processing in relation to sex and sexual orientation. In C. Mucignat-Caretta (Ed.), *Neurobiology of chemical communication* (pp. 517–528). Boca Raton, FL: CRC Press.

Schacht, A., & Sommer, W. (2009). Emotions in word and face processing: Early and late cortical responses. *Brain and Cognition, 69*(3), 538–550.

Schultz, J., & Pilz, K. (2009). Natural facial motion enhances cortical responses to faces. *Experimental Brain Research, 194*(3), 465–475.

Schupp, H. T., Junghöfer, M., Weike, A., & Hamm, A. (2003). Attention and emotion: An ERP analysis of facilitated emotional stimulus processing. *NeuroReport, 14*(8), 1107–1110.

Schupp, H. T., Öhman, A., Junghofer, M., Weike, A. I., Stockburger, J., & Hamm, A. O. (2004). The facilitated processing of threatening faces: An ERP analysis. *Emotion, 4*, 189–200.

Tettamanti, M., Buccino, G., Saccuman, M. C., Gallese, V., Danna, M., Scifo, P., ... Fazio, F. (2005). Listening to action-related sentences activates fronto-parietal motor circuits. *Journal of Cognitive Neuroscience, 17*(2), 273–281.

Thompson-Schill, S. L., Bedny, M., & Goldberg, R. F. (2005). The frontal lobes and the regulation of mental activity. *Current Opinions in Neurobiology, 15*(2), 219–224.

Thompson-Schill, S. L., D'Esposito, M., Aguirre, G. K., & Farah, M. J. (1997). Role of left inferior prefrontal cortex in retrieval of semantic knowledge: A reevaluation. *Proceedings of the National Academy of Sciences USA, 94*(26), 14792–14797.

Tranel, D. (2000). Non-conscious brain processing indexed by psychophysiological measures. *Progress in Brain Research, 122,* 317–332.

Tranel, D., Damasio, H., & Damasio, A. R. (1995). Double dissociation between overt and covert face recognition. *Journal of Cognitive Neuroscience, 7*(4), 425–432. doi:10.1162/jocn.1995.7.4.425.

Trautmann, S. A., Fehr, T., & Herrmann, M. (2009). Emotions in motion: Dynamic compared to static facial expressions of disgust and happiness reveal more widespread emotion-specific activations. *Brain Research, 1284,* 100–115.

Ungerleider, L. G., & Mishkin, M. (1982). Two cortical visual systems. In D. J. Ingle, M. A. Goodale, & R. J. W. Mansfield (Eds.), *Analysis of visual behavior* (pp. 549–586). Cambridge, MA: The MIT Press.

Van der Gaag, C., Minderaa, R. B., & Keysers, C. (2007). Facial expressions: What the mirror neuron system can and cannot tell us. *Social Neuroscience, 2*(3–4), 179–222. doi: 10.1080/17470910701376878.

Van Gelder, R. S., & Borod, J. E. (1990). Neurobiological and cultural aspects of facial asymmetry. *Journal of Communication Disorders, 23,* 273–286.

von dem Hagen, E. A. H., Passamonti, L., Nutland, S., Sambrook, J., & Calder, A. J. (2011). The serotonin transporter gene polymorphism and the effect of baseline on amygdala response to emotional faces. *Neuropsychologia, 49,* 674–680.

Vrtička, P., Sander, D., & Vuilleumier, P. (2013). Lateralized interactive social content and valence processing within the human amygdala. *Frontiers in Human Neuroscience, 6,* 1–12. doi: 10.3389/fnhum.2012.00358.

Vuilleumier, P., & Huang, Y-M. (2009). Emotional attention. *Current Directions in Psychological Science, 18,* 148–152.

Vuilleumier, P., & Pourtois, G. (2007). Distributed and interactive brain mechanisms during emotion face perception: Evidence from functional neuroimaging. *Neuropsychologia, 45*(1), 174–194.

Wartenburger, I., Kühn, E., Sassenberg, U., Foth, M., Franz, E. A., & van der Meer, E. (2010). On the relationship between fluid intelligence, gesture production, and brain structure. *Intelligence, 38,* 193–201.

Weisbuch, M., & Ambady, N. (2008). Affective divergence: Automatic responses to others' emotions dependent on group membership. *Journal of Personality & Social Psychology, 95,* 1063–1079.

Willems, R. M., & Hagoort, P. (2007). Neural evidence for the interplay between language, gesture, and action: A review. *Brain and Language, 101,* 278–289.

Wilson, M. (2002). Six views of embodied cognition. *Psychonomic Bulletin & Review, 9,* 625–636. doi:10.3758/BF03196322.

Wolff, W. (1933). The experimental study of forms of expression. *Journal of Personality, 2,* 168–173.

Zajonc, R. B. (1985). Emotion and Facial Efference: A Theory Reclaimed. *Science, 228,* 15–21.

Zajonc, R. B., Adelmann, K. A., Murphy, S. T., & Niedenthal, P. M. (1987). Convergence in the physical appearance of spouses. *Motivation and Emotion, 11,* 335–346.

3
Measuring Gestures

David B. Givens

Gestures

"we respond to gestures with an extreme alertness and, one might almost say, in accordance with an elaborate and secret code that is written nowhere, known by none, and understood by all" (Sapir, 1927, p. 556).

In standard American English a *gesture* is "A motion of the limbs or body made to express or help express thought or to emphasize speech" (Soukhanov, 1992, p. 762). The English word "gesture" derives from Latin *gerere*, "to behave." This chapter's scope is narrowed to gestures apart from the face.

Measurement

In gesture research, measurement involves assigning numbers to body movements and their constituent parts. Numerical measures may be spatial (physical) or temporal (chronological) in nature.

Spatial. The simplest spatial measurements are observational. A researcher assigns a binary value – a "one" or a "zero" – to a gesture to indicate its presence or absence, respectively, in the space of a communication venue such as a conversation. In Signal Detection Theory, four values or outcomes are possible for each individual sighting.

Imagine a researcher observing the shoulder-shrug gestures of a man and a woman seated together at a small coffee table. At some level of precision, there will be uncertainty as to whether or not a shrug actually occurred. If the man coughs and shrugs, for example, should that be counted as a shoulder-shrug? For any communication venue, four observational outcomes are possible. In Signal Detection parlance (Peterson et al., 1954), the first is a "hit": a shoulder-shrug occurs and the researcher sees and records it. The second is a "miss": a shrug occurs but the researcher neither sees nor records it. Third is a "false alarm": a shrug does not occur, but the researcher incorrectly sees and records one. And fourth is a "correct rejection": no shrug occurs and the researcher correctly notates its absence.

On the spatial side of measurement, most gesture research has entailed simple observations of this sort, namely, of a body movement's presence or absence in a given social interaction. Should the investigated movement be a shoulder-shrug, zeroes or ones may be recorded to represent the shrug's absence or presence. Later, additional numbers may be assigned to measure the frequency and magnitude of the shrugging motions, and to gauge how a pair's shrugs correlate together in time and with the couple's collateral nonverbal signs and spoken words.

Regarding measurement of a gesture's size and magnitude, researchers have paid less attention to a signal's strength and amplitude than to the simpler, binary metric of presence or absence. Four decades ago Bouissac (1973) proposed that human body movements be studied in terms of the three-dimensional volumes they occupy in space. This focus was intended to improve upon earlier notation systems, such as the hieroglyphic-like kinesic system of Birdwhistell (1952), which accounted principally for the presence or absence of body-motion cues, such as backward-leans, head-nods, and steepling cues, in interaction. Though Bouissac's volumetric measurement of gestures did not bear fruit, computers now make such measurements possible. Ning and colleagues, for example, have perfected a computerized motion detector that can be used to measure shoulder-shrug cues (Ning et al., 2006). Huazhong and et al. (2006) have designed a real time shoulder-shrug detector. Boker and colleagues (2009) have perfected a computerized avatar for use in measuring head movements in dyadic conversations.

Temporal. In temporal terms, the simplest gesture measurements are relative. A given body movement is observed to come before, during, or after another body-motion unit or event. A shoulder-shrug, for example, may come before, during, or after a spoken word or another nonverbal sign in the stream of behavior. The shrug's occurrence in time is measured not in absolute terms but in relation to its serial appearance in a timeline: preceding, coinciding with, or following a spoken word or body movement.

On the temporal side of measurement, most gesture research has entailed simple chronological measurements of this kind, namely, of a body movement's relative position in the observed behavioral sequence (see below: "Head-Shake Gestures"). It is likely that computer analyses will enable greater real time temporal measurements of gestures.

To explore the past, present, and future prospects of measuring gestures, we examine three classic body movements studied by Charles Darwin (1872/1998), the *head-nod*, the *head-shake*, and the *shoulder-shrug*.

Head-nod gestures

"Is the head nodded vertically in affirmation, and shaken laterally in negation?" (Darwin, 1872/1998, p. 23).

The human head-nod is a vertical, up-and-down (or down-and-up) movement that is often used to show agreement or comprehension while listening. The flexed-forward, lowering motion of the skull is also used to emphasize an idea, an assertion, or a key speaking point. Rhythmically raised and lowered as an affirmative sign, it is widely used throughout the world to show understanding, approval, and agreement. Emphatic head-nods while speaking or listening, on the other hand, may indicate feelings of conviction, excitement, or superiority, and sometimes anger or rage. Students of head-nodding often correlate the gesture with linguistic syntactical and semantic features of speech. Beginning with Darwin (1872/1998), many have assessed the emotional dimensions of nodding as well.

Anatomy

Eight muscles are key players in the head-nod. In the affirmative nod, longuscapitis, rectus capitis anterior, and longuscolli muscles (all supplied by cervical spinal nerves) flex the neck and head forward, while splenius (a deep muscle of the back, also supplied by cervical spinal nerves) and upper trapezius (supplied by cranial nerve XI) bend the head and neck backward. In the emphatic head-nod, forced expiration while stressing a word contracts muscles of the abdominal wall (oblique [supplied by the first cervical spinal nerve] and transverse muscles [supplied by intercostal nerves], and latissimusdorsi [supplied by cervical spinal nerves]), which depress the lower ribs and bend the backbone and head forward (Salmons, 1995, pp. 818–819). Electromyographic measurements show that the sternocleidomastoid muscles (supplied by cranial nerve XI) are involved in both flexion and extension of the neck (Salmons, 1995, p. 805).

Evolution

Measured in evolutionary terms, the emphatic head-nod may reach back ca. 280 million years ago to the beginning of reptiles. Paleocircuits for the reptilian up-and-down head-bobbing display (used aggressively by lizards today to affirm their physical presence in space and time) may underlie the nods we ourselves use to reinforce assertions and accent words (see below: *"(4) Reptilian-brain centers"*). The reptilian principle of isopraxis (MacLean, 1990), for instance, may explain why speakers and listeners often nod together in synchrony (see section on *"Video"*). Meltzoff (2002, p. 23) invokes mirror neurons to explain how human newborns from 42 minutes to 72 hours old (mean = 32 hours) can imitate adult emotional expressions and head-movement gestures.

Research

Though other types of affirmative head movements have been observed cross-culturally (LaBarre, 1947), the affirmative head-nod is well-documented as a nearly universal indication of accord, agreement, and understanding (Darwin, 1872/1998; Eibl-Eibesfeldt, 1970; Morris, 1994). Researchers have found cultural differences in the meaning of head-nod cues. Samovar and colleagues, for instance, report a key variance in the American and Chinese use of the sign. In the United States, head-nodding bespeaks agreement, whereas " ... the head nod is used by the Chinese to acknowledge the speaker, not to signal agreement with what is said" (Samovar et al., 2007, p. 302). Despite this difference, the nodding motion itself is an emotionally positive, affirmative signal in both countries.

According to Mehrabian (1972), " ... frequent head nodding, in addition to communicating liking to a listener, implies a less confident or submissive speaker" (p. 81). In a review of more than 70 research articles on human head movements, Harrigan (2005) found that nearly 80% dealt with nodding. Of the articles she reviewed, 55 dealt with the head-nod itself, 14 with the head-shake, eight with the head-tilt, and 25 with "any" head movement (Harrigan, 2005). These frequencies may be used as a crude measure of the importance researchers attribute to the head-nod as compared to other head-movement gestures.

Measured sequentially as units in the kinesic flow of behavior, Birdwhistell (1970) proposed three "kinemes" (gestures having linguistic-like properties) for head-nodding: " ... the 'one nod,' the 'two nod,' and the 'three nod' ... " (p. 100). He attempted – unsuccessfully – to calculate a measurement for the duration of the three-nod gesture, to distinguish it from the occurrence of three one-nod gestures. In a study of conversations, Nori and colleagues similarly proposed three values for the head-nod cue: "single," "double," and "repeated," noting that Japanese subjects tended to use single, while German subjects used more repeated head-nods (Nori et al., 2011, p. 414). In his study, Wilbur (2000) measured the relative position of head-nods as units in the flow of American Sign Language (ASL), finding that "large, slow nodding" marked a signer's "commitment to the truth" of an assertion, while "small, rapid noddings" marked a signer's "hedging [comparable to using 'sort of' and 'kind of' phrases in spoken English] or counterfactuals [i.e., untruthful assertions]" (p. 201).

Video. In a video study of head movements by native speakers of American English, McClave (2000) found that speaker head-nods were often closely followed by listener nods, within 0.7 seconds in the example given. Their close proximity in time, McClave concluded, is an indication that the latter nods were elicited or triggered by the speaker's head-nods. Listeners, she notes, are "extraordinarily sensitive" to such speaker nods (p. 855), which seem to function as gestural requests for listener input.

"During face-to-face conversation," Lee, Neviarouskaya, Prendinger, and Marsella (2009) write, "the speaker's head is continually in motion" (p. 9). More often than not, head-nods have a measurable emotional component as well. In a study of head-nod gestures using the Affect Analysis Model (AAM) of emotional recognition, Lee and colleagues (2009) found that head-nods most frequently occurred at the beginning of sentences, and with interjections, proper nouns, conjunctions, and adverbs. It is noteworthy that each of these occurrences is marked by some degree of emotion.

Beginning a new sentence implies feelings of self-assurance, namely, that it is now one's turn to speak. An interjection, meanwhile, is "A part of speech usually expressing an emotion, and capable of standing alone, such as *Ugh!* or *Wow!*" (Soukhanov, 1992, p. 941). Since proper nouns are used as names for "unique individuals, events, or places" (Soukhanov, 1992, p. 1452), they are likely to provoke more feelings than are elicited by ordinary nouns. Conjunctions mark momentary pauses between words, phrases, and sentences, pauses often brought on by indecision, uncertainty, and doubt. And finally, an adverb marked by a head-nod is usually an "intensifier": "A linguistic element, such as the adverb *extremely* or *awfully*, that provides force or emphasis" (Soukhanov, 1992, p. 939). Intensifiers enhance the emotional content of the words they modify.

In an observational study of head-nods in debate conversations, Poggi, D'Errico, and Vincze (2011) define the head-nod " ... as a vertical head movement in which the head, after a slight tilt up, bends downward and then goes back to its starting point" (p. 2). Poggi and her colleagues found that, for speakers, head-nods were used to emphasize words and phrases, and to request a confirmation of understanding from listeners. For listeners, nods were used to signal affirmation (i.e., to nod "yes"), agreement, approval, and submission. Regarding submission, the researchers conclude that " ... nodding communicates openness to interaction, by confirming the other's claims and accepting his opinion and goals. From this point of view, nodding still maintains its original ethological meaning, in which lowering your head in front of another, that [sic] makes you prone to his power over you, becomes a communicative act of submission ... " (Poggi et al., 2011, p. 11).

Bowing

Like Poggi and colleagues, other researchers have decoded the head-nod gesture as a form of bowing. As Morris (1994) writes, "Others see it [the head-nod] as an abbreviated form of submissive body-lowering – in other words, as a miniature bow" (p. 142). In naturalistic observations I have seen the head-nod grade into tandem bowing movements of the head and neck, in which the head does not nod at its joint on the first cervical vertebra (the atlas) but instead pushes forward with the neck to give more emphasis and visibility to the movement. Measured as more than a head-nod but less than a full-body bow from the waist, the thrusting head-and-neck gesture may be used to add agreement or emphasis across a greater distance (e.g., across a sales counter) than is normal in ordinary conversations.

In the full-body bow, one bends, curls, or curves the upper body and head forward. Around the world, people bow *a.* to greet, *b.* to defer, *c.* to show courtesy, and *d.* to pray. Bowing the trunk forward starts with the flexor muscles of the stomach's recti abdominis (supplied by thoracic spinal nerves), assisted by the backbone's erector spinae muscles (supplied by spinal nerves C1-S5). These muscle groups are supplied directly by spinal nerves rather than by more evolved nerve plexuses. The bow's submissive tone stems from the role these muscles and nerves originally played in curling the head and trunk forward into a protective vertebrate crouch.

The vertebrate crouch itself is formed of ancient bending motions designed to remove an animal from danger. A reflexive act controlled by the spinal cord, bending the body moves it away from hazards, reduces its exposed surface area, and makes it look "smaller." Nonverbally, flexed body movements used to crouch lower to the ground predate extension movements used to rise above the terrestrial plain (as in the *high-stand* display of dominance); thus, our remote ancestors crouched before they stood tall. Crouching can be traced to an avoider's response, which is tactile in origin rather than visual (as in the high-stand). So primitive is the crouch posture's flexor reflex that it exists even in immature fish and amphibian larvae. Stimulating the skin of these immature creatures leads to side-to-side bending movements, which, in a watery world, remove them from dangers signaled by touch.

The crouch posture is keyed to paleocircuits formed of primitive spinal-cord interneurons in charge of tactile withdrawal. Similar "tap withdrawal" movements have been observed even in spineless animals such as the nematode worm. Working through pools of interneurons controlling the muscular stretch reflex, the worm's body, like our own, automatically bends away from danger.

Neurology

To further account for the nervous system's role in gesture communication, we inventory six neuromuscular circuits, centers, and modules, each of which – individually and in varied combinations and proportions – is involved in sending (encoding) or receiving (decoding) nonverbal cues.

Arm-flapping.   For comparative purposes, and as a prologue to our neural inventory, consider the whimsical *arm-flapping* gesture once used by TV comedian Richard Bernard "Red" Skelton (1913–1997) to tell his classic "Gertrude and Heathcliff" jokes. Tightly flexing his arms, Skelton placed the fingertips of his right hand into his right armpit, and those of his left hand into the left armpit, and pantomimed rhythmic "flapping" movements as he told his seagull jokes. We bring in Skelton's gesture to ask a simple question: Why does our species, *Homo sapiens*, head-nod significantly more than it arm-flaps? For answers, we gauge the neural circuitry that underlies both cues.

(1) Spinal-cord reflexes. According to Ghez (1991), "The movements of which our motor systems are capable can be divided into three broad, overlapping classes": reflexive responses, voluntary movements, and rhythmic motor patterns (p. 534). As we saw above, the bowing version of the head-nod (used to greet and defer to others) has spinal-cord roots in the primitive tactile-withdrawal reflex. The submissive tone of the deferential head-nod (which begins with a downward nod, and may

be rhythmically repeated) stems from the role the neck muscles and nerves originally played in curling the head forward in a protective crouch. Thus, the spinal-cord reflex provides a neurological rationale for head-nodding in contexts of greeting and deference.

In contrast, Red Skelton's arm-flap has no such cord reflex governing it, and therefore is not used, like the head-nod, to greet, bow, or defer. The arm-flap is a voluntary rhythmic movement. At some point in his career, Skelton learned how to perform the gesture, and willfully and consciously arm-flapped for years in his comic routines until doing so became functionally automatic. "Once initiated," according to Ghez, "the sequence of relatively stereotyped movements [like arm-flapping] may continue almost automatically in reflex-like fashion" (Ghez, 1991, p. 534).

(2) Special visceral nerves. An innate quality of the affirmative ("yes") head-nod is its innervation by special visceral efferent nerves. A special visceral nerve is a nerve linked to a facial, jaw, neck, shoulder, or throat muscle that once played a role in eating or breathing. It is a cranial nerve whose original role in digestion and respiration renders it emotionally responsive today (Givens, 2013, 2014).

Special visceral nerves mediate those "gut reactive" signs of emotion we unconsciously send through head-nods, head-shakes, and shoulder-shrugs. Nonverbally, these nerves are special because the muscle contractions they mediate are less easily (i.e., voluntarily) controlled than are those of the skeletal muscles (which are innervated by *somatic* nerves). In Skelton's arm-flap, the arms' deltoid muscles contract through voluntary control of somatic spinal nerves C5 and C6. In versions of the affirmative head-nod (which begin with a nod upward), the upper trapezius muscle contracts to bend the head backward through special-visceral (emotional) control of cranial nerve XI, the accessory nerve. Special visceral control is also supplied to the sternocleidomastoid muscles (Salmons, 1995).

Associated with the *pharyngeal arches*, special visceral nerves control the branchiomeric muscles that once constricted, or dilated, "gill" pouches of the ancient alimentary canal. Special visceral nerves are emotionally responsive, while somatic nerves are emotionally rather neutral. The former mediate a range of emotional responses through efferent fibers of *a.* the trigeminal nerve (cranial V, for biting and chewing); *b.* the facial nerve (cranial VII, for facial expressions); *c.* the glossopharyngeal nerve (cranial IX, for swallowing); *d.* the vagus nerve (cranial X, for tone of voice); and *e.* the accessory nerve (cranial XI, for head-nodding, head-shaking, and the shoulder-shrug).

Neural blueprint for emotion.   The paleocircuits of special visceral nerves – which originally mediated muscles for opening and closing parts of the primitive gill apparatus in eating and breathing – are today linked to the limbic system. Before the mammalian brain (see below: "*(5) Mammalian-brain centers*"), life in the nonverbal world was automatic, preconscious, and predictable. Motor centers in the reptilian brain (see below: "*(4) Reptilian-brain centers*") reacted to vision, sound, touch, chemical, gravity, and motion sensory cues with preset body movements and pre-programmed postures. With the arrival of night-active mammals, ca. 180 million years ago, smell replaced sight as the dominant sense, and a newer, more flexible way of responding – based on emotion and emotional memory – arose from the olfactory sense. In the Jurassic period, the mammalian brain invested heavily in aroma circuits to succeed at night as reptiles slept. These odor pathways gradually formed the neural blueprint for what was later to become our limbic brain.

Smell carries directly to limbic areas of the mammalian brain via nerves running from the olfactory bulbs to the septum, amygdala, and hippocampus. In the aquatic brain (Givens, 2013), olfaction was critical for detecting food, foes, and mates from a distance in murky waters. Like an emotional feeling, aroma has a volatile or "thin-skinned" quality because sensory cells lie on the exposed exterior of the olfactory epithelium (i.e., on the bodily surface itself). Like a whiff of smelling salts, a sudden feeling may jolt the mind. The force of a mood is reminiscent of a smell's intensity (e.g., soft and gentle, pungent, or overpowering), and similarly permeates and fades. The design of emotion cues, in tandem with the forebrain's olfactory prehistory, suggests that the sense of smell is the neurological model for our emotions. The close kinship between special visceral nerves and the chemical senses (taste and smell) is what makes these nerves more emotionally sensitive than somatic nerves.

(3) Muscular interactions. Like the bowing head-nod, the emphatic nod begins with a downward movement that may be rhythmically repeated. The emphatic nod, however, is controlled by different neural circuits, including cervical spinal fibers (C6 to 8) and thoracic spinal fibers (T7 to 12). In this head-nod, forced expiration while stressing a word contracts anterolateral muscles of the abdomen which depress the lower ribs and bend the trunk (backbone) and head forward (Salmons, 1995). Some emphatic head-nods may be jointly controlled by these spinal circuits in tandem with the spinal-cord reflexes outlined above for the bowing head-nod. At present, there is no authoritative way to measure the proportionality of control between these two neural systems.

Additional muscular interactions affecting the head-nod include actions that produce the *head-shake* (see below: "Head-Shake Gestures"), sideward *head-tilt*, sideward *head-jerk*, and upward *head-toss*. Any or all of these common head movements may precede, coincide (combine or blend) with, or follow a given head-tilt and thereby modify its meaning, physical amplitude, appearance, and/or temporal placement in the stream of behavior. Alternately turning the head toward and away from one's speaking partner may interact with the head-nod as well. Computerized motion detectors will no doubt improve our measurement of such muscular interactions in the future.

(4) Reptilian-brain centers. Yet another control center for emphatic head-nods includes the basal ganglia of the reptilian brain, a motor control area MacLean (1990) originally identified as the "protoreptilian brain" or "R-complex." Collectively, the reptilian brain includes those early parts of the human brain which developed during the reptilian adaptation to life on land. Of particular interest are modules of the forebrain which evolved to enable reptilian body movements such as the head-nod, pushup, and high-stand display.

Fixed-action patterns. Among living reptiles, these stereotyped gestures and displays have been well studied in lizards. "A typical first display," Greenberg (2003) writes, "has been termed 'assertion,' and includes a distinctive pattern of vertical movements of the head performed with more-or-less amplitude (head-nods) that provides the definitive species-typical 'signature' display for many lizards, the green anole included" (p. 431). The green anole (*Anoliscarolinensis*) is among the best studied of all lizards. Its assertion ("I am here") display includes head-nods, frequently combined with push-ups (into high-stand postures) and showy extensions of the throat's colorful dewlap.

Earlier we hypothesized that paleocircuits for the reptilian up-and-down head-bobbing display may underlie the nods we ourselves use to reinforce assertions and accent words. In the anole lizard, head-bobbing is assessed as a *fixed-action pattern*. "A fixed-action pattern," Kupfermann writes, "resembles a reflex in that it is a behavioral response elicited by a specific stimulus and its expression does not require previous learning" (Kupfermann, 1991, pp. 989–990). Unlike a reflex, the behavioral response (e.g., an anole's head-nod) is more complex and is preceded by bodily orientation toward the specific stimulus (e.g., another anole lizard) that elicited its performance (Kupfermann, 1991).

Examples of fixed-action patterns in human beings include coughing, swallowing, and suckling. That human infants make downward head movements when accepting the breast (Morris, 1994) and in feeding (Salmons, 1995) may in some measure involve a mammalian fixed-behavior pattern. It is questionable at present whether fixed-action patterns underlie some versions of the head-nod. And yet, given the ubiquity of conversational head-nods performed by our species, it would be unwise to rule out the possibility of some degree of fixed-action influence.

Isopraxism. Earlier we cited research on imitative qualities of the human head-nod (McClave, 2000), namely, that watching a speaker nod may invoke nodding in a listener. Neurologically, some forms of human imitation may be found in circuits of the reptilian brain that mediate *isopraxism.*

The word *isopraxis* (Greek iso-, "same"; praxis, "behavior") was introduced by the neuroanatomist Paul D. MacLean in 1975. MacLean (1990) found isopraxis rooted in the reptilian brain's basal ganglia. Adding the -m ending, I began using a variant spelling of the word that first appeared in print in a United Press International story in 1981. According to Anne H. Soukhanov, former executive editor of *The American Heritage Dictionary*, "With the -m spelling, ordinary people might be inclined to use the word more" (Soukhanov, 1995, p. 90).

Isopraxism, Suokhanov (1993) writes, is "A non-learned neurobehavior in which members of a species act in a like manner" (p. 135). As defined in *The Nonverbal Dictionary*, isopraxism is "A deep, reptilian principle of mimicry, i.e., of copying, emulating, or aping a behavior, gesture, or fad" (Givens, 2013). It is "An impulsive tendency to, e.g., *a.* stand and clap as audience members nearby stand and applaud, or *b.* wear the same style of jewelry, clothing, or shoes" (Givens, 2013). Examples include *a.* the simultaneous head-nodding of lizards, *b.* the group gobbling of turkeys, and *c.* the synchronous preening of birds. In human beings, isopraxism " … is manifested in the hand-clapping of a theater audience and, on a larger scale, in historical mass migrations, in mass rallies, violence, and hysteria, and in the sudden widespread adoption of fashions and fads" (Soukhanov, 1993, p. 135).

Some researchers call isopraxism the *chameleon effect.* "The chameleon effect," Chartrand and Bargh (1999) write, "refers to nonconscious mimicry of the postures, mannerisms, facial expressions, and other behaviors of one's interaction partners, such that one's behavior passively and unintentionally changes to match that of others in one's current social environment" (p. 893). Call it mimicry, isopraxism, or the chameleon effect, in some instances the tendency for humans to head-nod in synchrony may be traced to subcortical circuits of the brain's basal ganglia.

(5) Mammalian-brain centers. Another head-nod variant is the *aha* nod of discovery. English "aha" is an interjection used " ... to express surprise, pleasure, or triumph" (Soukhanov, 1992, p. 36). The aha head-nod begins with an upward movement that may be rhythmically repeated. Performed after a speaker says, "This is a rubber tree," for instance, your unspoken aha nod would seem to say, "Ah, so this *is* a rubber tree!" Your nod signifies pleasure that a momentary uncertainty has been resolved.

Yet another head-nod variant is the nod of *certitude*. Like the emphatic head-nod, it begins with a downward movement and may be rhythmically repeated. Performed after a speaker says, "This is a rubber tree," your unspoken nod of certitude would seem to say, "Yes, this *is* a rubber tree!" You already knew that fact, and affirm to the speaker that you have a strong personal feeling that he or she has correctly identified the tree. Both head-nod types are mediated by reverberating emotion circuits of the mammalian brain.

Personal feelings of surprise, pleasure, triumph, and certitude originate in the limbic system, which includes those interlinked modules and pathways of the brain in charge of emotions and moods. Guyton (1996) describes the limbic system as the " ... entire neuronal circuitry that controls emotional behavior and motivational drives" (p. 752). Cytowic (1993) describes it as the emotional core of the human nervous system.

Mammalian emotion. As indicated above, by ca. 150 million years ago our mammalian forbears had entrusted their evolutionary future to a new and powerful form of arousal: emotion. In significant measure, the nerve network for emotions, feelings, and moods evolved from neural structures earlier committed to the chemical senses of taste and smell. Prior to the evolution of the mammalian brain, vertebrate body movements were primarily reflexive. Neither learning nor memory was required to crouch from a looming object, startle to a sound, or withdraw from a painful bite. With emotions came a new set of motivations for nodding the head. That the human brain is the most emotional vertebrate brain yet to evolve – the limbic brain grew proportionately with the neocortex (Armstrong, 1995) – can be inferred by the diversity and emotional content of our species' head-nods.

(6) Mirror-neuron imitation. In some instances the reptilian principle of isopraxism accounts for why watching a speaker nod may invoke nodding in a listener. Other neural dimensions of mutual nodding are

likely due to mirror neurons. Rotondo and Boker (2002), for example, have speculated on the role that mirror neurons play in the synchronization of gestures, such as the head-nod, in conversational interaction. For gestural imitation generally, there is agreement that mirror neurons play an important part (Williams et al., 2001; Meltzoff, 2002; Iacoboni 2008, 2009).

Mirror neurons were discovered in the 1990s in the premotor neocortex of macaque monkeys. Giacomo Rizzolatti and colleagues at the University of Parma identified neurons that activate when monkeys perform certain hand movements – such as picking up fruit – and also fire when monkeys watch other primates perform the same hand movements (Rizzolatti & Craighero, 2004). Subsequently, mirror neurons have been found in Broca's area and other parts of the human brain.

With respect to gestures and other nonverbal signs, mirror neurons provide brain circuitry that helps us intuit, decode, and understand their meanings. When we see a grasping-hand gesture, for instance, or hear an angry voice tone, mirror neurons set up a motor template – a prototype or blueprint in our own brain – that allows us to mimic the particular gesture or vocal tone. Additionally, through links to the mammalian brain's limbic system, mirror neurons enable us to decode the emotional nuances of the hand gestures we see and the tones of voice we hear. What has emerged from mirror-neuron research is that *we are seemingly wired to interpret the nonverbal actions of others as if we ourselves had enacted them.*

With respect to the head-nod, when we see a speaker nod in a conversation, mirror neurons help us feel the cue's emotional content as if we ourselves had nodded. Feeling the gesture's emotion (e.g., agreement, surprise, pleasure, triumph, or certitude), we may find ourselves nodding as well. In short, the motivation to imitate is the emotion felt through watching the head-nod itself. Thanks to mirror-neuron circuits, viewers not only see the head-nod but feel it as well.

Conclusion

A seemingly trivial gesture, the head-nod has many important meanings to convey. To repeat the observation of Lee and colleagues, "During face-to-face conversation the speaker's head is continually in motion" (Lee et al., 2009, p. 9). The head-nod is one of the most frequent motions seen in the conversational venue. With *a.* the involvement of diverse neuromuscular circuits, centers, and modules, *b.* emotional stimulation from special visceral nerves, and *c.* the gesture's interaction with allied movements such as the head-shake, head-toss, and head-turn, the human head-nod is an incredibly gifted communicator that always bears watching. Taking the measure of its neurological circuitry will enable researchers to assess the head-nod's use in contexts of detecting deception, in multicultural exchanges, and in face-to-face communication generally. Computerized avatars and motion detectors will enable increasingly precise measurements of the panhuman head-nod cue.

Head-shake gestures

" ... I shall endeavor to show that the opposite gestures of affirmation and negation, namely, vertically nodding or laterally shaking the head, have both probably had a natural beginning" (Darwin, 1872/1998, p. 65).

Students of gesture often assess the head-nod by gauging its contrast to the *head-shake* cue. In head-shaking, the head rotates right and left in the horizontal plane, often *a.* to disagree, *b.* to show incredulity or disbelief, and/or *c.* to show misunderstanding of a speaker's words. In an emotional conversation, a rhythmic head rotation may reflect one's personal convictions, condolences, sympathies, or feelings of grief. Thus, the head-shake may be used to show emotional disagreement, cognitive uncertainty, or emotional empathy – or all three feelings simultaneously.

Anatomy

Longus colli and splenius muscles (both supplied by cervical spinal nerves), in tandem with the sternocleidomastoid muscle (supplied by cranial nerve XI), rotate the head from side-to-side. The latter's prehistory as a branchiomeric muscle (originally used for respiration and feeding, and still controlled today by special visceral nerves) makes it responsive as a gut-reactive sign of refusal. Indeed, the first nonverbal nay-saying may occur when human babies head-shake to refuse proffered food and drink. As Morris (1994) writes, "When a baby does not want food, either at the breast or when being spoon-fed, it twists its head away sideways" (p. 144).

Research

According to Darwin (1872/1998), the head-shake is "probably" a universal sign of disapproval, disbelief, and negation (p. 65). Morris (1994) notes that the head-shake cue is geographically "widespread" (p. 144).

Rhesus monkeys, baboons, bonnet macaques, and gorillas similarly turn their faces sideward in aversion (Altmann, 1967). Children born deaf and blind head-shake to refuse objects and to disapprove when being touched by an adult (Eibl-Eibesfeldt, 1973). Evasive action shows in sideward head movements of young children to avoid the gaze of adults (Stern & Bender, 1974).

Students of gesture note certain "exceptions" to the rule that head-shaking signifies negation. The Bulgarian and Indian "head-bobble," for instance, resembles a head-shake but is used instead like a head-nod, that is, as an affirmative cue. The head-bobble itself, however, does not involve horizontal rotations of the head, as measured in the body's horizontal plane, but rather involves oscillating, sideward head-tilts, alternatively angling right and left, as measured in the body's coronal plane. Indeed, when measured in terms of the gesture's involved muscles and geometric-planar body movements, the bobble is actually a sideward head-tilt.

Measured anatomically, the sideward head-tilt involves *a.* the scalene muscles (supplied by cervical spinal nerves), which connect the neck bones (cervical vertebrae) to the upper two ribs, as well as *b.* the upper trapezius (supplied by cranial nerve XI), and *c.* the sternocleidomastoid (also cranial XI). Controlled by special visceral nerves, the latter two muscles are well equipped to express positive or negative emotions, feelings, and moods.

Gail, George, and Kris.   To measure the frequency and temporal positioning of head-shake gestures in interaction, I draw from data collected in three, eight-minute videos of dyadic conversations between subjects Gail, George, and Kris (Givens, 1976). The college-student volunteers – Gail (age 24), George (22), and Kris (20) – were native-born, English-speaking Americans of European descent, who were unacquainted with each other or with the researcher.

Subjects were told they were to be participants in a linguistic study of conversations (the nonverbal focus was undisclosed). Instructions were given to get to know the partner by "talking about school activities, hobbies, travel, movies, or whatever interests you." For each conversation the researcher turned on the video camera and left the room.

Videos were then carefully reviewed, and both the linguistic and nonlinguistic behaviors were recorded on data sheets (Givens, 1976, Table II, pp. 177–218). All nonverbal signs were synchronized to the speaking activity, recorded in standard English orthography. In temporal terms, the gestural measurements are relative rather than absolute, as each body movement was observed to come before, during, or after another body-motion unit or speech event, including words, voice quality, vocal register, and clause-terminal pitch. Results for the head-shake cue are outlined below.

Gail. In her eight-minute conversations with George and Kris, Gail performed 12 head-nods with George and 21 with Kris – but did not perform a single head-shake with either. Instead, she used a stronger sign of nonverbal negation, the *head-jerk*. A head-jerk is an abrupt, exaggerated head-tilt backward or tilt to the side. It is more energetic than a standard conversational head-tilt, and sometimes combines with an elevated, upper-lip expression suggestive of emotional contempt (i.e., a *sneer*).

Gail jerked her head backward and sideward twice with George and once with Kris. Head-jerks occurred when Gail disagreed strongly with a partner. With Kris, the head-jerk accompanied the word "yeah" as Gail said, "Well, yeah, except a lot of people think it's a little unfair ... " (Givens, 1976, p. 102). With George, a head-jerk accompanied by a derisively lifted upper lip (sneer) came with the word "except" as she said, "Yeah, well except for you don't have that many alternatives ... " (Givens, 1976, p. 103). George head-jerked four times with Gail as he argued with her, and once with Kris to accent a non-argumentative speaking point. Kris head-jerked only once in her conversations, to accent a non-argumentative speaking point with Gail.

Jerking the head rapidly upward, straight back or to one side, has been described by Darwin (1872/1998) as a component of sneering, scorn, or defiance, accompanied by raising the upper lip and "uncovering the canine tooth" (p. 246) in a snarl or sneer. Izard (1971) included "throwing back" the head in his description of contempt-scorn. Eibl-Eibesfeldt (1973) observed head-jerking and frowning in situations of anger in a deaf-and-blind-born child. The prime mover of the head-jerk is sternocleidomastoid, a neck muscle innervated by emotionally responsive special visceral nerves.

George. While speaking, George performed four head-shakes with Gail, and one with Kris. The first head-shake with Gail signified negation, and accompanied the spoken phrase "I'm not" (in "Don't worry, I'm not a male-chauvinist pig."). The second head-shake signified George's emotional investment in his belief that women (of the 1970s) had not achieved parity with men on the job (his affirmative shake came as he said, "It's really true."). His third head-shake was equally affirmative, occurring with "[It] really is [true]." The fourth, a head-shake of negation, came as George stated that he was not (like Gail) a campus political activist. In retrospect from 2013, the single head-shake noted in 1976 with Kris was a "false alarm," in Signal Detection terms, and may have been an exaggerated transition in George's direction of gaze (he turned his head away after responding, "Oh").

Kris. Kris performed six head-shakes with Gail, and six, as well, with George. Her first head-shake with Gail followed two major speech pauses (linguistic hesitations or nonfluencies) as she tried to explain the academic path through her dental hygiene program. The head-shake likely signaled uncertainty, and accompanied the phrase "you're almost separate." Since immediately after the shaking gesture Kris said, "I don't think you have to fill out distribution requirements ... " (Givens, 1976, p. 206), her first head-shake might also signify negation, as in "I don't know."

Definitely showing negation, Kris's second head-shake came with the word "not" as she told Gail, "I'm so apolitical it's not even funny anymore" (Givens, 1976, pp. 208–209). And again signifying negation, her third head-shake accompanied "never" as she told Gail, "I've never been really interested in [politics] ... " (Givens, 1976, p. 209). Kris's fourth head-shake, like the first one, signified uncertainty. It coincided with the phrase "sounds familiar" in a statement marked by hesitations and disfluencies. Gail asked Kris if she had heard about the recent case of a fired professor on campus, and Kris responded, "Yeah, I think, um, it sounds, it sounds familiar like ... " (Givens, 1976, p. 214). Kris's fifth head-shake co-occurred with the word "really," used as an interjection to convey emotional hopelessness about the political issue of firing professors at her school. And finally, Kris's sixth head-shake with Gail, accompanying her "not necessarily" phrase, was a clear sign of negation.

Kris's first head-shake with George came as a response to his question, "You're Kris?" The shake came immediately after Kris said, "Yeah," and accompanied the word "I" ("Yeah, I, I can remember faces, but I'm really bad on names."). Since the head-shake prefaced her disclosed inability to remember names, it may be interpreted as a sign of negation. This shake may also signify a degree of uncertainty reflected in the hesitation between her repeated "I" words, combined with emotion signified by its occurrence with an adverbial intensifier.

Kris's second head-shake with George, coinciding with "103," marked her uncertainty about the course number of a chemistry class she had taken ("I took, um, one-oh-three or whatever, some three credit thing here," Givens, 1976, pp. 181–182). Simultaneously, she accompanied her shake with an upper-lip-raise expression (sneer). Kris's third head-shake accompanied the word "wasn't" as a sign of negation ("When I came back, [Chemistry] one-sixty wasn't continued in the series in the same book," Givens 1976, p. 182). Kris's fourth head-shake with the phrase "twelve or something" marked uncertainty as to age in her future dental-assisting work ("I think I can clean teeth up to age twelve or something, I don't know . . ." Givens, 1976, p. 183).

Kris's fifth head-shake with George, coincident with the word "doesn't," marked negation as she said, " ... so sugar doesn't, you know, the price of sugar doesn't mean that much" (Givens, 1976, p. 184). And finally, her sixth head-shake with him marked uncertainty, accompanying the phrase, "friend of mine" (in "I think, um ['"um' is an interjection 'used to express doubt or uncertainty or to fill a pause when hesitating in speaking," Soukhanov, 1992, p. 1938], a friend of mine has, ah, graduated; did he have a B.A. or B.S.? I can't remember," Givens, 1976, p. 186). Her "can't" word adds a degree of negation, as well.

Measuring the head-shake cue

As with head-nods, taking the neurological measure of head-shake cues enables us to better understand their performance and meaning. Like the head-nod, the human head-shake exhibits a substantial degree of polysemy. Measuring the relative frequency of each of the cues in natural interaction, and gauging the neurological similarities and differences between the two cues, allows us to formulate a subset of discrete meaning categories for the human head-shake and head-nod.

Frequency of shakes and nods

Measured as percentages, of the 20 researcher-ascribed head-shake meanings above, 50% of the observed shakes signified *negation*, 30% signified *uncertainty*, and 20% signified *emotional intensity*. As for head-nods, of the 78 nods observed in the Gail, George, and Kris study, 59% were *affirmative*, and 23% were *emphatic* (*certitude* = 6%, *aha* = 5%, *simultaneous nodding* = 5%, with a *verbal pause* = 4%, and *intensifier* = 2%; due to rounding, figures add to more than 100%).

Comparative dimensions of nods and shakes

A comparative method helps us find similarities and differences between head-nod and head-shake variables. The levels of measurement are *nominal* (i.e., the categories we specify for each variable have names) and *ordinal* (the categories have names and can be rank-ordered in frequency).

For head-nod variables, the first category is *affirmative*. The English word "affirm" derives from the 7,000-year-old Indo-European root, dher-, "to hold firmly, support," and means "Asserting that something is true or correct, as with the answer 'yes': an *affirmative reply*" (Soukhanov, 1992, p. 30). In the videos, affirmative nods accompanied words and phrases such as "yeah," "oh yeah," "uh-huh," and "that's true." Along with emotionally positive affirmation itself, affirmative nods also played a role perhaps best characterized by the Japanese word, "aizuchi."

When Japanese converse, according to De Mente (2004), " ... they are conditioned to constantly encourage the person who is speaking by what is known as *aizuchi* (aye-zoo-chee), or 'chiming in,' meaning that they nod at regular intervals, say *hai* (hi), 'yes,' or make an affirmative 'uh' sound" (p. 18). With their affirmative head-nods, Gail, George, and Kris encouraged each other socially as well as emotionally. In many instances affirmative head-nods were given when a speaker, who had glanced away to begin an utterance, returned to a facing gaze at the end of the utterance as if seeking an aizuchi-style nod in return.

The second category of head-nod is *emphatic*. Compared to the emotional and social meanings of the affirmative nod, the meaning of emphatic head-nods is basically linguistic. In the video study, emphatic nods accompanied words that carried linguistic primary stress.

The first two head-nod categories account for 82% of the nods observed in the videos. They may be considered major categories when compared to the relatively minor categories of *certitude, aha, simultaneous, uncertainty* (with verbal pauses and disfluencies), and *intensifier* head-nods.

Compared to head-nods, head-shakes were far less frequently observed. A total of 21 shakes was noted in the 24 minutes of video interaction (one false alarm was noted as well). The first category for the head-shake variable is *negation*. Shakes of negation co-occurred with "doesn't," "never," "not," and "wasn't" words. In these instances the head-shakes starkly contrast with nods of affirmation, reflecting the polar-opposite contrast between yes and no. If "yes" has an emotionally positive valence, "no" is "used to express refusal, denial, disbelief, emphasis, or disagreement: '*No, I'm not going. No, you're wrong*'" (Soukhanov, 1992, p. 1226). Indeed, that yes and no, affirmation and negation, are so emotionally charged is in significant measure why our emotional brain devotes so many head movements to their expression.

The second head-shake category is *uncertainty*. Shakes of uncertainty co-occurred with such words and phrases as "um," "or whatever," and "I don't know." If negation has a strong emotional valence, uncertainty – itself an emotion (Kagan, 2007) – does as well. Though not often classified as an emotion per se, observations of shoulder-shrug gestures (see below: "Shoulder-Shrug Gestures") lead the author to categorize it as one.

Shoulder-shrug gestures

"When a man wishes to show that he cannot do something, or prevent something being done, he often raises with a quick movement both shoulders" (Darwin, 1872/1998, p. 264).

To shoulder-shrug is to lift, raise, or flex forward one or both shoulders in response *a.* to another person's statement, question, or physical presence; or *b.* to one's own inner thoughts, feelings, and moods. The shrug is one of 13 constituents of the larger shoulder-shrug display (Givens, 1977, 2013).

The shoulder-shrug is likely a universal sign of resignation, uncertainty, and submissiveness. Shrug cues may modify, counteract, or contradict verbal remarks. With the statement, "Yes, I'm sure," for instance, a lifted shoulder suggests, "I'm not so sure." A shrug gesture reveals misleading, ambiguous, or uncertain areas in dialogue and oral testimony, and thus may provide a *probing point*, that is, an opportunity to examine an unverbalized belief or opinion marked by the shrug (Givens, 2013). Additionally, when used to communicate submissiveness, shoulder-shrug cues play an important role in courtship (Givens, 2005).

Research

The shrug gesture originates from an ancient, protective crouch pattern innervated by paleocircuits designed for flexion withdrawal. The shoulder-shrug complex was originally identified by Darwin in 1872. Darwin noted instances of shrugging as a cue of helplessness in aboriginal Australia and North America, Africa, India, Malaya, and Micronesia. Shoulder-shrugging has been seen in South African adult and young adult baboons as a sign of fear and uncertainty, and as a response subsequent to the startle reaction (Hall & DeVore, 1972). Pulling in the shoulders is a response to spatial invasion (Sommer, 1969). The shrug is listed in two checklists of universal nonverbal signs: *a.* as "A fairly sudden raising of both shoulders" (Brannigan & Humphries, 1972, p. 60), and *b.* as "Raising both shoulders" (Grant, 1969, p. 533). Shrugging the shoulders is a submissive sign in children (McGrew, 1972).

From hundreds of face-to-face interviews conducted as a special agent for the FBI, nonverbal-communication specialist Joe Navarro (2012) found that shoulder-shrug movements indicated that speakers were uncertain, or lacked confidence in what they were saying. "As they answer a question," Navarro wrote, "they will say something such as, 'I am positive he wasn't here yesterday,' and as they do so, you see the shoulders or perhaps just one shoulder rise up slightly or slowly. This muted or slow inching up of the shoulders says, subconsciously, [that] I lack confidence in what I am saying" (Navarro, 2012).

Anatomy

The upper trapezius muscles (mediated by cranial nerve XI, a special visceral nerve) and levator scapulae muscles (mediated by cervical spinal nerves C3-5) lift the shoulder blades (scapulas). The trapezius (assisted by pectoralis major, p. minor [both mediated by cervical spinal nerves C5-8, and thoracic spinal nerve T1], and serratus anterior [mediated by C5-7]) medially rotates (i.e., ventrally flexes) the shoulders, as well. "The Trapezius of terrestrial vertebrates," Cartmill and colleagues write, "seems to be derived from a muscle sheet in fish that runs down from the back of the head to the top of the gill-arch bones. In a fish, this muscle lifts the whole set of gills up dorsally when it contracts" (Cartmill et al., 1987, p. 224).

Gail, George, and Kris.   In the videotape study, Gail and George shrugged five times each, and Kris shrugged 13 times. Shrugs marked pauses due to speaker uncertainty, and co-occurred with such uncertainty-connoting phrases as "I guess," "I don't know," "kind of," and "why not?" In seven instances the shoulder-shrug coincided with the English word "just." The shrug bears an interesting relationship to this word (in its adverbial usage), as in, "I don't know why I took the money – I just took it." In this sense, "just" conveys a feeling of powerlessness and uncertainty as to motive. The word also connotes "merely," as in "Just a scratch" (Soukhanov, 1992, p. 979). These diminutive features of the "just" word resonate with the cowering, cringing, and crouched aspects of the shoulder-shrug cue.

At one point in the video, Kris used shoulder-shrugs flirtatiously with George. After mutual laughter, George leaned forward and awkwardly extended his arms through his lap. Kris imitated him by joining her hands in her own lap, gazing submissively downward, and shrugging her shoulders. George responded with childlike sideward, swaying movements of his torso and shoulders; Kris then answered in a softer, ostensibly flirtatious tone of voice.

Neurology

As a branchiomeric muscle, the upper trapezius is emotionally responsive and may contract by other than conscious means. The upper trapezius is innervated by the accessory nerve (cranial XI), a special visceral nerve that also feeds into the voice box (or larynx). Thus, shoulder-shrugs and softer (submissive-like) vocal tones may be given at the same time. In her seemingly flirtatious exchange with George, Kris's shrugs were followed by a "depression in voice loudness below her normal level" (Givens, 1976, p. 184).

Conclusion

Measuring gestures involves assigning numbers to body movements and their constituent parts. In this chapter we have focused on three key gestures studied by Charles Darwin: the head-nod, head-shake, and shoulder-shrug. To date, numbers assigned by researchers to these three cues have been principally binary (presence or absence), proportional (percentage), and relational (occurring before, during, or after). Only rarely have the gestures been assigned volumetric (amplitude or intensity) numbers, and when assigned, the measurements have consisted of qualitative, nominal variables comparable to the Facial Action Coding System's (FACS) "trace," "slight," and "pronounced" variables for facial cues. Given the growing field of computerized avatar, motion-detection, and gesture-recognition research, amplitude measurements are likely to be more precisely quantifiable in the future.

We have broadened the concept of measurement in this chapter to include an accounting of neural dimensions of the head-nod, head-shake, and shoulder-shrug cues. Doing so enables us to explain why head, neck, and shoulder muscles have been recruited in our evolution as *Homo* – rather than other muscles of the body – for the expression of feelings of agreement, disagreement, submissiveness, and uncertainty. Charting the neural centers and pathways that underlie our nods, shakes, and shrugs – that is, taking their measure in the nervous system – reveals that evolution has clearly favored special-visceral over somatic nerves for emotional cues. This evolutionary postulate explains why, as Darwin concluded years ago, so many of humankind's emotional gestures are in widespread, if not universal, usage throughout the world.

The postulate also explains why these gestures are " ... in accordance with an elaborate and secret code that is written nowhere, known by none, and understood by all" (Sapir, 1927, p. 556).

References

Altmann, S. (1967). The structure of primate communication. In S. Altmann (Ed.), *Social communication among primates* (pp. 325–362).Chicago: University of Chicago Press.

Armstrong, E. (1995). Expansion and stasis in human brain evolution: Analyses of the limbic system, cortex, and brain shape. *65th James Arthur Lecture on the Evolution of the Human Brain.* New York: American Museum of Natural History.

Birdwhistell, R. (1952). *An introduction to kinesics.* Louisville: University of Louisville.

Birdwhistell, R. (1970). *Kinesics and context.* Philadelphia: University of Pennsylvania.

Boker, S. M., Cohn, J. F., Theobold, B., Matthews, I., Brick, T. R., & Spies, J. R. (2009). Effects of damping head movement and facial expression in dyadic conversation using real–time facial expression tracking and synthesized avatars. *Philosophical Transactions of the Royal Society, 364*(1535), 3485–3495. Retrieved from http://rstb.royalsocietypublishing.org/content/364/1535/3485.full

Bouissac, P. (1973). *La mesure des gestes: Prolegomenes à la semiotique gestuelle.* Mouton: The Hague.

Brannigan, C., & Humphries, D. (1972). Human non-verbal behaviour, ameans of communication. In N. G. Blurton-Jones (Ed.), *Ethological studies of child behaviour* (pp. 37–64). Cambridge: University Press.

Cartmill, M., Hylander, W. L., & Shafland, J. (1987). *Human structure.* Cambridge: Harvard University Press.

Chartrand, T. L., & Bargh, J. A. (1999). The chameleon effect: The perception-behavior link and social interaction. *Journal of Personality and Social Psycholology, 76*(6), 893–910.

Cytowic, R. E. (1993). *The man who tasted shapes.* New York: G.P. Putnam's Sons.

Darwin, C. (1998). *The expression of the emotions in man and animals* (3rd ed.). New York: Oxford University Press (Original work published 1872)

De Mente, B. L. (2004). *Japan's cultural code words.* North Clarendon, Vermont: Tuttle Publishing.

Eibl-Eibesfeldt, I. (1970). *Ethology: The biology of behavior.* San Francisco: Holt, Rinehart, and Winston.

Eibl-Eibesfeldt, I. (1973). The expressive behaviour of the deaf-and-blind-born. In M. von Cranach & I. Vine (Eds.), *Social communication and movement* (pp. 163–194). New York: Academic Press.

Ghez, C. (1991). The control of movement. In E. R. Kandel, J. H. Schwartz, & T. M. Jessell (Eds.), *Principles of neural science* (3rd ed., pp. 533–547). Norwalk, CT: Appleton & Lange.

Givens, D. B. (1976). *An ethological approach to the study of human nonverbal communication.* Doctoral dissertation, University of Washington. Ann Arbor: University Microfilms).

Givens, D. B. (1977). Shoulder shrugging: A densely communicative expressive behavior. *Semiotica, 19*(1/2), 13–28.

Givens, D. B. (2005). *Love signals: A practical field guide to the body language of courtship*. New York: St. Martin's Press.

Givens, D. B. (2013). *The nonverbal dictionary of gestures, signs & body language cues*. Spokane, Washington: Center for Nonverbal Studies Press. Retrieved from www.center-for-nonverbal-studies.org/6101.html

Givens, D. B. (2014). Nonverbal neurology: How the brain encodes and decodes wordless signs, signals, and cues. In A. Kostic & D. Chadee (Eds.), *Social Psychology of Nonverbal Communication* (pp. 9–30). New York: Palgrave-MacMillan Press.

Grant, E. (1969). Human facial expressions. *Man, 4*, 525–536.

Greenberg, N. (2003). Sociality, stress, and the corpus striatum of the green anolis lizard. *Physiology & Behavior, 79*, 429–440.

Guyton, A. C. (1996). *Textbook of medical physiology* (9th ed.). Philadelphia: W. B. Saunders.

Hall, K., & DeVore, I. (1972). Baboon social behavior. In P. Dolhinow (Ed.), *Primate patterns* (pp. 125–180). San Francisco: Holt, Rinehart, and Winston.

Harrigan, J. A. (2005). Proxemics, kinesics and gaze. In J. Harrigan, R. Rosenthal, & K. Scherer (Eds.), *New handbook of methods in nonverbal behavior research* (pp. 137–198). Oxford: Oxford University Press.

Huazhong, N., Tony, X. H., Yuxiao, H., Zhenqiu, Z., Yun, F., & Thomas, S. H. (2006). A realtime shrug detector. In *Proceedings of the International Conference on Automatic Face and Gesture Recognition*, 505–510.

Iacoboni, M. (2008). The mirror neuron revolution: Explaining what makes humans social/*Interviewer: Jonah Lehrer*. Retrieved from http://www.scientific american.com/article/the-mirror-neuron-revolut/

Iacoboni, M. (2009). Imitation, empathy, and mirror neurons. *Annual Review of Psychology, 60*, 653–670.

Izard, C.E. (1971). *The face of emotion*. New York: Appleton-Century-Crofts.

Kagan, J. (2007). *What is emotion?: History, measures, and meanings*. New Haven, CT: Yale University Press.

Kupfermann, I. (1991). Genetic determinants of behavior. In E. R. Kandel, J. H. Schwartz, & T. M. Jessell (Eds.), *Principles of neural science* (3rd ed., pp. 987–996). Norwalk, Connecticut: Appleton & Lange.

LaBarre, W. (1947). The cultural basis of emotions and gestures. *Journal of Personality, 16*, 49–68.

Lee, J., Neviarouskaya, A., Prendinger, H., & Marsella, S. (2009). Learning models of speaker head nods with affective information. *Proceedings of International Conference on Affective Computing and Intelligent Interaction* (ACII '09), (pp. 9–15). Amsterdam, The Netherlands: Institute of Electrical and Electronics Engineers.

MacLean, P, D. (1990). *The triune brain in evolution*. New York: Plenum Press.

McClave, E. Z. (2000). Linguistic functions of head movements in the context of speech. *Journal of Pragmatics, 32*, 855–878.

McGrew, W. C. (1972). Aspects of social development in nursery school children with emphasis on introduction to the group. In N. G. Blurton Jones (Ed.), *Ethological studies of child behaviour* (pp. 129–156). Cambridge: University Press.

Mehrabian, A. (1972). *Nonverbal communication.* New Jersey: Aldine Transaction.

Meltzoff, A. N. (2002). Elements of a developmental theory of imitation. In A. N. Meltzoff & P. Wolfgang (Eds.), *The imitative mind: Development, evolution, and brain bases* (pp. 19–41). Cambridge: Cambridge University Press.

Morris, D. (1994). *Bodytalk: The meaning of human gestures.* New York: Crown Publishers.

Navarro, J. (2012). What the shoulders say about us. [Web log message]. Retrieved from http://www.psychologytoday.com/blog/spycatcher/201205/what-the-shoulders-say-about-us

Ning, H., Han, T. X., Hu, Y., Zhang, Z., Fu, Y., & Huang, T. S. (2006). A realtime shrug detector. *Proceedings of the IEEE International Conference on Automatic Face and Gesture Recognition, 2006,* (pp. 505–510). Southampton, United Kingdom: Institute of Electrical and Electronics Engineers.

Nori, F., Lipi, A. A., & Nakano, Y. (2011). Cultural differences in nonverbal behaviors in negotiation conversations: Towards a model for culture-adapted conversational agents. In C. Stephanidis (Ed.), *Universal access in human-computer interaction* (pp. 410–419). Berlin: Springer-Verlag.

Peterson, W. W., Birdsall, T. G., & Fox, W, C. (1954). The theory of signal detectability. *Transactions of the IRE Professional Group on Information Theory, 4*(4), 171–212.

Poggi, I., D'Errico, F., & Vincze, L. (2011). 68 nods. But not only of agreement. In E. Fricke & M. Voss (Eds.), *68 Zeichen für Roland Posner. Ein Semiotisches Mosaik.* [68 signs for Roland Posner: A semiotic mosaic]. Retrieved from http://europa.uniroma3.it/dse/files/ed49e4be-3806-4a72-ac12-9178862e9e21.pdf.

Rizzolatti, G., & Craighero, L. (2004). The mirror-neuron system. *Annual Review of Neuroscience, 27,* 169–192.

Rotondo, J. L., & Boker, S. M. (2002). Behavioral synchronization in human conversational interaction. In M. I. Stamenov & V. Gallese (Eds.), *Mirror neurons and the evolution of brain and language* (pp. 163–171). Amsterdam: John Benjamins.

Salmons, S. (1995). Muscle. In P. L. Williams & L. H. Bannister (Eds.), *Gray's anatomy: The anatomical basis of medicine and surgery* (38th ed., pp. 737–900). New York: Churchill Livingstone.

Samovar, L. A., Porter, R. E., & McDaniel, E. R. (2007). *Communication between cultures.* Boston: Wadsworth.

Sapir, E. (1927). The unconscious patterning of behavior in society. In D. Mandelbaum (Ed.), *Selected writings of Edward Sapir* (pp. 544–559). Los Angeles: University of California Press.

Sommer, R. (1969). *Personal space: The behavioral basis of design.* Englewood Cliffs, NJ: Prentice-Hall.

Soukhanov, A. H. (Ed.). (1992). *The American heritage dictionary of the English language* (3rd ed.). New York: Houghton Mifflin Co.

Soukhanov, A. H. (1993). Word watch. *The Atlantic Monthly* (October), 135–138.

Soukhanov, A. H. (1995). *Word watch.* New York: Henry Holt.

Stern, D., & Bender, E. (1974). An ethological study of children approaching a strange adult. In R. Friedman et al. (Eds.), *Sex differences in behavior* (pp. 233–258). New York: John Wiley and Sons.

Thagard, P. (2010). *The brain and the meaning of life.* Princeton, NJ: Princeton University Press.

Wilbur, R. B. (2000). Phonological and prosodic layering of nonmanuals in American sign language. In K. Emmorey & H. L. Lane (Eds.), *The signs of language revisited: An anthology to honor Ursula Bellugi and Edward Klima* (pp. 190–214). Mahwah, NJ: Lawrence Erlbaum Associates, Inc.

Williams, J. H. G., Whiten, A., Suddendorf, T., & Perrett, D. I. (2001). Imitation, mirror neurons and autism. *Neuroscience & Biobehavioral Reviews, 25*(4), 287–295.

4

Nonverbal Elements of the Voice

Mark G. Frank, Darrin J. Griffin, Elena Svetieva, and Andreas Maroulis

The human voice is capable of making a wide variety of sounds. From a psychological point of view, what is interesting is that only some configurations of sounds are meaningful to others. There are the words we choose, which are combinations of sounds that symbolically represent various concepts we are trying to communicate. But even those sounds that compose words have variations that can impart meaning independent of those words – even to the point of changing their meaning entirely. The phrase "It's not what you said, but how you said it" exists in our parlance because we have come to recognize the reality that the nonverbal elements that accompany the spoken word are as important as the actual words in creating meaning. In fact, when we speak we unleash three distinct types of information upon listeners through our voices, of which one is verbal, while the other two are nonverbal. Thus we can separate the voice channel into three different subchannels. The first subchannel is the *verbal* subchannel, and consists of the actual words we speak. The second subchannel is the speech *style* subchannel, which consists of the patterns of pausing and other irregularities of speech that accompany the words spoken. The third subchannel is the speech *tone* subchannel, which consists of the acoustic properties of speech such as loudness and pitch. We consider the verbal, style, and tone aspects of speech *subchannels* because they are each capable of sending separate and unique messages; however, these subchannels are interdependent. This is not true of all nonverbal communication channels; for example, one can make a facial expression without uttering a sound, or gesture at someone without uttering a sound. However, once you utter a sound, each sound will be accompanied by a tone and a style. Moreover, a speech style must have a tone. Likewise, once words are articulated, they will have tone and style. Most of the time these three subchannels impart roughly the same message to a listener, but at other times they can impart different, even contradictory messages. For example, a person who has been told they need a painful dental procedure may respond to this diagnosis by saying "well, that sounds like fun." However, through shifting voice tones and speaking styles, the speaker can convey to his or her listener that they believe this procedure is quite the opposite of the specific spoken words that suggest this procedure will actually be enjoyable. The presence of these multiple subchannels permits things like sarcasm. But these nonverbal subchannels are about producing more than sarcasm; they can reveal information about our enduring demographic traits, such as our gender, approximate age, and even our native language. They also reveal information about transient states, such as emotions, attitudes, as well as cognitive load. This information can be "pushed" out due to some internal state such as an emotion, or "pulled" out from people due to the social circumstances surrounding them, or some combination of both (Scherer, 2003). All of these things can be communicated above and beyond the words one chooses to speak.

This chapter will focus on the nonverbal communication elements of speech, thus we will be deliberately ignoring issues with language and word usage. Of the three subchannels identified above, we will focus more on the style and tone. The style and tone of speech are often lumped together under the term *prosody*. But prosody, or the "music" of speech, is a subcategory of all the various noises we can make, such as disfluencies, pauses, laughs, yawns, and grunts, which are collectively called *paralanguage* (Trager, 1961; Duncan, 1969). Paralanguage tends to be a catch-all category for any information derived from the voice that is not the actual spoken word (Harrison & Knapp, 1972). What is important to note is that although we will review the science concerning nonverbal signals in the voice separately from the verbal, in reality it may be impossible to cleave them so neatly.

The mechanics of nonverbal signals in the voice

Typically speech starts with various thoughts in the brain, and then signals from the outer or neo cortex – Broca's speech area – activate the cortical motor strip which then signals the jaw, tongue, lips, vocal cords, larynx, and diaphragm to initiate the movements and air flow that produce the sounds that compose the words that represents the thoughts (Fry, 1979). Those sounds are created by air from the lungs being forced up through the trachea and into the glottis – at which point the air pressure underneath the glottis either releases to produce a variety of sounds, through combination of vibrations of the vocal folds, or movements of the tongue and lips. Thus through conscious control and practice, sounds get formed into the comprehendible patterns that compose words and statements.

There are other forces acting on this process as well. For example, if an emotion is aroused, then the inner limbic system of the brain sends signals that engage the autonomic and somatic nervous systems, which then alter blood flow, blood pressure, muscle tension, mucus secretion, respiration, and so forth (Furness, 2006). These physiological changes then alter the length and shape and smoothness of the movements of the various body parts that are responsible for the sounds of speech, thus changing the tone, energy, loudness, and other measurable elements of the voice (Scherer, 1989). Both of these brain systems can send signals simultaneously to the throat structures (Frank, 2003; Rinn, 1984). However, unlike other emotional signaling systems like the face – where there is a direct connection between the limbic system and facial muscle movements – the voice instead features more indirect connections to the muscles and other associated elements that surround the body parts that are responsible for speech. These small changes to any of the body elements can produce measurable acoustic changes in the voice, which strongly suggests that nonverbal measures that accompany speech may be a useful source of information about the speaker's transient states (Scherer, 1989).

Measurement of nonverbal voice characteristics

The sound of a human voice is composed of many distinct and measurable qualities that make each human voice sound, for the most part, unique (Nolan, 1983). It is these nonverbal elements that tend to make voices recognizable.

Although systems exist to measure the specific motor movements of speech – such as high speed photography (Kitzing, 1985) or even magnetic resonance imaging (MRI; Kim et al., 2009) – what are important psychologically are the acoustic parameters of speech. The acoustic parameters, or the sounds emitted, are what reflect an individual's intentions, and drive others' perceptions (Scherer, 2003). There are a number of quantifiable acoustic measures of nonverbal information that we can extract from the voice. These acoustic measures are much more easily measured due to the easy availability of speech analysis software (e.g., PRAAT; Boersma & Weenink, 2013). Research suggests one can compute vast numbers of measures on the voice, including compound and combined measures (e.g., Zwan et al., 2007). We of course remind the reader of the garbage in/garbage out principle, in that if the collected materials to be analyzed are poor or staged representations of spontaneous utterances, or the measures selected do not represent the essential ingredients of production and perception, then the resulting findings from any software analysis program will be misleading representations of reality (Frank, 2005).

The most frequently assessed characteristics, which have also been productive from a research point of view in that they predict various behaviors or emotional states, include both tonal and stylistic subchannel features. For example, the *tonal* features include:

Fundamental frequency

Often denoted as F_0, and referred to as pitch, F_0 is the measurement of the vocal frequency. Pitch changes are caused by a combination of air pressure upwards from below the larynx and the speed of vibration of the vocal folds (Lieberman, 1961). The length of the vocal folds also influences pitch, such that shorter folds produce higher pitch. Women and children – who are more likely to have shorter folds – also have higher pitched voices then men (Daniloff et al., 1980). Scientists have been interested in not only mean changes in pitch as indicators of various states, but also the variability in pitch over a statement (depending upon specific comparison between measurement periods, referred to as *jitter*, or *shimmer*; Lieberman, 1961; Murphy, 2000; Patel & Shrivastav, 2011; Sundberg et al., 2011).

Amplitude

Often erroneously referred to as *loudness* (because loudness is the subjective quality, whereas amplitude is a physical measurement), amplitude is the measure of the intensity or energy of the voice. Amplitude changes are caused by the combination of air pressure upwards from below the larynx and the tension of the larynx (Zemlin, 1968). Amplitude changes within a subject are often hard for scientists to measure accurately, because unless a microphone is attached at a constant distance from the mouth, any head movements will artificially change the amplitude of the signal measured. However, gross changes in loudness – shouting versus whispering – can be captured somewhat reliably even if the microphone is not at a controlled distance from the mouth.

Timbre

Often hard to measure, it is a representation of the *quality* of the voice. It is considered hard to measure because there are many possible characteristics that can go into the timbre, and many scientists see it as the measure of anything that is neither amplitude nor F_0 (McAdams & Bregman, 1979). Timbre can then be thought of as the difference in two voices when their loudness and pitch are identical. A number of factors can produce timbre changes, including different sorts of phonation (Daniloff et al., 1980), which modify the vibrations of the larynx. Often timbre differences are attributable to differences in the configuration of an individual's mouth, nose, throat, and so forth, along with their basic tension (Scherer, 1989). This is measured through changes in the harmonics as well (Simpson, 2009).

Resonance

Often measured by the presence of *formants* in the spectrum of a voice, these are the specific pronunciation sounds of different consonants, vowels and other sounds (Fant, 1960). They are differentially generated by slight changes in the positions and movements of the tongue, lips, larynx, and so forth.

There are other popular and productive nonverbal measures that we can extract from the voice within the *stylistic* subchannel:

Speech rate

This is usually measured as words per minute or words per second. A change in the speech rate can often indicate higher cognitive load or mental effort on the part of the individual (Sillars et al., 1982). It can also reflect the effects of an emotion, with a decrease for a lower arousal emotion like sadness or disgust, but an increase for higher arousal emotions like anger and fear (Johnson et al., 1986).

Response length

This is the amount of time a person spends talking. There is some evidence that when people are lying they choose to utter shorter statements (Zuckerman et al., 1981). Depressed patients, as well, utter shorter statements; this can be due to a higher cognitive load caused by lying, or somatic and psychiatric distress, causing the individual to inhibit much of his or her speech (e.g., Kenny & Williams, 2007).

Speech latency

This is the measurement of the time it takes someone to respond to another. It is the period that spans the end of one person's statement or question to the beginning of the other person's response. It is sometimes referred to as speech hesitation. Longer speech latencies – i.e., slower responses – have been shown to be reliable measures of higher cognitive load or mental effort (Goldman-Eisler, 1968; DePaulo et al., 2003).

Pauses

This is the time between spoken words. There are two types of pauses – *filled* and *unfilled*. A filled pause is when an individual fills the pause with noise, but not necessarily a word. For example, if someone says "um," or "ah," in between words. For example, "I went to the uh zoo." The "uh" fills that pause with sound. An unfilled pause simply does not have the sound involved. For example, "I went to the ... zoo." Scientists count the number, rate, and duration of pauses. When people are thinking on their feet, they tend to have more pauses (Goldman-Eisler, 1968).

Speech errors

These are various disfluencies or disturbances in speech, such as repeating words, stuttering, grammar errors, slips of the tongue, false starts, and any incoherent sounds that are uttered (Kasl & Mahl, 1965; Siegman & Feldstein, 1979). As with many of these other measures, they are typically measured as the rate of errors or disturbances per unit of time. An increase in the rate of these disturbances often indicates a higher cognitive load, and in particular, the disturbances marked by repeated particular words and phrases seem to be compelling (DePaulo et al., 2003).

Although scientists can measure all these *stylistic* qualities precisely, they often have trouble in the some of the *tonal* qualities (e.g., like timbre) given the large number of possible parameters than can be derived from vocal measures (Zwan et al., 2007). In face to face encounters with others it is often our less precise general impressions of the tone and style that influences our perceptions of them. Thus a person's voice may be described as dull, harsh or breathy, from which we infer other traits about them (Scherer, 1984). Likewise, we can detect pronunciation changes associated with accents, and then use that information to infer someone's ethnicity (e.g., Walton & Orlikoff, 1994).

Socially relevant information derived from the nonverbal subchannels of the voice

The tonal and stylistic qualities of the human voice provide a wide array of information about someone's appearance, personality, and emotional/cognitive state. Most of this information individuals process without conscious thought. A telephone call from a stranger evokes an instant mental image of the person speaking. Research shows people are surprisingly accurate at identifying strangers from voice; participants were able to match audio samples from strangers to their photographs at 76.5% accuracy, significantly higher than chance (50%; Krauss et al., 2002). However, there are a number of aspects of appearance one might be able to detect from voice; thus to make this manageable we have separated the characteristics into *enduring*, stable traits (e.g., age, gender) of the individual, *transient* dynamic states of the individual (e.g., emotions) and *interactive tools* of the individual (e.g., turn-taking cues).

Enduring traits

These refer to relatively stable demographic or personality characteristics of people. The first thing to note is that people are good at recognizing *identity*. When participants are presented with a 2.5-minute audio clip of someone speaking to whom the participant is familiar, then participants accurately identify them 98% of the time (Hollien et al., 1982). Other studies have shown that audio clips of familiar individuals saying "Hello! How are you?" are recognized nearly 100% of the time (Abberton & Fourcin, 1978). People are also accurate identifying famous people from voice, although on average not as well as familiar people from their lives. If someone has to come up with the name of the famous person from his or her own free recall, then people are 26.6% accurate; but when given a multiple choice listing of names to select, then accuracy rises to 69.9% (van Lancker et al., 1985). These high accuracy levels are likely due to the fact that no two individuals sound exactly alike. And of course one reason for that is that individuals differ in the size and position of their voice apparatus, which will have corresponding consequences for their typical levels of pitch, timbre, and resonance.

Age is another characteristic that is recognized accurately. A long ago study found that 4,000 listeners could estimate quite accurately the age of the nine unknown speakers on a radio broadcast (Pear, 1931). When participants in other studies were given voice samples and asked to match them to photos of the speaker, they were able to identify age quite well, and age was one of the strongest driving factors (Krauss et al., 2002). Research also suggests accurate age identification of male stimulus subjects through the vocal quality parameters and speech rate (Harnsberger et al., 2010). It appears that as we get older, voice pitch deepens – dramatically for males in puberty – but then stabilizes into adulthood, but then rises slightly after age 70 (Masaki & Seiji, 2008). Also, disturbances in fundamental frequency increase, and speech rate decreases, with age (Hummert et al., 1999). Surprisingly, perceived hoarseness in the voice is not a predictor of age (Gorham-Rowan & Laures-Gore, 2006).

Gender is detected at very high rates as well (Pear, 1931). Even when presented with just six vowel sounds per speaker, detectors were able to identify accurately gender 96% of the time (Lass et al., 1976). This is likely due to female voices being higher-pitched, but also more variable and with lower resonance than male voices (Ko et al., 2006). Interestingly, it appears that women tend to be more attracted to men with low-pitched voices, whereas men tend to be more attracted to women with higher-pitched voices (Collins & Missing, 2003; Vukovic et al., 2011).

Ethnicity is often identified based upon speaking accent – for example, a person speaks English with an Australian or a Greek accent. It can also betray where one was raised within a specific country, as in an American with a Texas or Buffalo accent. Identifying race within a culture is not as straightforward. Judges who were presented with a pair of sustained "a" sounds, taken from an African or Caucasian American speaker, were able to accurately classify them 60% of the time (Walton & Orlikoff, 1994). However, social class, as reflected in education levels, tends to be better and more reliably recognized than race (Harms, 1961). Social status, as reflected through dominance measures such as interruptions and softness of voice, are also reliably identified (Hall et al., 2005).

Personality is not as tightly tied to vocal qualities, but some types of personality seem to have certain characteristics that make them identifiable. For example, extraverts tend to talk more loudly, with a faster speech rate, shorter pauses, and more variable pitch than introverts (Lippa, 1998; Siegman, 1987). Dominance is also associated with lower pitch and greater loudness (Hall et al., 2005; Puts et al., 2006). Moreover, perceptions of trustworthiness and gender attitudes also are reliably identified by voice (Vukovic et al., 2011).

Transient states

Although the word "transient" may imply that something is not significant, in fact these characteristics have received the most attention of all in the nonverbal research literature on the voice. The most important transient characteristics of people include their emotions and mental processing efforts.

Emotions.   Research on human emotion has historically focused on facial expression, but a large literature also exists for research on vocal expression of *emotions*. Moreover, many of the same controversies arise in research on voice and emotion as in research on the face and emotion. For example, voice scientists debate which labels best describe the emotion family represented by a particular vocal tone (Scherer, 1986; Juslin & Laukka, 2003). Scientists also debate whether vocal expressions of the emotions are best understood as categorical entities with their own properties (e.g., Laukka, 2005; Scherer, 1984), or whether they are better and more parsimoniously understood as conveying varying amounts of the dimensions of arousal and pleasure (e.g., Bachorowski, 1999). This question has inspired a large chunk of the research on voice and nonverbal communication.

Emotions have been defined as bio-psycho-social responses designed to aid individuals to adapt to and cope with events that have immediate consequences for their welfare (Matsumoto et al., 2013). This is not limited to humans, as other animals express emotions, including vocalizations that communicate threats, danger, and the nature of relationships (e.g., Kitchen et al., 2003). There is compelling evidence that human facial expressions of emotion are universal; that is, expressed similarly and recognized across all cultures (e.g., Ekman, 2003). The question is whether the voice shows the same qualities. Darwin (1872/1998) thought so, and described many paralinguistic correlates of various emotional states. As signals from different parts of the brain to the muscles of facial expression (e.g., Rinn, 1984), different parts of the brain can independently send signals to the speech production apparatus in the throat. The fact that discrete emotional signals are sent should produce more bounded changes in the voice structures within each discrete emotion, which in turn would produce some distinguishing sound qualities corresponding to each emotion. This means individuals should agree on which emotion term should label a vocal portrayal of an emotion made by either a lay person or actor. If this is true, we would also expect people from many different cultures to agree as to which vocal portrayal represented which emotion. However, given that there are no direct inputs from the subcortical structures of the brain – typically responsible for emotion (reviewed by Rinn, 1984) – into the specific vocal apparatus, only in the supporting structures, we would likely expect the levels of agreement to be lower than those for the face because of the interposition of layers of body material or tissue between these components. This may muffle and muddle the correspondence between the emotion and the signal, and thus render their relationship less precise or strong than the relationship between the facial expression and emotion – which is exactly what the research literature shows (see review by Scherer, 2003).

A comprehensive review of the literature on voice and emotion examining the emotions of anger, fear, happiness, and sadness showed significantly greater than chance agreement for all four emotions, both within and across cultures (Juslin & Laukka, 2003). And, as suggested above, the agreement rates were typically less than the agreement rates reported for facial expressions and emotion, which are typically anywhere from 60–95% for expressions of anger, contempt, disgust, fear, happiness, sadness, and surprise, with the greatest agreement on happiness. The agreement rates for the vocal expressions of emotion ranged from approximately 54–70% for judgments made within a given culture, to approximately 32–64% for judgments made across cultures. We note two things about these data; first, that despite being lower, they were still significantly higher than chance agreement. Second, we have translated the actual agreement rates to percentage agreements (of which chance accuracy for these data is 14%), even though this paper reported Rosenthal and Rubin's (1989) pi statistic. Pi is a measure of agreement-controlling for the number of response alternatives – which then enables better comparisons across studies with different response options. Chance for pi is .50, and perfect agreement is 1.00. The original Juslin and Laukka (2003) paper reports pis ranging from .93 to .74. However, typically, judgment data like this had been reported as percentage agreements, so we recalculated these pis as percentage agreements (we assumed seven response options to make this back-calculation). This means that the percentage agreements reported here are good estimates, but not exact.

For both within and across cultures, the pattern was the same – the highest agreement levels were for the vocal expressions of anger and sadness, and the lowest agreement level was for happiness (although we are ignoring a tentative finding for an even lower rate for tenderness, because that was a single study with only three speakers; Juslin & Laukka, 2003). This pattern is opposite to what we typically find in facial expression research, where the highest agreement rate is almost always happy facial expressions. Although we should exercise some caution when comparing the relative importance of face and voice, as there are likely cultural factors that may push or pull for the different expressive channels. For example, when presented with facial and vocal expressions of emotion, the Japanese tend to appear to be a bit more influenced by voice than face, compared to the Dutch (Tanaka et al.,

2010). This was also a single study so we should be careful about generalizing from it. But the pattern of findings in cross-cultural research on voice and emotion is similar to findings on the face – that there appear to be universals on voice production of emotion, even when the groups are relatively isolated from western culture (e.g., Scherer et al., 1991; Bryant & Barrett, 2008). Interestingly, the combination of both voice and face in these studies produces the highest agreement rates; higher than either face or voice alone (Mortillaro et al., 2011).

Although anger, fear, happiness, and sadness have received the most study, smaller numbers of studies have examined agreement for emotions such as disgust, contempt, boredom, embarrassment, guilt, shame, and many shades of positive emotion, such as amusement, relief, contentment, and so forth. The results for these emotions are less consistent than the results for anger, fear, happiness, and sadness. For example, shame (Banse & Scherer, 1996) and guilt often do not show high agreement rates (e.g., 22%, with chance being 7%), although they are occasionally misclassified as sadness (Simon-Thomas et al., 2009). Disgust shows irregular agreement patterns, sometimes significantly high (93.5%; Sauter et al., 2010; Simon-Thomas et al., 2009) and sometimes insignificantly low agreement (15%; Banse & Scherer, 1996). This may be due to the techniques used to elicit disgust in the vocalists, as scientists have noted disgust utterances elicited by emotional films tend to feature significantly higher F_0 (i.e., fundamental frequency) whereas disgust elicited by actor portrayal tends to produce disgust utterances with significantly lower F_0 (Scherer, 1989). In contrast, embarrassment has shown lower, but still significant above-chance agreement (17%; Simon-Thomas et al., 2009), as has contempt (60%; Banse & Scherer, 1996; 34%; Simon-Thomas et al., 2009; 46%; Sauter et al., 2010).

Voice researchers have spent more time differentiating amongst different positive emotion states than facial expression researchers. Studies have shown that lay people's agreement rates for expressions of various positive emotions are significantly greater than chance for amusement (81%), relief (76%), interest (66%), enthusiasm (42%), pleasure (35%), awe (30%), and triumph (29%). Studies have also shown that there is not statistically significant agreement on compassion, gratitude, love, contentment, desire, or pride (Simon-Thomas et al., 2009). Other studies have reported the same high agreement for distinguishing amusement (76.5%), relief (64.7%), pleasure (58.8%), triumph (achievement; 70.6%), and in this case also contentment (46%; Sauter & Scott, 2007; 23.5%; Sauter et al., 2010). Interest has also had consistently high agreement levels, and so has its opposite – boredom, at similarly high rates (75% and 76%, respectively; e.g., Scherer, 1989; Banse & Scherer, 1996). The emotion of surprise expressed in the voice, although at times confused with fear, is also reliably detected (81.3%; Sauter et al., 2010).

There are other emotions, expressed through the voice, that have also been assessed – but under the labels of anxiety, stress, laughter, and crying. These are likely subsumed under the general rubric of fear, joy/happiness, and distress/sadness emotion family labels (see Matsumoto & Hwang, 2013 for a more detailed discussion of conceptual issues with labeling emotion). Regardless, studies have reported a number of interesting findings; for example, anxiety is better detected in the voice by itself as compared to in the face by itself (e.g., Harrigan et al., 2004). Some of the qualities associated with anxiety are similar to fear, such as speech disturbances, pauses, and stutters (Harrigan et al., 1994). Stress has usually been measured in the context of deception, with a variety of measures purported to measure vocal stress associated with telling a lie – although often to no avail (Hollien & Harnsberger, 2006). Laughter is seen in all cultures, yet the actual acoustic properties vary greatly, suggesting that laughter may serve a few different functions, ranging from extreme joy to nervousness (Grammer & Eibl-Eibesfeldt, 1990). Crying is also found in all cultures, tending to be mostly associated with sadness (Klineberg, 1940) – but can be seen at times at supposedly happy occasions (Vingerhoets & Cornelius, 2001).

Cognition

There are also nonverbal features in speech that tend to reflect an individual's higher mental effort, or *thinking*. These include longer speech latencies, slower speech, and more pauses (Greene & Ravizza, 1995). There is also some evidence to suggest that people engaged in higher mental effort also are less immediate, which includes speaking in a more monotone fashion (Kraut & Poe, 1980). Moreover, the cognitive appraisals that may underlie or trigger an emotion (e.g., Scherer, 2003) are also reliably detected from the voice (Laukka & Elfenbein, 2012). Even when cognitions are compromised by an external substance – such as alcohol causing intoxication – they are still detectable by voice (Hollien, et al., 2009).

Transient states – Methodological issues

The lower agreement rates for judging transient emotional states from voices, compared to judging them from faces, are likely due to a combination of different reasons. One reason, as discussed earlier, is that the biological elements of sound production are indirectly tied to the elements affected by emotional reactions. Another reason is methodological. First, vocal portrayals of a given emotion can vary greatly depending upon the method used to elicit it – e.g., disgust portrayals featured higher pitch when elicited by a film, yet featured lower pitch when self-generated by actors (Pittam & Scherer, 1993). Recordings of spontaneous vocal expression of emotion, taken from real life spontaneous emotion situations (e.g., airline pilots during panic situations; Kuroda et al., 1979), suffer from this same problem – the events that trigger the emotion differ drastically. These sorts of spontaneous samples also suffer from other problems inherent in using any natural spontaneous material, such as often poor-quality recordings, short samples, a single speaker, and uncertainty as to the true underlying emotional state of the speaker as they spoke (Scherer, 2003). Second, when researchers attempt to exert experimental control by employing actors to pose vocal emotions, they note much larger individual differences in people's abilities to pose an emotion in their voices as compared to posing emotions in their faces (Scherer, 1989). Thus the individual differences in expressing the prototype for each vocal emotion will likely be more variable. Third, this individual difference factor becomes particularly problematic because many studies feature only one or two stimulus speakers doing the vocal portrayals, thus any deviant or poor portrayal will have a disproportionate effect on suppressing the agreement rates (Scherer & Bänziger, 2010). Fourth, and consistent with the previous observation, voice researchers have not been able to document with great precision the exact parameters of each of the emotions expressed in the voice (Batliner et al., 2011). Much of this is likely due to both technical *capabilities* of and *limitations* in measuring the voice. Technical advances have allowed researchers to carve up and represent vocal signals in hundreds of ways; for example, F_0 is studied for emotions by measuring its mean, its variance, its range, its contours (change patterns), high-frequency energy, shift regularity, formants, formant precision, amplitude mean, range, variability (e.g., Banse & Scherer, 1996; Zwan et al., 2007), and other variables that are often hard to describe and still not quite settled by researchers (the same way that the construct of *timbre* is not quite settled; e.g., McAdams & Bregman, 1979). Furthermore, technological advances have enabled the discovery of new complex and detailed measures (e.g., new energy measures and/ or synthetic vocal recreations; e.g., Laukka, 2005). Thus the measurement tools used to study the voice are continually changing. Ironically, the fact that new measures are being uncovered actually speaks strongly to the technical *limitations* that plague the study of voice. Scientists have lamented that many unique paralinguistic characteristics of speech have yet to be quantified (Patel & Scherer, 2013). Thus the measurement canvas upon which scientists may apply their tools is also shifting. In contrast, scientists studying facial expressions only need to observe the facial muscles, of which there are only 46 possible facial muscle movements. Moreover, there are only two ways to measure facial expressions – visually, using a human (e.g., FACS; Ekman & Friesen, 1978) or computer-driven systems based on human coding (e.g., CERT; Bartlett et al., 2006), or physically with Electromyography (e.g., Fridlund et al., 1987). The final consideration when researching the tone qualities of each emotion is that almost all the measurements must be within-subject measurements (i.e., comparing a person's emotional tone with his or her neutral tone), as there are vast differences between individuals in voice pitch, timbre, and so forth.

In summary, given the indirect innervation of the vocal tract, the lack of consensus on the exact prototype of each emotional signal, and the myriad possible vocal measurements and characterizations of those measurements of each emotion, it is reasonable to expect that emotions expressed through the voice would not elicit the same levels of agreement as the face. Despite that, and the other methodological considerations when studying the voice, the research seems to have converged across posed, induced, and spontaneous vocal expressions of emotion to show that there are markers for each of the basic emotions in the voice, and that the pattern of results looks very similar to the pattern of results found when studying facial expressions of emotion.

Interactive tools in the voice

These characteristics refer to the subchannel paralinguistic characteristics of the voice (tone, style) that can be directed outward toward others, and thus affect interactions in some observable way. For example, the paralinguistic information associated with speech influences *comprehension* of information, such that people are more likely to remember information that is presented by a speaker with more variable pitch and amplitude in his or her speech than one who has less (e.g., Glasgow, 1952). People are more likely to be *persuaded* by people who not only vary pitch and amplitude, but also speak with fewer pauses, shorter latencies, and faster speech (Apple et al., 1979; Leigh & Summers, 2002; Miller et al., 1976). Related to this topic is the phenomenon of "motherese," in which a parent speaks with exaggerated pitch and amplitude changes that seem to be more effective in grabbing the attention of a prelinguistic child (Fernald, 1992). All parents throughout the world tend to use this type of exaggerated intonation to infants (and occasionally to animal pets), and it seems to be effective in conveying the rudiments of language to the prelinguistic child as well as garnering attention (Singh et al., 2009). To adults, then, it seems that varying intonations also captures attention, and thus may be the mechanism upon which more intoned speech is effective in persuasion – if one is listening more to the message, then one is more likely to be persuaded (Andersen, 1999).

Paralinguistic information is essential in managing conversations (e.g., *turn taking*) as well. Individuals make subtle adjustments in their voice pitch, amplitude, and style to signal that they are finished speaking (Duncan & Fiske, 1977). For example, when a speaker needs to request a turn he or she may accelerate their rate of backchannel ums and ahs to the current speaker, and/or may stutter starts with their initial word or sounds ("I ... I ... I ... "; Wiemann & Knapp, 1975). A speaker may maintain his or her speaking position by sensing when others wish to interject, and deploying various tone and style signals to keep the floor, such as increasing speech rate, loudness, and rate of filled pauses in order to prevent openings for the other to start talking (silence allows others a golden opportunity to cut in; Lallgee & Cook, 1969; Rochester, 1973). A speaker will indicate that he or she is finished by typically dropping their pitch and stretching their final word or syllable (Cappella, 1985). If it is a question to which one wishes an answer, then the pitch rises at the end. Thus throughout an interaction, parameters such as the patterns of pausing – seen as the "absence" of a behavior – are critical to the free flow of conversation (Mortensen, 2007).

Besides regulating turn taking, tone and style clues can mark interaction coordination between speakers (Gallois et al., 2005). The *communication adaptation theory* describes how members of an interaction will migrate toward the vocal style of the other (Giles & Powesland, 1975), and this can mark agreement between speakers; likewise, migrating away from vocal style often marks disagreement or even hostility (Salamin & Vinciarelli, 2012).

Finally, there is a perspective that argues that the main purpose of subchannel paralinguistic information is to *provoke* directly the behavioral reaction of others, rather than to be a basic expression of various internal emotional or other processes (Owren et al., 2003). This model argues that the evolutionary origins of the vocal signal and acoustics serve the organism by driving the emotional reactions of others; for example, laughter and crying have been shown to provoke strong emotional reactions (Hatfield et al., 1995; Neumann & Strack, 2000).

This may in fact be the case, as most of our nonverbal communication will affect others in unspecified ways, dependent upon context. We recognize that there is not only a biological and a psychological aspect to emotions, but a social component as well (Matsumoto et al., 2013). Thus this perspective on the tonal and stylistic issues in the voice may be true, but it does not require rejecting the perspective that these paralinguistic clues are manifestations of internal states.

Conclusion

Although all three subchannels of information in the voice are important, the two nonverbal subchannels – tone and style – have elements that are universally produced and recognized. The nonverbal elements associated with voice have been used to predict outcomes that other behavioral clues have not. We can identify people by their voices. Current trends in technology have now made available literally hundreds of possible parameters within the voice in much the same way that video technology enabled the more detailed examination of nonverbal behavior in the face and body. These advances will enable us to better understand the internal dynamics of an individual, as well as better understand the outer impressions of an individual – whether for right or wrong.

References

Abberton, E., & Fourcin, A. J. (1978). Intonation and speaker identification. *Language and Speech, 21*(4), 305–318. doi: 10.1177/002383097802100405.

Andersen, P. A. (1999). *Nonverbal communication: Forms and functions.* Mountain View, CA: Mayfield.

Apple, W., Streeter, L. A., & Krauss, R. M. (1979). Effects of pitch and speech rate on personal attributions. *Journal of Personality and Social Psychology, 37*(5), 715–727. doi: 10.1037/0022-3514.37.5.715.

Bachorowski, J. A. (1999). Vocal expression and perception of emotion. *Current Directions in Psychological Science, 8*(2), 53–57. doi: 10.1111/1467-8721.00013.

Banse, R., & Scherer, K. R. (1996). Acoustic profiles in vocal emotion expression. *Journal of Personality and Social Psychology, 70*(3), 614–636. doi: 10.1037/00223514.70.3.614.

Bartlett, M. S., Littlewort, G., Frank, M. G., Lainscsek, C., Fasel, I., & Movellan, J. R. (2006). Automatic recognition of facial actions in spontaneous expressions. *Journal of Multimedia, 1*(6), 22–35.

Batliner, A., Steidl, S., Schuller, B., Seppi, D., Vogt, T., Wagner, J., . . . Amir, N. (2011). Whodunnit – Searching for the most important feature types signalling emotion-related user states in speech. *Computer Speech & Language, 25*(1), 4–28. doi: 10.1016/j.csl.2009.12.003.

Boersma, P., & Weenink, D. (2013). PRAAT: Doing phonetics by computer (Version 5.3.65) [Computer software]. Retrieved from http://www.praat.org/.

Bryant, G. A., & Barrett, H. C. (2008). Vocal emotion recognition across disparate cultures. *Journal of Cognition and Culture, 8*(1–2), 135–148. doi: 10.1163/156770908x289242.

Cappella, J. N. (1985). Production principles for turn-taking rules in social interaction: Socially anxious vs. socially secure persons. *Journal of Language and Social Psychology, 4*(3–4), 193–212. doi: 10.1177/0261927x8543003.

Collins, S. A., & Missing, C. (2003). Vocal and visual attractiveness are related in women. *Animal Behaviour, 65*(5), 997–1004. doi: 10.1006/anbe.2003.2123.

Daniloff, R., Schuckers, G., & Feth, L. (1980). *The physiology of speech and hearing: An introduction.* Englewood Cliffs, NJ: Prentice-Hall.

Darwin, C. (1998). *The expression of the emotions in man and animals.* New York: Oxford University Press (Original work published 1872).

DePaulo, B. M., Lindsay, J. J., Malone, B. E., Muhlenbruck, L., Charlton, K., & Cooper, H. (2003). Cues to deception. *Psychological Bulletin, 129*(1), 74–118. doi: 10.1037/0033-2909.129.1.74.

Duncan, S. (1969). Nonverbal communication. *Psychological Bulletin, 72*(2), 118–137. doi: 10.1037/h0027795.

Duncan, S., & Fiske, D. W. (1977). *Face-to-face interaction: Research methods and theory.* Hillsdale, NJ: Erlbaum.

Ekman, P. (2003). *Emotions revealed* (2nd ed.). New York: Times Books.

Ekman, P., & Friesen, W. V. (1978). *The facial action coding system.* Palo Alto, CA: Consulting Psychologists.

Fant, G. (1960). *Acoustic theory of speech production.* The Hague, The Netherlands: Mouton.

Fernald, A. (1992). Human maternal vocalizations to infants as biologically relevant signals: An evolutionary perspective. In J. H. Barkow, L. Cosmides, & J. Tooby (Eds.), *The adapted mind: Evolutionary psychology and the generation of culture* (Vol. xii, pp. 391–428). New York: Oxford University Press.

Frank, M. (2005). Research methods in detecting deception research. In J. A. Harrigan, R. Rosenthal, & K. R. Scherer (Eds.), *The new handbook of methods in nonverbal behavior research* (pp. 341–368). Oxford: Oxford University Press.

Frank, M. G. (2003). Getting to know your patient: How facial expression reveals true emotion. In M. Katsikitis (Ed.) *The clinical application of facial measurement: Methods and meaning* (pp. 255–283). Dordrecht: Kluwer.

Fridlund, A. J., Ekman, P., & Oster, H. (1987). Facial expression of emotion. In A. Siegman & S. Feldstein (Eds.), *Nonverbal behavior and communication* (pp. 143–224). Hillsdale, NJ: Erlbaum.

Fry, D. B. (1979). *The physics of speech.* Cambridge, UK: Cambridge University Press.

Furness, J. B. (2006). *The enteric nervous system.* Malden, MA: Blackwell Publishing, Inc.

Gallois, C., Ogay, T., & Giles, H. (2005). Communication accommodation theory: A look back and a look ahead. In W. Gudykunst (Ed.), *Theorizing about international communication* (pp. 121–148). Thousand Oaks, CA: Sage.

Giles, H., & Powesland, P. F. (1975). *Speech style and social evaluation.* London: Academic Press.

Glasgow, G. M. (1952). A semantic index of vocal pitch. *Communication Monographs, 19*(1), 64–68.

Goldman-Eisler, F. (1968). *Psycholinguistics: Experiments in spontaneous speech.* London, New York: Academic Press.

Gorham-Rowan, M. M., & Laures-Gore, J. (2006). Acoustic-perceptual correlates of voice quality in elderly men and women. *Journal of Communication Disorders, 39*(3), 171–184. doi: 10.1016/j.jcomdis.2005.11.005.

Grammer, K., & Eibl-Eibesfeldt, I. (1990). The ritualisation of laughter. In W. A. Koch (Ed.), *Naturlichkeit der Sprache und der Kultur* (pp. 192–214). Bochum, Germany: Brockmeyer.

Greene, J. O., & Ravizza, S. M. (1995). Complexity effects on temporal characteristics of speech. *Human Communication Research, 21*(3), 390–421. doi: 10.1111/j.1468-2958.1995.tb00352.x.

Hall, J. A., Coats, E. J., & Smith LeBeau, L. (2005). Nonverbal behavior and the vertical dimension of social relations: A meta-analysis. *Psychological Bulletin, 131*(6), 898–924. doi: 10.1037/0033-2909.131.6.898.

Harms, L. S. (1961). Programmed learning for the field of speech. *Communication Education, 10*(3), 215–219.

Harnsberger, J. D., Brown Jr., W. S., Shrivastav, R., & Rothman, H. (2010). Noise and tremor in the perception of vocal aging. *Journal of Voice, 24*, 523–530. doi: 10.1016/j.jvoice.2009.01.003.

Harrigan, J. A., Suarez, I., & Hartman, J. S. (1994). Effect of speech errors on observers' judgments of anxious and defensive individuals. *Journal of Research in Personality, 28*(4), 505–529. doi: 10.1006/jrpe.1994.1036.

Harrigan, J. A., Wilson, K, & Rosenthal, R. (2004). Detecting state and trait anxiety from auditory and visual cues: A meta-analysis. *Personality and Social Psychology Bulletin, 30*(1), 56–66. doi: 10.1177/0146167203258844.

Harrison, R. P. & Knapp, M. L. (1972). Toward an understanding of nonverbal communication systems. *The Journal of Communication, 22*(4), 339–352.

Hatfield, E., Hsee, C. K., Costello, J., Weisman, M. S., & Denney, C. (1995). The impact of vocal feedback on emotional experience and expression. *Journal of Social Behavior and Personality, 10*(2), 293–313.

Hollien, H., & Harnsberger, J. (2006). *Voice stress analyzer instrumentation evaluation.* Final Report CIFA Contract – FA 4814-04-0011. Gainesville: University of Florida.

Hollien, H., Harnsberger, J. D., Martin, C. A., Hill, R., & Alderman, G. A. (2009). Perceiving the effects of ethanol intoxication on voice. *Journal of Voice, 23*, 552–559. doi: 10.1016/j.jvoice.2007.11.005.

Hollien, H., Majewski, W., & Doherty, E. T. (1982). Perceptual identification of voices under normal, stress and disguise speaking conditions. *Journal of Phonetics, 10*(2), 139–148.

Hummert, M. L., Mazloff, D., & Henry, C. (1999). Vocal characteristics of older adults and stereotyping. *Journal of Nonverbal Behavior, 23*(2), 111–132. doi: 10.1023/a:1021483409296.

Johnson, W. E., Emde, R. N., Scherer, K. R., & Klinnert, M. D. (1986). Recognition of emotion from vocal cues. *Archives of General Psychiatry, 43*(3), 280–283.

Juslin, P. N., & Laukka, P. (2003). Communication of emotions in vocal expression and music performance: Different channels, same code? *Psychological Bulletin. 129*(5), 770–814. doi: 10.1037/0033-2909.129.5.770.

Kasl, S. V., & Mahl, G. F. (1965). Relationship of disturbances and hesitations in spontaneous speech to anxiety. *Journal of Personality and Social Psychology, 1*(5), 425–433. doi: 10.1037/h0021918.

Kenny, M. A., & Williams, J. M. G. (2007). Treatment-resistant depressed patients show a good response to mindfulness-based cognitive therapy. *Behaviour Research and Therapy, 45*, 617–625.

Kim, Y. C., Narayanan, S., & Nayak, K. S. (2009). Accelerated 3D upper airway MRI using compressed sensing. *Magnetic Resonance in Medicine, 61*, 1434–1440. doi: 10.1002/mrm.21953.

Kitchen, D. M., Cheney, D. L., & Seyfarth, R. M. (2003). Female baboons' responses to male loud calls. *Ethology, 109*(5), 401–412. doi: 10.1046/j.1439-Q310.2003.00878.x.

Kitzing, P. (1985). Stroboscopy – A pertinent laryngological examination. *The Journal of Otolaryngology, 14*(3), 151–157.

Klineberg, O. (1940). *Social psychology* (Vol. 5). New York: Holt.

Ko, S. J., Judd, C. M., & Blair, I. V. (2006). What the voice reveals: Within- and between-category stereotyping on the basis of voice. *Personality and Social Psychology Bulletin, 32*(6), 806–819. doi: 10.1177/0146167206286627.

Krauss, R. M., Freyberg, R., & Marsella, E. (2002). Inferring speakers' physical attributes from their voices. *Journal of Experimental Social Psychology, 38*(6), 618–625. doi: 10.1016/s0022-1031(02)00510-3.

Kraut, R. E., & Poe, D. (1980). Behavioral roots of person perception: The deception judgments of customs inspectors and laymen. *Journal of Personality & Social Psychology, 39*(5), 784–798.

Kuroda, I., Fujiwara, O., Okamura, N., & Utsuki, N. (1979). Method for determining pilot stress through analysis of voice communication. *Aviation, Space, and Environmental Medicine, 47*(5), 528–533.

Lallgee, M. G., & Cook, M. (1969). An experimental investigation of the function of filled pauses in speech. *Language and Speech, 12*(1), 24–28.

Lass, N. J., Hughes, K. R., Bowyer, M., Waters, L. T., & Bourne, V. T. (1976). Speaker sex identification from voiced, whispered, and filtered isolated vowels. *Journal of the Acoustical Society of America, 59*(3), 675–678.

Laukka, P. (2005). Categorical perception of vocal emotion expressions. *Emotion, 5*(3), 277–295. doi: 10.1037/1528-3542.5.3.277.

Laukka, P., & Elfenbein, H. A. (2012). Emotion appraisal dimensions can be inferred from vocal expressions. *Social Psychological and Personality Science, 3*(5), 529–536. doi: 10.1177/1948550611428011.

Leigh, T. W., & Summers, J. (2002). Effects of salespersons' use of nonverbal cues. *Journal of Personal Selling and Sales Management, 22*(1), 41–53.

Lieberman, P. (1961). Perturbations in vocal pitch. *Journal of the Acoustical Society of America, 33*(5), 597–603.

Lippa, R. (1998). Gender-related individual differences and the structure of vocational interests: The importance of the people – Things dimension. *Journal of Personality and Social Psychology, 74*(4), 996–1009. doi: 10.1037/0022-3514.74.4.996.

Masaki, N., & Seiji, N. (2008). Changes in speaking: Fundamental frequency characteristics with aging. *Folia Phoniatrica et Logopaedica, 60*(3), 120–127.

Matsumoto, D., Frank, M., & Hwang, H. S. (2013). Reading people: Introduction to the world of nonverbal behavior. In D. Matsumoto, M. G. Frank, &

H. S. Hwang (Eds.), *Nonverbal communication: Science and applications* (pp. 3–14). Thousand Oaks, CA: Sage.

Matsumoto, D., & Hwang, H. S. (2013). Facial expressions. In D. Matsumoto, M. G. Frank, & H. S. Hwang (Eds.), *Nonverbal communication: Science and applications* (pp. 15–52). Thousand Oaks, CA: Sage.

McAdams, S., & Bregman, A. (1979). Hearing musical streams. *Computer Music Journal, 3*(4), 26–60.

Miller, N., Máruyama, G., Beaber, R. J., & Valone, K. (1976). Speed of speech and persuasion. *Journal of Personality and Social Psychology, 34*(4), 615–624. doi: 10.1037/0022-3514.34.4.615.

Mortensen, C. D. (2007). *Communication theory* (2nd ed.). New Brunswick, NJ: Transaction Publishers.

Mortillaro, M., Mehu, M., & Scherer, K. R. (2011). Subtly different positive emotions can be distinguished by their facial expressions. *Social Psychological and Personality Science, 2*(3), 262–271. doi: 10.1177/1948550610389080.

Murphy, P. J. (2000). Spectral characterization of jitter, shimmer, and additive noise in synthetically generated voice signals. *The Journal of the Acoustical Society of America, 107*(2), 978–988. doi: 10.1121/1.428272.

Neumann, R., & Strack, F. (2000). "Mood contagion": The automatic transfer of mood between persons. *Journal of Personality and Social Psychology, 79*(2), 211–223. doi: 10.1037/0022-3514.79.2.211.

Nolan, F. (1983). *The phonetic bases of speaker recognition. Cambridge studies in speech science and communication.* Cambridge, UK: Cambridge University Press.

Owren, M. J., Rendall, D., & Bachorowski, J. A. (2003). Nonlinguistic vocal communication. In D. Maestripieri (Ed.), *Primate psychology* (pp. 359–394). Cambridge, MA: Harvard University Press.

Patel, S., & Scherer, K. (2013). Vocal behavior. In J. A. Hall & M. L. Knapp (Eds.), *Nonverbal communication.* Berlin, Germany: De Gruyter Mouton.

Patel, S., & Shrivastav, R. (2011). A preliminary model of emotional prosody using multidimensional scaling. *Proceedings of interspeech* (pp. 2957–2960). Florence, Italy.

Pear, T. H. (1931). *Voice and personality.* Great Britain: Chapman & Hall.

Pittam, J., & Scherer, K. R. (1993). Vocal expression and communication of emotion. In M. L. Lewis & J. Haviland (Eds.), *Handbook of emotions* (pp. 185–197). New York, London: Guilford Press.

Puts, D. A., Gaulin, S. J. C., & Verdolini, K. (2006). Dominance and the evolution of sexual dimorphism in human voice pitch. *Evolution and Human Behavior, 27*(4), 283–296. doi: 10.1016/j.evolhumbehav.2005.11.003.

Rinn, W. E. (1984). The neuropsychology of facial expression: A review of the neurological and psychological mechanisms for producing facial expressions. *Psychological Bulletin, 95,* 52–77. doi: 10.1037/0033-2909.95.1.52.

Robinson, W. P. (1972). *Language and social behaviour.* Harmondsworth, Middlesex: Penguin Books.

Rochester, S. R. (1973). The significance of pauses in spontaneous speech. *Journal of Psycholinguistic Research, 2*(1), 51–81. doi: 10.1007/BF01067111.

Rosenthal, R., & Rubin, D. B. (1989). Effect size estimation for one-sample multiple choice-type data: Design, analysis, and meta-analysis. *Psychological Bulletin, 106*(2), 332–337. doi: 10.1037/0033-2909.106.2.332.

Salamin, H., & Vinciarelli, A. (2012). Automatic role recognition in multiparty conversations: An approach based on turn organization, prosody, and conditional random fields. *IEEE Transactions on Multimedia, 99*, 1–4. doi: 10.1109/TMM.2011.2173927.

Sauter, D., & Scott, S. (2007). More than one kind of happiness: Can we recognize vocal expressions of different positive states? *Motivation and Emotion, 31*(3), 192–199. doi: 10.1007/s11031-007-9065-x.

Sauter, D. A., Eisner, E., Calder, A. J., & Scott, S. K. (2010). Perceptual cues in nonverbal vocal expressions of emotion. *The Quarterly Journal of Experimental Psychology, 63*(11), 2251–2272. doi: 10.1080/17470211003721642.

Scherer, K. R. (1984). On the nature and function of emotion: A component process approach. In K. R. Scherer & P. Ekman (Eds.), *Approaches to emotion* (pp. 293–317). Hillsdale, NJ: Erlbaum.

Scherer, K. R. (1986). Vocal affect expression: A review and a model for future research. *Psychological Bulletin, 99*(2), 143–165. doi: 10.1037/0033-2909.99.2.143.

Scherer, K. R. (1989). Vocal correlates of emotional arousal and affective disturbance. In H. Wagner & A. Manstead (Eds.), *Handbook of social psychophysiology* (pp. 165–197). Oxford, England: John Wiley & Sons.

Scherer, K. R. (2003). Vocal communication of emotion: A review of research paradigms. *Speech Communication, 40*(1–2), 227–256. doi: 10.1016/s0167-6393(02)00084-5.

Scherer, K. R., & Bänziger, T. (2010). On the use of actor portrayals in research on emotional expression. In K. R. Scherer, T. Bänziger and E. B. Roesch (Eds.), *Blueprint for affective computing: A sourcebook* (pp. 166–178). Oxford: Oxford University Press.

Scherer, K. R., Banse, R., Wallbott, H. G., & Goldbeck, T. (1991). Vocal cues in emotion encoding and decoding. *Motivation and Emotion, 15*(2), 123–148. doi: 10.1007/bf00995674.

Siegman, A. W. (1987). The telltale voice: Nonverbal messages of verbal communication. In A. W. Siegman & S. Feldstein (Eds.), *Nonverbal behavior and communication* (2nd ed., pp. 351–433). Hillsdale, NJ, England: Erlbaum.

Siegman, A. W., & Feldstein, S. (1979). *Of speech and time. Temporal speech patterns in interpersonal contexts.* Hillsdale, NJ: Lawrence Erlbaum Associates.

Sillars, A. L., Coletti, S. E., Parry, D., & Rogers, M. A. (1982). Coding verbal conflict tactics: Nonverbal and perceptual correlates of the "avoidance-distributive-integrative" distinction. *Human Communication Research, 9*(1), 83–95. doi: 10.llll1j.1468-2958.1982.tb00685.x.

Simon-Thomas, E. R., Keltner, D. J., Sauter, D., Sinicropi-Yao, L., & Abramson, A. (2009). The voice conveys specific emotions: Evidence from vocal burst displays. *Emotion, 9*(6), 838–846. doi: 10.1037/a0017810.

Simpson, A. P. (2009). Phonetic differences between male and female speech. *Language and Linguistics Compass, 3*(2), 621–640. doi: 10.1111/j.1749-818X.2009.00125.x.

Singh, L., Nestor, S., Parikh, C., & Yull, A. (2009). Influence of infant-directed speech on early word recognition. *Infancy, 14*, 654–666.

Sundberg, J., Patel, S., Bjorkner, E., & Scherer, K. R. (2011). Interdependencies among voice source parameters in emotional speech. *IEEE Transactions on Affective Computing, 2*(3), 162–174. doi: 10.1109/T-AFFC.2011.14.

Tanaka, A., Koizumi, A., Imai, H., Hiramatsu, S., Hiramoto, E., & de Gelder, B. (2010). I feel your voice: Cultural differences in the multisensory perception of emotion. *Psychological Science, 21*(9), 1259–1262. doi: 10.1177/0956797610380698.

Trager, G. L. (1961). The typology of paralanguage. *Anthropological Linguistics, 3*(1), 17–21.

van Lancker, D., Kreiman, J., & Emmorey, K. (1985). Familiar voice recognition: Patterns and parameters. Part I: Recognition of backward voices. *Journal of Phonetics, 13*(1), 19–38.

Vingerhoets, A. J. J. M., & Cornelius, R. R. (2001). *Adult crying: A biopsychosocial approach* (Vol. 3). Philadelphia: Routledge.

Vukovic, J., Jones, B. C., Feinberg, D. R., DeBruine, L. M., Smith, F. G., Welling, L. L., & Little, A. C. (2011). Variation in perceptions of physical dominance and trustworthiness predicts individual differences in the effect of relationship context on women's preferences for masculine pitch in men's voices. *British Journal of Psychology, 102*(1), 37–48. doi: 10.1348/000712610X498750.

Walton, J. H., & Orlikoff, R. F. (1994). Speaker race identification from acoustic cues in the vocal signal. *Journal of Speech & Hearing Research, 37*(4), 738–745.

Wiemann, J. M., & Knapp, M. L. (1975). Turn taking in conversations. *Journal of Communication, 25*(2), 75–92.

Zemlin, W. R. (1968). *Speech and hearing science; anatomy and physiology.* Englewood Cliffs, NJ: Prentice-Hall.

Zuckerman, M., Koestner, R., & Driver, R. (1981). Beliefs about cues associated with deception. *Journal of Nonverbal Behavior, 6*(2), 105–114. doi: 10.1007/bf00987286.

Zwan, P., Szczuko, P., Kostek, B., & Czyżewski, A. (2007). Automatic singing voice recognition employing neural networks and rough sets. In M. Kryszkiewicz, J. Peters, H. Rybinski, & A. Skowron (Eds.), *Lecture notes in artificial intelligence: Proceedings of the international conference on rough sets and intelligent systems paradigms* (pp. 793–802). doi: 10.1007/978-3-540-73451-2_83.

5

The Expression and Perception of the Duchenne Smile

Sarah D. Gunnery and Judith A. Hall

The smile, as a nonverbal behavior, can be a quite confusing expression. People smile for many reasons and when experiencing many different emotions including embarrassment, anger, jealousy, and distress along with many kinds of positive affect (Ekman & Friesen, 1982; Keltner, 1995; Ansfield, 2007; Ambadar et al., 2009). Although people smile when they are feeling a range of different emotions, the smile is largely synonymous with happiness, and people are very good at perceiving when another person is feeling happy rather than one of the other emotions listed above.

Since French neurologist Duchenne de Boulogne first used electromyography (EMG) to document that when a person feels happy, crow's feet are achieved around the eyes, it has been widely understood that when a person is expressing true and genuine happiness this happiness is likely to be expressed in the eyes as well as in the mouth (Duchenne, 1862/1990). Until recently scientists believed that a smile only "reached the eyes" when the person was feeling genuinely happy (Ekman et al., 1990; Frank et al., 1993). This specific type of expression, named the Duchenne smile, is a smile that includes activation of the orbicularis oculi (cheek raiser) muscle that lifts the cheeks, creating crow's feet around the eyes, slight pouching under the eyes, a slight droop in the eyelid, and slight lowering of the outer eyebrow. Using language from the Facial Action Coding System (FACS; Ekman et al., 2002), the Duchenne smile consists of activation of Action Unit (AU) 12, the zygomatic major muscle (lip corner puller), and AU 6, the orbicularis oculi (cheek raiser). The non-Duchenne smile is a smile that lacks cheek raiser (AU 6) activation or a smile that, in more colloquial terms, does not reach the eyes. See Figure 5.1 for a photograph of a Duchenne and non-Duchenne smile.

This chapter will review the literature on the expression and perception of the Duchenne smile as well as include how smile intensity and

Figure 5.1 From left to right: a Duchenne smile and non-Duchenne smile. Photos courtesy of Veikko Surakka, Professor at University of Tampere, Finland

new findings on the deliberate production of the Duchenne smile may reshape how the previous literature is viewed. For clarity, throughout the remainder of the chapter people who express Duchenne smiles will be referred to as targets and those perceiving the Duchenne smiles will be referred to as perceivers.

Expression of the Duchenne smile

Since the first documentation, numerous studies have found a connection between the Duchenne smile and happiness. In a study using EMG, Ekman and Davidson (1993) found that production of the Duchenne smile was related to brain activation associated with enjoyment, while production of a non-Duchenne smile was not. In a study looking at smiling and deception (Ekman et al., 1988), targets watched either an enjoyable film or an upsetting film and were interviewed about how they were feeling while watching. Targets were instructed to always say that they were enjoying the film, and thus had to lie while watching the upsetting film. Targets produced more Duchenne smiles when talking about watching a film they actually enjoyed than when saying they were enjoying watching the upsetting film. This study was the foundation for many claims about how people are less able to produce a Duchenne smile when they are not feeling underlying positive affect, and is frequently cited as showing a strong connection between production of the non-Duchenne smile and deception or interpersonal manipulation.

In a further investigation of when people are more likely to produce a Duchenne smile, Jakobs et al. (1999) found that the context within which targets are exposed to mood-inducing stimuli is important in the expression of Duchenne smiles. Participants Duchenne smiled more when they heard stories that elicited strong positive emotion rather than moderate positive emotion. Participants also Duchenne smiled more when a friend rather than a stranger told them the story. The presence of the storyteller also increased Duchenne smiling (as compared to hearing the story over the phone, or a tape recording of the story) but this was only true when the story was being told by a friend, and not when being told by a stranger. Also looking at how different social contexts affected smile production, Mehu, Grammer, and Dunbar (2007) found that participants produced more Duchenne smiles when they were deciding how to share an amount of money than when they were having a conversation that did not involve sharing. This study also found that targets who smiled more during the sharing conversation also self-reported that they would be more likely to help a friend who was in financial need. Both of these studies showed that the situation is important in the production of the Duchenne smile, while providing more evidence that people Duchenne smile more when they are feeling positive affect.

Moving outside the laboratory to a real-life situation, Matsumoto and Willingham (2009) investigated the smiling behavior of blind and sighted athletes in response to winning or losing Judo matches in the Special Olympics and Olympics. Both blind and sighted athletes produced more Duchenne smiles when they won their medal match (gold and bronze) than when they were defeated (silver and fourth). This study indicated that people produce more Duchenne smiles when they win a match rather than lose it, independent of their overall place. People who won silver medals produced fewer Duchenne smiles than people who won bronze medals, indicating that the act of winning in the moment elicited more Duchenne smiles than overall ranking, reflecting the probable emotional state of the athletes – elation for winning gold and bronze and disappointment in losing the gold for those who received silver medals.

Two studies have investigated how people who produce more Duchenne smiles respond to different types of situations differently than those who produce fewer Duchenne smiles. In a study on grief and bereavement, participants who Duchenne smiled more were found to have fewer symptoms of grief (Bonanno & Keltner, 1997), and similarly in a study of physical pain perception, Zweyer et al. (2004) found that participants who Duchenne smiled more reported feeling less pain during a cold pressor task. This could be indicative of a third variable, such as general positive affect, being linked to both use of the Duchenne smile and how a person copes with grief and pain. Or, a person actually experiencing less grief or pain might promote positive affect and therefore the Duchenne smile.

These investigations of the Duchenne smile have mostly come out of the theory that there are seven basic emotions that are universally felt, expressed, and understood (Ekman et al., 1987; Fridlund et al., 1987). The Duchenne smile had been exclusively talked about in the facial expression literature as an expression that was outside of volitional control. This is illustrated best by the many studies that substitute the term Duchenne smile with genuine or enjoyment smile when they write about the expression (e.g., Peace et al., 2006). The Duchenne smile stood out as the nonvolitional expression that was the hallmark for the evolutionary argument for basic emotions. The theory that the Duchenne smile was the spontaneous and nonvolitional physical representation of genuine felt positive affect across cultures meant that there were basic emotions that humans possessed innately and that the wiring for the expression of these emotions was also innate (Matsumoto et al., 2008). Because it is obvious to researchers and laypeople alike that the other "basic" emotions can be produced deliberately by nearly anyone, the Duchenne smile stood alone in supporting the view that humans are pre-wired for emotional "read-out" due to its supposedly nonvolitional nature. However, the idea that the Duchenne smile is outside volitional control has recently been found to be incorrect (Gosselin et al., 2010; Gunnery et al., 2013; Krumhuber & Manstead, 2009), indicating that theories positing that smiles are social signals influenced by the context in which the smiler finds him or herself may also be supported by research on the Duchenne smile (Fridlund, 1994). While it is undoubtedly true that some Duchenne smiles are spontaneous and unwilled, others are not.

The deliberate Duchenne smile

An investigation of the Duchenne smiling literature turns up many reports of participants making deliberate Duchenne smiles, but these are alluded to as insignificant methodological details, or just not discussed as actually being evidence that it is possible for the Duchenne smile to be produced on purpose. Frank and Ekman (1993) reported that "up to 20% of the population can consciously contract the outer portion of their orbicularis oculi muscles (AU 6) and are thus capable of producing a false Duchenne marker" (p. 18); note, by calling it a false Duchenne marker the authors were categorizing these expressions differently than those expressions that are produced naturally. It is as though through producing the expression deliberately it is not a real Duchenne smile and would not communicate the same message. Frank and Ekman (1993) thus conflate the description of the expression with an a priori assumption about its origin and intent.

Levenson, Ekman, and Friesen (1990) uncovered more evidence for the deliberate Duchenne smile, though again not referring to it as such, by bringing unselected participants into the lab and asking them to contract a series of muscles either individually or in conjunction with other muscles. They found that 16% of participants were able to contract their cheek raiser muscle, and 25% of people were able to contract their cheek raiser muscle when their lip corner puller was also activated. Importantly, both of these figures are underestimates because they are the percentages of participants who could pose all the tested muscles, not just AU 12 and 6. Because Levenson et al. (1990) found that this combination was one of the two easiest to perform, one can assume that the percentage who could perform those two movements would be considerably higher than the 16% and 25% just stated. This is evidence that participants were able to both produce the Duchenne marker by itself and produce a Duchenne smile when asked to do so.

In another study, Ekman and Davidson (1993) found that 71% of a sample of unselected undergraduates could control the cheek raiser muscle in order to produce a Duchenne smile, a finding the authors called "quite unusual" (p. 343). Since this detail was irrelevant to the purpose of the study, it was not mentioned again, nor cited in any of Ekman's subsequent studies as evidence that a many people can produce the expressions when explicitly asked to do so.

There has also been evidence for the deliberate Duchenne smile from outside of Ekman's group. Schmidt, Ambadar, Cohn, and Reed (2006) found that 91% of their participants activated the cheek raiser muscle when asked to deliberately pose joy. In another study that instructed participants to deliberately appear happy, Smith, Smith, and Ellgring (1996) found that 100% of unselected expressors produced a Duchenne smile, a figure that dropped only to 82% in a group of patients with Parkinson's disease (who are known to have reduced expressive control).

Two studies of actors also suggest willful control of the Duchenne smile. Carroll and Russell (1997) studied expression in Hollywood movies and found a high rate of Duchenne smiling (74%) in scenes that were classified as "happy" based on contextual information. Gosselin, Kirouac, and Doré (1995) instructed trained actors to pose different emotions and found a Duchenne performance rate of 84% when posing happiness. Of course, it is possible that the actors in these studies were not deliberately putting on the Duchenne smile, but were self-inducing a positive emotion, with the Duchenne smile spontaneously ensuing from that. However, Gosselin, Kirouac, and Doré (1995) quoted result was for a condition in which the actors were explicitly told not to experience the emotion in question.

Krumhuber and Manstead (2009) were the first researchers to publish evidence for the deliberate Duchenne smile and call it evidence that people can deliberately produce a Duchenne smile. In a study investigating the differences between spontaneous and deliberate Duchenne smiles, Krumhuber and Manstead found that 83% of participants who were instructed to appear as if they were watching something funny while actually watching neutral stimuli produced a Duchenne smile. This did not significantly differ from the number of Duchenne smiles (70%) produced by participants who smiled naturally in response to amusing stimuli. This effectively showed that people were able to produce Duchenne smiles at will.

Following Krumhuber and Manstead (2009), Gosselin et al. (2010) found a similar result when asking participants to coactivate certain facial muscles. In a laboratory setting devoid of emotional stimuli, participants were instructed to activate AU 6 and AU 12 separately and coactivate AU 6 and AU 12. In their study, 60% of participants were able to activate AU 6. Half of the 60% activated AU 6 by itself, while the other 30% of participants activated AU 6 while coactivating another action unit, most commonly AU 12. Gosselin et al. (2010) also found that participants who were instructed to activate AU 12 also quite often coactivated AU 6.

Gunnery et al. (2013) provided further evidence that participants are able to deliberately put on a Duchenne smile. Unlike Krumhuber and Manstead (2009), this study used role-plays in which participants were instructed to smile as they would in different social situations where they wanted to express both genuine happiness and fake happiness, that is, masking some negative affect (masked disliking, masked fatigue, and masked disappointment) with a smile. Gunnery et al. (2013) found that across genuine and fake happiness scenarios 38% of participants' smiles were Duchenne.

Gunnery et al. (2013) took the study of the deliberate Duchenne smile a step further by exploring possible individual differences that exist between people who produce Duchenne smiles deliberately and those who do not. Participants who were able to deliberately put on the expression in the genuine happiness smiling role-plays were also more likely to use it in the fake happiness smiling role-plays, and also when asked to imitate a Duchenne smile that was shown in a photograph. This indicated consistency in the ability across different types of tasks. 23 of the participants in this study had also completed the deliberate Duchenne role-play task in a previous unpublished study conducted about one year earlier. Their performance on the task the year earlier was correlated with their performance in the new study, providing evidence that this individual difference shows consistency over time.

Perceptions of the Duchenne smile

Numerous studies have investigated, either in addition to or instead of documenting when and how Duchenne smiles are expressed, how they are perceived by others. Frank, Ekman, and Friesen (1993) found that people are more likely to categorize smiles with the Duchenne marker as true expressions of genuine enjoyment than smiles without the Duchenne marker. In a second study Frank et al. (1993) found that people rated targets showing Duchenne smiles as more positive on the aggregate of 15 bipolar trait pairs than people showing non-Duchenne smiles.

Following in the tradition of examining both how Duchenne smiles are perceived differently from non-Duchenne smiles and how people that are shown producing Duchenne smiles are perceived differently from people shown producing non-Duchenne smiles, Quadflieg, Vermeulen, and Rossion (2013) found that perceivers rated Duchenne smiles as being more amused, authentic, spontaneous, and intense, but ratings of the targets' personalities were more variable. Perceivers rated targets as more attractive, dominant, and intelligent but not more trustworthy when they Duchenne smiled rather than non-Duchenne smiled.

In a study that looked only at perceptions of the smiles rather than inferences about the smilers, Ambadar et al. (2009) found that smiles containing the Duchenne marker were more likely to be perceived as amused than polite, embarrassed, or nervous. The Duchenne smiles were also more likely to be open mouth smiles, to have larger maximum onset and offset velocity and longer duration, and to display more additional muscle movements that worked to counteract the lip corner puller, like a tightening in the lips. This study provides evidence that the Duchenne marker on its own may not be the best indicator of felt happiness, and that it is instead a combination of numerous characteristics of the smile.

Other studies exclusively investigated how the smiler is perceived. Mehu, Little, and Dunbar (2007) measured the difference in ratings of people showing neutral expressions and either Duchenne or non-Duchenne smiles and found that the differences in perceiver-rated generosity and extroversion for targets expressing Duchenne as compared to their neutral expression was greater than the difference between perceptions of targets producing a non-Duchenne smile and their neutral expression. Though the difference for Duchenne smiles did not differ significantly from the differences for non-Duchenne smiles there was a greater difference in ratings of attractiveness, agreeableness, neuroticism, and openness for Duchenne smiles than non-Duchenne smiles. The differences between people producing neutral expressions and non-Duchenne smiles was greater than the difference between ratings of people expressing neutral expressions and Duchenne smiles, though not significantly so, for ratings of conscientiousness and healthiness, and there were no difference between the difference scores for ratings of trustworthiness. When looking at these effects separately by gender of the target, the effect observed for generosity was mostly true for male faces. This study showed that, as was found in the later study by Quadflieg et al. (2013), there are some traits that are not vulnerable to the effects of the Duchenne smile.

Woodzicka (2008) showed that hireability for a job and competence were not two of these invulnerable traits. This study, looking at how people are perceived differently due to the type of smile they produced, found that targets in a mock interview setting who produced Duchenne smiles were rated as more hireable and competent than targets who produced non-Duchenne smiles (Woodzicka, 2008).

A set of studies looked at whether the type of smile affects how others view the clothing the target is wearing. T-shirts were rated more positively by perceivers when being worn by people who were producing Duchenne rather than non-Duchenne smiles (Peace et al., 2006). This finding goes beyond making ratings of the person showing a sort of contagion effect where an object associated with a Duchenne smiler is rated more positively than one associated with a non-Duchenne smiler. This effect went away when exposure time was limited to 150 ms, but was found again in a third study by Peace et al. (2006) that showed that when asked to rank rather than rate t-shirts, those worn by a person producing a Duchenne smile were still ranked higher than those worn by a person producing a non-Duchenne smile.

A separate type of perception study, that investigated how different types of smiles made perceivers feel, found that when perceivers viewed a block of Duchenne smiles before viewing a block of non-Duchenne smiles, the perceivers reported feeling more pleasure after seeing the block of Duchenne smiles than after seeing the block of non-Duchenne smiles (Surakka & Hietanen, 1998). This effect did not hold true for when they viewed the block of non-Duchenne smiles first, indicating that the order in which participants viewed the smiles mattered.

Difference in perceiver traits and manipulated states

Some studies looked at perceiver variables as moderators of how Duchenne and non-Duchenne smiles are perceived. In a study that investigated how participants' trait of sexual restrictedness affected how they classified Duchenne and non-Duchenne smiles, Sacco, Hugenberg, and Sefcek (2009) found that people who are sexually unrestricted are better able to differentiate between Duchenne and non-Duchenne smiles as measured by classification of Duchenne smiles as genuine and non-Duchenne smiles as deceptive. They hypothesized that people who are sexually unrestricted are better able to identify those who are sexually receptive rather than those who are smiling even though they are not sexually receptive, and that the Duchenne smile is a cue to sexual receptivity. There is limited data indicating that the Duchenne smile indicates sexual receptivity as opposed to the non-Duchenne smiles, and more research is needed to draw conclusions from this study.

In two studies that manipulated feelings of social exclusion and social inclusion through writing about previous experiences with the two feelings, Bernstein, Young, Brown, Sacco, and Claypool (2008) and Bernstein, Sacco, Brown, Young, and Claypool (2010) found that people who wrote about a time they felt socially excluded were more sensitive to the distinction between Duchenne and non-Duchenne smiles than those who wrote about a time they felt socially included or wrote about a neutral experience. Bernstein et al. (2008) came to this conclusion after having perceivers take part in a simple task where they had to say whether smiles were genuine or not. Bernstein et al. (2010) took this a step further by asking perceivers who had been manipulated to feel excluded, included, and neutral in the same way to rate how willing they would be to work with targets who were Duchenne smiling and non-Duchenne smiling. Perceivers who had written about a time they felt socially excluded were more likely to want to work with a person that they saw produce a Duchenne smile in a videotaped clip than a person that they saw producing a non-Duchenne smile.

There may also be cultural differences in how people perceive Duchenne and non-Duchenne smiles. Thibault, Levesque, Gosselin, and Hess (2012) found that Gabonese individuals living in Canada did not perceive Duchenne smiles as more authentic displays of happiness than non-Duchenne smiles. Chinese perceivers living in Canada perceived Duchenne smiles as more authentic than non-Duchenne smiles, but only when they were being displayed by French-Canadian targets indicating that people may learn how different cultures use the Duchenne marker to communicate happiness.

Age differences in perceptions

Studies investigating how perceptions of Duchenne and non-Duchenne smiles differ by age have found a mix of results. Gosselin, Perron, Legault, and Campanella (2002) found that children aged six to seven do not classify Duchenne smiles as genuine displays of happiness more than non-Duchenne smiles, but by age nine, children were classifying

Duchenne smiles as real happiness displays and non-Duchenne smiles as smiles used to fake happiness at equal levels as college-aged adults. Del Giudice and Colle (2007) found that young children (mean age of eight) used cues in the eyes to categorize smiles as authentic or inauthentic, but that they were unable to distinguish between AU 6 (the Duchenne marker) and AU 7 (defined by FACS as the lid tightener that makes a squinting appearance), meaning that they classified non-Duchenne smiles with AU 7 activation as authentic as well. Thibault, Gosselin, Brunel, and Hess (2009) found that children between the ages of four and 17 used the Duchenne marker to distinguish between authentic and inauthentic smiles but that younger children also relied on smile intensity while adolescents seemed to rely more exclusively on the Duchenne marker when making these judgments.

At the other end of the age spectrum, Slessor, Miles, Bull, and Phillips (2010) found that older adults (aged 65–81) were more likely to classify both non-Duchenne and Duchenne smiles as expressing happiness than younger adults (aged 17–36) but that both age groups were more likely to classify Duchenne smiles as indicating happiness than non-Duchenne smiles.

Perceptions of deliberate Duchenne smiles

Krumhuber and Manstead (2009) investigated differences in perceptions of Duchenne and non-Duchenne smiles as well as looking at perceptions of Duchenne smiles separately for smiles that were produced in a natural mood induction paradigm and those that were produced in a posed paradigm. Krumhuber and Manstead found that Duchenne smiles overall were rated more positively than non-Duchenne smiles. When looking at the difference between smiles elicited using videotapes that induce happy moods and those produced by asking targets to pretend as if they are watching funny or happy stimuli, it was found that videotapes of smiles elicited naturally were rated as more amused and genuine than Duchenne smiles that were elicited deliberately with a posing paradigm. These findings were true when perceivers only had access to videotapes of the top half of the target's face or the bottom half of the face, indicating that activation of the cheek raiser muscle may cause perceptual changes in the lip corner puller as well or that there are additional characteristics in the lip corner puller activation that co-vary with presence of the Duchenne marker. Krumhuber and Manstead posit that these could be differences in onset and offset, duration, and intensity of the smile, as temporal components of smiles have been shown to influence how genuinely they are perceived (Krumhuber & Kappas, 2005).

Gunnery et al. (2013) also conducted a perception study on the smiles produced in their deliberate (role-playing) Duchenne smiling paradigm, and found that deliberate Duchenne smiles were rated as showing more genuine happiness than the deliberate non-Duchenne smiles. While this study did not include naturally produced smiles as a comparison it is further evidence that the perceptual difference still exists between Duchenne and non-Duchenne smiles when they are produced deliberately.

Meta-analysis of differences in perception studies

30 perception studies were meta-analyzed to find the mean effect size of the differences in perceptions of Duchenne and non-Duchenne smiles (Gunnery & Ruben, 2014). The Pearson correlation was used as the effect size metric. The correlation was positive if Duchenne smiles were perceived more positively than non-Duchenne smiles, and negative if non-Duchenne smiles were perceived more positively than Duchenne smiles. Following effect size extraction all analyses were completed using the Comprehensive Meta-Analysis software package (Borenstein, Hedges et al., 2005).

The meta-analysis found that Duchenne smiles and people producing Duchenne smiles are rated more positively than non-Duchenne smiles and people producing non-Duchenne smiles with a mean effect size of $r = .34$ (30 studies, combined $Z = 18.80$, $p < .001$) in the meta-analysis the term "positively" was used as a general term to describe the numerous dependent variables (e.g., authentic, genuine, real, attractive, trustworthy) measured across the individual studies. A moderator analysis revealed that a number of stimulus related, perceiver related, and methodology related variables moderated the effect.

Stimulus specific moderators

The term *stimulus specific moderators* refers to whether the study used static photographs or dynamic video stimuli, whether stimuli were elicited naturally through affect inductions or were elicited using a posing paradigm, and whether Duchenne and non-Duchenne smiles were matched for intensity within each study's stimuli.

The meta-analysis showed that the perceptual difference between Duchenne and non-Duchenne smiles was greater when the stimuli were dynamic rather than static. The mean effect size for static stimuli was significantly above zero indicating that static Duchenne smiles are still perceived more positively than static non-Duchenne smiles. This is more evidence pointing to other dynamic characteristics of smiles providing important perceptual information about the type of smile.

Stimuli that were elicited naturally rather than using posing paradigms produced a greater mean effect size. This indicates that when the targets were instructed how to smile or asked to produce the expression when they were not feeling happy, there was less of a perceptual difference between Duchenne and non-Duchenne smiles (though perceptions of Duchenne and non-Duchenne smiles were still significantly different when looking at only studies that used posing paradigms). This is likely the result of some other visual difference, such as more intense or symmetric Duchenne smiles, that occurs when the smiles are elicited naturally.

Also, when Duchenne and non-Duchenne smiles were matched for intensity, there was a lower effect size than when they were not matched for intensity. This means that the Duchenne marker is likely not the only cue being used to make these judgments. The relationship between smile intensity and presence of the Duchenne marker is discussed later in the chapter.

Overall, perceivers' perceptions of Duchenne and non-Duchenne smiles were most different when stimuli included the kind of smiles that appear in natural social interaction, meaning they were dynamic, not posed, and unmatched for intensity.

Perceiver specific moderators

Gender and age of the perceivers were analyzed as moderators. The correlation between the percentage of perceivers that were female and effect size was not significant, $r(27) = .20$, $p = .32$. This indicates that having more female perceivers does not moderate the effect, meaning that the effect is the same regardless of the targets' gender. Gender of perceiver was also examined within some studies by the original investigators. Only a minority of individual studies reported testing for a gender difference, and all those (e.g., Krumhuber & Manstead, 2009; Sacco et al., 2009) that did report this analysis did not find a significant difference between males and females.

In line with what was found in individual studies (e.g., Gosselin et al., 2002), the meta-analysis showed that studies with college-aged and older perceivers had larger effect sizes than studies with perceivers under the age of 17.

Methodological moderators

The meta-analysis compared studies that used between-subjects analyses with studies that use within-subjects analyses, meaning whether the study compared how one group perceived Duchenne smiles to how another group perceived non-Duchenne smiles or if they measured differences between how one group perceived both Duchenne and non-Duchenne smiles. This moderator analysis indicated that effect sizes originating from between-groups analyses were smaller than effect sizes originating from within-group analyses. Finding that effect sizes from between-groups analyses were smaller than effect sizes from within-groups analyses is in line with the nature of how these effect sizes are specifically extracted. Effect sizes from studies that used a within-group design had assumedly smaller error terms because of the nature of a repeated-measures design.

Secondly, the meta-analysis compared studies that measured dependent variables dichotomously (e.g., was the smile authentic or inauthentic?) with studies in which the dependent variable was measured continuously (e.g., rate on a scale from 1 to 7 how authentic the smile is). When dependent variables were measured using dichotomous rather than continuous response scales, the difference between the perceptions of Duchenne and non-Duchenne smiles was greater, meaning that when perceivers were forced to categorize smiles as having a certain characteristic or not (i.e., genuine or not genuine) or the smiler as being one way or not (e.g., amused or not amused), the difference between positivity ratings for Duchenne and non-Duchenne smiles was greater than when they were able to rate the smile or smiler on a continuous scale (e.g., from not at all genuine to very genuine). When looking at the mean effect sizes for these subgroups individually, both had effect sizes that were significantly greater than zero, but significant moderator analysis reveals that when given the opportunity to use a scale to make the rating, perceivers still rated Duchenne smiles more positively, but there was likely more variability in their responses due to use of a continuous scale.

The last methodological moderator analyzed was whether the study's dependent variable was specific to characteristics of the Duchenne smile (i.e., authentic, genuine, and enjoyment) or was a trait inference about the smiler (i.e., attractive, competent, persuasive). This analysis showed that there was no difference in perceptions of Duchenne and non-Duchenne smiles when perceivers were asked to rate attributes that were specific to the Duchenne smile, such as how genuine the smile was, rather than make trait inferences about the smiler, such as how competent the smiler was. This points to the Duchenne smile having an overall halo effect, meaning that the person who displays a Duchenne smile is seen more positively than the person who non-Duchenne smiles with the same strength as the perceptual difference between the actual smiles.

Social outcomes of Duchenne smiles

There are many studies on the social outcomes of smiling, without the distinction between types of smiles. Some of these findings show that people who smile more are seen as more attractive (Otta et al., 1996), are given more leniency after an academic infraction (LaFrance & Hecht, 1995), and are seen as more cooperative and therefore are more likely to be trusted (Scharlemann et al., 2001). However, there is limited evidence on the social outcomes of Duchenne smiles in particular. People reported greater customer satisfaction after a simulated interaction with a service provider who Duchenne smiled than a service provider who non-Duchenne smiled (Grandey et al., 2005). Also, people were more likely to cooperate with others who displayed a Duchenne smile rather than a non-Duchenne smile in a trust game (Johnston et al., 2010).

More research is needed on what impressions Duchenne smiling creates in natural circumstances and what kind of behavioral impact it might have. Also, because of the growing evidence that substantial minorities (and in some studies, majorities) of people possess the ability to deliberately produce a Duchenne smile, there is need for research that connects deliberate Duchenne smiling as measured in a laboratory paradigm with Duchenne smiling under natural circumstances. In a natural circumstance, it is difficult and perhaps impossible to determine whether smiles are deliberate or spontaneous. However, people who are able to produce a deliberate Duchenne smile are more likely to use a Duchenne smile in an unstructured social interaction (Gunnery & Hall, 2011), indicating a likelihood that at least some of the smiles produced in social interactions are deliberate. This constitutes preliminary evidence that the skill is used in real-life situations and not just in a laboratory paradigm. In addition to replicating this finding, it is important to find out what kinds of social outcomes accrue to individuals who have the capacity to make a Duchenne smile deliberately.

Gunnery and Hall (2014) addressed both of these goals in the context of a persuasion task. The persuasion task was a taste perception paradigm (Feldman et al., 1999) in which targets sipped a sweet, pleasant-tasting juice and a very tart, unpleasant-tasting juice and in both cases had to smile and persuade another person to drink the juice. Targets then completed a deliberate Duchenne smiling paradigm (the same task described above with reference to Gunnery et al., 2013) to measure their ability to deliberately produce a Duchenne smile. Trained coders applied the FACS to determine whether smiles in the taste task were Duchenne or non-Duchenne. Finally, naïve perceivers watched videotapes of the taste tasks and rated how likely they would be to try the juice. Results replicated the previous finding that people who can deliberately Duchenne smile use the Duchenne smile more in social interactions, by showing that targets who were able to deliberately produce a

Duchenne smile when role-playing genuine happiness were more likely to use a Duchenne smile when persuading an experimenter to drink the sweet-tasting juice. Furthermore, this study found that targets who were better able to produce a Duchenne smile deliberately were more persuasive than targets who had less of this ability, and this was true both when persuading to drink the pleasant juice and when persuading to drink the unpleasant juice. However, targets only successfully used the Duchenne smile to persuade after drinking the pleasant-tasting juice (as determined by a mediation analysis). These findings indicate that people who have the ability to deliberately produce a Duchenne smile are perceived as more persuasive, and that they only use the Duchenne smile to persuade in a context where use of the Duchenne smile does not contradict their current affective state. This raises the interesting question of why people who were more able to make deliberate Duchenne smiles were more persuasive with the unpleasant juice even though their Duchenne smiling in the taste task was not responsible for this effect (according to mediation analysis). One possibility is that the expressive control that enabled them to make Duchenne smiles successfully at will also enabled them to produce other cues (for example in their voice tone) that served their persuasive goals.

Expression, perception, and smile intensity

In 2002, Ekman, Friesen and Hagar published a new edition of their FACS manual that included new guidelines for coding the cheek raiser as present when it is accompanied by a high intensity lip corner puller. This addition was made to the coding manual because it had been made clear that it was possible for crow's feet to appear around the eyes when the lip corner puller was of a great enough intensity without the cheek raiser muscle independently being activated. Put simply, this means that it was possible that many of the crow's feet coded in studies before 2002 as the Duchenne marker were just artifacts of more intense smiles. While Ekman and Rosenberg (2005) commented that this is a small possibility, they also made the statement that findings from studies before 2002 likely still hold true. This statement was made without support from the literature.

There is, in fact, a real possibility that many studies prior to 2002 need reconsideration. This concern applies both to production studies and perception studies. In a production study, typically the researcher's goal would be to show that when people are truly happy they produce Duchenne smiles, thus validating Ekman's theory of the function of the Duchenne smile (e.g., Ekman et al., 1988). However, it is possible simply that when people are truly happy they smile more intensely, which incidentally creates the crow's feet that are the Duchenne hallmark.

The problem is similar with perception studies. Before the above-mentioned criteria were added to the FACS manual, Hess, Kappas, McHugo, and Kleck (1989) found that smiles where the lip corners are pulled back further creating bigger, or in FACS terms more intense, smiles are perceived as indicating more happiness. As noted above when summarizing the meta-analysis of perception studies, some studies matched for intensity in their stimuli (e.g., Quadflieg et al., 2013) and some did not (e.g., Woodzicka, 2008). If the Duchenne smiles in a study's stimuli are of a higher intensity than the non-Duchenne smiles, any differences in perceptions of Duchenne and non-Duchenne smiles could be due to the differing intensities and not the Duchenne marker per se. This could be the case both if more positive characteristics are attributed to people displaying more intense smiles than less intense smiles and if perceivers categorize smiles of greater intensity as real or genuine while smiles of lesser intensity are categorized as fake or polite. The Duchenne and non-Duchenne smile stimuli appearing on the BBC Science website (that have been used in a number of perceptions studies e.g., Bernstein et al., 2008) illustrate this point nicely (BBC, n.d.). The stimuli in this online quiz that are categorized as genuine and thus Duchenne are of higher intensity than those categorized as fake and thus non-Duchenne. Thus, numerous studies in the earlier Duchenne literature are potentially compromised by the possible presence of Duchenne expressions than confound AU 12 intensity with AU 6 activation.

Now there is evidence that the new coding criteria do not make the problem go away. The new edition of FACS in 2002 added that either a slight drop in the corner of the eyebrow, a slight pouching effect under the eye, or a slight droop in the eyelid need to be observed in addition to crow's feet in order for the Duchenne marker to be coded as present as an independent muscle movement. This revision to the coding criteria is intended to solve the problem of smile intensity as a confounder or a rival explanation for Duchenne smile effects. However, while one could speculate about the findings of studies prior to 2002, there is evidence that even with new coding techniques, there is still a strong correlation between intensity of the smile and presence of the Duchenne marker (e.g., Gunnery et al., 2013).

Actually, one should not be surprised by the connection between smile intensity and presence of the Duchenne marker, as they are both used to show more enjoyment. A person who is truly happy is likely to make a more intense smile, and such a person is likely to activate crow's feet at the corners of the eyes. That this correlation exists is not a failure of the FACS coding system; however, it remains problematic in the study of Duchenne smiling. The updated coding techniques in the 2002 revision of the FACS manual were intended to reduce this confound by ensuring that any appearance of wrinkles around the eyes is the result of the Duchenne marker being activated and not an artifact of a more intense smile (Ekman & Rosenberg, 2005). However, as mentioned above, these coding techniques require that a viewer is able to recognize slight and subtle changes in facial anatomy, and the standard in the field for achieving this ability requires numerous hours of training and coding in FACS. If one must undergo a significant amount of training to be able to differentiate between coincidental crow's feet that are an artifact of a big smile and crow's feet that are the result of activation of the cheek raiser muscle, this is likely not a skill that the average perceivers who took part in this chapter's reviewed studies would possess. This leads one to believe that perceivers may be relying more on smile intensity than the Duchenne marker to make these judgments. At the very least, the correlation between smile intensity and the Duchenne marker, even with the new FACS coding criteria, poses a very significant challenge to smile researchers.

Conclusion

To conclude, there are robust findings showing that when people are happy they produce more Duchenne smiles than non-Duchenne smiles and that people perceive Duchenne smiles as more positive than non-Duchenne smiles. Recent findings that the Duchenne smile can be produced deliberately mean that it cannot be assumed that Duchenne smiles are spontaneous readouts of felt positive affect (Buck, 1985). This indicates that there is not a bidirectional relationship between the Duchenne smile and happiness. People who feel happy are likely to Duchenne smile, but those who Duchenne smile are not necessarily happier.

In a similar way, the relationship between smile intensity and presence of the Duchenne marker puts the validity of many production and perception studies into question. There are other smile characteristics (e.g., duration, intensity, symmetry) that may hold more weight in distinguishing when a person is truly feeling happy.

References

Ambadar, Z., Cohn, J. F., & Reed, L. (2009). All smiles are not created equal: Morphology and timing of smiles perceived as amused, polite, and embarrassed/ nervous. *Journal of Nonverbal Behavior, 33*, 17–34.

Ansfield, M. E. (2007). Smiling when distressed: When a smile is a frown turned upside down. *Personality and Social Psychology Bulletin, 33*(6), 763–775.

BBC. (n.d.) Spot the fake smile. Retrieved from http://www.bbc.co.uk/science/humanbody/mind/surveys/smiles/

Bernstein, M. J., Sacco, D. F., Brown, C. M., Young, S. G., & Claypool, H. M. (2010). A preference for genuine smiles following social exclusion. *Journal of Experimental Social Psychology, 46*, 196–199.

Bernstein, M. J., Young, S. G., Brown, C. M., Sacco, D. F., & Claypool, H. M. (2008). Adaptive responses to social exclusion: Social rejection improves detection of real and fake smiles. *Psychological Science, 19*, 981–983.

Bonanno, G. A., & Keltner, D. (1997). Facial expressions of emotion and the course of conjugal bereavement. *Journal of Abnormal Psychology, 106*, 126–137.

Borenstein, M., Hedges, L., Higgins, J., & Rothstein, H. (2005). *Comprehensive meta-analysis* (2nd ed.). Englewood, NJ: Biostat.

Buck, R. (1985). Prime theory: An integrated view of motivation and emotion. *Psychological Review, 92*, 389–413.

Carroll, J. M., & Russell, J. A. (1997). Facial expressions in Hollywood's portrayal of emotion. *Journal of Personality and Social Psychology, 72*, 164–172.

Del Giudice, M., & Colle, L. (2007). Differences between children and adults in the recognition of enjoyment smiles. *Developmental Psychology, 43*, 796–803.

Duchenne, B. (1862/1990). *The mechanism of human facial expression or an electro-physiological analysis of the expression of the emotions* (A. Cuthbertson, Trans.). New York: Cambridge University Press.

Ekman, P., & Davidson, R. J. (1993). Voluntary smiling changes regional brain activity. *Psychological Science, 4*, 342–345.

Ekman, P., Davidson, R. J., & Friesen, W. V. (1990). The Duchenne smile: Emotional expression and brain physiology: II. *Journal of Personality and Social Psychology, 58*, 342–353.

Ekman, P., & Friesen, W. V. (1982). Felt, false, and miserable smiles. *Journal of Nonverbal Behavior, 6*, 238–258.

Ekman, P., Friesen, W. V., & Hager, J. C. (2002). *The facial action coding system* (2nd ed.). Salt Lake City, UT: Research Nexus eBook.

Ekman, P., Friesen, W. V., & O'Sullivan, M. (1988). Smiles when lying. *Journal of Personality and Social Psychology, 54*, 414–420.

Ekman, P., Friesen, W. V., O'Sullivan, M., Chan, A., Diacoyanni-Tarlatzis, I., Heider, K., ... Tzavaras, A. (1987). Universals and cultural differences in the judgments of facial expressions of emotion. *Journal of Personality and Social Psychology, 53*, 712–717.

Ekman, P., & Rosenberg, E. L. (2005). *What the face reveals: Basic and applied studies of spontaneous expression using the facial action coding system (FACS)* (2nd ed.). New York, NY: Oxford University Press.

Feldman, R. S., Tomasian, J. C., & Coats, E. J. (1999). Nonverbal deception abilities and adolescents' social competence: Adolescents with higher social skills are better liars. *Journal of Nonverbal Behavior, 23*, 237–249.

Frank, M. G., & Ekman, P. (1993). Not all smiles are created equal: The differences between enjoyment and nonenjoyment smiles. *Humor, 6*, 9–26.

Frank, M. G., Ekman, P., & Friesen, W. V. (1993). Behavioral markers and recognizability of the smile of enjoyment. *Journal of Personality & Social Psychology, 64*, 83–93.

Fridlund, A. J., Ekman, P., & Oster, H. (1987). Facial expressions of emotion. In A. W. Siegman & S. Feldstein (Eds.), *Nonverbal behavior and communication* (2nd ed., pp. 143–223). Hillsdale, NJ: Lawrence Erlbaum Associates, Inc.

Fridlund, A. J. (1994). *Human facial expression: An evolutionary view*. San Diego, CA: Academic Press.

Gosselin, P., Kirouac, G., & Doré, F. Y. (1995). Components and recognition of facial expression in the communication of emotion by actors. *Journal of Personality and Social Psychology, 68*, 83–96.

Gosselin, P., Perron, M., & Beaupré, M. (2010). The voluntary control of facial action units in adults. *Emotion, 10*, 266–271.

Gosselin, P., Perron, M., Legault, M., & Campanella, P. (2002). Children's and adults' knowledge of the distinction between enjoyment and nonenjoyment smiles. *Journal of Nonverbal Behavior, 26*, 83–108.

Grandey, A. A., Fisk, G. M., Mattila, A. S., Jansen, K. J., & Sideman, L. A. (2005). Is "service with a smile" enough? Authenticity of positive displays during service encounters. *Organizational Behavior and Human Decision Processes, 96*, 38–55.

Gunnery, S. D., & Hall, J. A. (2011). *The deliberate Duchenne smile: Evidence for expressive control and individual differences*. Unpublished manuscript. Department of Psychology, Northeastern University, Boston, Massachusetts.

Gunnery, S. D., & Hall, J. A. (2014). The Duchenne smile and persuasion. *Journal of Nonverbal Behavior, 38*, 181–194.

Gunnery, S. D., Hall, J. A., & Ruben, M. A. (2013). The deliberate Duchenne smile: Individual differences in expressive control. *Journal of Nonverbal Behavior, 37*, 29–41.

Gunnery, S. D., & Ruben, M. A. (2014). Perceptions of Duchenne and non-Duchenne smiles: A meta-analysis. Manuscript submitted for review.

Hess, U., Kappas, A., McHugo, G. J., & Kleck, R. E. (1989). An analysis of the encoding and decoding of spontaneous and posed smiles: The use of facial electromyography. *Journal of Nonverbal Behavior, 13*, 121–137.

Jakobs, E., Manstead, A. S., & Fischer, A. H. (1999). Social motives, emotional feelings, and smiling. *Cognition and Emotion, 13*, 321–345.

Johnston, L., Miles, L., & Macrae, C. N. (2010). Why are you smiling at me? Social functions of enjoyment and non-enjoyment smiles. *British Journal of Social Psychology, 49*, 107–127.

Keltner, D. (1995). Signs of appeasement: Evidence for the distinct displays of embarrassment, amusement, and shame. *Journal of Personality and Social Psychology, 68*, 441–454.

Krumhuber, E., & Kappas, A. (2005). Moving smiles: The role of dynamic components for the perception of the genuineness of smiles. *Journal of Nonverbal Behavior, 29*, 3–24.

Krumhuber, E. G., & Manstead, A. R. (2009). Can Duchenne smiles be feigned? New evidence on felt and false smiles. *Emotion, 9*, 807–820.

LaFrance, M., & Hecht, M. A. (1995). Why smiles generate leniency. *Personality and Social Psychology Bulletin, 21*, 207–214.

Levenson, R. W., Ekman, P., & Friesen, W. V. (1990). Voluntary facial action generates emotion-specific autonomic nervous system activity. *Psychophysiology, 27*, 363–384.

Matsumoto, D., Keltner, D., Shiota, M. N., O'Sullivan, M., & Frank, M. (2008). Facial expressions of emotion. In M. Lewis, J. M. Haviland-Jones, & L. Barrett

(Eds.), *Handbook of Emotions* (3rd ed., pp. 211–234). New York, NY: Guilford Press.

Matsumoto, D., & Willingham, B. (2009). Spontaneous facial expressions of emotion of congenitally and noncongenitally blind individuals. *Journal of Personality and Social Psychology, 96*, 1–10.

Mehu, M., Grammer, K., & Dunbar, R. I. (2007). Smiles when sharing. *Evolution and Human Behavior, 28*, 415–422.

Mehu, M., Little, A. C., & Dunbar, R. M. (2007). Duchenne smiles and the perception of generosity and sociability in faces. *Journal of Evolutionary Psychology, 5*, 183–196.

Otta, E., Abrosio, F., & Hoshino, R. (1996). Reading a smiling face: Messages conveyed by various forms of smiling. *Perceptual and Motor Skills, 82*, 1111–1121.

Peace, V., Miles, L., & Johnston, L. (2006). It doesn't matter what you wear: The impact of posed and genuine expressions of happiness on product evaluation. *Social Cognition, 24*, 137–168.

Quadflieg, S., Vermeulen, N., & Rossion, B. (2013). Differential reliance on the Duchenne marker during smile evaluations and person judgments. *Journal of Nonverbal Behavior, 39*, 69–77.

Sacco, D. F., Hugenberg, K., & Sefcek, J. A. (2009). Sociosexuality and face perception: Unrestricted sexual orientation facilitates sensitivity to female facial cues. *Personality and Individual Differences, 47*, 777–782.

Scharlemann, J. W., Eckel, C. C., Kacelnik, A., & Wilson, R. K. (2001). The value of a smile: Game theory with a human face. *Journal of Economic Psychology, 22*, 617–640.

Schmidt, K. L., Ambadar, Z., Cohn, J. F., & Reed, L. I. (2006). Movement differences between deliberate and spontaneous facial expressions: Zygomaticus major action in smiling. *Journal of Nonverbal Behavior, 30*, 37–52.

Slessor, G., Miles, L. K., Bull, R., & Phillips, L. H. (2010). Age-related changes in detecting happiness: Discriminating between enjoyment and nonenjoyment smiles. *Psychology and Aging, 25*, 246–250.

Smith, M. C., Smith, M. K., & Ellgring, H. (1996). Spontaneous and posed facial expression in Parkinson's disease. *Journal of the International Neuropsychological Society, 2*, 383–391.

Surakka, V., & Hietanen, J. (1998). Facial and emotional reactions to Duchenne and non-Duchenne smiles. *International Journal of Psychophysiology, 29*, 23–33.

Thibault, P., Gosselin, P., Brunel, M., & Hess, U. (2009). Children's and adolescents' perception of the authenticity of smiles. *Journal of Experimental Child Psychology, 102*, 360–367.

Thibault, P., Levesque, M., Gosselin, P., & Hess, U. (2012). The Duchenne marker is not a universal signal of smile authenticity—But it can be learned! *Social Psychology, 43*, 215–221.

Woodzicka, J. A. (2008). Sex differences in self-awareness of smiling during a mock job interview. *Journal of Nonverbal Behavior, 32*, 109–121.

Zweyer, K., Velker, B., & Ruch, W. (2004). Do cheerfulness, exhilaration, and humor production moderate pain tolerance? A FACS study. *Humor, 17*, 85–120.

6
Emotional Recognition, Fear, and Nonverbal Behavior

Aleksandra Kostić and Derek Chadee

Facial expressions of emotions

Nonverbal communication plays a prominent role in human social behavior. It is defined as "communication effected by means other than words" since it goes without saying that words are the principal means of verbal communication (Knapp & Hall, 2010, p. 5). In most cases, this can be a useful definition although, in some ways, it reduces the role and importance of the numerous functions of nonverbal behavior. Those who wish to understand human social behavior must carefully "disentangle" and decode nonverbal signals given by the interlocutors (facial expression, gestures, posture, bodily contact, tone of voice, proximity), and then view these signals in the context of the entire communication, including verbal.

A nonverbal signal or sign is an element of a person's behavior which is "received" by the sense organs of another person, and which influences this other person's behavior. These are distinctive forms of behavior containing *meaning*, which may be sent to the interlocutor willingly or which may represent only unconscious (automatic) behavioral or physiological responses of a person (Argyle, 1988). Many studies have found that there is some similarity in the use of nonverbal signals by people and animals, confirming that these signals have an evolutionary origin (Darwin, 1872/1998; Altmann, 1968; Thorpe, 1972; Chevalier-Skolnikoff, 1973; van Hooff, 1973; Redican, 1982; Burrows et al., 2006).

Various nonverbal signals may communicate varying messages: some of them may reveal emotional states and interpersonal attitudes, others may illustrate and synchronize speech, regulate interaction, transmit information on the participants in the interaction, and provide feedback. One of the most important functions of nonverbal communication is the *expression of emotional states* of a person (Argyle, 1988). In spite of the fact that various bodily signals can also communicate information on how someone feels, the face – a highly expressive region – represents the most important, primary area of nonverbal emotion signaling. Charles Darwin's book *Expression of the Emotions in Man and Animals* (1872/1998), which presented his theoretical positions and empirical observations on the origins, form, and interpretation of facial emotional expressions in people and animals, was certainly quite inspirational for all subsequent research of facial expressions. Darwin was convinced that the communicative potential of the face has a phylogenetic basis, i.e., evolutionary origin (Darwin, 1872/1998). Later studies have tried to corroborate or refute Darwin's theory and many researchers have become interested in studying facial expression and recognition of emotional signals provided by the face. There have been numerous discussions on the origins of facial expressions, on whether the external, facial indication of an internal emotional condition should be viewed as *communication* or *expression* of emotion. It turns out that only a full understanding of the nature, function and multi-signal potentials of facial expressions enables us to make a clear distinction between emotion and its related phenomena (Ekman, 1997).

It is well known that emotions represent important determinants of human life. They permeate almost all social relations and have the power to make these relations strong or fragile. Emotions unite and disunite people, changing the way in which they understand behavior – their own and that of others. Facial expressions of emotions represent a visible form of expressing feelings and interpersonal attitudes that contain emotions, which is an important condition for developing "emotional and social intimacy" (Ekman, 2003). For this reason, facial expressions have an invaluable role in social interactions, enabling successful social interaction and effective interpersonal communication (Masten et al., 2008), as well as successful intercultural adjustment (Hee Yoo et al., 2006). Accurate recognition of the facial expressions of emotions is central to the understanding of feelings, intentions, expectations, and behavior of other people (Silvia et al., 2006; Kostić, 2013). Facial expressions of positive and negative emotions are powerful sources of important social information (Darwin, 1872/1998; Ekman, 1993; Keltner & Ekman, 2000). In the last few decades, systematic studies of facial expressions of emotions have resulted in some important insights which have practical implications for actual social life (Matsumoto & Hwang, 2011). One such discovery was that of the *universal nature* of facial expressions of emotions.

Based on his many years of study of emotion and its expression, Ekman (1997, p. 337) is convinced "that all expressions of emotion are unintended, that they are never made willingly or intentionally." He specifically stresses that this statement pertains to all facial expressions of emotion, but not to all facial movement. When someone, for instance, experiences fear, impulses are automatically sent and reach facial muscles. The person cannot stop this process. He or she may attempt to interfere with the work of the facial muscles to prevent the visibility of the fear expression but cannot do anything to stop the movement of neural impulses from reaching the facial muscles. Results of these studies prompt us to reach the following conclusion: although the facial expressions of emotion may be very informative, they do not emerge from the person's *intention* to communicate a message. It is only natural to call these facial signals expressions because they are part of the emotion; they are signs that a person is experiencing an emotion. The question of whether and how much the expressions are informative and communicative is not the question of their origins, but rather that of the way in which facial expressions appear and get used in our social life (Ekman, 1997).

Taking into account empirical findings of numerous studies, one may conclude that the facial expressions of primary emotions are inborn, a product of evolution, that they represent spontaneous expressions of experienced emotions, which do not require any learning (Ekman, 2003; Matsumoto & Hwang, 2011). In Ekman's opinion, the capacity to accurately recognize facial emotional expressions is also predetermined, although in early childhood "preset instructions may be damaged or destroyed by severely disturbed early experience" (Ekman, 2003, p. 219). Many studies have established that facial expressions of basic emotions are a reliable source of inference of experienced emotions, which is corroborated by very strong concurrence of observers in both civilized and primitive cultures (Ekman et al., 1969; Izard, 1971; Ekman & Friesen, 1971).

The capacity to recognize relevant social signals is made possible by the "activation of cortical regions in the temporal lobe which participate in the reception of socially relevant stimuli, while the amygdala, right somatosensory cortex, orbitofrontal cortex and cingular cortex take part in binding the perception of such stimuli to motivation, emotion, and cognition" (Nešić, 2008, p. 54). Becker (2012) identifies two activities of the amygdala that may enable a quicker idenitification of emotinally-relevant stimuli. First, when the amygdala detects emotional valence, this may influence the momentary direction of the person's attention directed towards the particular emotional stimulus. Second, detection of emotional valence may also result in increased awareness (Armony et al., 1997), as there are "direct connections from the amygdala to perceptual cortices" involved in this process (Amaral et al., 2003). In turn, this may increase the gain of those perceptual units responsible for processing the emotional stimulus (Phelps & LeDoux, 2005). The crucial role of the amygdala in emotional face processing is corroborated by studies of both normal participants and brain-damaged patients (Cristinzio et al., 2007).

Emotional recognition research

Limitations of early research

Research into the accuracy of perceiving facial emotional expressions has a 100-year history. In their attempts to determine whether observers are capable of accurately decoding facial expressions of emotion, researchers have found inconsistent results. Analyzing one of the most comprehensive overviews of studies which had dealt with the accuracy of emotion recognition (Bruner & Tagiuri, 1954), Ekman, Friesen and Ellsworth (1982) found crucial errors in the presentation and interpretation of results suggesting that facial expressions of emotion are *not a reliable* source of information.

Summing up the discussion on the negative findings of accuracy studies overviewed by Bruner and Tagiuri (1954), Ekman and colleagues (1982) concluded that most of the analyzed studies suffered from numerous shortcomings. Typically, they used drawings and artistic sketches rather than recordings of actual behavior, in some studies data analysis was overly simplified, while some researchers unfoundedly expected that selected situations would always cause one and the same emotional reaction. For all these reasons, Ekman and colleagues (1982) concluded that the analyzed studies had not been able to provide a reliable answer to the question of accuracy of emotional assessment. Studying how justified the common impression is that the face is not a reliable source of information on emotion, Ekman and colleagues refuted the validity of evidence available by that time, revealing the causes for the discrepancies in results, and at the same time provided undeniable evidence that one *can* use facial behavior in order to make inferences of emotion. One should add that this conclusion is predominantly based on the critical analysis of studies which used posed, rather than spontaneous facial expressions of emotion as stimuli.

Research into origins of facial expressions of emotion

Scholars have attempted to explain the origin of facial expressions and develop an understanding of their nature. Following Darwin's theory (Darwin, 1872/1998), some have vouched for the principle of evolution and conducted comparative studies to provide evidence for the universality of facial expressions. Others, like the anthropologist Birdwhistell (1970), put emphasis on the primary influence of learning and cultural specificity of facial expressions, stressing major differences among cultural groups. Both have studied the same domain of behavior, yet their results were different: the former insisted on the *universality*, the latter on the *specificity* of facial expressions. This was only to be expected as their theoretical interpretations of the origin of facial expressions, of the interaction of facial elements and the role of the social environment, were different. Evolutionists emphasized the dominant role of inborn, instinctive mechanisms determining expressive facial movements (Darwin, 1872/1998; Tomkins, 1962; Izard, 1971; Eibl-Eibesfeldt, 1972), while cultural relativists (Klineberg, 1940; LaBarre, 1947; Birdwhistell, 1970; Mead, 1975) claimed that facial expressions were, most of all, a result of learning specific to the given culture.

Too much emphasis put on the role of either biological or cultural origins of facial expressions appears to have been a limitation for both a nativistic as well as for a relativistic approach. Researchers neglected the significance of those factors which had not been considered as dominant in their research. The most important limitation of those two approaches was that a proper perception and categorisation of specific facial configurations became unreliable. Despite obvious anatomical differences, facial configurations were interpreted as being either the same or similar. Some researchers, mostly anthropologists, did not have adequate tools for a precise description of facial behavior. It made a differentiation of facial expression of emotions from facial illustrators, regulators, and emblems difficult (Ekman et al., 1982). Certain facial behaviors were verbally labelled in the same way despite the fact that they did not have the same function. Some authors were convinced that they studied the same facial activities without having checked whether the same labels covered the same meanings – which was, obviously, caused by those linguistic imprecisions (Kostić, 2010).

Since the first research on the universality of facial expressions (Tomkins, 1962; Izard, 1971; Ekman, 1972), more than one hundred studies have been conducted, testing judgments of facial emotional expression (Matsumoto, 2001; Matsumoto & Hwang, 2011). Researchers have gathered strong empirical evidence not only for the universality of facial expressions but also for universal recognition of emotion (Elfenbein & Ambady, 2002a). Results of more than 75 studies have shown that facial emotional expressions of spontaneously experienced primary emotions were *identical*, irrespective of all differences, including culture (Matsumoto et al., 2008). Knapp and Hall (2010) list five categories of studies which looked into the biological groundedness of expressions. Facial manifestations have been studied of *deaf and blind* persons (Eibl-Eibesfeldt, 1973, 1975; Pitcairn & Eibl-Eibesfeldt, 1976; Galati et al., 1997; Galati et al., 2001; Galati et al., 2003), of *newborns* (Izard, 1977, 1991; Field et al., 1982; Camras et al., 1993), of *identical twins* (Farber, 1981; Viken et al., 1994), of *apes* (Darwin, 1872/1998; Thorpe, 1972; Chevalier-Skolnikoff, 1973; van Hooff, 1973; Preuschoft, 1995; Bard, 2003). Numerous *cross-cultural studies* (Ekman et al., 1969; Ekman & Friesen, 1971; Izard, 1971; Eibl-Eibesfeldt, 1972; Ekman, 1972; Fridlund et al., 1987; Ekman, 1994), investigated interpretations of expressions of emotion in participants from various cultures, and found high levels of agreement in the identification of emotional categories.

Matsumoto and Hwang (2011) point out the impressive value of the findings on the universality of facial expressions since the studies in question have been conducted by various researchers, coming from all parts of the world, using a variety of methodological approaches. They have all reached the same conclusions, and their research corroborates the universal nature of the facial expressions of seven primary emotions: joy, fear, sadness, surprise, contempt, disgust, and anger.

Contemporary research

Contemporary researchers dealing with the recognition of emotional facial expressions are today focused less on the nature, origin, and form of facial behaviors, and more on the interaction of emotion and related phenomena, as well as on factors influencing the process of perceiving emotion. There is a strong tendency to assess the applicability of obtained results, especially viewed against different categories of population suffering from organic damage to particular neuronal structures relevant for the perception of emotion. The goal is to understand and minimize problems in the process of perceiving and decoding emotions. Thus, with the development of neuroscience, interest in the neurophysiological grounds of expressing and perceiving emotions has grown. Likewise, the increase of aggressive behavior has motivated more research on factors influencing the speed of recognizing anger as opposed to recognizing happiness. To follow are some studies exemplifying new perspectives in the research of recognition of facial emotional expression.

For example, Duchaine et al. (2003) have studied the recognition of emotion in a prosopagnosic. Their research supports the idea that there are various mechanisms enabling an independent process of perceiving facial identity as compared with the process of the perception of facial expressions of emotion. Although the subject performed in a very impaired manner on facial identity tests, her performance in the tests of emotion recognition showed results which were within normal values. They conclude that their research provides an important support for models in which identity recognition and emotion recognition are performed by separate processes.

In another study, Kirsh and Mounts (2007) tested the how quickly facial emotional expressions of happiness and anger were recognized. They viewed this process as a function of violent video game play. Typically, happy faces were identified more quickly than were angry ones (the happy-face advantage). Results suggest that if one plays a violent video game, this can result in a reduction in the happy-face advantage, which should be seriously considered when one devises models of aggressive behavior.

Phelps (2006) discusses new approaches to studying and understanding cognition in cognitive neuroscience, stressing its interactions with emotion, which is not typical of the traditional approaches. She suggests that the role of the human amygdala should be better studied in domains such as: emotion learning, emotion and memory, emotion's influence on attention and perception, processing emotion in social stimuli, and changing emotional responses. Understanding human behavior entails the research of neural systems which suggest that there is a close interaction between emotional and cognitive processes. Recent research leads one to believe that studies of cognition cannot be separated from studies of emotion.

Becker's study (2012) looked into whether negative emotional photographs would be identified more slowly than positive ones. The question asked in this study was: does the emotional valence of a photograph influence the time required to originally identify the contents of the image? Results have shown "that the detection of an image as negative impedes rather than assists the rapid identification of that image's identity" (Becker, 2012, p. 1249). In order to understand in what way emotional stimuli influence processing, one should study the mechanism behind the tendency of negative images to hold attention longer than positive ones.

Research on fear recognition

Fear is an emotion that has been the subject of numerous studies – more than any other primary emotion. Ekman (2003, p. 152) thinks that this could be explained by the fact that fear is easy to induce by any situation which the person interprets as immediately threatening, whether the potential injury is physical or psychological.

During the experience of fear, visible, distinctive changes appear in each of the three facial areas. The eyebrows are raised and drawn to one another; the eyes are open, the upper eyelids elevated, and the lower ones tense; the mouth may be open, and the lips barely visibly extended towards the ears (Ekman & Friesen, 2003, p. 50). The facial expression of fear does not inform the observer of "the cause", even though one may assume that the cause may be found in the situational context.

Strong empirical confirmation of the universality of the facial expressions of primary emotions, including the expression of fear, as well as high agreement in their recognition, has diverted the attention of contemporary researchers towards questions on which there has been no concord and which have been neglected and disputed, providing no reliable answers. As for recent studies of the recognition of fear, present-day researchers are interested in the neurophysiological and biochemical basis of fear recognition, especially in cases of lesions in the neural structures responsible for processing this emotion. In other words, the research is turning toward fear recognition and neural responses to facial and vocal expressions of fear. The studied populations include maltreated children, patients with amygdala damage after encephalitis or with bilateral amygdala lesions, and those with the post-traumatic stress disorder. Examples of such studies follow.

Masten et al. (2008) conducted an early study of the recognition of facial emotions in children who had been maltreated and also had high rates of post-traumatic stress disorder. Maltreatment in childhood can produce deficits in typical emotion processing, and at the same time, can cause the development of post-traumatic stress disorder. The results of this study show that maltreated children respond more quickly than controls during the process of naming emotional facial expressions. This particularly applied to their perception of fearful faces. When compared with children who had not been ill-treated, maltreated children with and without PTSD showed faster response times during the process of identification of frightened faces. Researchers reported no differences between these groups of children while they named and identified other facially-expressed emotions, except fear. Therefore, maltreated children showed an increase in sensitivity and capacity to identify fearful faces, which was shown in significantly faster reaction times than the times of control children. These scholars therefore conclude that it is possible that atypical processing could find its roots in childhood maltreatment.

The study by Broks and colleagues (1998) focuses on five post-encephalitic people. These participants had average intelligence. Of them, four had damage in the amygdala region, while one person had hippocampal damage, but their amygdala was relatively preserved. The results of this study showed that temporal lobe damage involving the amygdala impaired the recognition of fear. In terms of the basic emotions (happiness, surprise, fear, sadness, disgust, and anger), and in comparison with the control group, three patients were able to normally recognize all emotions, except fear. Results of emotion recognition in the three patients were in full opposition to the results of the participants whose amygdala region was relatively spared. This points to the important role which the amygdala may have in the recognition of fear.

In terms of the neural responses to facial and vocal expressions of fear and disgust, Phillips and colleagues (1998) have confirmed the importance of the preservation of the amygdala. In their study, participants with lesions in this neural structure were more impaired in responses to the facial expression of fear than disgust. A converse situation was found in participants suffering from Huntington's disease. The study tested the perception of fear and disgust from facial and vocal expressions. Results corroborated earlier neuropsychological findings, as it turned out that the two types of fearful stimuli stimulated the amygdala. The perception of facial expressions of disgust resulted in the activation of the anterior insula and the caudate-putamen, while vocal expressions of disgust did not seem to activate any of these neural regions. This provides support to the thesis that there is a different localization of neural substrates of fear and disgust.

The study by Calder and Young (2005) tried to look into the details behind the mechanism of facial identity and facial expressions. Calling upon the dominant position from earlier studies, according to which facial identity and facial expression utilize differentiated functional and neuronal mechanisms and pathways, Calder and Young noticed that this model was not as strongly supported as one might expect. Namely, they list other possible models which attempt to explain the process of recognizing facial identity and facial expressions.

Scott et al. (1997) dedicated their study to hampered recognition of fear and anger in bilateral amygdala lesions. They stress the well-known fact that the amygdala represents a medial temporal lobe structure which studies have shown has to do with neural emotion substrates. Although selective bilateral damage to the amygdala occurs quite rarely, this patho-logical phenomenon can tell us a lot about the impaired functions of this neural structure. Some studies show that impairment in the amygdala hinders social perception, which creates problems with recognizing two basic emotions: fear and anger. It turns out that the amygdala is a very important neural structure for the interpretation of negative emotions, particularly that of fear. The question that still remains unanswered is the following: does this impairment equally influence the perception of visual and vocal signals of fear? It is still quite difficult to provide an answer to this one, especially since this study had only one participant.

Poljac and Montagne (2011) studied how fear and sadness were perceived by persons who suffered from post-traumatic stress disor-der (PTSD). Starting from the fact that spontaneous facial expressions provide us with reliable information related to a person's emotional condition, researchers stress that it is important to be able to correctly interpret the facial signals of the interlocutor. It is well known that the ability to accurately assess emotions is hampered in neurological and psychiatric disorders. This research shows that this tendency applies with PTSD, as well: this disorder also seems to go hand-in-hand with changes in the ways in which particular emotions are processed in the brain. This particular study tested emotional processing in war veterans who showed symptoms of PTSD, after they had been exposed for a long period to traumatic events related to combat situations. Persons with this syndrome are known to have difficulties in experiencing and iden-tifying emotions, and this was additionally confirmed by this study – in which researchers were focused on the ability of participants to rec-ognize the facial expressions of six basic emotions (happiness, anger, fear, surprise, disgust, and sadness). The major findings suggest that par-ticipants with post-traumatic stress disorder were less able to recognize two emotions in particular: fear and sadness.

Another study which has dealt with impaired recognition of facial expressions of fear due to bilateral damage to the amygdala was under-taken by Adolphs and colleagues (1995). These scholars found that only bilateral, and not unilateral damage to the amygdala could hamper, and even totally compromise the recognition of fearful facial expres-sions. The case here is that of insensitivity to the intensity of the fear expressed by the face. These researchers also confirmed that there was a double dissociation between the recognition of facial expressions of fear and recognition of facial identity, although both processes can be hampered quite independently. Preliminary results of this study there-fore suggest that the role of the amygdala extends to both recognition and *also* recall of fearful facial expressions.

Although these studies have found significant interactions among the factors influencing the mechanism of fear perception, as well as the role of neural structures responsible for the processing of this emotion, and have thus expanded our knowledge in this domain, the small number of participants remains their central limitation.

Emotional recogition and levels of general fear

The relationship between emotional recognition and general fear dichotomized into abstract fear was researched in a 2013 Trinidad study utilizing a sample of 317 undergraduate students, which assessed, among other factors, the relationship between emotional recognition and pragmatic fear, abstract fear and stimuli valence and arousal. The study was undertaken by the ANSA McAl Psychological Research Centre. The sample consisted of 85% females with a mean age of 21.7 years. The results showed a relationship between pragmatic fear and fear recognition and a relationship between abstract fear and anger recognition. Both pragmatic and abstract fear were created out of a general fear scale derived from Scherer's (1988) categories (see Chadee & Ng Ying, 2013).

Emotion recognition was measured using images selected from the *International Affective Picture System* (IAPS, Lang et al., 1997) database. Respondents were exposed to five images for each emotion. The Self-Assessment Manikin (SAM, Lang, 1985), which adopts humanoids, was used to measure affective ratings on three dimensions (hedonic valence, arousal, and dominance) associated with each image. Bradley and Lang (2007) noted that "judgments of the hedonic valence indicate which motivational system is engaged [...] judgements of arousal index the intensity of its activation" (p. 30). Dominance ratings measure sense of control, and gains relevance in social/environmental contexts (Lang, 1988). Pragmatic fear is a global/general fear focusing on events that are tangible, such as fear of loss of income, fear of vehicular accident, fear of health problems. On the other hand, abstract fear is a global/general fear focusing on the intangible, such as fear of the unknown, fear of supernatural events happening to you, fear of solitude, fear of relational break-up.

Specifically, the findings show that when pragmatic fear ($\beta = .087$, $p > .05$), abstract fear ($\beta = -.126$, $p < .05$), stimuli arousal ($\beta = .14$, $p < .01$), and valance (($\beta = -.176$, $p < .01$) were used as predictors of anger recognition, except for pragmatic fear, the other factors were significant predictors of anger recognition ($R^2 = .07$, $F (5, 312) = 4.41$, $p < .001$). Persons low in abstract fear and valence and high in arousal were more likely to recognize anger. High abstract fear appeared to inhibit the recognition of anger. On the other hand, when pragmatic fear (β = .129, p<.05), abstract fear (β = .064, p>.05), and stimuli arousal (β = .213, p<.01) were used as predictors of fear recognition, except for abstract fear, the other two factors were positive significant predictors of fear recognition (R^2 = .156, F (5, 312) = 11.55, p<.001). The higher pragmatic fear and arousal, the more likely the prediction of fear recognition.

From an evolutionary psychological perspective human beings are genetically wired to protect themselves and identify danger cues. Integral to this survival process are both fear and anger (Davidson et al., 2004; Doty et al., 2013). Doty and colleagues (2013) argue that anger displayed by others is perceived as a more threatening cue than fear, which sends an indirect message of potential danger. Hence, recognitions of these two emotions are more easily distinguished than those of other emotions. Their findings show a positive relationship between trait anxiety and recognition of fear and a correlation between neuroticism and fear recognition. Persons high in pragmatic fear may have a greater sensitivity to issues, and research needs to explore the relationship between this kind of fear and neuroticism. This relationship may assist in refining our understanding of emotional recognition and the mediating role of personality in fear. However, the literature has underscored the importance of the amygdala in both fear and anger recognition. Specifically, Pichon, de Gelder, and Grezes (2009) found that both emotions elicit "similar activity in amygdala, posterior temporal cortices, dorsomedial and inferior frontal cortices" and conclude that the signal of threat associated with these two emotions resulted in these brain activities creating higher sensitivity.

Future research utilizing the propensity to be influenced by a particular emotion should also take into consideration idoscycracies of the particular culture, including ethnic and other kinds of differences. The debate by Elfenbein and Ambady (2002a, 2002b, 2003) will definitely inform these considerations, including their strongly-argued position of the emotion recognition in-group advantage. Though there are compelling research findings supporting the universal emotion recognition thesis rooted in evolution, the cultural equivalence model (see Tomkins, 1962; Ekman, 1972; Mesquita & Frijda, 1992; Soto & Levenson, 2009), there is also equally convincing support for the in-group advantage thesis, the cultural advantage model.

Elfenbein and Ambady (2002a) suggest that there are nuances created by norms emerging from the cultural variation in rules of display and decoding. The functional value of these cultural nuances is to ensure the appropriate expression and decoding of emotions. Therefore, members of the in-group will be at an advantage in the recognition and interpretation of the nuances. Nuances or cultural driven facial expressions, they argue, are also articulated in language, with in-group members being more likely to identify same-group vocal expressions. The in-group advantage concept was previously articulated in the literature as ethnic bias (see Markham & Wang, 1996; also Elfenbein & Ambady, 2002b). Elfenbein and Ambady (2002b) also identified a number of moderating factors to assist in the understanding of emotional recognition across cultures and these factors are exposure between cultures including the adopted style of emotional expressions; majority or minority status within the culture; attributes of studies; and demographic factors. Citing Henley (1997) the authors recognize that minority members may be more likely to familiarize themselves with the nonverbal nuances than members of the majority. However, they also noted that Hall and colleagues (1997) found a greater nonverbal cue sensitivity in the high-status groups disputing the minority effect. These findings question the universality hypothesis that the face is the main emotion cue source and emotions expressed facially are easily recognizable across cultures.

In closing, we refer to Merluzzi (2014), who notes that though the face may provide important cues and is often the first avenue for identifying emotions, a focus on other body features also provides useful sensory information in recognition. He further articulates that emotional, cultural, situational, and psychological contexts, when taken into consideration, refine the emotion identification proceess.

References

Adolphs, R., Tranel, D., Damasio, H., & Damasio, A. R. (1995). Fear and the human amygdala. *The Journal of Neuroscience, 15*(9), 5879–5891.

Altmann, S. A. (1968). Primates. In T. A. Sebeok (ed.), *Animal communication* (pp. 466–522). Bloomington: Indiana University Press.

Amaral, D. G., Behniea, H., & Kelly, J. L. (2003). Topographic organization of projections from the amygdala to the visual cortex in the macaque monkey. *Neuroscience, 118*, 1099–1120.

Argyle, M. (1988). *Bodily communication.* London: Methuen.

Armony, J. L., Servan-Schreiber, D., Cohen, J. D., & LeDoux, J. E. (1997). Computational modelling of emotion: Explorations through the anatomy and physiology of fear conditioning. *Trends in Cognitive Science, 1*, 28–34.

Bard, K. A. (2003). Development of emotional expressions in chimpanzees (Pan troglodytes). *Annals of the New York Academy of Sciences, 1000*, 88–90.

Becker, M. W. (2012). Negative emotional photographs are identified more slowly than positive photographs. *Attention, Perception, & Psychophysics, 74*(6), 1241–1251.

Birdwhistell, R. L. (1970). *Kinesics and context.* Philadelphia: University of Pennsylvania Press.

Bradley, M. M. & Lang, P. J. (2007). The International Affective Picture System (IAPS) in the study of emotion and attention. In J. A. Coan & J.B. Allen (eds), *Handbook of emotion elicitation and assessment* (pp. 29–46). New York, NY: Oxford University Press.

Broks, P., Young, A. W., Maratos, E. J., Coffey, P. J., Calder, A. J., Isaac, C. L., Mayes, A. R., Hodges, J. R., Montaldi, D., Cezayirli, E., Roberts, N. & Hadley, D. (1998). Face processing impairments after encephalitis: Amygdala damage and recognition of fear. *Neuropsyhologia, 36*(1), 59–70.

Bruner, J. S. & Tagiuri, R. (1954). The perception of people. In G. Lindzey (ed.), *Handbook of social psychology* (Vol. 2, pp. 634–654). Reading, MA: Addison-Wesley.

Burrows, A. M., Waller, B. M., Parr, L. A., & Bonar, C. J. (2006). Muscles of facial expression in the chimpanzee (Pan troglodytes): Descriptive, comparative, and phylogenetic contexts. *Journal of Anatomy* (2), 153–168.

Calder, A. J. & Young, A. W. (2005). Understanding the recognition of facial identity and facial expression. *Nature Reviews Neuroscience, 6,* 641–651.

Camras, L. A., Sullivan, J., & Michel, G. (1993). Do infants express discrete emotions? Adult judgments of facial, vocal and body actions. *Journal of Nonverbal Behavior, 17,* 171–186.

Chadee, D. & Ng Ying, N. K. (2013). Predictors of fear of crime: general fear versus perceived risk. *Journal of Applied Social Psychology, 43*(9), 1896–1904.

Chevalier-Skolnikoff, S. (1973). Facial expression of emotion in nonhuman primates. In P. Ekman (ed.), *Darwin and facial expression.* New York: Academic Press.

Cristinzio, C., Sander, D., & Vuilleumier, P. (2007). Recognition of emotional face expressions and amygdala pathology. *Epileptologie, 24,* 130–138.

Darwin, C. (1998), *The expression of the emotions in man and animals* (3rd ed.). New York: Oxford University Press. (Original work published 1872)

Davidson, R. J., Maxwell, J. S., & Shackman, A. J. (2004). The privileged status of emotion in the brain. *Proceedings of the National Academy of Sciences, USA, 10,* 11915–11916.

Doty, T. J., Japee, S., Ingvar, M., & Ungerleider, L. G. (2013). Fearful face detection sensitivity in healthy adults correlates with anxiety-related traits. *Emotion, 13*(2), 183–188.

Duchaine, B. C., Parker, H., & Nakayama, K. (2003). Normal recognition of emotion in a prosopagnosic. *Perception, 32,* 827–838.

Eibl-Eibesfeldt, I. (1972). Similarities and differences between cultures in expressive movements. In R. A. Hinde (ed.), *Nonverbal communication.* Cambridge: Cambridge University Press.

Eibl-Eibesfeldt, I. (1973). The expressive behavior of the deaf-and-blind born. In M. von Cranach & I. Vine (eds), *Social communication and movement.* New York: Academic Press.

Eibl-Eibesfeldt, I. (1975). *Ethology: The biology of behavior* (2nd ed.). New York: Holt, Rinehart & Winston.

Ekman, P., Sorenson, E. R. & Friesen, W. V. (1969). Pan-cultural elements in facial displays of emotions. *Science, 164,* 86–88.

Ekman, P. & Friesen, W. V. (1971). Constants across cultures in the face and emotion. *Journal of Personality and Social Psychology, 17,* 124–129.

Ekman, P. (1972). Universals and cultural differences in facial expressions of emotion. In J. Cole (ed.), *Nebraska symposium on motivation* (Vol. 19). Lincoln, NE: University of Nebraska Press.

Ekman, P. & Friesen, W. V. (1982). Facial action coding system. In: P. Ekman (ed.), *Emotion in the human face* (2nd ed.). Cambridge: Cambridge University Press.

Ekman, P., Friesen, W. V., & Ellsworth, P. (1982). Does the face provide accurate information? In P. Ekman (ed.), *Emotion in the human face* (2nd ed.). Cambridge: Cambridge University Press.

Ekman, P. (1993). Facial expressions and emotion. *American Psychologist, 48*(4), 376–379.

Ekman, P. (1994). Strong evidence for universals in facial expressions: A reply to Russell's mistaken critique. *Psychological Bulletin, 115*, 268–287.

Ekman, P. (1997). Should we call it expression or communication? *Innovations in Social Science Research, 10*, 333–344.

Ekman, P. (2003). *Emotions revealed: recognizing faces and feelings to improve communication and emotional life.* New York: Times Books, Henry Holt and Company, LLC.

Ekman, P. & Friesen, W. V. (2003). *Unmasking the face: A guide to recognizing emotions from facial clues.* Los Altos, CA: Malor Books.

Elfenbein, H. A., & Ambady, N. (2002a). On the universality and cultural specificity of emotion recognition: A meta-analysis. *Psychological Bulletin, 128*, 203–235.

Elfenbein, H. A., & Ambady, N. (2002b). Is there an in-group advantage in emotion? *Psychological Bulletin, 128*, 243–249.

Elfenbein, H. A., & Ambady, N. (2003). Universals and cultural differences in recognizing of emotions. *Current Directions in Psychological Sciences, 12*(2), October, 159–164.

Farber, S. L. (1981). *Identical twins reared apart: A reanalysis.* New York: Basic Books.

Field, T. M., Woodson, R., Greenberg, R. & Cohen, D. (1982). Discrimination and imitation of facial expression of neonates. *Science, 218*, 179–181.

Fridlund, A. J., Ekman, P., & Oster, H. (1987). Facial expressions of emotion: Review of literature, 1970–1983. In A. W. Siegman & S. Feldstein (eds), *Nonverbal behavior and communication* (2nd ed.). Hillsdale, NJ: Erlbaum.

Galati, D., Scherer, K. R., & Ricci-Bitti, P. E. (1997). Voluntary facial expression of emotion: Comparing congenitally blind with normally sighted encoders. *Journal of Personality and Social Psychology, 73*, 1363–1379.

Galati, D., Miceli, R., & Sini, B. (2001). Coding and judging the facial expression of emotions in congenitally blind children. *International Journal of Behavioral Development, 25*, 268–278.

Galati, D., Sini, B., Schmidt, S., & Tinti, C. (2003). Spontaneous facial expressions of emotions: Comparing congenitally blind and sighted children aged between eight and eleven. *Journal of Visual Impairment and Blindness, 97*(7), 418–428.

Hall, J. A., Halberstadt, A. G., & O'Brien, C. E. (1997). Subordination and non-verbal sensitivity: A study and synthesis of findings based on trait measures. *Sex Roles, 37*, 295–317.

Hee Yoo, S. H., Matsumoto, D., & LeRoux, J. (2006). The influence of emotion recognition and emotion regulation on intercultural adjustment. *International Journal of Intercultural Relations, 30*, 345–363.

Henley, N.M. (1997). *Body politics: power, sex and nonverbal communication.* Englewood Cliffs, NJ: Prentice-Hall.

Izard, C. E. (1971). *The face of emotion.* New York: Appleton-Century-Crofts.

Izard, C. E. (1977). *Human emotions.* New York: Plenum.

Izard, C. E. (1991). *The psychology of emotions*. New York: Plenum Press.

Keltner, D., & Ekman, P. (2000). Facial expression of emotion. In M. Lewis & J. Haviland-Jones (eds), *Handbook of emotion* (pp. 236–249). New York: Guilford Press.

Kirsh, S. J. & Mounts, J. R. W. (2007). Violent video game play impacts facial emotion recognition. *Aggressive Behavior, 33,* 353–358.

Klineberg, O. (1940). *Social psychology*. New York: Henry Holt.

Knapp, M. L. & Hall, J. A. (2010). *Nonverbal communication in human interaction* (7th ed.). Boston, MA: Wadsworth, Cengage Learning.

Kostić, A. (2010). *Govor lica – značenja facijalnih ponašanja [Facetalk – meanings of facial behaviors]*. Filozofski fakultet u Nišu i "Punta" – Niš [Faculty of Philosophy, Nis]. ISBN 978-86-7379-193-7.

Kostić, A. (2013). Opažanje emocija [Recognition of emotions]. In Đ. Đurić, M. Franceško & A. Kostić (eds), *Pojedinac u društvenom okruženju – uvod u socijalnu psihologiju [Individual in Social Environment – Introduction to Social Psychology]* (pp. 158–177). Fakultet za pravne i poslovne studije, Novi Sad i "Tampograf" [Faculty of Legal and Business Study, Novi Sad].

LaBarre, W. (1947). The cultural basis of emotions and gestures. *Journal of Personality, 16,* 49–68.

Lang, P. J. (1985). The Cognitive Psychophysiology of Emotion: Anxiety and the Anxiety Disorder. Hillsdale, NJ: Lawrence Erlbaum.

Lang, P. J. (1988). What are the data of emotion? In V. Hamilton, G. H. Bower, & N. H. Frijda (eds), *Cognitive perspectives on emotion and motivation* (pp. 173–191). Dordrecht, The netherlands: Kluwer Academic Publishers.

Lang, P. J., Bradley, M. M., & Cuthbert, B. N. (1997). *International Affective Picture System (IAPS): affective ratings of pictures and instruction manual* (Technical Report A-6). Gainesville, FL: NIMH Center for the Study of Emotion and Attention.

Markham, R. & Wang, L. (1996). Recognition of emotion by Chinese and Australian children. *Journal of Cross-Cultural Psychology, 27*(5), 616–643.

Masten, C. L., Guyer, A. E., Hodgdon, H. B., McClure, E. B., Charney, D. S., Ernst, M., Kaufman, J., Pine, D., & Monk, C. S. (2008). Recognition of facial emotions among maltreated children with high rates of post-traumatic stress disorder. *Child Abuse & Neglect, 32*(1), 139–153.

Matsumoto, D. (2001). Culture and emotion. In D. Matsumoto (ed.), *The handbook of culture and psychology* (pp. 171–194). New York: Oxford University Press.

Matsumoto, D., Keltner, D., Shiota, M. N., Frank, M. G., & O'Sullivan, M. (2008). What's in a face? Facial expressions as signals of discrete emotions. In M. Lewis, J. M. Haviland, & L. Feldman Barrett (eds), *Handbook of emotions* (pp. 211–234). New York: Guilford Press.

Matsumoto, D., & Hwang, H. S. (2011). Reading facial expressions of emotion., *Psychological Science Agenda, 25*(5). Retrieved from http://www.apa.org/science/about/psa/2011/05/facial-expressions.aspx.

Mead, M. (1975). Review of *Darwin and facial expression. Journal of Communication, 25*(1), 209–213.

Merluzzi, A. (2014). Nonverbal accents: Cultural nuances in emotional expression. *Observer, 27*(4). Retreive from http://www.psychologicalscience.org/index.php/publications/observer/2014/april-14/nonverbal-accents.html.

Mesquita, B. & Frijda, N. H. (1992). Cultural variations in emotions: A review. *Psychological Bulletin, 112,* 179–204.

Nešić, M. (2008). Neurofiziološka osnova komunikacije [Neurophysiology of communication]. In A. Kostić (ed.) *Govor bez reči [Talk without words]* (53–74). Filozofski fakultet, Univerzitet u Nišu i Niš: "Punta".

Phelps, E. A. & LeDoux, J. E. (2005). Contributions of the amygdala to emotion processing: From animal models to human behavior. *Neuron, 48*, 175–187.

Phelps, E. A. (2006). Emotion and cognition: Insights from studies of the human amygdala. *Annual Review of Psychology, 57*, 27–53.

Phillips, M. L., Bullmore, E. T., Howard, R., Woodruff, P. W. R., Wright, I. C., Williams, S. C. R., Simmons, A., Andrew, C., Brammer, M. & David, A. S. (1998). Investigation of facial recognition memory and happy and sad facial expression perception: An fMRI study. *Psychiatry Research: Neuroimaging Section, 83*, 127–138.

Pichon, S., de Gelder, B., & Grezes, J. (2009). Two different faces of threat: Comparing the neural systems for recognizing fear and anger in dynamic body expressions. *NeuroImage, 47*, 1873–1883.

Pitcairn, T. K. & Eibl-Eibesfeldt, I. (1976). Concerning the evolution of nonverbal communication in man. In M. E. Hahn & E. C. Simmel (eds), *Communicative behavior and evolution*. New York: Academic Press.

Poljac, E., & Montagne, B. (2011). Reduced recognition of fear and sadness in post-traumatic stress disorder. *Cortex, 47*(8), 974–980.

Preuschoft, S. (1995). *'Laughter' and 'smiling' in macaques: An evolutionary perspective*. Utrecht, Netherlands: University of Utrecht.

Redican, W. K. (1982). An evolutionary perspective on human facial displays. In P. Ekman (ed.), *Emotion in the human face* (2nd ed.). Cambridge: Cambridge University Press.

Scott, S. K., Young, A. W., Calder, A. J., Hellawell, D. J., Aggleton, J. P., & Johnson, M. (1997). Impaired auditory recognition of fear and anger following bilateral amygdala lesions. *Nature, 385*, 254–257.

Silvia, P. J., Allan, W. D., Beauchamp, D. L., Maschauer, E. L., & Workman, J. O. (2006). Biased recognition of happy facial expressions in social anxiety. *Journal of Social and Clinical Psychology, 25*(6), 585–602.

Soto, J. A. & Levenson, R. W. (2009). Emotion recognition across cultures: The influence of ethnicity on empathic accuracy and physiological linkage. *Emotion, 9*, 874–884.

Thorpe, W. H. (1972). The comparison of vocal communication in animals and man. In R. Hinde (ed.), *Nonverbal communication*. Cambridge: Cambridge University Press.

Tomkins, S. S. (1962). *Affect, imagery, consciousness* (Vol. 1, *The positive affects*). New York: Springer.

van Hooff, J. A. R. A. M. (1973). A structural analysis of the social behaviour of a semi-captive group of chimpanzees. In M. von Cranach & I. Vine (eds), *Social communication and movement*. New York: Academic Press.

Viken, R. J., Rose, R. J., Kaprio, J., & Koskenvuo, M. (1994). A developmental genetic analysis of adult personality: Extraversion and neuroticism from 18 to 59 years of age. *Journal of Personality and Social Psychology, 66*, 722–730.

Part II
Applied

7

Nonverbal Firsts: When Nonverbal Cues Are the Impetus of Relational and Personal Change in Romantic Relationships

Valerie Manusov, Tony Docan-Morgan, and Jessica Harvey

Nonverbal cues occur in all of our interactions, but they are particularly important in our close relationships (Noller, 2006). People show affection, distrust, love, disappointment, and myriad other messages through nonverbal modes of communicating with their loved ones (see, for e.g., Guerrero, 1997; Floyd, 2006). They also reflect how people define their relationship with one another (i.e., as romantic, as unequal, as formal) (Burgoon & Hale, 1984). People may, for example, enact their relationship as an intimate one by gazing at one another in a loving way or holding hands in public (Andersen et al., 2006). Or they may show that a relationship is uncertain, with intimate behaviors used tentatively. In such cases, the nonverbal cues are functioning as reflections of what the relationship means to, or how it is defined by, the people in those relationships.

But nonverbal cues can also evoke change in a relationship (Manusov & Milstein, 2005; Docan-Morgan, Manusov & Harvey, 2013). That is, they can – or can be perceived to – bring something about that was not there before. When they do so, the actions can be seen as "relational firsts": behaviors or other nonverbal cues that begin something new for the people in the relationship or for the relationship itself. This paper has as its goal to look more closely at the occurrence of these relational firsts. Specifically, our aim is to discern the types of behaviors reported to be transformative in relationships that are defined by a relational partner as romantic (before and/or after the behavior occurred). We also explore what firsts were brought about through the behaviors and look at the ways in which participants judged these events. Before doing so, however, we discuss more fully the conception of nonverbal cues as

153

potentially transformative in relationships, looking first at the larger concept of turning points.

Turning points in relationships

The idea that things can change quickly and through one event has been explored by a range of relational scholars. Identified in various ways – as transition points (Levinger, 1983), critical events (Planalp & Honeycutt, 1985), transition phases (Masheter & Harris, 1986), and relational transitions (Conville, 1988) – they are most commonly conceptualized as *relational turning points*. Bolton (1961) was the first to use this term and defined turning points as "breakthrough points at which some ambiguous matter 'jells,' jump points where there is a sudden surge in affective involvement, points of decommitment from past relations or identities, etc." (p. 237). Graham (1997) later reiterated that, "[b]y definition, turning points capture a critical moment, an event or incident that has impact or import" (p. 351). Baxter and Bullis (1986) likewise identified relational turning points as "any event or occurrence that is associated with change in a relationship" (p. 470).

Researchers who study relational turning points have been concerned primarily with identifying the types of events that create turning points within different forms of relationships (e.g., romantic relationships, families, friendships) and with particular results (e.g., levels of commitment, relational satisfaction, and closeness) (see, e.g., Baxter & Bullis, 1986; Golish, 2000; Johnson et al., 2003; Johnson et al., 2004; Surra & Huston, 1987). From this research, scholars have learned that turning points take a number of forms (e.g., Graham, 1997, in looking at turning points in post-divorce relationships found that mourning a family member and the former spouse moving away can be salient turning points). Only some of these relational turning points can be defined as firsts, however.

The study where firsts in romantic relationships were most clear was Baxter and Bullis's (1986) investigation. Their participants noted several firsts that were important moments of change in the course of their relationships. These included the first kiss, the first time they stated that they loved one another, the first time they had sex, and the first time that they met one another's family. In all cases, the "firstness" was important to their impact on the participants. Whereas these types of actions (e.g., saying "I love you") will likely be repeated many times over the course of a relationship, the *first times* that they happened are typically the most memorable and the ones that are likely to have the largest effect on a relationship's progression (i.e., become a turning point). Something like "moving away" may also be a turning point, but it can be so whether it was the first, second, or tenth time it occurred. Thus, only a subset of turning points can be described as relational firsts.

Nonverbal cues as turning points

As noted, researchers who study turning points have focused their attention on discerning the nature and impact of turning points rather than investigating whether specific behaviors may become turning points. Within their focus on the events and their outcomes, however, some researchers have found nonverbal cues to emerge as a behavior that made up or was part of turning points. As was seen, in their investigation of romantic partners, for example, Baxter and Bullis (1986) noted that two behaviors associated with *touch* – first kiss and first sex – were important events in escalating relationship commitment. They also found other turning points associated to some degree with *physical space*, often discussed as a form of nonverbal communication. In particular, their participants identified physical separation (e.g., vacations, overseas trips) and living together as relational turning points. Other researchers have found that space, in various forms, works as a turning point in other types of close relationships (e.g., Golish, 2000; Johnson et al., 2003). Although limited in scope, these results provide evidence that nonverbal cues may change or transform something, such as level of commitment, in relationships.

In addition to helping indicate what nonverbal cues may bring about change, some of the cues found in previous research also suggest that, on occasion, these turning points may also be firsts. As noted, Baxter and Bullis (1986) found that the first time their participants kissed or had sex with a partner altered the degree of commitment that they had to the relationship. In this way, the first appearance of certain nonverbal cues or acts may be important triggers of change within a relationship.

But there may be other types of firsts. That is, nonverbal cues are interesting communicatively because, among other features, they typically have to be interpreted (Manusov, 1990, 2002). For example, a kiss may be perceived as a sign of romantic interest; it can also, within our cultural repertoire of meanings, be interpreted as a sign of friendly affection or as a greeting/departure ritual with little or no relational implications. Given this ability to make sense of the same behavior in different ways, it may be that certain cues occurred in a relationship but the parties to that relationship may never have before interpreted them in a particular way (e.g., a kiss as romantic rather than as friendly). The first time a behavior is interpreted differently may also be an important relational first tied to nonverbal cues.

Understanding the ways in which nonverbal cues may function as turning points requires a more specific investigation than what has been done previously. Given that nonverbal cues are a central part of relationships (Andersen et al., 2006; Noller, 2006), and given their ability to be transformative in those relationships (Docan-Morgan et al., 2013), we argue that it is important to look more closely at the form of those behaviors and the types of firsts they entail. As such, we ask the following two research questions:

RQ$_1$:   What types of nonverbal cues do people report working as change agents in relationships defined (either before or after the behavior occurred) as romantic?

RQ$_2$:   What types of firsts are reported to be created with nonverbal cues?

As noted at the start of this chapter, nonverbal cues may be positive or negative forces in relationships (they may also be neutral, reflecting the status quo; Guerrero & Floyd, 2006). They can also bring about change that is judged positively or negatively (i.e., they can have different valences attached to them). Given this contention, and the exploratory nature of this investigation, it is necessary to look at the judgments given to the behaviors and what those judgments may bring about. We therefore pose the following questions:

RQ$_3$:   Are there differences in the valence attributed to certain behaviors that act as firsts in relationships?

RQ$_4$:   With what other judgments is the valence of a nonverbal first associated?

We work to answer these questions through the means explained next.

Methods

Participants

The data from this study were derived from a larger survey of nonverbal turning points collected in 2007. After Institutional Review Board and instructor approval, students were recruited from eight classes, two of which were very large courses that enroll a range of students from across the university. 301 people from these classes took part in the survey. Of these, 270 recalled a nonverbal event that they described as a turning point, although we eliminated 15 of these whose descriptions did not appear to actually include a nonverbal turning point (in some cases, the cue involved was not a nonverbal cue; in most cases, however, the respondent discussed a nonverbal cue as meaningful but not one that was transformative/produced change).

From this set of data ($N = 255$), we identified those respondents who discussed a cue that occurred in a romantic relationship (either at the time of the cue's occurrence or after it happened) and those whose descriptions represented a first (i.e., the initial time a particular cue was used, the first time it was interpreted in a particular way, etc.). There were 127 respondents meeting these criteria, and they were included in the present analyses. Of these respondents, 89 were female, and 38 were male. Their average age was 20.85. One person indicated that he/she was African American or Black, one listed American Indian or Alaska Native, 20 reported being Asian, two categorized themselves as Hispanic or Latino, 88 noted being White or Caucasian. Fourteen respondents indicated being "other," and most of these respondents said that they were mixed race.

Procedure

Students who chose to take part in this study were asked to go to a web address where they could access our survey. The system assessed their enrollment status and whether or not they had already taken the survey. Viable respondents were given this information:

> The following survey was created to examine the types of nonverbal behaviors that occur in close relationships with others (e.g., parents, friends, romantic partners, work associates). Nonverbal behaviors are actions like touch, facial expressions, the use of time, and vocal tones that may communicate things to others.

> We would like you to think about a time in a relationship you had/have with another person where you feel a type of nonverbal behavior occurred that really stood out to you in some way. More specifically, we would like you to recall a type of nonverbal behavior enacted by you or another person that you felt changed something between you and that other person. This turning point could be positive or negative. But, it should be an event that was meaningful to you in the relationship.

If they were able to recall such a time, they were then asked to complete the following two questions:

> What was the behavior (or behaviors) and what was the meaning you interpreted for the behavior? Describe the story of this behavior and what changes the behavior brought about.

> Why was this nonverbal behavior and/or the change particularly meaningful to you?

Respondents were also asked to rate, on a scale of 1 (*very negative*) to 5 (*very positive*), how positive or negative the event was to them; how negatively or positively they viewed their relationship prior to and after the event; how negatively or positively they felt about the other person prior to and after the event; and how negatively or positively they felt about themselves prior to and after the event. Further, participants checked what nonverbal behaviors were involved in the event (they could choose one or more behaviors from a list we provided; these cues were eye behavior, facial expressions, touch, hand gestures, voice, physical space, use of time, and "other"). They also indicated their relationship with the other person at the time of the occurrence and at the present, along with other demographic information.

Results

Research question one: Behaviors

As noted, we asked respondents to check off any of seven nonverbal cues that they recalled being a part of the first event. That means that any cue could have a frequency from 0 to 127. The cue indicated most commonly was touch (*n* = 76), which was reported to have occurred in over half of the respondents' events. This was followed in frequency by eye behavior (*n* = 66), which was also reported by more than half of the sample, space (*n* = 59), and facial expression (*n* = 54). Less common were vocal cues (*n* = 34), time (*n* = 24), and hand gestures (*n* = 18). Whereas all of these behaviors could or did make up a part of a nonverbal turning point, some were more frequent than were others. In the next section, we highlight in what situations these cues were likely to be used based on our respondents' reports.

Research question two: Nonverbal firsts

Our primary concern in this study was to assess what firsts occurred through nonverbal means. To answer this question, the first author looked over all the entries for the 127 respondents. Five primary categories emerged in this analysis. These are (1) first behaviors indicating a romantic relationship, (2) first time becoming aware of degree of caring, (3) first signals of problems in relationship, (4) first (and last) negative behavior that led to sudden dissolution, and (5) first reflections of untrustworthiness. The other two authors reviewed these categories, comparing them to the data set, and they concurred with their labels and occurrence. We discuss each of these categories in turn and highlight the behaviors most commonly associated with them in our data.

First behaviors indicating a romantic relationship. In our respondents' reports, we read many accounts of how a single behavior, used for what the respondent recalled was the first time, instantly changed the relationship or the perception of the relationship between the two individuals. There was some variety in the behaviors, but most typically they were handholding, prolonged gaze, kisses, closer proximity, and "changes" in touch behavior.

In most of the situations described by our participants, the behavior was received positively and started a romantic relationship. In a few instances, however, it indicated to the respondent that they or another person had romantic feelings that were unreciprocated. These latter situations reportedly resulted in either the termination of the existing relationship or awkwardness in the relationship. We discuss the "successful" examples first.

The accounts of behavioral firsts that led to changes in romantic relationships tended to be straightforward and suggested that the behaviors were relatively unambiguous for the respondents. They were also welcomed by the behaviors' recipients. Following are some examples of this clarity. The first three of these are examples of the importance that touch seemed to play – particularly handholding – in relationships that were reported to have moved from friendship to romantic. We use added italics to emphasize the fit within the primary behaviors involved and other relevant information.

Before my significant other and I started dating, we hung out as friends a few times after meeting in college. He's always been the one to call me and ask me to hang out, though I didn't know then how I really felt about him. One night I went over to his house for a movie night. He somehow *found my hand and held it* through all the movies and that was the first time that anything romantic happened between us, and I found out he had feelings for me and the fact that I *never let go* let him know that I felt the same way, without having said a word.

In this example, the respondent's report reflects the newness of the behavior and her interpretation, and the ways in which she acted that helped confirm to the other that she interpreted and accepted the behaviors he used as indicators of romantic interest.

As another respondent reported,

> I had a good friend in high school who later became a long-term boy-friend. I had no idea that he was interested in pursuing a more inti-mate relationship until one evening when we were walking through the hallways at an after-school event and *he wrapped his arm around me to rest his hand on my hip*. From that act alone, I realized that he wanted to be "more than friends," and *our relationship was changed from that moment on*.

In this example, the behavior indicated to its recipient the feelings that the "sender" had; she then chose to "accept" the behavior, and its acceptance reflected the respondent's acceptance of the new relational definition. In the following, the touch confirmed the respondent's beliefs about the toucher's feelings and, perhaps more importantly, allowed her to make a different judgment of her own.

> Before my boyfriend and I started dating, I knew he liked me but I wasn't sure if I felt the same way. After hanging out for a few weeks I realized I wanted to be more than just friends. He played football in high school and after a game I was sitting on the ground with a group of friends waiting for the guys to exit the field. He came up to me and put his hand out to help me up, I grabbed it and I didn't let go. *I held his hand* and this signaled to him that I was interested and wanted to be more than friends. That was an important part of our relationship because *it was really the beginning, it was the first time we held hands and it was a perfect moment*.

In all of these cases, and despite having somewhat different qualities, the particular form of touch was said to have occurred for the first time and signaled a clear shift from friendship to romance, one that was reciprocated. These individuals had interacted with one another in many other circumstances. But, for them, it was the unique cue, occurring for the first time, and one that they associated with an intimate, romantic relationship, that shifted the relationship from friendship to love the moment the behavior and their interpretation of it occurred.

As discussed, our respondents reported that other behaviors played a similar role. As with Baxter and Bullis (1986), these include first kisses:

The most recallable moment was the first time my girlfriend kissed me. I picked her up at her house, we had dinner, bla bla bla, and *she kissed me at the end of the day*. It was very meaningful to me. [I interpreted] it *as a willingness to continue our relationship into a deeper relationship*. The changes that this behavior brought was significant, we end[ed] up getting [into a] deeper romantic relationship afterwards.

First behaviors indicating romance and changing relationships to romantic also often involved protracted gaze or gaze that suggested desire:

There was a time when I was watching a movie with another person. We were very good friends, but our relationship had not progressed past that. However when the movie was over, with the lights off, we sat together on a couch and *just spent many minutes just looking at each other*. These behaviors brought about the feeling that our friendship was about to become a bit more serious than it had been and perhaps progress to another level.

Overall, and as noted, the entries that fit in this category were marked by clarity of interpretation and, in most cases, reciprocation of the behavior. There were, however, instances in which the behavior was reported to be ambiguous, unambiguous but not wanted, and/or that the other did not respond with like actions. These situations tended to result, according to the respondents, in either awkwardness/discomfort or a move away from being friends. Following are some examples. Interestingly, they include some of the same behaviors as in the examples that moved to a romantic relationship.

The behavior was: after hanging out with a girl for the night, we *kissed* goodnight when I dropped her off at her house. The meaning to be interpreted was that she saw the hanging out as a date, and the kiss afterward meant she had feelings for me. The behavior brought about *a change in my view towards the relationship*. I became skeptical and *we slowed our hanging out together*.

Another stated,

I have a really good guy friend who recently started exhibiting nonverbal behaviors that made me think he might like me. He does things such as *stand closer to me than he used to*, etc. Mostly proximity things. Like I said, we are really good friends, but I don't think I want it to be any more than that, so it's kind of awkward now.

These latter entries were not common, but they reflected that the same actions – kisses, close personal distance – may have very different outcomes, depending on the reciprocity of the behaviors and feelings. Overall, for our respondents, nonverbal cues, most notably touch, proximity, and/or gaze, occurring for the first time changed the nature of the relationship between individuals, usually in a direction reported to be desired by both relational members. They did so in ways that were very memorable for the respondents, suggesting their centrality in the relational shift.

First time becoming aware of another's degree of caring. This category reflects a set of behaviors that occurred largely in existing romantic relationships. Their firsts referenced behaviors by their partner that occurred typically in situations of stress or distress that arose during the course of those relationships. For these participants, their partners' behaviors let them know/believe for the first time just how much they cared for them or how close they had become. In all cases, the behaviors, and the shifts that followed them, were presented positively.

In our data, touch arose again in this category as particularly important. Unlike the nature of the touch in the category just discussed, in these cases, the primary form of touch was a hug. In some cases, the change reported was an assessment of the other's deepening feelings that was triggered from the behavior:

I was really upset the other day after I heard some news and my boyfriend came over to me and *held me and gently rubbed my back* to comfort me. This was the first time that he has seen me really upset and he was really comforting in my time of need which *showed me that he really cared about me.*

Similarly,

When I was talking about an issue with my boyfriend, and he began to cry. The meaning that I interpreted from this behavior was that it was so important to him that he showed all of his *emotion on his face,* and cried and from that *I knew he truly cared.*

In other cases, the behavior brought about a strengthening of one's own feelings toward the relational partner:

> When I was frustrated by the results of the competition, my boy-friend came up to me and gave me a *big hug*. This hug presented me with the feelings of being loved as well as encouragement. After this event, I *value him more* and cherish the memories together more.

Others implicated changes for both relational members:

> Despite having just admitted to lying to, and cheating on, my partner for several years, I *cried while my partner embraced me* for about twenty minutes. My actions indicated my deep remorse, while my partner's actions indicated her willingness to forgive and be understanding of my mistakes, all without words. The experience ultimately *brought us much closer together, solidified the bond between us and symbolized a strengthened commitment to one another*. I have since been entirely faithful and honest with my partner, as has she in return.

Likewise,

> The behavior was a *hug* and the meaning I interpreted for the behav-ior was close comfort and a nonverbal way of letting me know some-one was there for me when I needed them the most. The reason why I remember the hug so clearly is because of the value and meaning [I] placed upon [it]. It was given to me by my partner of two years, who was with me after hearing the news of a close friend's death. *The behavior of him really brought us closer together and created a tighter bond.*

Overall, these entries were very consistent: The interactants were already in romantic relationships; but the actions – particularly hugs – during certain types of events were reported to have opened the respondents' eyes to how close the relationship was, or they worked to bring them closer.

First signals of problems in relationships. Whereas the initial two relational firsts were largely positive and relationship *building*, with behaviors and interpretations that were seen as beneficial (Prager & Buhrmester, 1998), these next three types of firsts are tied in more with relational decline. In this category, respondents talked about a cue that first triggered their perception that their relationship was *problematic* in some way. In some cases, the cues were said to have allowed the participants to repair their relationships. In most instances, however, the cues were said to be the first of many that led up to a relational break-up. Indeed, these entries often seemed more about a series of behaviors (or non-behaviors).

Specifically, the participants often commented on the *lack of a behavior* (e.g., no eye contact, ignoring behavior [which presumably was determined by lack of gaze, not responding, and the like], and not talking [silence]). The themes were consistent whether they were discussing their own or their partner's behaviors. Here are some examples:

> Me and this girl [were] seeing each other for a while, and after I lost interest in her I started to *avoid eye contact* and *didn't really smile* much which made her think that I wasn't interested in her anymore.

The following mirrors the non-occurrence of certain behaviors, particularly gaze, highlighting, importantly, that its absence was remarkable particularly because it was the opposite of behaviors that occurred earlier in their relationship:

> The behavior was *a lack of eye contact* when I was talking with him. I interpreted this to mean that he was not interested in what I was talking about and/or not focused on me but what was past me. *In the beginning of the relationship eye contact was more consistent,* however as the relationship continued it became less focused. The *change the behavior brought about was my lack of interest/effort in maintaining the relationship status.* This was because of I felt my thoughts were less appreciated by him and I didn't want to be with someone who didn't listen to me.

In some cases, the behaviors (or lack of behaviors) were interpreted without difficultly, as in the following:

> I could totally tell by her body language and physical appearance around me. *She wouldn't try to look pretty* for me anymore, and *she would not look into my eyes* that way that she had in the past.

In other examples, however, the behaviors or their absence were perceived as ambiguous but suggested that there might be a relational shift:

> The most obvious situation that sticks out to me is in a previous relationship when the other person *stopped talking to me.* When we

were around each other their *body language* suggested something was either wrong or awkward and it sent mixed signals to me. When I did try to initiate conversation I was either *ignored* or else given enough attention until I could be ignored again. This confusion resulted in mixed communication and interpretations about our true feelings since neither of us actually talked.

In most of these entries, the nonverbal cues that often mark the beginning of relationships became absent, and their absence largely reflected the end of a relationship, either clearly or with some ambiguity. Avoidance of eye contact, silence, and "ignoring," rather than immediate, engaged, intimate, behavior was common in this group of entries and marked the beginning (or the first signal) of the relationship's decline.

First (and last) negative behavior that led to sudden dissolution. Whereas the previous category differs somewhat from the others, as the discussions tended to blend several interactions that reflected waning interest, a few entries were centered on a particular behavior that was said to have ended a relationship immediately. Typically, these were behaviors that can be defined as rude, angry, or violent. The following entry reflects the "first and only" behavior, in this case a hand gesture, needed to finish off a relationship:

My ex-boyfriend *gave me the finger once* and I realized that, *that was the end of our relationship* because no one should treat me that way.

Likewise, vocal tones were reported to have changed the way other participants thought about their relationships and to be the specific trigger for ending a relationship

Well there was this one time when my boyfriend *raised [his] tone* on me when talking about a certain issue ... And although I was very calm ... I later *broke this relationship up because of that one time.*

Touch and proxemics also were reported to have played a role:

My ex-boyfriend had been drinking when we started to get into an argument. We were at a party and all of a sudden he started *yelling* at me. I walked up to him to just hug him and tell him that this is stupid when we *pushed me against the wall and walked away. This behavior obviously changed our relationship for the worse* and when he did this to me I felt as though he didn't give a care in the world about my feelings or hurting me.

This respondent noted elsewhere in her responses that her boyfriend's action ended their relationship right away.

Overall, and although this was a somewhat infrequent category, one nonverbal cue used for the first (and last) time could break a relationship immediately. In some cases, the end did not come right away. But in all of these instances, it was seen as an unacceptable behavior after which the respondents said they could no longer be in relationship with the other person.

First perceptions of distrust.   In some of the entries in the previous category of firsts, the respondents alluded to their view that the behavior reflected something about the person that they did not like. Their focus was on the behavior, however, as the instigator of change. In this final, and related, category, participants wrote about how the first appearance of certain behaviors began to *change their view of the other person*, which in turn led to the relational decline. Specifically, they began to believe that the other person was not trustworthy. In many of the cases, the participants appeared to be looking for/at signs of deceit.

Almost all of these entries referenced eye behavior specifically, with some discussion about facial expressions and silence. Here are some examples, the first of which includes a participant talking about her own relationship, although she did so in second person:

> The behavior is the *pause and looking away* when you ask someone a question. This to me means that they are worried about telling the truth or are considering lying. It makes me *worried about the reliability of what the person* will say.

A second talks about her reaction to her boyfriend's behavior when he came home from a trip. When she refers to "they," she means her boyfriend, but she may have been trying to avoid stating anything about his identity:

> But from the behavior, *smiles and avoidance of talking* about the trip I became skeptical ... I was growing scared and curious about what I was missing. It occurred to me that this person might have cheated on me. I asked about this girl and I was given excuses and diverted answers. *They hardly looked me in the eye* ... I had never been so hurt,

our relationship was never the same because they lost my trust and other events made us finally separate.

Likewise,

> A while back my boyfriend and I were having an argument. I told him that I thought he was still in love with his ex girlfriend. When I asked him this, there was *no shock in his face or reaction in his eyes*. He kind of *looked away and down* and replied no. I could tell he was not telling me the truth because of his non verbal behavior. He wasn't looking at me in the eye and wasn't outraged that I had assumed such a thing. His reaction and behavior simply made it more clear that he still had feelings for her.

In these two examples, the participants referenced the behavior signaling the others' behaviors that suggested that the others had been cheating. In some cases, the reference was to a different form of dishonesty/ negative behavior that was separate from their relationship but was indicative of a problematic aspect or characteristic of the other person:

> I used to regularly date a guy who seemed to be the typical "prince charming" that all guys seem to be when you first start dating. Everything was going well until one day in particular he *wouldn't look me in the eyes* when engaging in basic conversation. He'd constantly look down and away or even past me. Turns out that was right around the time when he was getting into various drugs and stealing money from his mother for them. *Not being able for him to keep eye contact was the first thing that made me distrust him.*

These final firsts, then, reference the cues that led the respondents to think less of the one engaged in the behavior. Most of the time, the cues were seen as reasons that they should not trust the other person. Not all of the relationships reportedly ended because of these cues, but they certainly changed in quality. In some cases, the participants reported that it led to the end of the relationship, but in a few, it led to talking more openly in order to get their relationship – and their perception of the other – to a better place.

Research questions three and four: Valence

These qualitative entries just reported reflect well that the respondents evaluated the valence of the events. To assess more specifically how the events that included certain behaviors were perceived (RQ$_3$), we ran t-tests comparing the assessments of positivity/negativity of the event (on a five point scale, with five more positive) by (1) those who "checked off" that the behavior occurred as compared to (2) those who did not. That is, the t-test compared people who indicated that the cue was part of the interaction(s) with people who did not note it on their overall judgment of the interaction. Only one of these tests was significant: Given the qualitative data just reported, it is not surprising that interactions in which touch occurred tended to be judged as more positive ($M = 4.11$, $SD = 1.34$) than were interactions in which it did not ($M = 2.66$, $SD = 1.49$), $t(124) = 5.65$, $p < .001$. In most cases, touch included hand holding, kisses, and other forms of affectionate touch (Floyd, 2006), and these were typically in events that were reported to have led to the start of a romantic relationship or a deepening of an existing one. None of the other six behaviors was a part of interactions judged consistently as more positive or negative when they occurred as compared to the judgments of interactions in which they did not occur.

Our final research question (RQ$_4$) asked about the other ways in which valence judgments may have had an impact on the respondents. Whereas our data do not allow us to make causal claims, they do suggest the possible effects of the behaviors' valence on other important personal and relational outcomes.

Specifically, we used Pearson correlations to assess the relationship between judgments of the event's valence with participants' perception of how positively or negatively they viewed their relationship, the other, and themselves after the event. All of the correlations were significant: with the relationship after, $r = .88$, with perception of the other, $r = .80$, and with perception of themselves, $r = .64$, $p < .001$, one-tailed tests. As a comparison, there was no significant correlation between perceptions of the relationship, $r = .03$, or themselves, $r = -.07$, *prior to* the event and their judgments of their event, although there was a relatively small and significant relationship between their judgment of the other before the event and their judgment of the event, $r = .29$, $p = .04$. These findings suggest that the events were connected strongly to other post-event judgments.

Discussion

In this study, we looked at whether nonverbal cues could be considered firsts in relationships, relationships that were defined at one time as, or could potentially become defined as, "romantic." We did so by assessing people's reports of nonverbal cues that they could recall having changed something between them and another person. Many of these reports suggested that the first occurrence of certain behaviors altered the respondents' relationships and/or perceptions of another person. We categorized some of these changes as *advancing relationships*, specifically the behavioral firsts that were reported to have changed a non-intimate relationship into a romantic one or that helped the respondents see the degree of closeness that they shared with their partners. Others were related to *relational demise*, with first cues leading to an awareness of relational problems, a relationship's "sudden death" (Duck, 1994), or to distrust of the other person.

In our data, we saw both positive and negative turning points instigated by nonverbal firsts, and the judgments of the nature of these firsts were very important. In particular, positive and negative valence judgments of the first were correlated with judgments of the relationship overall as well as assessments of the other person and themselves. These correlations were very strong, suggesting that the magnitude of the tie between the event and other judgments was great. That is, when an interaction was rated as very positive, people also judged their relationship positively, saw themselves more favorably, and thought better of the other; as the valence of the interaction decreased, all of the these other judgments decreased as well, even their judgments of themselves

The judgments of valence were also tied to particular behaviors, although typically in complex ways. Except for a few instances of negative touch (e.g., pushing away), the most straightforward interpretations had to do with touch, and events in which touch occurred were evaluated much more positively than events in which it did not. Given the affectionate nature of most of the touches mentioned (Floyd, 2006), such as hugging, hand holding, and kissing, it is not surprising that they were judged so positively. In particular, a rather common claim about touch is that it "is a signal in the communication process that, above all other communication channels, most directly and immediately escalates the balance of intimacy" (Thayer, 1986, p. 8). Perhaps above all other nonverbal cues, touch has been shown to facilitate dramatic "surge[s] in affective involvement" to use Bolton's (1961, p. 237) terms.

Other cues, however, were assessed with more disparity, depending on the nature and context of the behavior. For example, eye behavior, the cue mentioned most commonly by these respondents, was sometimes labeled positively (i.e., sustained eye contact was common in stories of shifts to romantic relationships), and other times it was seen as negative (i.e., avoidance of gaze was common in events that suggested there was something problematic in the relationship or with the other person). Our form of analysis focused on similarity rather than difference, because we did not anticipate the importance of a behavior's absence playing such a large role and, therefore, that the particular behavior *as a category* would be judged with such diversity. Thus the large category of eye behavior, along with some of the other cues, would be better split into the use or avoidance of to see more consistent ties with perceived event valence. The same is likely for facial expressions, where, in particular, the nature of the smiles reported to be used could be a part of affection or distrust. When vocal cues were mentioned, they were more often done so with some negativity, so the same diversity may not be seen there.

We argue from these data, then, that nonverbal cues have the potential to trigger change in perceptions and relationships (for a larger discussion of types of change, see Docan-Morgan et al., 2013), at least for United States young people in pre-marriage relationships. This transformative potential of nonverbal cues may take many forms (see Manusov & Milstein, 2005), but the current study centers particularly on the behaviors' first appearance or absence (or the first notice of their appearance or absence) and their ability to sometimes quickly and profoundly alter the course of a relationship. This is significant because it shows how just one behavior or set of behaviors enacted at one point in time can have, reportedly at least, very significant influences. As such, it shows clearly the potential of nonverbal cues in relationships.

In doing this analysis, we hope to have extended the relational turning point literature in both focusing on the saliency of firsts as important forms of turning points and highlighting that the nature of nonverbal communications – as particularly indicative of meaningful behaviors in close relationships – makes them potentially memorable turning points or change triggers. That is, they are not only meaningful in themselves, but nonverbal cues, although sometimes subtle and easy to miss, may actually be "big" actions in relational change.

Note

A previous version of this paper was presented to the Interpersonal Communication Interest Group, Western States Communication Association. Colorado Springs, CO, February, 2008.

References

Andersen, P. A., Guerrero, L. K., & Jones, S. M. (2006). Nonverbal behavior in intimate interactions and intimate relationships. In V. Manusov & M. L. Patterson (Eds.),*The Sage handbook of nonverbal communication* (pp. 259–277). Thousand Oaks, CA: Sage.

Baxter, L. A., & Bullis, C. (1986). Turning points in developing romantic relationships. *Human Communication Research, 12,* 469–493.

Bolton, C. D. (1961). Mate selection as the development of a relationship. *Marriage and Family Living, 23,* 234–240.

Burgoon, J. K., & Hale, J. L. (1984). The fundamental topoi of relational communication. *Communication Monographs, 51,* 193–214.

Conville, R. L. (1988). Relational transitions: An inquiry into their structure and function. *Journal of Social and Personal Relationships, 5,* 423–437.

Docan-Morgan, T., Manusov, V., & Harvey, J. (2013). When a small thing means so much: Nonverbal cues as turning points in relationships. *Interpersona: An International Journal on Personal Relationships, 7,* 110–124.

Duck, S. W. (1994). *Meaningful relationships: Talking, sense, and relating.* Thousand Oaks, CA: Sage.

Floyd, K. (2006). *Communicating affection: Interpersonal behavior and social context.* Cambridge, England: Cambridge University Press.

Golish, T. D. (2000). Changes in closeness between adult children and their parents: A turning point analysis. *Communication Reports, 13,* 79–97.

Graham, E. E. (1997). Turning points and commitment in post-divorce relationships. *Communication Monographs, 64,* 350–368.

Guerrero, L. K. (1997). Nonverbal involvement across interactions with same-sex friends, opposite-sex friends, and romantic partners: Consistency or change? *Journal of Social and Personal Relationships, 14,* 31–58.

Guerrero, L. K., & Floyd, K. (2006). *Nonverbal communication in close relationships.* Mahwah, NJ: Erlbaum.

Johnson, A. J., Wittenberg, E., Haigh, M., Wigley, S., Becker, J., Brown, K., & Craig, E. (2004). The process of relationship development and deterioration: Turning points in friendships that have terminated. *Communication Quarterly, 52,* 54–67.

Johnson, A., Wittenberg, E., Villagran, M., Mazur, M., & Villagran, P. (2003). Relational progression as a dialectic: Examining turning points in communication among friends. *Communication Monographs, 70,* 230–249.

Levinger, G. (1983). Development and change. In H. H. Kelley et al. (Eds.), *Close relationships* (pp. 315–359). San Francisco, CA: Freeman.

Manusov, V. (1990). An application of attribution principles to nonverbal messages in romantic dyads. *Communication Monographs, 57,* 104–118.

Manusov, V. (2002). Thought and action: Connecting attributions to behaviors in married couples' interactions. In P. Noller & J. A. Feeney (Eds.), *Understanding marriage: Developments in the study of couple interaction* (pp. 14–31). Cambridge: Cambridge University Press.

Manusov, V., & Milstein, T. (2005). Interpreting nonverbal behavior: Representation and transformation frames in Israeli and Palestinian coverage of the 1993 Rabin-Arafat handshake. *Western Journal of Communication, 69,* 183–201.

Masheter, C., & Harris, L. M. (1986). From divorce to friendship: A study of dialectic relationship development. *Journal of Social and Personal Relationships, 3,* 177–189.

Noller, P. (2006). Nonverbal communication in close relationships. In V. Manusov & M. L. Patterson (Eds.), *The Sage handbook of nonverbal communication* (pp. 403–420). Thousand Oaks, CA: Sage.

Planalp, S., & Honeycutt, J. (1985). Events that increase uncertainty in personal relationships. *Human Communication Research, 11,* 593–604.

Prager, K., & Buhrmester, D. (1998). Intimacy and need fulfillment in couple relationships. *Journal of Social and Personal Relationships, 15,* 435–469.

Surra, C., & Huston, T. L. (1987). Mate selection as a social transition. In D. Perlman & S. Duck (Eds.), *Intimate relationships: Development, dynamics, and deterioration* (pp. 88–120). Beverly Hills: Sage.

Thayer, S. (1986). Touch: Frontier of intimacy. *Journal of Nonverbal Behavior, 10,* 7–11.

8

Beyond Facial Expression: Spatial Distance as a Factor in the Communication of Discrete Emotions

Ross Buck and Mike Miller

This chapter examines the role of nonverbal behavior other than facial expressions in displaying and communicating emotion. Our thesis is that a wider variety of displays than are often considered are responsible for communicating a broad assortment of specific emotions, and that one of the primary variables important in this is the spatial distance in the ecology of an organism at which a given emotion is typically displayed. The emotions most associated with facial expressions – the classic *primary affects* including at least happiness, sadness, fear, anger, surprise, and disgust – best function as displays at moderate personal distances. At intimate distances, a variety of emotions including love, lust, gratitude, anger, and sympathy can be reliably communicated through displays involving pheromones and touch. At longer social and public distances, social and moral emotions including pride/arrogance/triumph, guilt/shame/humiliation, envy/jealousy/resentment, and pity/scorn/contempt are communicated through larger and more substantial body postures and gestures associated with ancient dominance and submission displays. Finally, the GREAT emotions (gratitude, respect, elevation, appreciation, and trust) are signaled at a dyadic level via mutually contingent responsiveness and interpersonal synchrony. In addition, vocal prosody has the capability of expressing emotions over a wide variety of distances, from a sigh to a scream. Our analysis allows for the explication of the nonverbal display and communication of an expanded range of specific emotions, consistent with recent and emerging research in affective neuroscience concerning the brain organization of emotions. We combine this analysis of nonverbal emotion communication with a classic and comprehensive approach to interpersonal communication which has not emphasized its emotional aspects: the interpersonal adaptation theory (IAT) of Burgoon, Stern, and Dillman (1995).

Defining emotion

Emotion is traditionally defined in terms of three elements: subjective experience or *affect*; communicative *display*; and physiological *arousal* (Kleinginna & Kleinginna, 1981). These aspects have been termed Emotion I, II, and III, respectively (Buck, 1985). In *The Expression of the Emotions in Man and Animals* (1872/1998), Darwin argued that the display of emotion is essential to social organization across many species including human beings. However, for much of the last century, the concept of emotion was largely ignored in the social and behavioral sciences because its affective aspect seemed fundamentally subjective and therefore beyond the comprehension of objective science.

Facial expression and the renaissance of emotion research

This changed significantly in 1969 with publication in *Science* of the work of Ekman, Sorenson, and Friesen, demonstrating that isolated tribespeople from the New Guinea highlands could accurately identify posed facial expressions of Westerners associated with the primary affects of happiness, sadness, fear, anger, surprise, and disgust; and that Westerners could accurately identify the tribespeoples' posed expressions. The Ekman et al. (1969) findings were made in the context of Silvan Tomkins' (1962–1963) affect theory, which among other things held that the subjective experience of emotion derived from feedback from facial expressions, or *facial feedback*. Thus it initially appeared that the concept of emotion could be related, in principle, to objectively observable and measureable events – facial expressions. The 1969 paper resulted in a renaissance in the study of emotion. Over the years, Ekman, Friesen, and colleagues developed the Facial Action Coding System (FACS) for the objective coding of facial expression, which has in turn spawned a great diversity of automatic coding systems including some controlling artificial facial expressions in androids (Ekman and Friesen, 1978).

At the same time, evidence that facial feedback is the origin of subjective emotional experience has been questioned (e.g., Buck, 1980; Rinn, 1984) and alternative means have been found to study heretofore hidden processes associated with subjectively felt feelings and desires. Much of this has involved the identification of psychoactive drugs and the increased understanding of the neurochemical systems underlying them (e.g., Panksepp, 1998; Pert, 1997). Specific neurochemical systems, particularly involving peptide molecules, have been associated with a variety of subjective feelings and desires, including feelings of elation, depression, anxiety, panic, stress, and nurturance. These are often studied in animals, but new methods have become available for human studies including the introduction of neurochemicals in nasal sprays enabling powerful double-blind research designs. These advances have made it possible to separate the conceptualization and measurement of subjective experiences from the conceptualizations and measurement of displays.

Emotional education

Although the Ekman et al. (1969) result greatly advanced the empirical study of emotion, much research has suggested that the three aspects of emotion – affect, display, and arousal – often do not occur together. People who are overt in their emotional response often show smaller physiological responses than less expressive persons: the internalizing-externalizing phenomenon (Buck & Boone, 2009a, 2009b). Also, it is well known that people often attempt to hide their "true feelings," altering the display of their actual emotions or displaying emotions they do not feel. This has sometimes led to questioning whether the concept of emotion actually exists as a meaningful phenomenon that is accessible to objective science (e.g., Dixon, 2012). However, upon reflection there are compelling reasons to expect that these three aspects of emotion *should not* relate to one another in any simple way.

During normal social development, the three aspects affect, display, and arousal are differently accessible to a responder (e.g., a child) and interaction partners (e.g., a parent). Affect is accessible only for the child, the display is most accessible to the parent, and neither child nor parent has very good access to arousal without special measuring equipment (Buck, 1999). For this reason, a little boy may learn that parents tolerate his aggressive behavior, while a girl may learn that similar behavior is "unladylike" and punished. Similarly, the boy for example may learn that expressions of fear and sadness are not tolerated ("big boys don't cry"), while they are allowed for girls. In both cases, in this process of *emotional education* the punished display is inhibited, perhaps causing stress-related physiological responses and lack of accurate labeling and understanding of the relevant affective state. This can cause both the externalizing-internalizing phenomenon (the child who learns to label and display the appropriate state openly experiences less stress) and the phenomenon of *alexithymia* (no words for mood), where the child does not learn to label and understand accurately the causes of the affective state (Buck, 1993; Nemiah & Sifneos, 1970).

Beyond the face: Display and communication as defining aspects of emotion

Although the face is clearly important in the display and communication of emotion, it is not the only channel of emotion display. A wide variety of behaviors has been included in the "body language" that is involved in nonverbal communication, and many of these are relevant to the display and communication of emotion. In this chapter, we aim first to summarize some of this work and to point out its implications both to the theory of emotion and to nonverbal communication. More specifically, we note that the display and communication of emotion occurs in ecological context – in the context of the relationship of a sending organism and receiving organism within the terrestrial environment – and that a critical variable in this context is the physical distance between sender and receiver. Second, we consider the implications of this expanded view of emotional display and communication to the theory of emotion.

Spatial distance and the ecological context of display and communication

In his classic work *The Hidden Dimension* (1966), Edward T. Hall distinguished four distances according to the sensory impact of an interaction partner. In the closest *intimate* distance (within 18″), the sensory presence of the partner is overwhelming. Odors, including sexual and other body odors, are perceptible and do not carry the social taboos that pertain to odors perceptible at greater distances. Touch, carrying with it the perception of body heat by conduction, is relatively easy; and radiant heat is perceptible without touch. Vision is blurred and perception of the face is distorted. Aurally, expression is through grunts, groans, murmurs, sighs, and whispers. In the second *personal* distance (18″ – 4′), the perception of body odors is taboo, radiant heat is not perceptible, and touch requires deliberate effort. Visually, the face is seen clearly, and whole body movements are seen in peripheral vision. Aurally, casual conventional conversations can occur. In the *social* (4′ – 10′) and *public* (10′ +), distances, odor, touch, and radiant heat are insignificant, although interactions often begin with a handshake in which both reach out. Visually, the finer details of the face are lost but eye behaviors associated with eyebrow movements can be perceived. Upper body gestures are seen clearly at social distances; and at public distances, as the face becomes less distinct the whole body is clearly seen. Aurally, conversation becomes difficult, requiring a loud voice or vocal amplification.

Thus, there are dramatic differences in the impact of different channels of emotional display at these four distances. It seems reasonable to suggest that these channels are associated with the expression and communication of distinctly different specific emotions. Facial expression is suited to personal more than intimate distances, where the face is overwhelmed by other stimuli, relatively difficult to perceive, and distorted. Going from social to public distances, the relative efficacy of facial expression in accurately displaying and communicating emotion should gradually fall, as the relative efficiency of gestures and larger body movements becomes more informative. The following paragraphs discuss emotional display and communication at intimate and social/public distances.

The intimate context: Pheromones and touch

Pheromonal communication

Pheromones are traditionally defined as chemical substances secreted by a sender individual that trigger behavioral and social responses in receiver individuals of the same species. They have been studied in species ranging from single-celled prokaryotes to vertebrates, although their functioning in human beings is controversial. Some pheromones have been observed to show remarkable conservation across evolution: for example the peptide Gonadotropin Releasing Hormone (GnRH) functions as a sexual pheromone in unicellular yeast (*Saccharomyces cerevisiae*), is a sexual neurotransmitter in rats, and has been implicated in erotic affect in human beings (O'Day & Horgen, 1981; Loumaye, Thorner & Catt, 1982; Panksepp, 1998; Kohl et al., 2001; Kohl & Francoeur, 2012).

Pheromones have been extensively studied in insects, and pheromonal communication has been demonstrated to underlie the complex social structures of such familiar creatures as termites, ants, and bees. In familiar animals such as dogs and cats, the actions of pheromones are particularly evident in territorial and sexual behaviors. No human pheromones have been identified with certainty. Putative human pheromones include *androstadienone*, a metabolite of testosterone present in male sweat, urine, and seminal fluid; and *copulins*, which increase in women in the vaginal fluid prior to ovulation (Michael et al., 1975).

Responses to pheromones have been associated with the vomeronasal organ (VNO), a small olfactory sensory structure in the nasal septum that is detectable by endoscopy. The VNO sends input to the amygdala and hypothalamus, bypassing brain centers involved in higher cognitive processing. The VNO has been widely considered to be vestigial and nonfunctional in adult human beings (Mast & Samuelsen, 2009), and there are suggestions that pheromonal communication may be mediated by other structures in human beings (e.g., Frasnelli et al., 2011).

Despite the uncertainty regarding the VNO, evidence remains for pheromonal communication in human beings (see Wysocki & Preti, 2004, for review). Pheromones fulfill several roles in human communication. *Primer* pheromones display endocrine and reproductive states. Martha McClintock and colleagues reported evidence that the menstrual cycles of co-habiting women can become synchronized, a phenomenon termed the McClintock effect (McClintock, 1971; Hummer & McClintock, 2009). Although controversial, the reality of the phenomenon is now generally accepted (Wysocki & Preti, 2004). Pheromones also appear to serve *signal* functions in humans, often associated with the immune system. The major histocompatibility complex (MHC) is a protein present on the membrane of all body cells that is slightly different for every individual, and therefore can function to identify cells belonging in the body. Similarity in MHC structure varies with the degree of genetic relatedness. MHC also plays a major role in the determination of body odor. When women smell t-shirts worn by men for five days without washing, their ratings of the attractiveness of the odor increases with the degree of difference between their own MHC complex and that of the man. This has been suggested as an incest avoidance mechanism signaling mating compatibility (Ober et al., 1997). The "odor print" associated with MHC also seems to signal kin and biological recognition (e.g., between mother and child), social dominance/submission, and possibly sexual orientation (Berglund et al., 2006).

Other functions ascribed to human pheromones include *releaser* functions, in which the pheromone directly elicits an immediate response, and *moderator* functions, where the pheromones exert their influence less directly by altering mood. Direct releaser functions have been relatively difficult to demonstrate in human beings, perhaps the clearest examples being the appetitive responses of the newborn to the milk and breast of the mother (Contreras et al., 2013). There is also evidence that pheromones are involved in sexual attraction: smelling androstadienone has produced higher levels of salivary cortisol (CORT) in women (Wyart et al., 2007). Wyart and colleagues also replicated other work showing that smelling androstadienone was associated with larger changes in rated positive mood and sexual arousal, as well as composite physiological arousal.

There is considerable evidence of the moderating effects of human pheromones on mood (e.g., Chen & Haviland-Jones, 1999). This is of particular interest because an evolution from releaser to modulator functions is consistent with the general increase in behavioral flexibility that may be a central function of experienced affect (Buck, 1985, 1999, 2014). Rather than inflexibly controlling behavior, the moderating function allows the pheromone to *cajole* behavior – to persuade or wheedle the individual, as it were – thus giving the individual the ultimate power of choice. Sexual affect allows the individual choice of how to respond: the affect is controlled by the pheromone, but the receiver's response to it is not.

Tactile communication

Much like the modalities of facial expression and vocalics, research pertaining to human touch as an agent for emotive exchanges spans multiple fields of inquiry, ranging from the neurological sciences to the social sciences. Findings from these fields offer similar support that emotions can be encoded into touch expressions by senders and decoded by receivers; emotions such as lust, anger, fear, happiness, sadness, disgust, love, gratitude, and sympathy have all been shown to be communicable via touch (Clynes, 1977; Hertenstein et al., 2006; Hertenstein et al., 2009). The next section provides two emergent explanations for how and why emotion is communicated by the modality of touch. This is followed by a discussion of the intimate body distance required for touch and subsequent emotions best conveyed at that distance.

Some scholars theorize that humans have evolved emotive touch communication by way of prosocial exchanges. They suggest that reliable and mutually rewarding tactile signals of altruism may have emerged over long-term interactions because they help to identify cooperative individuals who present a high likelihood for pleasurable exchanges (Frank, 2002; Sober, 2002; Hertenstein et al., 2006, 2009). From this perspective, infants and adults alike experience and exchange emotions through touch based on the positive or negative emotions they associate with the exchanges. Hertenstein et al. (2006) provided evidence for this perspective by having participants engage in a blind touch experiment where they sat across from one another, separated by a black curtain. The experiment entailed the sender using their hand to express twelve emotions by touching a receiver anywhere from their elbow to their fingertips; senders were free to choose any form of touch they wanted and receivers were blind to the touch since their arms were pushed through the curtain onto the senders' side of a table separating them. Results indicated that participants from both the United States and Spain were able to decode the emotions of anger, fear, disgust, love, and sympathy at better than chance levels using blind touch and also when viewing touch interactions that were recorded during the experiment; the emotions of happiness, sadness, embarrassment, envy, pride, surprise, and gratitude were not decoded at above chance levels. Further evidence came from Hertenstein et al. (2009) who expanded the regions where senders could touch receivers. In the follow-up study senders were able to touch blindfolded receivers anywhere on their body (intimate regions were excluded) again using a free form touch or a touch of their choosing. Using full body touch the emotions of happiness, anger, fear, sadness, disgust, love, gratitude, and sympathy were decoded by receivers at above chance levels. In summary, the research by Hertenstein and colleagues provides evidence that touch communicates specific emotions directly. The findings have been framed around the notion that humans have evolved cooperative, altruistic, mutual systems of emotion exchange using touch (Keltner et al., 2006).

Others have suggested that the duration and shape of human touch expressions coincide with universal, algorithmic brain responses, which in turn coincide with specific emotions (Clynes, 1977, 1988; Morrison et al., 2010). For example, Morrison and colleagues (2010) showed that the human brain processes touch that is viewed similarly to touch that is actually experienced, and suggested that humans may have a biological capacity (i.e., the touch system is designed) to predict emotions, intentions, and future interactions based on viewing or enacting touch. This perspective suggests that tactile communication works like a lock and key system, whereby a touch that most closely resembles a universal form related to an emotion (e.g., love) has the greatest potential to unlock that emotion for both the sender and receiver.

Clynes' (1977) theory of *sentics* offers potential universal time and shape touch expressions that coincide with the emotions of anger, hate, love, joy, sadness, sex, and reverence. These emotions were chosen based upon their relationship to emotions or feeling states experienced while playing or listening to music and their contagion nature (e.g., like laughter they are "contagious" when expressed). To test sentic theory Clynes (1977) measured emotion expression by having participants fantasize a given emotion and then express it by pushing down on a button attached to a *sentograph* which measured the horizontal and vertical pressure of the touch movement over time. Participants pushed the button multiple times to generate an aggregate expression and were cued at quasi-randomly timed intervals to push down. The rationale behind using only a simple touch was to eliminate potentially extraneous degrees of freedom associated with more complex movements; the choice of a finger according to Clynes (1977) is inconsequential, and he reported that a paraplegic participant generated the expected time shape forms by pushing down on the sentograph button with the head (Clynes, 1977). Clynes' research on communicating emotions using touch provided evidence that individuals in various cultures (Australia, Bali, Japan, and a remote Australian Aboriginal tribe) not only generated similar time shape forms when expressing anger, hate, love, joy, sadness, sex, and reverence but were also able to decode emotions by watching a video-taped finger expressing the emotions at better than chance levels. Clynes concluded that the touch-emotion system develops much in the same way that our organs develop and is ultimately coded into our DNA.

The evolutionary and pressure duration/shape perspectives on emotion communication and touch are not incompatible and may in fact work together to represent two separate systems working together, with one system informing the other. For example, it may be that humans have an innate biologically designed tactile-emotion system yoked tightly to the time shape forms that Clynes discovered using the sentograph. In addition, the tactile-emotion system described by Hertenstein and colleagues which utilized free form touch may, in many cases, represent larger adaptations of Clynes' time shape forms. Hence free form touch may indeed be indicative of a psychologically evolved manner of expressing emotions through physical contact. With these theoretical interpretations in mind we move forward to consider the role that proximity plays in restricting and/or enhancing emotion communication via touch, for physical contact is of course contingent upon proximity.

Spatial distance and the communication of emotions through touch

Using mock interactions with mannequins (for senders) and videotapes of these interactions (for receivers) App, McIntosh, Reed, and Hertenstein (2011) showed that the communicative efficacy of specific emotion displays is related to the modality in which they are displayed along with the social function of the display. Examining the nonverbal channels of body, face, and touch, they found that three emotions clusters, based on efficiency in sending and receiving, formed around each of the three channels. From these data and in conjunction with the perspective that the communication of emotions is most strongly tied to the communicator's social goals, they formed three categories for each cluster of emotions and its counterpart display channel: facial displays were labeled survival-focused and contained the emotions anger, disgust, fear, happiness, and sadness; body displays were labeled social status, comprised of embarrassment, guilt, pride, and shame; and lastly, touch displays were labeled intimate and contained the emotions love and sympathy. In all, the study by App et al. (2011) showed that the efficiency of communicating certain emotions shares a relationship with display modalities and can be explained using an evolutionary perspective focused on the link between emotions and social functions. As the authors indicated, there are other plausible interpretations of their findings and the external validity of the study was hindered by the use of mannequins and video tape footage. With these limitations in mind, we offer an additive rather than alternative explanation for the emotions found to relate most strongly to tactile communication. In conjunction with social functions we believe a stronger emphasis on spatial distance and the ecological constraints and opportunities it affords helps expand the proposed social evolutionary theoretical framework.

Physical touch provides a direct pathway from human to human for emotional expression and displays. We use touch at differing stages of development to directly convey intimate feelings and emotions associated with procreation (lust), nurturance (love and sympathy), threat (anger), and exploration (trust). Enactment and reception of trust may be a manifestation of accurately communicating or not communicating the first four emotions and building a close relationship (Dunbar, 2010). In the case of each physical behavior, touch is a minimum requirement; that is, breastfeeding, grooming, sexual intercourse, and rough and tumble play all require extended patterns of touch. By extension, the emotional corollaries of the aforementioned behaviors, lust, love, sympathy, anger, and trust, may best be conveyed, communicated, and consummated at distances that afford physical touch.

Distinguishing emotions conveyed at close distances can be confusing because touch often has some degree of equipotentiality (communicative outcomes can be reached by a variety of behaviors) and equifinality (a variety of meanings can be ascribed to the same behavior) (App et al., 2011). Because of this, quickly distinguishing variations in micro time shape expressions seems particularly useful to both humans and primates. To extrapolate this proposition and integrate it with the evolutionary social function perspective we can examine the potential confusion of a gentle loving touch with a gentle lustful touch, e.g., as friendly and encouraging or as sexually invasive. Consider being touched on the shoulder with a gentle squeeze, context aside; you can interpret the emotional motivation driving this type of touch in several ways. Because all contextual cues during touch are not always available it seems that a touch-emotion system would benefit from and even necessitate a fast process for quickly identifying emotions at intimate distances. A growing body of research indicates that, through grooming, animals form what are consistently referred to as nonsexual friendship (Dagg, 2011), suggesting that these animals distinguish touch that is sexual versus nonsexual. Interestingly, research suggests that rhesus macaques are unable or chose not to distinguish between grooming touch and sexual touch and often the former is exchanged for the latter (Massen et al., 2010). Moving back to the shoulder touch case involving humans, we no doubt benefit from being able to distinguish emotion motivations of physical contact sans a detailed assessment of all contextual cues due to the threat and speed at which touch with malicious intent could become harmful. A consideration of rough and tumble play and actual fighting offers another situation characterized by close physical contact where subtle variations in movements and pressure can quickly alter the playful nature of an exchange to one in which touch motivated by anger escalates the exchange. Despite the potential for this escalation, human children and a myriad of other animals engage in such play, often times easily negotiating the forms of touch and pressure necessary to not emotionally escalate their social exchange (Goodall, 1986; Burghardt, 2005; Pellegrini, 1991).

Touch of course does not happen in a relational vacuum and therefore the notion of a fast process of distinguishing certain emotions that requires the elimination of all distance between communicators is made more useful by combining the evolutionary social goals perspective. We suggest that the micro movements related to emotions persist in humans but have been translated into efficient macro touch movements that still maintain a relationship to the basic emotions related to touch (i.e. lust, love, sympathy, anger, and trust). One example of how a species has adapted a more macro expression of sympathy and/ or love in addition to grooming comes from the research on New World monkeys. Specifically, spider monkeys with close social ties have been documented exchanging embraces similar to human hugs (Schaffner & Aureli, 2005).This is suggestive that spider monkeys may have taken the simple micro touch motions associated with grooming (soft brush to the side and firm pull) and evolved them to more macro expressions that serve less of a hygienic function. Indeed, scholars have pointed out that primates groom one another far longer than is necessary to maintain proper hygiene (Dunbar, 2010) thus an alternate emergent touch to express love or sympathy that takes less time but elicits and conveys the same emotion is adaptive for the species.

The social/public context: Body movement and posture

At larger distances, other displays take over the functions of nonverbal communication. At personal distances facial expressions function best, as noted previously. At social and public distances, body movement and gesture take the lead, as it were, in nonverbal emotional communication. This is particularly evident in the ancient displays of dominance and submission that have organized the social behaviors of animals for many millions of years, including non-vertebrates such as lobsters and crayfish (see, e.g., Livingstone et al., 1980).

In contrast to the relatively widespread agreement concerning primary affects engendered by agreement regarding their display, there is little agreement among emotion theorists about social emotions such as pride, guilt, shame, envy, or jealousy; or moral emotions such as triumph and humiliation. Often these are considered to be "higher level" emotions, requiring complex cognitive processes involving a sense of self in comparison with abstract standards of conduct; indeed, they are often termed "self-conscious" emotions (e.g., Tracy & Robins, 2004).

If one considers that social and moral emotions typically occur in the context of social comparisons, it implies that the social and moral emotions of one person are not independent of those of others. More specifically, specific social and moral emotions can be seen to exist together in dynamic systems that emerge naturally in situations of relative success and failure of a person (P) vis-à-vis a comparison other (CO). For example, if P succeeds relative to CO, P experiences what is termed in English *pride/arrogance* relative to CO and regards CO with *pity/scorn*. The relatively unsuccessful CO experiences *guilt/shame* relative to P and regards P with *envy/jealousy*. We suggest these as four twin *primary social emotions*: "twins" in the sense that they tend to co-occur. Moral emotions are associated with learned expectations expressed in notions of distributive and retributive justice, that specify how good and bad outcomes, respectively, *should* be meted out (Homans, 1966). They provide the affective motivational force – the "fire" – underlying the sense of justice, creating powerful analogs of social emotions: specifically, *triumph/modesty*; *humiliation/indignation*; *admiration/resentment*; and *contempt/sympathy* are suggested as primary moral emotions (Buck, 2014).

We suggest that dominance and submission display universal social and moral emotions: dominance behaviors signal the sender's Pride/Arrogance and Pity/Scorn toward the CO, submission behaviors signal the sender's Guilt/Shame and Envy/Jealousy toward the CO. Thus dominance-submission behaviors display all of the social emotions simultaneously: a *system of social emotions*. Pride has been associated with a dominant posture with the torso out and the chest expanded; and shame with the opposite, submissive posture with slumped shoulders (Tracy & Matsumoto, 2008; Matsumoto & Hwang, 2012). All else equal, moral emotions tend to be stronger than social emotions and are associated with more powerful dominance and submission displays: for example, winning an Olympic game (Triumph) has been associated, like Pride, with torso out and the expanded chest, but unlike Pride, there is also a facial grimace with the head tilted forward and the arms raised in a punching motion; and there is a vocal shout or utterance possibly to signal intimidation. Losing (Humiliation) in contrast is associated with a more powerful version of the shame display, with the same slumped submissive posture but with hiding of the face and possibly weeping: the "agony of defeat" (Matsumoto & Hwang, 2012).

Emergent dynamic system of social and moral emotions

We suggest that the universal social and moral emotions emerge naturally and directly in the context of interpersonal interaction, particularly rough and tumble play. They emerge in animals as well as humans based upon the extent of their sociality; and have even been observed in animals who have established relationships with individuals of another species (e.g., lion and coyote, Great Dane and deer, goat and horse; Flanagan & Fleming, 2012). They are displayed in dominance and submission behaviors. As Figure 8.1 illustrates, the relative success of a person P is associated with feelings of Pride/Arrogance and a tendency to regard less successful comparison persons (COs) with Pity/Scorn. In turn, the relatively less successful partner tends to feel Guilt/Shame and to regard the successful comparison person with Envy/Jealousy.

Social emotions involve social comparisons of relative gain and loss, while moral emotions additionally involve considerations of fairness. Outcomes perceived as fair minimize conflict, while outcomes perceived as unfair exacerbate conflict. Eight primary moral emotions emerge during interpersonal interaction, where the issue is not only the relative success and failure of P and CO, but whether that success or failure was perceived to be deserved. The success of person P is associated with Triumph if seen as deserved, and Modesty if seen as undeserved (moments of triumph are often moderated by expressions of modesty). In contrast, failure on the part of person P is associated with Humiliation if regarded as fair – the agony of justified defeat – but with bitter Indignation if regarded as unfair. Relative success on the part of a comparison other is regarded with Admiration if perceived as fair, but acrimonious Resentment if perceived as unfair. Relative failure of a CO,

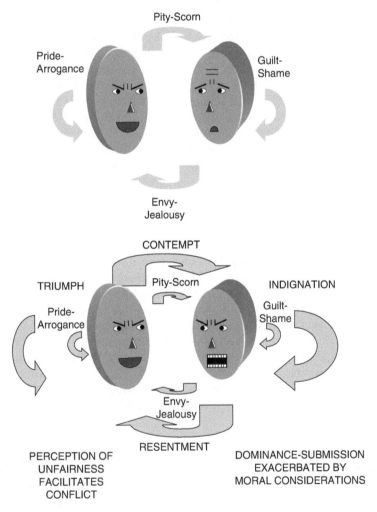

Figure 8.1 Emergent dynamic systems of social and moral emotions

on the other hand, is regarded with Contempt if perceived as fair, and Sympathy if perceived as unfair (Buck, 2014). The emergent dynamic systems of social and moral emotions are illustrated in Figure 8.1.

GREAT emotions of Gratitude, Respect, Elevation, Appreciation, and Trust

The social and moral emotions relate to situations in which there is comparison and potentially conflict between individuals: where one occupies a "one-up" and the other a "one-down" position in some regard. They do not occur when the relationship of two persons is equal and lacking conflict. Such essentially cooperative relationships bring us to another class of social/moral emotions, which, using their English terms in an appropriate acronym, we term the GREAT emotions: Gratitude, Respect, Elevation, Appreciation, and Trust. Not only do the GREAT emotions occur in an egalitarian relationship, but also their expression and communication do maintains that equality. Also, whereas the social and moral emotions tend to involve stress, the GREAT emotions buffer stress, functioning to maintain a social bioregulation associated with physical health and wellness.

GREAT emotions must be mutually shared. This sharing is so natural that it is virtually invisible: we tend to notice the GREAT emotions only in their absence. In ordinary life, they are expressed in rituals of politeness. For example, in contrast with the interactants in Figure 8.1, those experiencing the GREAT emotions are mutually supportive of one another (see Figure 8.2). Individual 1 regards individual 2 with the GREAT emotions, which supports the identity and self-image of individual 2; while individual 2 reciprocates by regarding individual 1 with the GREAT emotions, thus supporting their identity and self-image. This mutual sharing is a hallmark of the GREAT emotions: in effect you must give in order to get (Buck, 2004). Whereas social and moral emotions tend to occur at times of conflict, and are not entirely comfortable for either party, in the exchange of the GREAT emotions the mutual support is comfortable and perhaps confers much the stress-buffering aspect of social support (Buck, 1993).

Far from being rare or unusual, the GREAT emotions are ubiquitous but generally fly below the radar of consciousness and are rarely noticed, evident for example in conventional displays of politeness and good manners. In these simple interactions, we essentially tell one another that we mutually acknowledge that we in effect are "in it together" and support one another. While the presence of such polite accommodation

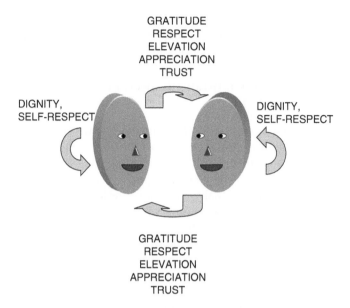

GRATITUDE
RESPECT
ELEVATION
APPRECIATION
TRUST

DIGNITY,
SELF-RESPECT

DIGNITY,
SELF-RESPECT

GRATITUDE
RESPECT
ELEVATION
APPRECIATION
TRUST

Figure 8.2   Emergent dynamic system of GREAT emotions (Gratitude, Respect, Elevation, Appreciation, and Trust)

may be so universally expected as to be unnoticed, certainly the ABSENCE of an expected display of politeness is noticed and responded to with remarkable strength and negativity as a sign of disrespect.

Mutually contingent responsiveness and the GREAT emotions

Just as social and moral emotions are nonverbally displayed and communicated via dominance and submission behaviors, and biological emotions via pheromones, touch, and facial expression, the GREAT emotions are nonverbally displayed and communicated via mutually contingent responsiveness: behaviors of interpersonal synchrony, mirroring, and reciprocity. Mutually contingent responsiveness fosters the emergence of *primary intersubjectivity*, in which each interaction partner is automatically attuned to the subjective state displayed by the other (Trevarthen, 1979). Given mutually contingent responsiveness, primary intersubjectivity takes place automatically, directly, naturally, and unconsciously. It is at this point that we seek to integrate the present analysis with a classic theory of interpersonal communication: *Interpersonal adaptation theory.*

Interpersonal adaptation theory

Interaction adaptation theory has been designed to predict communicative responses to nonverbal displays. Literature relevant to interpersonal adaptation theory (IAT) dates back to motor mimicry research (Hull, 1933) and spans biological, affective/arousal, social, communicative, and cognitive paradigms. This section follows the path of theoretical perspectives laid out by Burgoon et al. (1995) in their original conceptualization of IAT. Specifically, as the theory's name implies, it takes on an interactive sender and receiver (e.g., communicative) perspective.

Matching

IAT considers an initial group of "matching" theories that include interactional synchrony (Cappella, 1991; Condon & Ogston, 1966; 1967), motor mimicry (Allport, 1968), and mirroring (Kendon, 1970), all of which place biology at the root of interaction adaptation. These theories highlight an often preconscious, reflexive human drive to reciprocate others during interactions (e.g. match vocal tones, facial expressions, and expressed emotions). Burgoon et al. (1995) used these theories to illustrate the biological need-driven component of human interaction and adaptation; recognizing that although the need to mimic or reciprocate can be thought of as largely universal and involuntary, it is also influenced by environmental and social factors.

Affect arousal

The next theories that bear on IAT stem from interpersonal communication research and center on the influence of arousal and affect in driving approach and avoidance tendencies in interactions. Unlike the "matching" theories, affect and arousal theories such as affiliative conflict theory (Argyle & Cook, 1976), dialectical models (Baxter, 1992), and arousal labeling theory (Patterson, 1976) tend to predict reciprocity and compensation rather than just reciprocity. This group of theories adds psychological components to the previous mentioned biological models and brings the push-and-pull tensions of human communication to the forefront.

Social norms

Following an appraisal of these theories, Burgoon et al. (1995) considered the social-norm models such as the norm of reciprocity (Gouldner, 1960), communication accommodation theory (Giles, Coupland, & Coupland, 1991), and social exchange theory (Roloff & Campion,

1985). The first two tend to emphasize reciprocity in interactions or express conditions which make reciprocity likely. Communication accommodation theory, on the other hand, offers a social model in which interactants may be motivated to converge or diverge based on factors like in-group or out-group status. Social-norm models further layer the interpersonal adaptation landscape by emphasizing the influence of conformity pressures.

Communication and cognition

The final theories that bear on the development of IAT are labeled by Burgoon et al. (1995) as communication and cognitive models. They include theories like the sequential-functional model (Patterson, 1983), expectancy violation theory (EVT) (Burgoon & Hale, 1988), and cognitive valance theory (CVT) (Andersen, 1998). These theories approach interactions from a functionalist perspective. That is, they focus on the communicative purposes or outcomes of interactions as the determinants of communication that is reciprocal or not.

As a whole, all of the aforementioned theories make interaction predictions for reciprocity or divergence based on differing driving forces that vary by external and internal conditions. Interpersonal adaptation theory (IAT) is informed by the theoretical tenets and empirical support of these perspectives offering a predictive, communicative theory, driven by an aggregate weight of multiple forces.

Interaction position

Three key elements proposed by IAT make up what is referred to as one's interaction position (behavioral predisposition for interaction behaviors) (Burgoon et al., 1995). Interaction positions stem from what is *required*, *expected*, and *desired* from interpersonal interactions, that is, what is biologically needed, socially anticipated, and individually wanted (based on mood or personality). The IAT model examines interactions by adding up an individual's required (r), expected (e), and desired (d) interactions and then calculating an interaction position (IP), (IP = r + e + d). Following this, an individual's IP is compared to the actual interaction (A) that takes place.

The IAT model also addresses one's interaction position based upon predispositions toward individuals (e.g., how much an individual is liked). It is posited that when liked individuals' actual behaviors (A) are higher than one's interaction position (IP), approach behaviors result. The same scenario for disliked individuals results in avoidance behaviors. In addition, when liked individuals actual behaviors (A) are less than one's interaction position (IP), compensatory or maintenance behaviors result, whereas in the case of disliked individual's actual behaviors (A) being less than one's interaction position (IP), compensatory or maintenance behaviors are avoided (Burgoon et al., 1995).

Lastly, IAT indicates that any of the three key interaction position variables can dominate. That is, in any given situation with a particular individual, that which is required, expected, or desired can take precedent. For example, in the case of massaging between cross-sex friends, emotionally needy friends might be expected to have interaction positions that reflect most strongly the element of "desired" (the model represents emphasized elements via capital letters, thus this example would be represented as IP = r + e + D). The ability to give weight to individual interaction position variables increases the predictive and modeling power of IAT.

IAT and the GREAT Emotions

Interaction adaptation theory is particularly well suited to consider individuals' adaptive emotional responses related to gratitude, respect, elevation, appreciation, and trust. Consider three Olympic swimmers competing for one gold medal. Only one can win the race and the medal but all of them will likely emote something to the winner post-race either deliberately or not. To predict the emotion displays of the two losers we can use IAT to first examine the interaction position (IP) of each swimmer toward, for sake of argument, the eventual winner. Following this we can predict triumphant and elevated body postures displayed by the winner and then, based on each swimmer's IP toward the winner, we can predict whether or not they will reciprocate with a GREAT emotion display or not.

More specifically, consider that swimmer 1 (Goodkind) wins the race, swimmer 2 (Limon) loses and has a negative IP toward Goodkind, and lastly swimmer 3 (Mirron) loses and has a positive IP toward Goodkind. Utilizing IAT we can further elucidate the Limon and Mirron's interaction position (IP) toward Goodkind by considering their individual requirements, expectations, and desires. The following illustrate their individual interaction positions within the given ecological context.

Swimmer Limon's Interaction position toward Goodkind at the Olympics.

Required (r): Limon has been competing against Goodkind for ten years and never won a race. He gets very anxious and stressed out when interacting with Goodkind.

Expected (e):   He expects that this is his last chance to beat Goodkind and expects to win.

Desired (d):   Limon would like nothing more than to have Goodkind experience the disappointment that he himself has experienced.

Swimmer Mirron's Interaction positions toward Goodkind at the Olympics.

Required (r):   Mirron and Goodkind are friends and training partners. Mirron is physically comfortable and happy interacting with Goodkind.

Expected (e):   Mirron has never beat Goodkind and does not expect to win the race.

Desired (d):   Mirron would be pleased to have his friend win a gold medal.

Based upon IAT, a bodily expression of triumph by Goodkind after winning the race would result in a GREAT emotion reciprocation or matching from Mirron; he might express respect for his swim training partner. In turn, the same triumphant bodily expression viewed by Limon would result in compensation and a lack of convergence of a GREAT emotion; he may instead show the bodily displays of shame, envy, and humiliation. In this example, the swimmers' emotional reactions to Goodkind are a result of small or large disparities between their IP (predispositions for higher involvement and immediacy, coupled with liking or affiliation) and the actual (A) emotional immediacy display being enacted by Goodkind along with the display's associated level of involvement (see Figure 8.3).

The example in Figure 8.3 is a simple offering of the predictive modeling power of IAT in regards to social and moral emotion displays and subsequent reactions. As Burgoon and Hale (1998) suggest, more complex interaction models can be used such as longitudinal modeling (e.g. Markov chain analysis) or recursive, dyadic modeling (see Powers et al., 2011 for a relevant example) in conjunction with IAT to predict the impact of prior or subsequent displays and reactions. Additionally a consideration could be made and modeled regarding the influence of each of the three components of the swimmer's interaction positions. It may be that at the Olympics what is required (biologically needed) carries more emotional weight due to the magnitude of the event. Moreover IAT appears useful in predicting and examining the

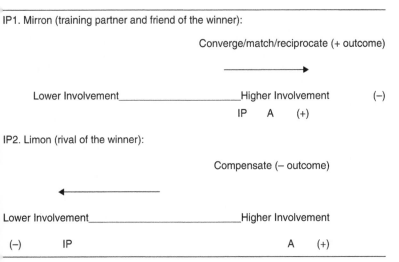

IP1. Mirron (training partner and friend of the winner):

Converge/match/reciprocate (+ outcome)

Lower Involvement_____Higher Involvement   (–)

                                        IP   A   (+)

IP2. Limon (rival of the winner):

Compensate (– outcome)

Lower Involvement_____Higher Involvement

(–)   IP   A   (+)

Figure 8.3 Emotional reactions to a triumphant display by a swim race winner
Source: Adapted from Burgoon, Stern, and Dillman (1995, p. 273).

probability of reciprocity in regards to the expression of gratitude, respect, elevation, appreciation, and trust.

References

Allport, G. W. (1968). The historical background of modern social psychology. In G. Lindzey & E. Aronson (Eds.), *Handbook of social psychology* (2nd ed., pp. 1–80). Reading, MA: Addison-Wesley.

Andersen, P. A. (1998). The cognitive valence theory of intimate communication. In M. Palmer & G. Barnett (Eds.), *Progress in communication sciences vol. XIV. Mutual influence in interpersonal communication: Theory and research in cognition, affect, and behavior* (pp. 39–72). Stamford, CT: Ablex Publishing Corporation.

App, B., McIntosh, D., Reed, C., & Hertenstein, M. (2011). Nonverbal channel use in communication of emotion: How may depend on why. *Emotion, 11,* 603–617.

Argyle, M., & Cook, M. (1976). *Gaze and mutual gaze.* Cambridge: Cambridge University Press.

Baxter, L. A. (1992). Forms and functions of intimate play in personal relationships. *Human Communication Research, 18,* 336–363.

Berglund, H., Lindstrom, P., & Savic, I. (2006). Brain response to putative pheromones in lesbian women. *PNAS Proceedings of the National Academy of Sciences of the United States of America, 103,* 8269–8274. doi: 10.1073/pnas.0600331103.

Buck, R. (1980). Nonverbal behavior and the theory of emotion: The facial feedback hypothesis. *Journal of Personality and Social Psychology, 38*(5), 811–824. doi: 10.1037/0022-3514.38.5.811.

Buck, R. (1985). Prime theory: An integrated view of motivation and emotion. *Psychological Review, 92*(3), 389–413. doi: 10.1037/0033-295X.92.3.389.

Buck, R. (1993). Emotional communication, emotional competence, and physical illness: A developmental-interactionist view. In H. Traue & J. W. Pennebaker (Eds.), *Emotional expressiveness, inhibition, and health* (pp. 32–56). Seattle, WA: Hogrefe and Huber.

Buck, R. (1999). The biological affects: A typology. *Psychological Review, 106*(2), 301–336.

Buck, R. (2004). The gratitude of exchange and the gratitude of caring: A developmental-interactionist perspective of moral emotion. In R. A. Emmons & M. McCullough (Eds.), *The psychology of gratitude* (pp. 100–122). New York: Oxford University Press.

Buck, R. (2014). *Emotion: A biosocial synthesis.* New York, NY: Cambridge University Press.

Buck, R., & Boone, R. T. (2009a). Internalizer. In D. Sander & K. Scherer (Eds.), *Oxford companion to emotion and the affective sciences* (p. 222). New York: Oxford University Press.

Buck, R., & Boone, R. T. (2009b). Externalizer. In D. Sander & K. Scherer (Eds.), *Oxford companion to emotion and the affective sciences* (p. 169). New York: Oxford University Press.

Burghardt, G. M. (2005). *The genesis of animal play: Testing the limits.* Cambridge, MA: The MIT Press.

Burgoon, J., & Hale, J. (1988). Nonverbal expectancy violations: Model elaboration and application to immediacy behaviors. *Communication Monographs, 55*(1), 58–79.

Burgoon, J., Stern, L. A., & Dillman, L. (1995). *Interpersonal adaptation: Dyadic interaction patterns.* Cambridge: Cambridge University Press.

Cappella, J. N. (1991). The biological origins of automated patterns of human interaction. *Communication Theory, 1,* 4–35.

Chen, D., & Haviland-Jones, J. (1999). Rapid mood change and human odors. *Physiology & Behavior, 68,* 241–250.

Clynes, M. (1977). *Sentics, the touch of the emotions.* New York: Anchor Press.

Clynes, M. (1988). Generalized emotion, how it is produced and sentic cycle therapy. In M. Clynes & J. Panksepp (Eds.), *Emotions and psychopathology* (pp. 107–170). New York, NY: Plenum Press.

Condon, W. S., & Ogston, W. D. (1966). Sound film analysis of normal and pathological behavior patterns. *Journal of Nervous and Mental Disease, 143,* 338–247.

Condon, W. S., & Ogston, W. D. (1967). A segmentation of behavior. *Journal of Psychiatric Research, 5,* 221–235.

Contreras, C. M., Gutierrez-Garcia, A. G., Mendoza-Lopez, R., Rodriguez-Landa, J. F., Bernal-Morales, B., & Diaz-Marte, C. (2013). Amniotic fluid elicits appetitive responses in human newborns: Fatty acids and appetitive responses. *Developmental Psychobiology, 55,* 221–231. doi: 10.1002/dev.21012.

Dagg, A. (2011). *Animal friendships.* New York: Cambridge University Press.

Darwin, C. (1998). *The expression of the emotions in man and animals* (3rd ed.). New York: Oxford University Press (Original work published 1872).

Dixon, T. (2012). "Emotion": The history of a keyword in crisis. *Emotion Review, 4,* 338–344.

Dunbar, R. (2010). The social role of touch in humans and primates: Behavioral function and neurobiological mechanisms. *Neuroscience and Biobehavioral Reviews, 34,* 260–268. doi: 10.1016/j.neubiorev.2008.07.001.

Ekman, P., & Friesen, V.W. (1978). *Facial Action Coding System (FACS): A technique for the measurement of facial action* (pp. 19–46). Palo Alto, CA: Consulting Psychologists Press.

Flanagan, S. (Writer), & Fleming, S. K. (Director). (2012). Animal Odd Couples [Television series episode]. In F. Kaufman (Executive producer), *Nature.* New York: Public Broadcasting System.

Ekman, P., Sorenson, E. R., & Friesen, W. V. (1969). Pan-cultural elements in facial displays of emotion. *Science, 164*(3875), 86–88.

Frank, R. H. (2002). Altruism in competitive environments. In R. J. Davidson & A. Harrington (Eds.), *Visions of compassion* (pp. 182–211). New York: Oxford University Press.

Frasnelli, J., Lundström, J. N., Boyle, J. A., Katsarkas, A., & Jones-Gotmann, M. (2011). The vomeronasal organ is not involved in the perception of endogenous odors. *Human Brain Mapping, 32,* 450–460.

Giles, H., Coupland, J., & Coupland, N. (1991). *Contexts of accommodation.* Cambridge: Cambridge University Press.

Goodall, J. (1986). *The chimpanzees of Gombe: Patterns of behavior.* Cambridge, MA: Belknap Press.

Gouldner, A. W. (1960). The norm of reciprocity: A preliminary statement. *American Sociological Review, 25,* 161–178.

Hall, E. T. (1966). *The hidden dimension.* Garden City, NY: Doubleday.

Hertenstein, M., Keltner, D., App, B., Bulleit, A., & Jaskolka, A. (2006). Touch communicates distinct emotions. *Emotion, 6,* 528–533. doi: 10.1037/1528-3542.6.3.528.

Hertenstein, M., Holmes, R., Keltner, D., & McCullough, M. (2009). The communication of emotion via touch. *Emotion, 9,* 566–573. doi: 10.1037/a0016108.

Homans, G. C. (1966). *Social behavior: Its elementary forms.* New York: Harcourt, Brace & World.

Hull, C. L. (1933). *Hypnosis and suggestibility.* New York: Appleton-Century.

Hummer, T. A., & McClintock, M. K. (2009). Putative human pheromone androstadienone attunes the mind specifically to emotional information. *Hormones and Behavior, 55,* 548–559.

Keltner, D., Horberg, E. J., & Oveis, C. (2006). Emotional intuitions and moral play. *Social Justice Research, 19,* 208–217.

Kendon, A. (1970). Movement coordination in social interaction: Some examples described. *ActaPsychologica, 32,* 100–125.

Kleinginna, P. R., & Kleinginna, A. M. (1981). A categorized list of motivation definitions, with a suggestion for a consensual definition. *Motivation and Emotion, 5*(3), 263–291. doi: 10.1007/BF00993889.

Kohl, J. V., Atzmueller, M., Fink, B., & Grammer, K. (2001). Human pheromones: integrating neuroendocrinology and ethology. *NeuroEndocrinological Letters, 22,* 309–321.

Kohl, J. V., & Francoeur, R. T. (2012). *The scent of eros: Mysteries of odor in human sexuality* [E-book]. Retrieved from http://bookstore.iuniverse.com/Products/SKU-000574070/The-Scent-of-Eros.aspx.

Livingstone, M. S., Harris-Warrick, R. M., & Kravitz, E. A. (1980). Serotonin and octopamine produce opposite postures in lobsters. *Science, 208*(4439), 76–79.

Loumaye, E., Thorner, J., & Catt, K. J. (1982). Yeast mating pheromone activates mammalian gonadotropins: Evolutionary conservation of a reproductive hormone? *Science, 218*(4579), 1323–1325. doi: 10.1126/science.6293058.

Massen, J., Sterck, E., & de Vos, H. (2010). Close social association in animals and humans: functions and mechanisms of friendship. *Behaviour, 147*, 1379–1412. doi: 10.1163/000579510X528224.

Mast, T. G., & Samuelsen, C. L. (2009). Human pheromone detection by the vomeronasal organ: Unnecessary for mate selection? *Chemical Senses, 34*, 529–531.

Matsumoto, D., & Hwang, H. S. (2012). Evidence for a nonverbal expression of triumph. *Evolution and Human Behavior, 33*, 520–529.

McClintock, M. K. (1971). Menstrual synchrony and suppression. *Nature, 229*(5282), 244–245. doi: 10.1038/229244a0.

Michael, R. P., Bonsall, R. W., & Kutner, M. (1975). Volatile fatty acids, "copulins", in human vaginal secretions. *Psychoneuroendocrinology, 1*, 153–163.

Morrison, I., Löken, L., & Olausson, H. (2010). The skin as a social organ. *Experimental Brain Research, 204*(3), 305–314. doi: 10.1007/s00221-009-2007-y.

Nemiah, J. C., & Sifneos, P. E. (1970). Psychosomatic illness: Problem in communication. *Psychotherapy and Psychosomatics, 18*, 154–160.

O'Day, D. H., & Horgen, P. A. (1981). *Sexual interactions in eukaryotic microbes.* New York: Academic Press.

Ober, C., Weitkamp, L. R., Cox, N., Dytch, H., Kostyu, D., & Elias, S. (1997). HLA and mate choice in humans. *American Journal of Human Genetics, 61*, 497–504.

Panksepp, J. (1998). *Affective neuroscience: The foundations of human and animal emotions.* New York: Oxford University Press.

Patterson, M. L. (1976). An arousal model of interpersonal intimacy. *Psychological Review, 83*, 231–249.

Patterson, M. L. (1983). *Nonverbal behavior: A functionalist perspective.* New York: Springer-Verlag.

Pellegrini, A. (1991). A longitudinal study of popular and rejected children's rough-and-tumble play. *Early Education & Development, 2*, 205–213. doi: 10.1207/s15566935eed0203_3.

Pert, C. B. (1997). *Molecules of emotion: Why you feel the way you feel.* New York: Scribner.

Powers, S. R., Rauh, C., Buck, R., Henning, R., & West, T. V. (2011). The effect of video feedback delay on frustration and emotion communication accuracy. *Computers in Human Behavior, 27*, 1651–1657.

Rinn, W. (1984). The neuropsychology of facial expression: A review of the neurological and psychological mechanisms for producing facial expressions. *Psychological Bulletin, 95*, 52–77.

Roloff, M. E., & Campion, D. E. (1985). Conversational profit-seeking: Interaction as social exchange. In R. L. Street, Jr. & J. N. Cappella (Eds.), *Sequence and pattern in communicative behavior* (pp. 161–189). London: Edward Arnold.

Schaffner C. M., & Aureli F. (2005). Embraces and grooming in captive spider monkeys. *International Journal of Primatology, 26*, 1093–1106. doi: 10.1007/s10764-005-6460-6.

Sober, E. (2002). Kindness and cruelty in evolution. In R. J. Davidson & A. Harrington (Eds.), *Visions of compassion: Western scientists and Tibetan Buddhists examine human nature* (pp. 46–65). New York: Oxford University Press.

Tomkins, S. S. (1962–1963). *Affect, imagery, consciousness* (Vols. 1 & 2). New York: Springer.
Tracy, J. L., & Matsumoto, D. (2008). The spontaneous display of pride and shame: Evidence for biologically innate nonverbal displays. *Proceedings of the National Academy of Sciences of the United States of America, 105,* 11655–11660.
Tracy, J. L., & Robins, R. W. (2004). Putting the self into self-conscious emotions: A theoretical model. *Psychological Inquiry, 15,* 103–125.
Trevarthen, C. (1979). Communication and cooperation in early infancy: A description of primary intersubjectivity. In M. Bullowa (Ed.), *Before speech: The beginning of human communication* (pp. 321–347). Cambridge, UK: Cambridge University Press.
Wyart, C., Webster, W. W., Chen, J. H., Wilson, S. R., McClary, A., Khan, R. M., & Sobel, N. (2007). Smelling a single component of male sweat alters levels of cortisol in women. *Journal of Neuroscience, 27,* 1261–1265.
Wysocki, C. J., & Preti, G. (2004). Facts, fallacies, fears, and frustrations with human pheromones. *The Anatomical Record, 281A*(1), 1201–1211. doi: 10.1002/ar.a.20125.

9
Theoretical Foundation for Emotion-Based Strategies in Political Campaigns

Albert Mehrabian

The literature on political campaigns has dealt with the function of emotions and, to a lesser degree, with individual differences in susceptibility to various types of emotional appeals in such campaigns. Studies have included analyses of differential effects of the more emotional television medium versus alternatives such as newspapers (Hyeon & Becker, 1987), positive effects of generally low-distress social conditions on voter turnout (Joubert, 1995), adverse effects of neuroticism on political participation (Peterson & Maiden, 1992–1993), and temperament and adjustment–maladjustment correlates of political orientation (Mehrabian, 1996c). Political strategies that assumed centrist positions on issues (Davis, 1987) or those that employed ambiguous rhetoric (Dacey, 1979) were shown to be effective and are relevant also because the communication vacuum created by such tactics increased the significance of non-issue oriented emotional messages conveyed with nonverbal behavior, props, and buzz-words.

Relative influences of emotions versus cognitions (or ideology) have also been of particular interest. In analyzing the pro-Wallace vote in the 1964 Presidential primary and general elections, Rogin (1969) found that pro-Wallace factions were emotionally, rather than ideologically, motivated and that potential opponents, in attempting to remain non-ideological, failed to oppose Wallace with sufficient conviction. In short, absence of ideological conviction in both the pro- and anti-Wallace camps appears to have strengthened the role of emotions in those elections. Also dealing with differential roles of cognitive and affective factors in voting behavior, Granberg and Brown (1989) used data from US presidential elections of 1972, 1976, 1980, and 1984. Although both cognitive and affective factors were found to determine voting direction, affective factors exerted the stronger influence of the two. Thus, data from these two studies suggested that affective and emotional factors yielded strong effects on voting behavior, particularly when ideological issues were minimized.

For example, affective and emotional political approaches to problems of poverty might be couched in terms of emphases on the suffering, hunger, vulnerability, or general deprivation of the poor and the necessity for more welfare spending. Ideological/cognitive approaches, in contrast, would emphasize the justification for self-sufficiency via educational and training programs for the poor or for reducing the monetary rewards that encourage greater dependency of the poor.

Christ (1985) found three basic dimensions of emotional response (pleasure-displeasure, arousal-nonarousal, and dominance-submissiveness) useful for differentiating decided and undecided voter preferences. Using the same three emotion scales, Masterson and Biggers (1986) quantified political advertisements and found that voting direction could be predicted from the emotional responses. Barber (1968) used two semantic differential dimensions of positive-negative evaluation (a correlate of pleasure-displeasure) and activity-passivity (a correlate of arousal-nonarousal) to classify presidential styles into four types and to describe the differential appeal of presidents.

Considering the demonstrated importance of emotions in political processes, the present study was designed to draw on existing work to yield general answers to the following questions: "What emotion-based campaign strategies are most likely to succeed in any election?" and "What emotion-based campaign strategies are most likely to succeed with different segments of the general population?" Answers to these two basic questions were provided using findings obtained with the Pleasure-Arousal-Dominance (PAD) Emotion Model and the Pleasure-Arousability-Dominance (PAD) Temperament Model, respectively (Mehrabian, 1995, 1996b). An outline of the PAD Emotion Model is needed as background and is supplied below.

The PAD emotion model

Although originally derived from studies of meaning, the semantic-differential factors of evaluation, activity, and potency (EAP) were later found to be applicable to the description of highly diverse stimuli, such as paintings, self-descriptions, or sonar signals (Osgood et al., 1957; Snider & Osgood, 1969). The study of meaning dealt with high-level cognitive functions, whereas the EAP helped identify the lowest common denominators of cognitive operations, that is, vague associations or emotions. Accordingly, the PAD emotion scales were developed to map the EAP factors onto the domain of emotions.

Pleasure-displeasure (P), the emotional correlate of positive-negative evaluation, distinguishes gradations of positive versus negative affective states (e.g., elation, comfort, security versus boredom, anxiety, anger). Arousal-nonarousal (A), the emotional counterpart of active-passive stimuli, refers to level of mental alertness and/or physical activity. Low arousal is exemplified by sleep, sleepiness, meditation, or quiet rest; moderate arousal is associated with a casual conversation or a leisurely walk, and high arousal accompanies concentrated mental activity, as when solving an abstract problem, or various forms of physical exercise or sports competition. Dominance-submissiveness (D), the converse of stimulus potency, is defined in terms of feelings of control and influence over one's activities and surroundings versus feelings of being controlled by circumstances and others (Mehrabian, 1995).

Theoretical rationale and experimental support for the PAD Emotion Model were described by Mehrabian (1995, 1997). A convenient way to visualize this model is to think of the pleasure-displeasure, arousal-nonarousal, and dominance-submissiveness dimensions and corresponding scales as three axes of a three-dimensional space. Specific emotions constitute points in this three-dimensional space and can be defined precisely in terms of their coordinates on the three axes. For example, transforming PAD scores so they range from -1 to $+1$ yielded averaged pleasure, arousal, and dominance coordinates for some sample emotions, as follows: bored ($-.65, -.62, -.33$), loved ($.87, .54, -.18$), sleepy ($.20, -.70, -.44$), violent ($-.50, .62, .38$), puzzled ($-.41, .48, -.33$) (Mehrabian, 1995). Thus, it is seen that boredom involves displeasure, low arousal, and submissiveness; being loved involves pleasure, high arousal, and submissiveness; and violence involves displeasure, high arousal, and dominance. Furthermore, magnitudes of the pleasure, arousal, and dominance coefficients for each emotional state provide a reasonably precise definition of that state with reference to the three PAD axes.

The following general labels are useful for describing the octants of three-dimensional PAD space. Abbreviated notations $+P$ and $-P$ for pleasure versus displeasure, $+A$ and $-A$ for high versus low arousal, and $+D$ and $-D$ for dominance versus submissiveness are used in these definitions.

$$\text{Exuberant-Bored} = (+P+A+D) \text{ vs. } (-P-A-D)$$
$$\text{Dependent-Disdainful} = (+P+A-D) \text{ vs. } (-P-A+D)$$

$$\text{Relaxed-Anxious} = (+P-A+D) \text{ vs. } (-P+A-D)$$
$$\text{Docile-Hostile} = (+P-A-D) \text{ vs. } (-P+A+D).$$

Sample emotional states representing the octants are given in Table 9.1 below.

It is noteworthy that analysis of the Positive and Negative Affect scales (PANAS) in terms of the PAD Emotion Model showed the Positive Affect Scale to approximate the Exuberant pole of the Exuberant-Bored dimension, and the Negative Affect Scale to approximate the Anxious pole of the Relaxed-Anxious dimension, in PAD space. The theoretically calculated correlation between the Exuberant-Bored and Anxious-Relaxed dimensions, as defined above, was low and negative ($r = -.33$) and explained the puzzling near-independence of two scales purported to measure "Positive Affect" and "Negative Affect," respectively. Mutual

Table 9.1 General preferences for each of eight basic categories of emotion

Emotion Category and Definition	Preference Mean	Preference Rank
Exuberant, +P+A+D (admired, bold, carefree, excited, mighty, triumphant)	6.40	2
Relaxed, +P–A+D (at ease, comfortable, casual, satisfied, secure, unperturbed)	6.20	2
Docile, +P–A–D (consoled, protected, reverent, sleepy, tranquilized, humble)	6.33	2
Dependent, +P+A–D (amazed, fascinated, grateful, impressed, loved, respectful)	5.89	4
Disdainful, –P–A+D (indifferent, unconcerned, selfish-uninterested, uncaring)	3.37	5
Bored, –P–A–D (despairing, fatigued, lonely, sad, subdued, listless)	2.95	6.5
Hostile, –P+A+D (angry, catty, defiant, insolent, nasty, enraged)	2.72	6.5
Anxious, –P+A–D (bewildered, distressed, in pain, aghast, insecure, upset)	1.95	8

Note: The eight basic categories correspond to octants in PAD space and are defined in terms of adjectives listed alongside each category. Abbreviated notations +P and –P represent pleasant and unpleasant, +A and –A represent aroused and unaroused, and +D and –D represent dominant and submissive, emotional states. The preference scale for which means are given in the second column ranges from 1 (least preferred) to 8 (most preferred). Preference means are ranked in the third column. Means that did not differ significantly are assigned the same rank. Thus, preferences for Exuberant, Relaxed, and Docile states did not differ significantly and were ranked highest (average rank of 2). These were followed by Dependent states (ranked 4), Disdainful states (ranked 5), Bored and Hostile states that were tied (ranked 6.5 each), and Anxious states that were ranked lowest (8).

independence of these two scales was achieved only because the Positive Affect Scale did not include a general and balanced representation of pleasant (exuberant, dependent, relaxed, docile) states; nor did the Negative Affect Scale include a general and balanced representation of unpleasant (bored, disdainful, anxious, hostile) states. In short, both scales lacked validity (Mehrabian, 1997).

Most and least preferred emotional conditions

Examination of the eight broad groups of emotional states, the octants, noted above shows four basic types of positive affect: exuberant, dependent, relaxed, docile. There are also four basic types of negative affect: bored, disdainful, anxious, hostile.

Using a large and emotionally-balanced sample of everyday situations, Mehrabian, Wihardja, and Ljunggren (1997) obtained the following correlations between emotions elicited by, and preferences for, various situations. Preference with pleasure-displeasure, r(1598) = .77, p<.01; preference with arousal-nonarousal, r(1598) = −.14, p<.01; preference with dominance-submissiveness, r(1598) = .12, p<.01. The latter correlations showed that, in general, preferences were greater for more pleasant, less arousing, and more controllable (i.e., dominance-inducing) situations. The latter study also showed that pleasure, arousal, and dominance interacted in determining preferences of situations.

Table 9.1 below has been constructed to encapsulate the findings reported by Mehrabian et al. (1997). Net results of the main and interaction effects of the PAD dimensions on preferences are summarized in Table 9.1. The preference scale used for reporting means in the second column of Table 9.1 ranged from 1 (least preferred) to 8 (most preferred). Preference means were ranked, as reported in the third column. Means that did not differ significantly were assigned the same rank. Thus, preferences for Exuberant (+P+A+D), Relaxed (+P−A+D), and Docile (+P−A−D) states did not differ significantly and were ranked highest (average rank of 2). These were followed by Dependent (+P+A−D) states (ranked 4), Disdainful (−P−A+D) states (ranked 5), Bored (−P−A−D), and Hostile (−P+A+D) states that did not differ significantly (ranked 6.5 each), and Anxious (−P+A−D) states that were ranked lowest (8).

Effective emotional messages in political campaigns

As illustrated in the study by Masterson and Biggers (1986), advertisements of political campaigns can be evaluated in terms of their PAD components. More generally, any campaign strategy can be examined in terms of its implied emotional promises and threats: (a) positive emotional outcomes for voters ensuing election of a candidate or passage of a recommended referendum measure and (b) negative emotional outcomes for voters resulting from election of an opposing candidate or defeat of a recommended referendum measure.

Key to formulation of a successful campaign strategy is knowledge of differential preferences among the four basic positive and four basic negative affective states of the PAD Emotion Model. Findings obtained with the model across a wide-ranging selection of everyday situations by Mehrabian et al. (1997) are summarized in Table 9.1 and show general levels of preference for each of the eight basic emotional states. The latter summary of preference levels for various major emotional conditions has significant implications regarding choices of types of emotional messages in political campaigns (e.g., various kinds of promises of favorable, or threats of harmful, outcomes resulting from a particular vote).

Specifically, we can extrapolate from the data summarized in Table 9.1 and suggest the following hypotheses. To be successful, the personality, communication style, issue positions, background setting (e.g., accompanying physical decor indoors, or type of outdoor setting used in advertisements), family, friends, and/or close political associates of a candidate need to elicit the following feelings from the electorate: exuberant ($+P+A+D$, e.g., bold, carefree, triumphant, excited, admired), relaxed ($+P-A+D$, e.g., comfortable, satisfied, secure, at ease, unperturbed), or docile ($+P-A-D$, e.g., consoled, protected, reverent, tranquilized). Similar emotional associations need to be generated to a favored referendum measure. Elicitation of dependent ($+P+A-D$) feelings from voters, though probably useful, is less likely to be effective.

Additional hypotheses would suggest that campaign strategies simultaneously cast opposition candidates and opposed initiatives as generating anxious ($-P+A-D$, e.g., bewildered, in pain, upset, distressed, insecure), hostile ($-P+A+D$, e.g., insolent, defiant, catty, angry, nasty), or bored ($-P-A-D$, e.g., despairing, fatigued, lonely, sad) feelings. Hypotheses regarding efficacy of messages that would attach feelings of disdain ($-P-A+D$) in voters to opposition-sought outcomes might be more problematic, though also worthy of pursuit.

Relations between induced positive emotional reactions to a candidate and campaign effectiveness have been noted (e.g., Atkin & Heald, 1976). Also, data are available on the effectiveness of positive and negative political advertising and rebuttals to such messages (e.g., Roddy & Garramone, 1988; Garramone et al., 1990; Johnson-Cartee & Copeland, 1991). Additional studies of positive and negative messages could compare the efficacy of various categories of positive associations with favored candidates (e.g., promises of exuberant, relaxed, or docile feelings) versus categories of negative associations with opposing candidates (i.e., threatened conditions implying anxiety, anger, or boredom). One difficulty with messages designed to elicit unpleasant emotions (e.g., fear, apprehension, anger) from voters is that they can produce unpleasant emotional associations to the messenger. Such detrimental effects of negative associations are reduced, however, by having persons or organizations that are ostensibly independent of, and far removed from, a candidate deliver the messages (e.g., Garramone, 1985).

A multitude of techniques can be used to elicit the preceding affective reactions from voters. For example, to communicate exuberance, the communication style and mannerisms of a candidate can be pleasant, varied and expressive, and full of confidence. To communicate relaxation, they can be pleasant, slow-paced, consistent, predictable, relaxed, and confident. PAD values of major elements of social style (e.g., subtle verbal cues such as speech rate, voice volume, speech errors and hesitations, amount of speech, amount of intonation, and nonverbal cues such as body orientation, proximics, posture, movements, gestures, facial expressions) were reviewed by Mehrabian (1981). PAD values can be assessed also for competing designs, colors, subject-matter, concepts, and "buzz-words" that are considered for advertisements, thus yielding a highly systematic approach to the use of limited campaign funds. For example, available findings relating colors to emotions can be used to associate positive feelings with a candidate or to associate negative feelings with his opposition (e.g., Valdez & Mehrabian, 1994).

If a strategy of exuberance, rather than of relaxation, is more fitting to the character and circumstances of a candidate, findings supporting the information rate/arousal hypothesis (Mehrabian & Russell, 1974) can be used to craft highly arousing communications. Thus, higher information-rate (i.e., more complex, varied, novel, and surprising) candidate clothing, grooming, and behaviors, backdrops used in advertising, position orientations, and speech style (i.e., rapid and varied in intonation) would be used to elicit greater arousal from the electorate. The importance of music in the political process has been noted (e.g., Kincheloe, 1985). Musical selections used to accompany advertisements or candidate appearances can be designed to be pleasant and of high information (i.e., exciting) or pleasant and of low information (i.e., calming and relaxing). Furthermore, musical selections can be designed to invigorate and elicit dominance (e.g., with the audience singing or marching) or to induce submissiveness (e.g., with fanfare accompanying a candidate to signify high status).

Examples of broad-based political messages that fit each of the eight octants of emotion space are given in Table 9.2. In addition, specific positions on various political issues, often determined by broad-based political philosophies, can also be analyzed in terms of the PAD framework. This is illustrated with the tentative PAD values assigned to various political issues (e.g., taxation) in Table 9.3. It is seen that PAD components of any issue depend strongly on the target group in question. Thus, for instance, PAD values of taxation for workers and entrepreneurs differ considerably from those for individuals who subsist on government largess. Despite consensus reactions such as those illustrated in Table 9.3, political campaigns can avail themselves of considerable latitude to frame an issue so as to highlight desired emotional connotations. Thus, for instance, a conservative approach to the issue of government regulations would probably cast it as oppressive, arbitrary, and costly (i.e., as anger or anxiety provoking), whereas a liberal approach would depict it as providing safety and security (i.e., relaxation, docility).

The PAD Emotion Model can be used also to illustrate campaign strategies based on broad-based political philosophies, such as libertarian

Table 9.2 Broad-based political message samples representing each of the PAD octants

---

Exuberant: "We will turn this into a nation of prosperity and change by paving the way for individual initiative and advancement. What's more, we will all have fun while we do it." "I will be your servant!"

Relaxed: "Our goals are to minimize crime, increase security, and virtually eradicate worries about poverty and lack of health care."

Docile: "When we implement our programs, you will be cared for, nurtured, and protected in every way."

Dependent: "You need us, our policies, and our proposed programs and institutions to be prosperous, happy, healthy, and safe."

Disdainful: "Our opponents' policies will create a society where alienation, indifference, and self-interest reign supreme."

Bored: "Their policies will create a society where everyone must be content with the same limited, monotonous, and listless existence. There will be no opportunities and no challenges, only the lowest levels of achievement for most."

Hostile: "Their proposed policies will polarize groups and generate antagonism, hate, and prejudice."

Anxiety: "Beware of policies that are bound to produce pain and insecurity for most and destitution for those who cannot care for themselves – policies that guarantee poor health and neglect of the elderly and the underprivileged."

Table 9.3   Ratings of major political issues and conditions in terms of their pleasure, arousal, and dominance values

Issue	PAD Values
High taxes (taxpayers)	−P+A−D
Arrogant and non-responsive government (those in power)	−P−A+D
Government-imposed regulations (the regulated)	−P−D
Social security (for beneficiaries)	+P−A
Medicare (for beneficiaries)	+P−A
School loans (for beneficiaries)	+P−A
Environmental regulations (for those paying costs)	−P−D
Environmental regulations (for those unaffected by costs)	+P
High crime rates (non-criminal population)	−P+A−D
Excessive government police powers (the governed)	−P+A−D
Economic prosperity (workers and entrepreneurs)	+P+A+D
Economic opportunities (workers and entrepreneurs)	+P+A+D
Unrestrained capitalism (for workers and entrepreneurs)	+A+D
"War on drugs" (for users)	−P+A−D
"War on drugs" and associated costs (for non-users)	−P
Political corruption (for citizens)	−P−D
Unrestrained freedom of speech and communication in all media (for citizens)	+A+D

Note: Abbreviated notations +P and −P represent pleasant and unpleasant, +A and −A represent aroused and unaroused, and +D and −D represent dominant and submissive, emotional states. Estimates of the salient PAD values corresponding to each issue are supplied and are referenced in terms of specific segments of the population. Thus, for instance, high taxes are referenced to taxpayers; corresponding PAD values for non-taxpayers would differ substantially.

or totalitarian positions. The libertarian philosophy emphasizes freedom (i.e., primarily dominance and secondarily pleasure and arousal), whereas the totalitarian philosophy is typically justified by depicting the alternatives as involving high risk of failure and abandonment (i.e., anxiety, distress, insecurity). Thus, a libertarian candidate would need to portray his/her issue positions as yielding freedom along with increased opportunities for success, advancement, rapid economic growth, and generally varied and exciting social and economic conditions (in short, +P+A+D). Opposing positions would, in turn, be depicted as producing massive coercive forces beyond individual control and yielding frustration and anxiety (−P+A−D) or anger and rebellion (−P+A+D). Alternatively, and with somewhat less effectiveness, totalitarian rule can be portrayed as producing regimentation, mediocrity, and uniformity of behaviors and outcomes (−P−A−D). In contrast, the totalitarian approach to a campaign would seek to emphasize relaxation, comfort, and security (+P–A+D) as benefits of such a regime, with chaos, anarchy, abandonment, and consequent anxiety, distress, and pain (–P+A–D) as alternatives to a strong central government.

The PAD Temperament Model

Effectiveness of political campaigns that are targeted at various segments of the general population (e.g., different demographic groups) requires knowledge of shared emotional characteristics within each targeted group. The PAD Temperament Model provides a reasonably comprehensive and precise framework for such analyses (e.g., Mehrabian, 1996a, 1996b). It was developed based on a fundamental distinction between emotions, feelings, and affect (i.e., transitory states that can change rapidly over the course of a day) versus individual emotional predispositions or temperament (i.e., emotional traits that are generally stable and unchanging over periods of years). Within the PAD Temperament Model, individual differences are conceptualized in terms of three nearly independent and stable emotional predispositions: trait pleasure-displeasure, trait arousability, and trait dominance-submissiveness. Trait pleasure-displeasure refers to a generalized tendency to dwell upon positive (negative) affective states; trait arousability refers to characteristic strength and duration of emotional arousal to positive or negative stimuli; trait dominance-submissiveness is defined in terms of a generalized tendency to feel in control of one's activities and surroundings versus feeling that situations and others have greater control.

Octant labels provided above for the PAD Emotion Model (exuberant-bored, relaxed-anxious, dependent-disdainful, docile-hostile) are applicable as well for describing the octants of PAD temperament space. Consistent with the octant definitions, measures of extroversion and affiliation were found to be weighted by high trait pleasure, high trait arousability, and high trait dominance (i.e., +P+A+D), neuroticism and anxiety were found to be weighted by (–P+A–D), dependency was weighted by (+P+A–D), and aggression was weighted by (–P+A+D) (Mehrabian & O'Reilly, 1980).

In a study of relations between PAD temperament variables and desired ideal environments (Mehrabian, 1998–1999), participants generally showed significantly stronger preferences for environments that increased pleasure and dominance, but not arousal. That is, environments that produced feelings of exuberance or relaxation were preferred the most, corroborating findings obtained by Mehrabian et al. (1997) and summarized in Table 9.1. Mehrabian (1998–1999) also found positive correlations between temperament pleasantness (arousability, dominance) and pleasure (arousal, dominance) sought in the ideal environment. One explanation of this finding is that more pleasant (arousable, dominant) temperament attributes are more likely to be confirmed and expressed in pleasant (arousing, dominance-inducing) settings. Thus, beyond generally stronger preferences by all for more pleasant and more controllable situations, individuals were attracted more to situations that conveyed emotions similar to their temperaments.

Findings on temperament-environment affinity related to results bearing on similarity/attraction and on emotional resonance. Byrne (1971) interpreted his highly general findings of a strong linear relation between self/other attitude similarity and attraction in terms of a reinforcement paradigm: Similar attitudes in a relationship are likely to result in positive mutual reinforcements (+P), whereas dissimilar attitudes generate negative reinforcements (–P). Findings obtained by Sigelman and Sigelman (1982) on political candidate/voter similarity were consistent with Byrne's hypothesis in showing a pro-female bias among women, pro-White male bias among White males, and pro-Black bias among Black people. Along similar lines, Winter's (1987) analysis of American presidents suggested that the electoral success of presidents could be attributed to congruence or match between a president's motive profile and that of voters at election time. Finally, according to a hypothesis of emotional resonance between voter and message, voters who frequently felt a particular emotion (e.g., anger, fear, pity, hope) were more likely to be persuaded by messages containing the corresponding feelings. Findings supported the hypothesis for two of four emotions, pity and anger (Roseman et al., 1986). The temperament-environment affinity hypothesis, however, differed in one important respect from the similarity/attraction or resonance hypotheses in that predictions of affinity or similarity applied to variance beyond that accounted for by generally greater preferences across all participants for more pleasant and more controllable situations (e.g., messages).

Consideration of similarity/attraction and emotional resonance would imply that campaign messages emphasize similarity, proximity, or unity (e.g., "We" instead of "I"; "My friends" instead of "Ladies and Gentlemen"; "Our shared goals" instead of "My goals"). Also, prevailing emotional inclinations of voters vis-à-vis a particular political issue can be used to select a specific, and congruent, type of positive (e.g., exuberant, relaxed, docile) or negative (anxious, hostile, bored) message bearing on the issue.

Voter temperament in relation to successful emotional messages

Extrapolating findings on temperament-environment affinity or reso-nance to the political arena suggests that voters' political choices are likely to depend on their inferences (based, in part, on communications they receive during political campaigns) regarding the emotional con-sequences of those choices. Thus, compared with those having unpleas-ant temperaments, persons with pleasant temperaments are more likely to favor candidates or propositions that are depicted as yielding pleas-ing physical, social, and economic conditions. Similarly, more arousable individuals are more likely to favor candidates or propositions that are portrayed as yielding high-information (i.e., complex, varied, novel, and surprising) conditions. Also, more dominant persons are more likely to favor candidates or propositions that are effectively depicted as producing conditions where they will feel more dominant.

Temperament components of a substantial number of major per-sonality dimensions, reviewed by Mehrabian (1996b), help illustrate differential effectiveness of political messages for different groups. Personality characteristics of nurturance and of agreeableness were weighted positively by trait pleasure; mysticism (i.e., a predisposition to believe in vague, incomprehensible, magical, and esoteric concepts and hypotheses without foundation) was weighted positively by trait arousability; autonomy and "exhibition" (i.e., wanting to be the center of attention) were weighted positively by trait dominance, whereas sen-sitivity to rejection and conformity were weighted negatively by trait dominance.

Many personality scales were weighted by two or more of the PAD fac-tors. Some important examples were: Extroversion (.21P +.17A +.50D), achievement (.13P +.60D), conscientiousness (.25P +.19D), affiliation (.47P +.24A or .44P +.20A +.26D), dependency (.20P +.23A −.34D), emo-tional empathy (.23P +.59A), arousal seeking (.14P +.26A +.55D), intellect or sophistication (.14P +.20A +.48D), inclination to engage in sports and physical activity (.26P +.40D), neuroticism (−.26P +.49A −.25D), trait anx-iety (−.43P +.29A −.37D), depression (−.42P +.09A −.37D), shyness (−.29P +.13A −.56D), aggression (−.36P +.20A +.28D) (Mehrabian, 1996b).

As shown in Table 9.4, PAD weights of various personality dimen-sions can be used to predict differential affinity of various personality types to the content, style, and promises of political messages. Thus, nurturing, agreeable, and affiliative persons are especially likely to favor and be swayed by messages that emphasize (a) pleasant outcomes of a favorable vote and (b) unpleasant outcomes of an unfavorable vote. Also, autonomous, exhibitionistic, extroverted, achievement oriented,

Table 9.4 Temperament-based affinity to political messages containing promises of Pleasure (Arousal, Dominance)

Individual difference	Magnitude of Affinity to Promises of		
	pleasure	arousal	dominance
Nurturing	High		
Agreeable	High		
Mystic		High	
Autonomous			High
Sensitive to rejection			Low
Conforming			Low
Middle-aged, young adult (vs. Elderly)			High
Male (vs. Female)			High
Female (vs. Male)		High	
High achiever	High		High
Conscientious	High		High
Aggressive	Low	High	High
Extroverted	High		High
Affiliative	High	High	
Emotionally empathic	High	High	
Dependent	High	High	Low
Arousal seeking	High	High	High
Sophisticated	High	High	High
Physically active	High		High
Neurotic	Low	High	Low
Anxious	Low	High	Low
Depressed	Low		Low
Lonely	Low		Low
Shy	Low	High	Low

aggressive, arousal seeking, sophisticated, and physically active persons are especially likely to respond favorably to messages that emphasize (a) dominance (e.g., individual control, freedom, lack of restraints) as the outcome of a favorable vote and (b) submissiveness (e.g., external controls and influences on individual behaviors and opportunities) as the consequence of an unfavorable vote. In particular, in comparison to individuals possessing pleasant plus dominant temperament characteristics (e.g., achiever, conscientious, arousal seeker, extrovert, sophisticate, physically active), those with unpleasant and submissive traits (e.g., neurotic, anxious, shy, depressed, lonely) are less likely to be motivated by messages and issue orientations that promise pleasure and dominance.

When considering that more arousable persons are likely to seek more arousing conditions, it is important to note that there was no overall general preference for more arousing conditions, whereas more pleasant and more controllable (i.e., dominance-inducing) conditions were generally preferred more (Mehrabian, 1998–1999). Thus, affiliative, emotionally empathic, mystic, arousal seeking, dependent, anxious, and neurotic persons are especially likely to respond favorably to messages that emphasize (a) high-information consequences (e.g., complexity, variety, or novelty of situations that would ensue from favorable votes) and (b) low-information consequences (e.g., simplicity, uniformity, monotony) of unfavorable votes. Furthermore, the latter effects are likely to be substantially enhanced when arousability plus pleasantness (or dominance) of temperament finds an affinity to messages that promise high arousal plus pleasure (or dominance). Thus, arousing plus pleasant messages are more likely to appeal to the emotionally empathic and affiliative than to the anxious or neurotic. Similarly, messages implying enhanced arousal plus dominance are more likely to appeal to arousal seekers and sophisticates than to the dependent, anxious, and neurotic.

Demographic correlates of preferences for emotional messages

Age-based affinities.　Mehrabian and Blum (1996) investigated temperament differences as a function of age. Participant age ranges were 16–67 (Study 1), 20–85 (Study 2), and 18–64 (Study 3). Their results showed no differences in trait pleasure or trait arousability across the age span. However, the elderly were found to be significantly less dominant than young adults or the middle-aged. Consistent with the temperament components of achieving tendency ($.13P + .60D$), the elderly also were found to be significantly less achievement-oriented than young adults or the middle-aged.

General findings bearing on temperament-environment affinity and these age-based temperament differences can be used to anticipate the efficacy of political messages of dominance that are targeted at various age groups. Considering that elderly were found to be less dominant and less achievement-oriented than young adults or the middle-aged (Mehrabian and Blum, 1996), one could hypothesize that messages of freedom, lack of restraint, and increased opportunities for economic and social mobility (i.e., dominance) are more likely to appeal to young adults or the middle-aged than to the elderly.

Gender-based affinities.　Mehrabian and O'Reilly (1980, equation 27) had found men to be significantly less arousable and more dominant than women. Mehrabian and Blum (1996) employed an improved and matched sample of 166 married couples, aged 20–85 years. Consistent with the earlier study, they found that the husbands were significantly less arousable and more dominant than the wives. In addition, both studies showed gender differences in arousability to be larger than gender differences in dominance.

Arousability (i.e., heightened emotional responsiveness or emotional reactivity to positive and/or negative events) has been found to be a strong positive correlate of emotional empathy (e.g., Mehrabian et al., 1988). Thus, greater arousability of women compared with men was also consistent with findings showing that women were more emotionally empathic than men (Eisenberg & Lennon, 1983; Mehrabian et al., 1988).

One can extrapolate from the preceding results on gender differences in temperament (Mehrabian & O'Reilly, 1980; Mehrabian et al., 1988; Mehrabian & Blum, 1996), to hypothesize the following gender-based affinities to various types of political messages. The first hypothesis is that, compared with men, women are likely to show a stronger affinity to political messages that contain or promise greater complexity, variety, and novelty. Thus, political candidates who have expressive and flamboyant mannerisms, speech styles, grooming, clothing, and messages are more likely to appeal to women than to men. A second hypothesis is that candidates and issues that emphasize freedom (e.g., fewer restrictions and external constraints on behavior and opportunities, less limitation on social and economic mobility) are more likely to appeal to men than to women.

Stress effects on voter susceptibility to emotional contagion

Paulhus and Lim (1994) showed that white noise (which generates stress, distress, or discomfort and can be summarized as $-P+A-D$) reduced participants' cognitive differentiation: under white noise, compared with no noise, participants' judgments of others became more polarized on evaluation (a correlate of pleasure-displeasure) and evidenced reduced emphasis of target activity (i.e., arousing quality) and potency (i.e., dominance) levels. Similarly, in studies of person impression formation, Mano (1992) showed that distress ($-P+A-D$) evoked simpler decision rules and more polarized evaluations. In related work, Lewinsohn and Mano (1993) found that less pleasant mood ($-P$) was associated with less deliberation and less thorough evaluation of choices in decision making.

Mehrabian, Stefl, and Mullen (1996–1997) defined and measured a personality dimension of Globality-Differentiation in terms of fusion versus differentiation of (a) reality and fantasy (e.g., psychopathology versus adjustment), (b) cognition, emotion, and behavior (e.g., emotional thinking, impulsivity), and (c) self and other (e.g., attribution of subjective attitudes and desires to others). More global, or less differentiated, individuals were found to have less pleasant, more arousable, and less dominant (−P+A−D) temperaments. The negative relation between characteristic (i.e., temperament or emotional trait) levels of −P+A−D and cognitive differentiation paralleled findings by Paulhus and Lim (1994) and Mano (1992) showing a negative relation between transitory (i.e., emotional state) levels of −P+A−D and differentiation. Furthermore, polarization of evaluations and simultaneous reduction of cognitive differentiation can be seen as being due to greater influence of emotions on cognitions (the intermingling of cognition, emotion, and behavior, as assessed in the Globality-Differentiation Scale).

Implications of the preceding findings for the political process are that the emotion constellation labeled "anxious" (−P+A−D) in the PAD models, whether induced situationally or associated with characteristic emotional predispositions, is likely to result in less complex and more emotionally driven political judgments. That is, political messages or tactics that repeatedly produce anxious feelings (e.g., bewilderment, distress, pain, insecurity, fear) in voters are likely to magnify the influence of voter emotions on voter political judgments. Additional related effects are expected to include greater polarization of competing groups and simplification of decision rules and belief systems (e.g., increased single-issue voting, greater reliance on candidates' physical features and communication styles than on candidates' ideological positions).

Mehrabian et al. (1996–1997) also defined and measured "mysticism" as a tendency to believe without foundation, that is, to embrace magical, esoteric, superstitious, or fanciful ideas and hypotheses. Their findings showed a positive relation between mysticism and trait arousability. Thus, it may be inferred that more arousable voters are likely to be influenced more easily by unfounded statements and claims or by blatantly exaggerated promises or threats based on distortions of fact or faulty logic. Related findings by Mehrabian (1998) showed that voter preferences were easily and consistently influenced by lopsided and bogus poll reports. First, obtained "bandwagon effects" (i.e., voting along with the majority on the basis of previously heard poll data) illustrated the general role of emotional contagion in the political process. Second, and in reference to the positive mysticism/arousability relation, the same study also showed that bandwagon effects (or susceptibility to emotional contagion) were more pronounced for more arousable or less dominant individuals. Thus, high arousability (a positive correlate of mysticism) and high arousability plus low dominance (two of the three temperament components of globality-differentiation) were positive correlates of susceptibility to emotional pressures generated by a crowd. Extrapolating from these findings and drawing on parallels between PAD temperament and PAD emotion variables, it may be hypothesized that political messages that induce states of higher arousal and/or lower dominance in voters elicit greater voter conformity to accurately or inaccurately depicted majority positions.

Political participation

The PAD models are helpful for analysis of differences in degree of political participation. Evidence bearing on relations between emotional states and political participation is sparse, although it suggests a positive relation between positive feelings and political participation. Findings by Joubert (1995) showed a negative relation between social distress (i.e., $-P+A-D$) and voter turnout. Arvizu and Garcia (1996) found positive relations between Latino voting participation and income $(+P)$ and home ownership $(+P)$. Bazargan, Kang, and Bazargan (1991) found self-assessment of health $(+P)$ to be a positive correlate of political participation for elderly Caucasians. Craig (1987) discussed the positive relation between political indifference and negative affect $(-P)$ toward parties. Also, Peterson and Franzese (1988) found negative relations of sexual abuse and fear of abuse $(-P+A-D)$ with political involvement. Finally, Iyengar and Ansolabehere (1995) provided extensive documentation showing that negative political advertising $(-P)$ not only reduced voter turnout, but was used intentionally by campaign strategists to keep voters away from the polls.

More evidence is available on relations of temperament variables with political participation. Peterson and Maiden (1992–1993) found neurotics $(-P+A-D)$ had low levels of interest in the political process, whereas those with an internal locus of control $(+D)$ were interested participants. Cox (1980) also found a positive relation between internal control $(+D)$ and feelings of political capability. Reimanis (1982) found anomie (i.e., anxiety, disorientation, or $-P+A-D$) and external control $(-D)$ related negatively to political activity. Tolor and Siegel (1989) found a negative relation between a personality scale of boredom proneness $(-P-A-D)$ and political participation. Bazargan et al. (1991) found life satisfaction $(+P)$ related positively to political participation for elderly African Americans. Carmines (1991) found adolescents' self-esteem $(+P+D)$

and internal locus of control (+D) were positive correlates of political involvement. Finally, Lippert, Schneider, and Zoll (1978) found that reductions in neuroticism (−P+A−D) brought about by military service were correlated with increases in political involvement.

The common denominator of the preceding findings is that displeasure (−P), submissiveness (−D) and particularly combinations thereof (e.g., anxiety or −P+A−D, low self-esteem or −P−D, boredom or −P−A−D) (either as induced by social conditions or as temperament-based proclivities) are conducive to reduced interest in broader social issues affecting one's immediate community or the nation at large. In contrast, pleasant plus dominant temperament characteristics, shown to be components of personality traits such as extroversion, sophistication, conscientiousness, achievement, arousal seeking, affiliation, and nurturance (Mehrabian, 1996b), are likely to produce greater concern and involvement with civic affairs.

Considering the parallels between emotions and temperament, it is expected that political messages that produce feelings of pleasure and dominance (i.e., freedom, opportunity, prosperity, absence of coercive government) also are likely to result in generally higher levels of political participation. In line with findings by Iyengar and Ansolabehere (1995), already noted, one implication of these observations is that attempts at attracting uninvolved voters are more likely to succeed with positive campaign messages than with negative ones.

Conclusions

The PAD Emotion Model and associated scales can be used as a general, yet precise, tool to assess the emotional impact of any aspect of a candidate's behavior, appearance, background and history, issue positions, general political orientation, or message context (i.e., physical or social setting where the message is delivered). Similar assessments can be made of political advertisements advocating passage of any referendum measure.

Data summarized in Table 9.1 showed that message content or promised results that elicit exuberant, relaxed, or docile feelings from voters were likely to be the most effective. Alternatively, threats that election of an opposing candidate or passage of an unfavored referendum would result in conditions conducive to anxiety (anger, boredom) were also likely to be effective. Sample broad-based messages representing the various octants in PAD space were given in Table 9.2 and sample issue positions and corresponding emotions were illustrated in Table 9.3. Use of the PAD Temperament Model also provided some general guidelines to evaluate the effectiveness of various types of emotional messages for different groups. Findings bearing on temperament-environment affinity (i.e., attraction of individuals to settings that facilitated reinforcement and expression of their temperament characteristics) were extrapolated to the political arena as follows: Individuals with more pleasant (arousable, dominant) temperaments are more likely to prefer promises that their favorable votes will produce pleasant (arousing, controllable) social and economic conditions.

Available data bearing on the PAD temperament components of major personality scales and individual differences were used to illustrate applications of this hypothesis. Affinities of various groups to messages containing promises of pleasure, arousal, or dominance were detailed in Table 9.4. Observations regarding age and gender differences were illustrative. Messages of freedom from government-imposed restraints and of increased economic and social opportunities were seen as being less attractive to the elderly than to young adults and the middle-aged. Such messages were also seen as being more attractive to men than to women, whereas messages that contain or promise greater complexity, variety, and novelty were viewed as being more attractive to women than to men.

Effects of anxiety (stress, distress, fear, bewilderment), as an emotional state or as a characteristic emotional predisposition, on political judgments were also considered. Findings showed negative correlations between anxiety (as a state), or anxiety (as a trait), and cognitive differentiation. These and related findings suggested that anxiety is conducive to increased influence of emotions on political judgments, simplification of decision rules and political beliefs, and greater conformity to accurately or inaccurately depicted beliefs of the majority.

Finally, individual predispositions to anxiety and distress were found to discourage individuals from political participation, whereas feelings of control and influence enhanced participation. This suggested that attempts to attract uninvolved voters could probably benefit more from use of positive, than of negative, campaign strategies.

References

Arvizu, J. R., & Garcia, F. C. (1996). Latino voting participation: Explaining and differentiating Latino voting turnout. *Hispanic Journal of Behavioral Sciences*, *18*, 104–128.

Atkin, C., & Heald, G. (1976). Effects of political advertising. *Public Opinion Quarterly*, *40*, 216–228.

Barber, J. D. (1968). Classifying and predicting presidential styles: Two "weak" presidents. *Journal of Social Issues*, *24*, 51–80.

Bazargan, M., Kang, T., & Bazargan, S. (1991). A multivariate comparison of elderly African Americans' and Caucasians' voting behavior: How do social, health, psychological, and political variables affect their voting? *International Journal of Aging & Human Development, 32,* 181–198.

Byrne, D. (1971). *The attraction paradigm.* New York: Academic Press.

Carmines, E. G. (1991). Psychological antecedents of adolescent political involvement: Personal competence and political behavior. *International Journal of Adolescence & Youth, 3,* 79–98.

Christ, W. G. (1985). Voter preference and emotion: Using emotional response to classify decided and undecided voters. *Journal of Applied Social Psychology, 15,* 237–254.

Cox, H. (1980). The motivation and political alienation of older Americans. *International Journal of Aging and Human Development, 11,* 1–12.

Craig, S. C. (1987). Neutrality, negativity, or both? A reply to Wattenberg. *Political Behavior, 9,* 126–138.

Dacey, R. (1979). The role of ambiguity in manipulating voter behavior. *Theory and Decision, 10,* 265–279.

Davis, S. (1987). A test of candidate equilibrium. *Political Behavior, 9,* 29–48.

Eisenberg, N., & Lennon, R. (1983). Sex differences in empathy and related capacities. *Psychological Bulletin, 94,* 100–131.

Garramone, G. M. (1985). Effects of negative political advertising: The roles of sponsor and rebuttal. *Journal of Broadcasting and Electronic Media, 29,* 147–159.

Garramone, G. M., Atkin, C. K., Pinkleton, B. E., & Cole, R. T. (1990). Effects of negative political advertising on the political process. *Journal of Broadcasting and Electronic Media, 34,* 299–311.

Granberg, D., & Brown, T. A. (1989). On affect and cognition in politics. *Social Psychology Quarterly, 52,* 171–182.

Hyeon, C. C., & Becker, S. L. (1987). Media use, issue/image discriminations, and voting. *Communication Research, 14,* 267–290.

Iyengar, S., & Ansolabehere, S. (1995). *Going negative: How campaign advertising shrinks and polarizes the electorates.* New York: Free Press.

Johnson-Cartee, K. S., & Copeland, G. A. (1991). *Negative political advertising: Coming of age. Hillsdale,* NJ: Lawrence Erlbaum Associates.

Joubert, C. E. (1995). Relationship of voters' turnout to indices of social distress. *Psychological Reports, 76,* 98.

Kincheloe, J. L. (1985). The use of music to engender emotion and control behavior in church, politics and school. *Creative Child & Adult Quarterly, 10,* 187–196.

Lewinsohn, S., & Mano, H. (1993). Multi-attribute choice and affect: The influence of naturally occurring and manipulated moods on choice processes. *Journal of Behavioral Decision Making, 6,* 33–51.

Lippert, E., Schneider, P., & Zoll, R. (1978). The influence of military service on political and social attitudes: A study of socialization in the German Bundeswehr. *Armed Forces and Society, 4,* 265–282.

Mano, H. (1992). Judgments under distress: Assessing the role of unpleasantness and arousal in judgment formation. *Organizational Behavior and Human Decision Processes, 52,* 216–245.

Masterson, J. T., & Biggers, T. (1986). Emotion-eliciting qualities of television campaign advertising as a predictor of voting behavior. *Psychology: A quarterly Journal of Human Behavior, 23,* 13–19.

Mehrabian, A. (1981). *Silent messages: Implicit communication of emotions and attitudes* (2nd ed.). Belmont, CA: Wadsworth.

Mehrabian, A. (1995). Framework for a comprehensive description and measurement of emotional states. *Genetic, Social, and General Psychology Monographs, 121,* 339–361.

Mehrabian, A. (1996a). Analysis of the Big-five personality factors in terms of the PAD temperament model. *Australian Journal of Psychology, 48,* 86–92.

Mehrabian, A. (1996b). Pleasure-arousal-dominance: A general framework for describing and measuring individual differences in temperament. *Current Psychology: Developmental, Learning, Personality, Social, 14,* 261–292.

Mehrabian, A. (1996c). Relations among political attitudes, personality, and psychopathology assessed with new measures of libertarianism and conservatism. *Basic and Applied Social Psychology, 18,* 469–491.

Mehrabian, A. (1997). Comparison of the PAD and PANAS as models for describing emotions and for differentiating anxiety from depression. *Journal of Psychopathology and Behavioral Assessment, 19,* 331–357.

Mehrabian, A. (1998). Effects of poll reports on voter preferences. *Journal of Applied Social Psychology, 28,* 2119–2130.

Mehrabian, A. (1998–1999). Relations of home preference with temperament and with prevailing emotional conditions in everyday life. *Imagination, Cognition and Personality, 18,* 43–58.

Mehrabian, A., & Blum, J. S. (1996). Temperament and personality as functions of age. *International Journal of Aging & Human Development, 42,* 251–269.

Mehrabian, A., & O'Reilly, E. (1980). Analysis of personality measures in terms of basic dimensions of temperament. *Journal of Personality and Social Psychology, 38,* 492–503.

Mehrabian, A., & Russell, J. A. (1974). A verbal measure of information rate for studies in environmental psychology. *Environment and Behavior, 6,* 233–252.

Mehrabian, A., Stefl, C. A., & Mullen, M. (1996–1997). Emotional thinking in the adult: Individual differences in mysticism and globality-differentiation. *Imagination, Cognition and Personality, 16,* 325–355.

Mehrabian, A., Wihardja, C., & Ljunggren, E. (1997). Emotional correlates of preferences for situation-activity combinations in everyday life. *Genetic, Social, and General Psychology Monographs, 123,* 461–477.

Mehrabian, A., Young, A. L., & Sato, S. (1988). Emotional empathy and associated individual differences. *Current Psychology: Research & Reviews, 7,* 221–240.

Osgood, C. E., Suci, G. J., & Tannenbaum, P. H. (1957). *The measurement of meaning.* Urbana, IL: University of Illinois Press.

Paulhus, D. L., & Lim, D. T. K. (1994). Arousal and evaluative extremity in social judgments: A dynamic complexity model. *European Journal of Social Psychology, 24,* 89–99.

Peterson, S. A., & Franzese, B. (1988). Sexual politics: Effects of abuse on psychological and sociopolitical attitudes. *Political Psychology, 9,* 281–290.

Peterson, S. A., & Maiden, R. (1992–1993). Personality and politics among older Americans: A rural case study. *International Journal of Aging & Human Development, 36,* 157–169.

Reimanis, G. (1982). Relationship of locus of control and anomie to political interests among American and Nigerian students. *Journal of Social Psychology, 116,* 289–290.

Roddy, B. L., & Garramone, G. M. (1988). Appeals and strategies of negative political advertising. *Journal of Broadcasting and Electronic Media, 32*, 415–427.

Rogin, M. (1969). Politics, emotion, and the Wallace vote. *British Journal of Sociology, 20*, 27–49.

Roseman, I. J., Abelson, R. P., & Ewing, M. F. (1986). Emotion and political cognition: Emotional appeals in political communication. In R. R. Lau & D. O. Sears (Eds.), *Political Cognition.* (pp. 279–294). Hillsdale, NJ: Erlbaum.

Sigelman, L., & Sigelman, C. K. (1982). Sexism, racism, and ageism in voting behavior: An experimental analysis. *Social Psychology Quarterly, 45*, 263–269.

Snider, J. G., & Osgood, C. E. (Eds.). (1969). *Semantic differential technique.* Chicago: Aldine.

Tolor, A., & Siegel, M. C. (1989). Boredom proneness and political activism. *Psychological Reports, 65*, 235–240.

Valdez, P., & Mehrabian, A. (1994). Effects of color on emotions. *Journal of Experimental Psychology: General, 123*, 394–409.

Winter, D. G. (1987). Leader appeal, leader performance, and the motive profiles of leaders and followers: A study of American presidents and elections. *Journal of Personality and Social Psychology, 52*, 196–202.

10

The Impact of Nonverbal Behavior in the Job Interview

Denise Frauendorfer and Marianne Schmid Mast

In human resources, employee selection plays a major role. Given that an organization functions only with its members, the selection of a member who contributes the most and best to the productivity is aspired to (Guion & Highhouse, 2006). Thus, the selection has a powerful impact on the company's outcome, going both ways: as much as a good selection can have a positive impact, a bad selection can have a negative impact on the company.

While a wide array of different employment selection tools are used such as ability tests, personality tests, and assessment centers (Gatewood et al., 2011), the job interview is the most frequently used selection tool across countries, jobs, and levels (McDaniel et al., 1994; Salgado et al., 2001). Recruiters value the job interview to a large extent because they believe that a better hiring decision can be made after having met the applicant in person than from evaluating the applicant's biographical data or test scores only (Gatewood et al., 2011). Moreover, research has shown that recruiters tend to trust their first impressions more than objective tests (Dipboye, 1994). Thus, to get in contact with the applicant and to draw inferences about him or her based on his or her interpersonal behavior seems to be an aspect desired by practitioners.

Because the job interview is a dyadic social interaction in which the applicant and the recruiter normally meet for the first time, the non-verbal cues such as one's smiling, nodding, eye contact, body posture (i.e., visual cues), but also voice pitch, speaking rate, and speaking time (i.e., paralinguistic or vocal cues) play an important role. Both the applicant and the recruiter try to form a first impression of their interaction partner. In case of the applicant's behavior, the recruiters try to infer different characteristics relevant for the job such as a specific personality profile, certain skills, job-relevant competences, but also motivation, values, leadership, and company attraction (Gatewood et al., 2011). Although this information can be drawn from the verbal behavior, the nonverbal behavior is often more important (Arvey & Campion, 1982) because useful information expressed nonverbally can very often not be expressed verbally (Schlenker, 1980). For instance, if an applicant emphasizes in a job interview being very stress resistant while at the same time nervously fidgeting in the chair, the recruiter might have the impression that this applicant might not be the right person for a job in which stress resistance is an important competence.

When using nonverbal behavior to form a first impression, different questions can be raised such as: How is the applicant's nonverbal behavior linked to the recruiter's hiring decision? What information is conveyed by the applicant's nonverbal behavior? Which applicant nonverbal cues are used to infer certain characteristics? How accurate are the inferences based on the nonverbal behavior? And, what is the impact of the recruiter's nonverbal behavior on the applicant? We first introduce results concerning the link between the applicant's nonverbal behavior and recruiter evaluation and then present the Brunswikian lens model (Brunswik, 1956), based on which we summarize the literature focusing on the role of the applicant's (i.e., sender) nonverbal behavior, the recruiter's (i.e., perceiver) perception, and the judgment accuracy of the recruiter. In a last section we review literature on recruiter nonverbal behavior and how it influences the perception and behavior of the applicant.

The applicant's nonverbal behavior and job interview outcomes

It is widely accepted that the first impression of the applicant by the recruiter is not only based on *what* the applicant says but also on *how* the applicant answers the recruiter's questions (Imada & Hakel, 1977). In other words, applicants convey a first impression through their expressed nonverbal behavior during the job interview. For instance, an applicant who shows a high amount of smiling and uses extensive hand gestures might give the impression of being an extraverted person. This first impression can affect different outcomes, such as how favorably the applicant is evaluated.

Research shows that there is a positive relation between applicant *positive nonverbal behavior* and recruiter evaluation. Positive nonverbal behavior can be defined as immediacy behavior which elicits proximity and liking in the interaction partner as for example a high level of eye contact, smiling, confirmative nodding, hand gestures, and variation in pitch and speaking rate (Guerrero, 2005). Applicants who used more immediacy behavior (i.e., eye contact, smiling, body orientation toward interviewer, less personal distance) were perceived as being more suitable for the job, more competent, more motivated, and more successful than applicants using less immediacy behavior (Imada & Hakel, 1977). Forbes and Jackson (1980) showed that selected applicants maintained more direct eye contact, smiled more, and nodded more during the job interview than applicants who were not selected for the job. Moreover, applicants who maintained a high amount of eye contact with the recruiter, who showed a high energy level, were affective, modulated their voice, and spoke fluently during the job interview were more likely to be invited for a second job interview than applicants revealing less of those nonverbal behaviors (McGovern & Tinsley, 1978). Parsons and Liden (1984) found that speech patterns such as articulation, voice intensity, and pauses predicted recruiter hiring decision, above and beyond objective information (e.g., school and extracurricular activities). Also, selected applicants showed more eye contact and more facial expression during the job interview than non-accepted applicants (Anderson & Shackleton, 1990). Finally, applicants who showed authentic smiles were evaluated more favorably than applicants with a fake or neutral smiling behavior (Krumhuber et al., 2009).

The impact of applicant immediacy nonverbal behavior on job interview outcome has also been investigated in relation to other factors, such as job or applicant characteristics. For instance, applicants who avoid eye contact with the recruiter when applying for a low-status job (blue-collar job) are not evaluated significantly less favorably compared to applicants gazing regularly at the recruiter. In contrast, applicants who avoid eye contact with the recruiter are significantly less favorably evaluated (compared to applicants gazing regularly at the recruiter) when applying for a high-status job (white-collar job) (Tessler & Sushelsky, 1978). Moreover, applicant smiling behavior has a negative impact on jobs which are more "masculine" (e.g., newspaper reporter) and for which the job holder is expected to smile less (Ruben et al., 2012).

In terms of applicant characteristics, applicants high in communication apprehension who used more nonverbal avoidance behavior (i.e., less talking, less eye contact, less fluent talking) were less effective in mock job interviews and were perceived as less suitable for the job than applicants with low levels of communication apprehension (Ayres et al., 1998). And, applicant gazing had a reversed effect for male compared to female applicants (Levine & Feldman, 2002). The more the male applicant maintained eye contact with the recruiter the less he was liked, whereas the more the female applicant gazed at the recruiter the more she was liked.

Applicant nonverbal behavior as an impression management (IM) strategy

Whether nonverbal behavior can be used consciously by applicants to convey a favorable impression has been debated. While some argue that nonverbal behavior is more spontaneous, less under control, and thus less conscious than verbal behavior (Peeters & Lievens, 2006), others argue that even if people are not always fully aware of their nonverbal behavior, they are still able to regulate it, especially for self-presentation purposes (Stevens & Kristof, 1995). Research that confirms the former view shows that even if applicants were told to convey a favorable impression (i.e., using more positive nonverbal behavior) during the job interview, they did not express more or less nonverbal behavior than applicants who were told to be as honest as possible (Peeters & Lievens, 2006). Contrary to this, applicants can use their nonverbal behavior as an impression management (IM) strategy. In this case, they consciously modify their nonverbal behavior in order to positively impress the recruiter (Steven & Kristof, 1995). Nonverbal IM typically includes positive nonverbal cues such as applicant smiling, gazing, affirmative nodding, and gesturing.

In the nonverbal IM literature, applicant nonverbal behavior is mostly measured based on self-report questionnaires rather than on coding of actual behavior. This approach rests on the assumption that positive nonverbal behavior is used in a conscious way to convey a favorable impression. Applicants are asked how much they think they smiled during the job interview or how often they think they had eye contact with the recruiter (Stevens & Kristof, 1995; Kristof-Brown, 2000; Tsai et al., 2005). Using such self-reports of applicant nonverbal behavior, the results look very similar to those obtained by more objective behavioral observation methods: The more the applicant reported using nonverbal IM during the job interview the more favorably he or she was evaluated by the recruiter (Steven & Kristof, 1995). Also, nonverbal IM had a remarkable impact on the recruiter's hiring decision when the job interview was less structured compared to a structured job interview (Tsai et al., 2005). Finally, nonverbal IM positively influenced perceived recruiter similarity: the more the applicant expressed positive nonverbal behavior during the job interview the more he or she was perceived by the recruiter as being similar whereas nonverbal behavior IM did not increase the perceived qualification of the applicant (Kristof-Brown et al., 2002).

Overall, there are only few studies that did not show an effect between applicant nonverbal immediacy behavior and a favorable hiring decision (Kristof-Brown et al., 2002; Sterrett, 1978) and meta-analyses reveal a clear net effect showing that the more the applicant uses nonverbal immediacy behavior, the better the interview outcome for the applicant (i.e., better chances of getting hired or of being evaluated positively): $r_w = .40$ (Barrick, Shaffer, & DeGrassi, 2009) and $r_w = .34$ (Frauendorfer & Schmid Mast, 2014b).

How to explain the applicant nonverbal behavior-hiring decision link

Why does the applicant's nonverbal behavior influence how the applicant is evaluated? Different explanations are provided by the literature.

First, Forbes and Jackson (1980) suggest that the nonverbal behavior helps the recruiter to judge the applicant more correctly, as the pre-screening of the applicants might not have delivered much information about how the applicants differ from each other in terms of competences, education, or work experience. Thus, specific nonverbal cues might make the differences among applicants more salient, especially in a rather homogenous group of applicants. This is the so-called *salience hypothesis*. Investigating mentally impaired individuals, research confirms this salience hypothesis in that in a group of mentally impaired applicants (who were homogenous in their ability to respond and to articulate), their nonverbal behavior explained a greater portion of the variance in the recruiter's hiring decision than in a group of mentally impaired applicants who were heterogeneous (ranging from people who could not answer questions to people who were responsive) (Sigelman & Davis, 1978; Sigelman et al., 1980). Thus, in a situation of homogenous applicants, the focus is rather on the nonverbal behavior, because this helps to differentiate between similar individuals (Edinger & Patterson, 1983).

A second explanation is based on the *reinforcement theory*, claiming that recruiters have made their decision already at the very beginning of the job interview and reinforce their first impression of the applicant during the job interview based on the applicant's behavior (Webster, 1964). In this case, the nonverbal behavior of the applicant is nothing other than the response to the recruiter's reinforcement during the job interview. This means that the recruiter's first impression can cause the applicant to behave in a manner that confirms the recruiter's impression (behavioral confirmation; Snyder & Swann, 1978; Darley & Fazio, 1980). According to Forbes and Jackson (1980) this second explanation does not necessarily contradict the first one, because the first impression drawn by the recruiter could be based on the salient nonverbal behavior of the applicant at the very beginning of the job interview.

A third explanation considers the *immediacy hypothesis* claiming that through nonverbal immediacy behavior (e.g., eye contact, smiling, hand gestures, closer interpersonal distance), applicants reveal more proximity and perceptual availability which entails positive affect in the recruiter and therefore leads to a better evaluation (Imada & Hakel, 1977). Put differently, liking might act as a mediator in the relation between applicant nonverbal behavior and hiring decision (Edinger & Patterson, 1983). Also, the explanation based on the *immediacy hypothesis* goes hand in hand with the *reinforcement theory* in that the positive affect elicited in the recruiter can result in reinforcement towards the applicant.

Differences in nonverbal behavior expression

Research has not only shown that the applicant's nonverbal behavior has a positive impact on job interview outcomes, but also that the frequency of nonverbal behavior expression varies according to the situation and among individuals. How frequently certain nonverbal behaviors are exhibited in a job interview depends on different factors, such as the situation, the applicant personality, the applicant gender, and the applicant race, among other factors.

Situational factors. Situational factors that are typically considered in the job interview are the type of job interview (past-behavioral vs. situational) and the degree of structure in the job interview (structured vs. unstructured). Past-behavioral means that the recruiter addresses questions to the applicant about specific situations in the past with the intention of knowing how the applicant behaved in those situations. In situational job interviews recruiters ask applicants about possible future situations and how they think they would behave in those situations (e.g., Campion et al., 1994; Janz, 1982; Motowidlo et al., 1992). Structured job interviews mean that the recruiter addresses standardized questions to the applicant and evaluates the applicant according to standardized criteria. In contrast, unstructured job interviews do not follow any preset procedure (McDaniel et al., 1994). Investigating the frequency of nonverbal behavior IM in different types of job interviews, no significant difference was found between past-behavioral and situational interviews. In both types the same amount of nonverbal impression management was used (Peeters & Lievens, 2006). However, when investigating the structure of the job interview, significant differences were found in terms of specific nonverbal cues, such as applicant self-touch (Goldberg & Rosenthal, 1986). Applicants in the unstructured condition (chat for a few minutes about no specific topic) revealed more self-touch (hair, face, arm, and hand) than applicants in the formal job interview condition. Men showed more face touching and women showed more hair touching. Future research might want to focus on systematic research to obtain a clearer picture about the effects of different situations on the use of nonverbal behavior by applicants.

Personality factors. Investigating the relation between applicant's personality and the applicant's nonverbal behavior during the job interview, research shows that more agreeable applicants express more positive nonverbal behavior during the job interview (i.e., smiling and maintaining eye contact) (Kristof-Brown et al., 2002), especially when applicants are told beforehand to evoke a favorable impression (Peeters & Lievens, 2006). Moreover, high self-monitoring women maintained more eye-contact with the recruiter than low self-monitoring men and women (Levine & Feldman, 2002). And, high self-monitoring applicants used more nonverbal behavior during the job interview in general, than low self-monitoring applicants (Peeters & Lievens, 2006). However, this was only the case if applicants had specific instructions to use more nonverbal behavior. When there were no such instructions, applicant self-monitoring was unrelated to applicant nonverbal behavior (Peeters & Lievens, 2006). So far only little research focused on personality differences in the context of the applicant's nonverbal behavior. Especially personality traits such as extraversion and conscientiousness might be interesting to investigate in the future, because they have been shown to predict future job performance. It might be crucial for the recruiter to know how highly extraverted and conscientious applicants express those traits nonverbally.

Gender differences. There are also gender differences concerning the use of nonverbal cues, such as smiling, gazing, interpersonal touch, interpersonal distance, and vocal behavior during the job interview. For instance, female applicants smile and nod more than male applicants (Van Vianen & Van Schie, 1995; Frauendorfer et al., 2014b). In one study conducted in our lab, female applicants also provided more visual back-channeling (i.e., nodding while speaking), spoke faster and louder, and varied more in their speech loudness than did male applicants. In terms of pitch variation, results were inconsistent; in one of our studies men revealed higher pitch variation than women whereas in another study, the reversed effect emerged. For gazing and speaking time, there seems to be no gender difference (Frauendorfer et al., 2014b; Van Vianen & Van Schie, 1995). Moreover, male applicants keep a larger interpersonal distance from (male) recruiters than do female applicants from (female) recruiters (Levine & Feldman, 2002). In sum, results on gender differences are very similar to the ones found in the general population (Hall, 1984; Dixon & Foster, 1998; Hall & Carter, 2000).

Race differences. In terms of race differences, white applicants maintained more eye contact with the recruiter of both races than did black applicants. Moreover, black and white applicants gazed more at the white recruiter than at the black recruiter (Fugita et al., 1974). The least amount of eye contact was exchanged when both the applicant and the recruiter were African American and the most eye contact was exchanged when the applicant and the recruiter were European American (Fugita et al., 1974). Thus, white people use more eye contact in job interviews than do black people. The latter might have other nonverbal IM strategies to make a good impression (Pelligrini et al., 1970). However, because research on race diversity and nonverbal behavior in job interviews is rare, there is a great need of current research focusing on nonverbal behavior and different ethnicities in the job interview context. Doing so would provide us with a clear insight into how race affects the use of applicant nonverbal behavior.

Summary of role of the applicant's nonverbal behavior in the job interview

Applicant nonverbal behavior seems to have a remarkable impact on the job interview outcome. The more immediacy (or positive) nonverbal behavior the applicant shows during the job interview, the more positive recruiter evaluations of the applicant are. Moreover, different explanations of why applicant immediacy nonverbal behavior positively influences job interview outcomes can be found in the literature: the salience hypothesis, the reinforcement hypothesis, or the immediacy hypothesis. Although these explanations have different rationales, they are not necessarily mutually exclusive. They might be considered as an integrative way of explaining the nonverbal behavior-hiring decision link. Finally, which nonverbal behavior is expressed depends on different factors, such as the situation, the personality, the gender, or the race of the applicant. In the next section we will present a Brunswikian perspective investigating what the applicant's nonverbal behavior expresses and what recruiters infer when basing their judgment on the applicant's nonverbal behavior.

Brunswikian perspective towards encoding and decoding

So far, several questions remain unanswered, such as what exactly it is that *recruiters* infer from nonverbal cues, or which nonverbal cues express applicant characteristics, and how accurate recruiters are at inferring applicants' characteristic when basing their judgment on the applicant's nonverbal behavior. Before we present the Brunswikian lens model (1956), it is important to look at which applicant characteristics are normally inferred by recruiters who try to gain a first impression about applicants.

The most frequently measured constructs in the selection process are applicant personality traits and cognitive ability (Van Vianen & Van Schie, 1995; Ng & Sears, 2010) because they have shown to predict later job performance (Barrick & Mount, 1991; Dunn et al., 1995; Schmidt & Hunter, 1998; Nicholls & Visser, 2010; Tews et al., 2011). While cognitive ability and conscientiousness predict job performance in all job categories (Schmidt & Hunter, 1998), extraversion is a valid predictor for jobs requiring social interactions (Barrick & Mount, 1991). Moreover, applicant personality traits do not only influence future job performance but also have an impact on the job interview outcome. For instance, applicants with a high level of extraversion, openness to experience, and conscientiousness use more social preparation (e.g., talking to others) before the job interview and are therefore more successful in the job interview (Caldwell & Burger, 1998). Thus, applicant personality traits are crucial in the job interview context because they are the most frequently assessed characteristics (besides general mental ability) and they have shown to predict the job interview outcome and job performance.

The Brunswikian lens model (1956) posits that target characteristics are expressed through the target's nonverbal behavior on which in turn the perceiver bases his or her judgment. Thus, the nonverbal behavior mediates the relation between the target's characteristics and the perceiver's judgment. *Encoding* means the relation between the actual target characteristics and the corresponding expressed nonverbal behavior and *decoding* means the relation between the target's nonverbal behavior and the perceiver's judgment. Encoding gives information about how a given target characteristic is expressed in behavioral cues (i.e., cue validity) whereas the decoding process gives information about which behavioral cues the perceiver uses for his or her judgment (i.e., cue utilization). Finally, the relation between the perceiver's judgment and the target's characteristic is an indicator of judgment accuracy. The more cue validity and cue utilization are similar, the higher the accuracy of the perceiver's judgment (Sommers et al, 1989; Ambady et al., 1995; Gifford, 2011). Based on the lens model, the following sections review the literature on cue utilization, cue validity, and judgment accuracy in the job interview.

Recruiter assessment through applicant nonverbal behavior

On which nonverbal cues does the recruiter base his or her judgment (i.e., cue utilization according to the Brunswikian lens model)? One study, for instance, has shown that the more the applicant showed eye contact and was facially expressive, the more he or she was perceived as being *interesting, relaxed, strong, successful, active, mature, enthusiastic, sensitive, pleasant, dominant,* and *liked* (Anderson & Shackleton, 1990). And, applicants showing more postural change were perceived as more *enthusiastic* and more applicant head movement was perceived as being more *sensitive*. Moreover, constructs such as *social skills* of an applicant were inferred based on the applicants' amount of gesturing, and time talked and applicant's *motivation* for the job was based on the applicant's smiling, gesturing, and time talked (Gifford et al., 1985). The more applicants used these nonverbal cues the more they were perceived as being socially skilled and motivated. Also, a high amount of applicant eye contact predicted perceived *competence* and *personal strength* whereas more positive facial expressions predicted perceived *liking* and *motivation* (Anderson, 1991). Finally, in one of the studies conducted in our lab, applicant *extraversion* was inferred based on numerous applicant vocal cues (i.e., more applicant speaking time, less short utterances – such as "mmhh," "ah" – less speaking turns, and a higher speaking rate), *openness* was inferred through more speaking time, *neuroticism* was negatively related to speaking time and positively related to number of turns during the job interview, *agreeableness* was inferred based on visual cues (i.e., more smiling and gazing behavior), and vocal cues (i.e., higher speaking rate, higher variation in speaking rate, and more speaking fluency), and *conscientiousness* was positively related to more nodding behavior and higher speaking rate. *Intelligence* was inferred based on more nodding, speaking time, a higher speaking rate, less short utterances (i.e., "mmhh," "ah"), and less turns (Frauendorfer et al., 2014b).

Investigating composites of nonverbal cues, DeGroot and Gooty (2009) found that perceived applicant *conscientiousness* and *openness to experience* were positively related to a composite of applicant visual cues (i.e., overall index of physical attractiveness, amount of smiling, gazing at the recruiter, hand movement, and body movement towards the recruiter). And, perceived applicant *extraversion* was positively related to a composite of applicant vocal cues (i.e., overall index of pitch, pitch variability, speech rate, pauses, and amplitude variability). Moreover, perceived applicant *conscientiousness, openness to experience*, and *extraversion* mediated the positive relation between applicant nonverbal behavior (i.e., visual and vocal cues) and the job interview outcome. The more the applicant revealed vocal and visual cues the more he or she was perceived as being conscientious, open, and extraverted which in turn lead to a more favorable evaluation (DeGroot & Gooty, 2009). Thus, personality traits are not only inferred based on single applicant nonverbal cues but also based on composites of different nonverbal cues.

Table 10.1 provides an overview of studies investigating nonverbal cues upon which diverse applicant personality traits and characteristics are assessed. As can be seen, applicant eye contact and facial expressiveness are used to assess most applicant characteristics (e.g., success, dominance, personal strength, likability). Interestingly, characteristics which are similar to each other such as intelligence and conscientiousness are assessed based on the same nonverbal cues, as for instance, applicant nodding and speech rate. Moreover, extraversion and neuroticism are assessed mostly based on vocal nonverbal behavior, whereas conscientiousness is mostly assessed via visual nonverbal cues (except for speaking rate). And, when inferring applicant agreeableness, both visual and vocal nonverbal behavior is used. Finally, openness seems to be least often assessed by applicant nonverbal behavior.

Applicant traits and skills expressed in nonverbal behavior

Which applicant nonverbal cues convey the applicant's personality traits and skills during a job interview? To date, there has been little research conducted answering this question. Because the illustration of cue validity in job interviews is highly relevant for the present review, we will briefly summarize research conducted in non-job interview situations. We focus on so called zero-acquaintance situations because in the job interview, typically, the recruiter meets the applicant for the first time.

One study, for instance, shows that *extraversion* is expressed by a powerful voice, a friendly expression, smiling, and head movements, *agreeableness* is indicated by a high voice, friendly expression, less frequent hand and head movements, and *neuroticism* is expressed via

Table 10.1 Overview of studies investigating the relation between nonverbal behavior, inferred applicant personality traits, and actual (applicant) characteristics

(Applicant) nonverbal cues	Inferred applicant characteristics	Actual (applicant) characteristics
Visual nonverbal behavior[1]	Conscientiousness, openness	
Eye contact	Interesting, relaxed, strong, successful, active, mature, enthusiastic, sensitive, pleasant, dominant, liked, competent, strong, *agreeableness*	*Conscientiousness*, intelligence[2]
Facial expressiveness	Interesting, relaxed, strong, successful, active, mature, enthusiastic, sensitive, pleasant, dominant, liked, motivated	*Extraversion*[2], *agreeableness*[2], *neuroticism* (−)[2]
Smiling	Motivation, *agreeableness*	*Agreeableness*, *extraversion*[2]
Gestures	Social skills, motivation	Social skills, *agreeableness* (−)[2]
Nodding	*Conscientiousness*, intelligence	−
Postural change	Enthusiastic	
Head movement	Sensitive	*Extraversion*[2], *agreeableness* (−)[2]
Fidgeting behavior		Intelligence (−)[2]
Trunk recline		Motivation
Vocal nonverbal behavior[1]	Extraversion	
Speaking time	Social skills, motivation, *extraversion*, *openness*, *neuroticism* (−), intelligence	Social skills, *extraversion*, *neuroticism* (−), *conscientiousness*, intelligence (−)
Speaking turns	*Extraversion* (−), *neuroticism*, intelligence (−), communication skills (−)	−
Speaking rate	*Extraversion*, *agreeableness*, *conscientiousness*, intelligence	*Extraversion*
Speaking rate variation	*Agreeableness*	*Extraversion*
Speaking fluency	*Agreeableness*	−
Short utterances	*Extraversion* (−), intelligence (−)	−
Audio back-channeling	−	*Openness, agreeableness*
Pitch[3]	−	*Neuroticism, agreeableness*[2], *openness* (−)[2], intelligence (−)[2]
Voice energy	−	*Openness, extraversion*[2], *neuroticism*[2], *conscientousness*[2], *neuroticism* (−)[2]

Note: This overview summarizes the studies mentioned in the present review (Gifford, et al., 1985; Anderson & Sheckleton, 1990; Anderson, 1991; Borkenau & Liebler, 1992; Murphy et al., 2003; DeGroot & Gooty, 2009; Frauendorfer et al., 2014b). Characteristics in italic refer to the big five personality traits (Costa & McCrae, 1992).
[1] Results of DeGroot and Gooty (2009) investigating visual and vocal nonverbal behavior as composites.
[2] Results from non-job interview studies (Borkenau & Liebler, 1992; Murphy et al., 2003).
[3] High value in pitch means a higher voice. A positive correlation therefore indicates that the more the applicant characteristic is present the more it is expressed through a higher voice.

a powerful voice (Borkenau & Liebler, 1992). Another study reports *extraversion* being correlated with a friendly expression, smiling, and a powerful voice, *conscientiousness* with a powerful voice, *neuroticism* with a less friendly expression and a weak voice, and *openness* and *intelligence* with a low voice (Borkenau & Liebler, 1995). In yet another study, *intelligence* was mostly expressed through less fidgeting behavior and more eye contact with the interaction partner (Murphy et al., 2003).

Research on cue validity in the job interview is scarce. Using the Brunswikian lens model approach, Gifford et al. (1985) found that applicant *social skills* were positively related to gestures and time talked during the job interview. Moreover, applicant *motivation* was revealed through trunk recline (Gifford et al., 1985). Based on two studies conducted in our lab, a high level of applicant *extraversion* was encoded by more speaking time, higher speaking rate, and more speaking rate variation, a high level of applicant *openness* was revealed by more audio back-channeling (i.e., short utterances while recruiter is speaking) and a louder voice, a higher level of applicant *neuroticism* was shown by less speaking time and higher pitch, a higher level of applicant *agreeableness* is revealed through more audio back-channeling and more smiling, and a higher level of applicant *conscientiousness* was encoded by a higher amount of speaking time and more eye contact with the recruiter (Frauendorfer et al., 2014b). Finally, applicant's *intelligence* was revealed through less speaking time.

The right side of Table 10.1 provides an overview of studies investigating the nonverbal behavior that is indicative of actual applicant characteristics. As can be seen, extraversion is mostly expressed through vocal nonverbal behavior. And, constructs similar to each other such as intelligence and conscientiousness are expressed through the same nonverbal cues (i.e., speaking time).

Conclusions have to be drawn carefully because there is little research so far investigating the link between actual applicant personality traits and expressed applicant nonverbal behavior. Moreover, Gifford (2006) argues that the encoding process faces different complexities. For instance, not all nonverbal behaviors might be relevant in all situations. That is, dominant nonverbal behavior might be less relevant in job interviews for a position in accounting than for a position in management. Also, the encoding might depend on the interaction partner, as the target might not encode the same nonverbal cues facing different interaction partners. There might be differences in encoding, depending on how the interaction partner behaves, for instance (e.g., Kanki, 1985; Kenny, 1994). We will indeed show, later in this chapter, that the recruiter's nonverbal behavior can affect how the applicant behaves nonverbally as well as the outcome of the job interview for the applicant.

The relation between nonverbal behavior and personality can also vary between different combinations of traits; for instance, a person who is sociable *and* shy reveals different nonverbal behaviors than somebody who is sociable *but not* shy. Certain personality traits might also be encoded by a combination of different nonverbal behaviors (e.g., looking at the interaction partner while speaking) rather than by one specific nonverbal cue alone. Encoding might also differ between males and females, with a given personality trait encoded by one non-verbal behavior for one sex but not holding up for the other. Finally, personality encoding might differ between cultures. Thus, the lens model approach is affected by different factors that can influence the validity of the inferences drawn. This might be a reason for the fact that it is not yet clear whether the nonverbal behavior explains vari-ance above and beyond applicant competencies and verbal content, or whether it lowers the validity of the hiring decision (Harris, 1989).

When comparing cue validity and cue utilization in job interviews, it clearly emerges (based on Table 10.1) that extraversion and neu-roticism are assessed based on valid vocal nonverbal cues. Applicant agreeableness, however, is inferred from applicant eye contact, smiling, speaking rate, speaking rate variation, and speaking fluency whereas agreeableness is actually expressed by applicant smiling only. Openness is inferred based on visual and vocal behavior, whereas it is actually expressed through audio back-channeling only. Given this, the ques-tion can be asked how accurate recruiters are when inferring applicant characteristics. For many personality characteristics, they seem to use the "wrong," meaning non-diagnostic cues.

Accuracy of recruiter inferences

There is evidence that recruiters perform quite well when assessing applicants based on only short excerpts of a job interview. For instance, Blackman (2002a) found that participants in the role of a recruiter were accurate at assessing the applicant's personality traits after a mock job interview. Also, recruiters were accurate at assessing applicants' person-ality traits based on 30-minute job interviews (Barrick et al., 2000). And, Gifford et al. (1985) showed that socials skills were accurately assessed by recruiters after having watched a videotape of a job interview.

Even after being provided with only a short glimpse of the applicant behavior, recruiters are able to accurately assess personality traits: Judges predicted applicant personality traits based on 10-second (Prickett et al., 2000) and two-minute slices of a mock job interview (Schmid Mast et al., 2011). Moreover, we have shown that recruiters were able to correctly infer the applicant's future job performance as well as their personality traits, after having watched a 40-second thin-slice of an applicant answering two job interview questions (Frauendorfer & Schmid Mast, 2014a). Interestingly, the first impression might not become more accurate when the thin-slice behavior is extended. Research outside the context of the job interview suggests that there is no significant difference in judgment accuracy when the judgment is based on 30-second or five-minute excerpts (Ambady & Rosenthal, 1992, 1993; Murphy, 2005).

Research on situational (e.g., job interview structure) and personal (e.g., years of experience of the recruiter) factors influencing judgment accuracy has shown that personality is more accurately assessed in face-to-face job interviews than in telephone interviews, in which no visual nonverbal behavior is available (Blackman, 2002a). The author argues that more behavioral information is available in the face-to-face interview, which results in higher accuracy judgment. Moreover, personality judgment was more accurate in unstructured compared to structured job interviews (Blackman, 2002b). This relation was mediated by the amount of applicant talking during the job interview. Thus, the unstructured job interview might put the applicant more at ease, which increases the quantity of disclosed behavior (speaking time) and this in turn makes personality judgments about the applicant more accurate. Interestingly, we found that additional information, such as a photograph on an applicant's resume, does not impact assessment accuracy. Personality traits and intelligence of the applicant were assessed significantly accurately, regardless of whether the applicant's resume contained a photograph or not (Schmid Mast et al., 2014). And, recruiter experience was unrelated to personality judgment accuracy (Schmid Mast et al., 2011; Frauendorfer & Schmid Mast, 2014a).

Applicant nonverbal behavior does not only provide the recruiter with information about the applicant's personality traits or intelligence, but can also demonstrate whether the applicant uses deceptive IM strategies. Especially the nonverbal behavior (compared to the verbal behavior) is indicative of whether the applicant is dishonest or not (DePaulo, 1992). Deceptive IM strategies are known to be used by applicants in order to polish their competency profile (Gilmore & Ferris, 1989; Levashina & Campion, 2007). This dishonest strategy might decrease job interview validity (Delery & Kacmar, 1998; Gilmore et al., 1999; Levashina & Campion, 2006; Marcus, 2006). In other words, the recruiter might miss a highly qualified applicant while selecting a less qualified applicant who used deceptive IM. Research so far has shown that recruiters are able to correctly detect lies and that they are better at this than laypeople (Roulin et al., 2014; Schmid Mast et al., 2011), however, their level of detecting honest answers is higher than their level of detecting dishonest answers (Roulin et al., 2014).

In sum, recruiters are quite good at correctly assessing applicant's personality and at detecting deceptive answers based on the applicant's nonverbal behavior. Situational factors such as the structure and the type of the job interview have a remarkable impact on both accurate personality judgment and lie detection. The role of personal factors regarding the recruiter, such as years of experience, shows an unclear picture with respect to accuracy in personality judgment and lie detection.

Recruiter nonverbal behavior

The recruiter's behavior is a crucial factor in the job interview as it is one of the main reasons for the applicant to accept a job offer (Glueck, 1973). The better the general impression the applicant has of the recruiter, the more favorably the company is perceived by the applicant and therefore the more likely the applicant is to accept the job. Moreover, the recruiter's nonverbal (and verbal) behavior is constantly interpreted by the applicant to obtain signs regarding their chances of obtaining the job (Rynes & Miller, 1983; Connerley & Rynes, 1997). This can be explained by the fact that applicants often have only little information about the job offer and they use the recruiter's behavior as a signal to learn more about the employment's characteristics. Indeed, it is shown that recruiter (nonverbal) behavior only has an impact on company attraction when the applicant has little information about the job and the company (Rynes & Miller, 1983; Powell, 1984). Moreover, the more the recruiter shows nonverbal behavior such as maintaining eye contact and smiling, the better the impression the applicant forms about the recruiter and the job (Keenan & Wedderburn, 1975; Gilmore & Ferris, 1989; Turban, Forret, & Hendrickson, 1998). And, the more nonverbally friendly the recruiter behaves during the job interview, the more the applicant makes positive inferences about the organization (Goltz & Giannantonio, 1995). Recruiter listening skills – most likely conveyed through nonverbal behavior (e.g., smiling, nodding, and facial expression) – have a positive impact on the applicant's willingness to accept the job offer (Harn & Thornton, 1985). Also, the recruiter's nonverbal behavior affects the applicant's evaluation of the recruiter and the applicant's nonverbal behavior. The more the recruiter interrupts the applicant during the job interview, the less the recruiter is perceived as being an empathic listener by the applicant (McComb & Jablin, 1984). And, interviewees rate interviewers as least attractive, give the shortest answers, and sit furthest away from the interviewer when the interviewer does not maintain eye contact (Kleinke et al., 1975).

Recruiter nonverbal behavior does not only have an impact on the applicant's perception, but also on how the applicant is perceived by strangers. For instance, outside observers perceived the applicant as liking the recruiter more when the recruiter shook the applicant's hand at the beginning of the job interview (Staneski et al., 1977). And, the more the recruiter showed nonverbal approval behavior (i.e., smiling, eye contact, and gesturing) the more the applicant was rated (by neutral observers) as being comfortable and as having conveyed a better impression (Washburn & Hakel, 1973; Keenan & Wedderburn, 1975; Keenan, 1976). Thus, there are also inferences made about the applicant, based on the recruiter's behavior only.

Research investigating moderators that influence the relation between recruiter nonverbal behavior and applicant behavior shows that recruiter nonverbal behavior (cold vs. warm) had a more pronounced impact on applicants with low self-esteem than it had on applicants with high self-esteem (Liden et al., 1993). Low self-esteem applicants performed significantly better (based on verbal and nonverbal behavior) when the recruiter showed warm nonverbal behavior compared to a recruiter showing cold nonverbal behavior, whereas for high self-esteem applicants the recruiter behavior (cold vs. warm) did not influence the applicant's performance. In sum, recruiter nonverbal behavior has a remarkable impact on the applicant perception of the recruiter and the company as well as on the applicant behavior.

Implicit stereotypes and the self-fulfilling prophecy

Often, recruiter nonverbal behavior is elicited by (gender or racial) stereotypes recruiters might harbor. This in turn can influence the applicant's performance during the job interview (Word et al., 1974; Anderson & Shackleton, 1990). For instance, European American interviewers revealed less immediacy behavior (in terms of physical distance, forward lean, eye contact, and shoulder orientation), more speech errors, and spoke less when facing a black applicant compared to when facing a white applicant (Word et al., 1974). This recruiter behavior in turn had a negative impact on the applicant's behavior, as a subsequent study by the same authors showed. Less recruiter immediacy behavior, more recruiter speech errors, and less recruiter speaking time decreased applicants' job interview outcomes, whereas applicants interviewed by a recruiter with nonverbal approval behavior (i.e., smiling, head nodding, and eye contact) performed better in the job interview. In this study both applicants and interviewers were white (Word et al., 1974). This is in line with the behavioral *confirmation theory* claiming that a perceiver's beliefs (e.g., recruiter) can cause the target (e.g., applicant) to behave in a manner that confirms the perceiver's beliefs (i.e., self-fulfilling prophecy; Snyder & Swann, 1978; Darley & Fazio, 1980) and this relation tends to be mediated by recruiter nonverbal behavior. In the same vein, research shows that the more a male recruiter possesses an implicit gender bias, the less well a female applicant performs in a job interview (Latu et al., 2013). The mechanism through which this effect happens is most likely linked to the recruiter emitting subtle nonverbal cues that convey expectations of incompetence to female applicants who then confirm these expectations – maybe also on an implicit level. In the aforementioned study, male recruiters tended to communicate their implicit gender stereotypes through their interruption behavior. The more the recruiter harbored implicit gender stereotypes the more he tended to interrupt the female applicant, which in turn led to a lower applicant job interview outcome (Latu et al., 2013). And, sexual harassment behavior of the recruiter (i.e., showing flirting behavior) influenced female applicants, as they spoke less fluently, gave lower quality answers, and asked fewer job-relevant questions than when the recruiter did not show sexual harassment behavior (Woodzicka & LaFrance, 2005).

In sum, recruiter stereotypes towards the applicant seem to be transmitted through recruiter nonverbal behavior, which in turn can decrease the applicant's performance during the job interview. In other words, recruiter nonverbal behavior can be responsible for the subtle transfer of recruiter attitudes towards the applicant.

Summary

Research shows a clear link between applicant nonverbal behavior and recruiter hiring decision. In particular, immediacy nonverbal behavior, such as a high amount of applicant smiling, nodding, eye contact, hand gestures, and pitch variation, is positively related to recruiter evaluation. While one line of research has focused on nonverbal behavior measured based on objective observations (e.g., Fugita et al., 1974; Forbes & Jackson, 1980; Anderson & Shackleton, 1990), another line of research has assessed nonverbal behavior based on self-reports which reflect the applicant's subjective perception of to what extent he or she expressed certain nonverbal behaviors during the job interview (Kristof et al., 2002). Both methods reveal a positive link between applicant nonverbal immediacy behavior and recruiter hiring decision.

The literature has also evidenced factors influencing the extent to which different nonverbal behaviors are expressed in the job interview. These factors include the situation, the personality, the gender, and the race of the applicant. Depending on these factors, one might use more or less nonverbal behavior during the job interview (Fugita et al., 1974; Van Vianen & Van Schie, 1995; Peeters & Lievens, 2006).

Based on the Brunswikian lens model approach (1956) it becomes evident that many more nonverbal cues are used to infer applicant's personality traits than are cues actually revealing these traits. This is line with previous research showing that many more nonverbal cues are used to infer dominance, for instance, than are actually indicative of dominance (Hall et al., 2005). However, even if recruiters use more nonverbal cues than are actually related to applicant characteristics, recruiters are still accurate in assessing applicants (Schmid Mast et al., 2011; Frauendorfer & Schmid Mast, 2014a; Schmid Mast et al., 2014).

Research has not only focused on the applicant's nonverbal behavior in the job interview, but also on the recruiter's nonverbal behavior and its impact on the applicant's perception. Overall, the more the recruiter reveals warm nonverbal behavior (e.g., smiling, maintaining eye contact, and confirming the applicant with head nods) the better is the impression the recruiter conveys and the higher is the likelihood of the applicant accepting the job offer (e.g., Keenan & Wedderburn, 1975; Harn & Thornton, 1985; Turban, 1992; Goltz & Giannantonio, 1995). Nonverbal behavior of the recruiter can also be responsible for a subtle delivery of stereotypical expectations and attitudes. For instance, interruption behavior of the recruiter can lead to a decrease in the applicant's job interview performance, in case where the applicant is not confirming (implicit) racial or gender stereotypes (Word et al., 1974; Latu et al., 2013).

Outlook

So far, most research investigating social perception in the job interview process has focused on the recruiter's inference, providing information about which nonverbal cues the recruiters use to infer certain applicant personality traits. By doing so, the lens model approach as a whole has been neglected. That is, cue utilization, cue validity, and assessment accuracy have rarely been investigated in one and the same study (except Gifford et al., 1985). However, only if the lens model approach is considered as a whole can all sides of the lens be investigated and compared. Moreover, recruiters seem to use the nonverbal cues that are not diagnostic to assess applicants – in a sense they use the wrong cues – and are still accurate in assessing applicants' personality. It remains therefore largely unknown how the recruiters make those correct inferences. Future research might want to refer increasingly to the lens model approach, which will enable researchers to compare adequately the cue utilization with cue validity and assessment accuracy (Gifford, 2011) and to assess an even wider array of nonverbal behaviors or nonverbal behavior composites.

One way of facilitating the nonverbal behavior coding necessary for this would be to welcome methodological innovation by using devices which automatically sense and extract the nonverbal behavior of the applicant. Even if the present book chapter is based on ample research about nonverbal behavior in the job interview, studies which investigate a wide array of nonverbal behavior of the applicant are still scarce. Behavioral research remains a time- and cost-intensive endeavor in which human coders have to view the same social interaction over and over again, in order to accurately code different behaviors (Reis & Charles, 2000; Furnham, 2008). We have shown that nonverbal behaviors can be automatically sensed and extracted during the job interview (Frauendorfer et al., 2014) and strongly encourage researchers to invest in such promising methods so that behavioral data collection can be conducted as efficiently as possible. *Automated social sensing* is typically done in two steps: first, the applicant's behavior is sensed and recorded based on ubiquitous computing; second, the applicant's nonverbal behavior is extracted automatically based on computational models and algorithms (Gatica-Perez et al., 2007). "Ubiquitous computing" stands for a computer environment that adapts to the human environment. It does not therefore require the human to enter the computer environment, but the computer and the sensing devices are implied in the everyday environment; the surrounding becomes "smart." The automated extraction of nonverbal behavior is conducted based on algorithms which are developed by computer scientists (Basu, 2002; Ba & Odobez, 2011; Biel, Aran, & Gatica-Perez, 2011).

The advantage of automated social sensing is that numerous different nonverbal cues from several interaction partners can be extracted at the same time and over long recording periods. Moreover, the automated extraction is very quick. Large amounts of data can be processed once the algorithms for data extraction are developed. Also, automated social sensing has shown to be accurate as long as the setup of the devices fulfills the pre-defined conditions, such as the lightning of the room and camera angles.

Using automated social sensing, we have been able to show that similar results are obtained when extracting the applicant's nonverbal behavior automatically compared to when the nonverbal behavior is coded manually. Automatically sensed and extracted applicant immediate nonverbal behavior such as gazing, speech fluency, and tempo variation predicted recruiter hiring decision (Frauendorfer et al., in press). In a further step, we have aimed to show that automated social sensing can also be used as a valid tool in personnel selection. In other words, we were interested in whether the automatically extracted nonverbal behavior of the applicant would also predict future job performance, especially when the job contains social interactions as a main characteristic, such as sales. Based on previous research showing that the nonverbal behavior of sales people predicts job performance (Leigh & Summers, 2002; Peterson, 2005; Wood, 2006; Taute et al., 2011), we assumed that for sales, the applicant's nonverbal behavior revealed during the job interview might be indicative of future job performance. And indeed, using a door-to-door sales job, we found that the applicant's vocal nonverbal cues such as speaking time, audio back-channeling, and speech fluency all together predicted objectively-measured job performance (Frauendorfer et al., 2014a). Even if more research has to be done on the usage of automated social sensing in job interviews, we have shown the first evidence that such a novel method can be predictively valid.

Conclusion

Nonverbal behavior in the job interview is crucial as it has a high impact on various outcomes. Whereas the applicant's nonverbal behavior influences how the recruiter evaluates the applicant, the recruiter's nonverbal behavior affects the applicant's perception and even the applicant's performance. Moreover, the applicant nonverbal behavior-hiring decision link has been shown to be influenced by factors such as the situation, personality, gender, and race. Finally, recruiters use more nonverbal cues to infer certain applicant characteristics than are actually indicative of the actual applicant characteristics.

Future research on nonverbal behavior could be facilitated by novel methods such as using automated social sensing which decreases time and cost investment enormously. Automated social sensing and other automated methods should therefore encourage researchers to conduct further behavioral studies in this area.

References

Ambady, N., Hallahan, M., & Rosenthal, R. (1995). On judging and being judged accurately in zero acquaintance situations. *Journal of Personality and Social Psychology, 69,* 518–529.

Ambady, N., & Rosenthal, R. (1992). Thin slices of expressive behavior as predictors of interpersonal consequences: A meta-analysis. *Psychological Bulletin, 111,* 256–274.

Ambady, N., & Rosenthal, R. (1993). Half a minute: Predicting teacher evaluations from thin slices of nonverbal behavior and physical attractiveness. *Journal of Personality and Social Psychology, 3,* 431–441.

Anderson, N. R. (1991). Decision making in the graduate selection interview: An experimental investigation. *Human Relations, 44,* 403–417.

Anderson, N. R., & Shackleton, V. J. (1990). Decision making in the graduate selection interview: A field study. *Journal of Occupational Psychology, 63,* 63–76. doi: 10.1111/j.2044-8325.1990.tb00510.x.

Arvey, R. D., & Campion, J. E. (1982). The employment interview: A summary and review of recent research. *Personnel Psychology, 35,* 281–322. doi: 10.1111/j.1744-6570.1982.tb02197.x.

Ayres, J., Keereetaweep, T., Chen, P.-E., & Edwards, P. A. (1998). Communication apprehension and employment interviews. *Communication Education, 14,* 1–17.

Ba, S., & Odobez, J.-M. (2011). Multiperson visual focus of attention from head pose and meeting contextual cues. *IEEE Transactions on Pattern Analysis and Machine Intelligence, 3,* 101–116.

Barrick, M. R., & Mount, M. K. (1991). The Big Five personality dimensions and job performance: A aeta-analysis. *Personnel Psychology, 44*(1), 1–26. doi: 10.1111/j.1744-6570.1991.tb00688.x.

Barrick, M. R., Patton, G. K., & Haugland, S. N. (2000). Accuracy of interview judgments of job applicant personality traits. *Personnel Psychology, 53*(4), 925–951. doi: 10.1111/j.1744-6570.2000.tb02424.x.

Barrick, M. R., Shaffer, J. A., & DeGrassi, S. W. (2009). What you see may not be what you get: Relationships among self-presentations tactics and ratings of interview and job performance. *Journal of Applied Psychology, 94,* 1394–1411.

Basu, S. (2002). *Conversational scene analysis.* Cambridge, MA: MIT Department of EECS. Retrieved from http://alumni.media.mit.edu/~sbasu/papers.html

Biel, J.-I., Aran, O., & Gatica-Perez, D. (2011, July). *You are known by how you vlog: Personality impressions and nonverbal behavior in YouTube.* Paper presented at the Proc. Int. AAAI Conference on Weblogs and Social Media, Barcelona, Spain.

Blackman, M. C. (2002a). The employment interview via telephone: Are we sacrificing accurate personality judgments for cost efficiency? *Journal of Research in Personality, 36,* 208–223.

Blackman, M. C. (2002b). Personality judgment and the utility of the unstructured employment interview. *Basic & Applied Social Psychology, 24,* 241–250.

Borkenau, P., & Liebler, A. (1992). Trait inferences: Sources of validity at zero acquaintance. *Journal of Personality and Social Psychology, 62*(4), 645. doi: 10.1037/0022-3514.62.4.645.

Borkenau, P., & Liebler, A. (1995). Observable attributes as manisfestations and cues of personality and intelligence. *Journal of Personality, 63,* 1–25.

Brunswik, E. (1956). *Perception and the representative design of psychological experiments*. Los Angeles: University of California Press.

Caldwell, D. F., & Burger, J. M. (1998). Personality characteristics of job applicant and success in screening interviews. *Personnel Psychology, 51*, 119–136.

Campion, M. A., Cheraskin, L., & Stevens, M. J. (1994). Career-related antecedents and outcomes of job rotation. *Academy of Management Journal, 37*, 1518–1542.

Connerley, M. L., & Rynes, S. L. (1997). The influence of recruiter characteristics and organizational recruitment support on perceived recruiter effectiveness: Views from applicants and recruiters. *Human Relations, 50*(12), 1563–1586. doi: 10.1023/a:1016923732255.

Darley, J. M., & Fazio, R. H. (1980). Expectancy confirmation processes arising in the social interaction sequence. *American Psychologist, 35*, 867–881.

Delery, J. E., & Kacmar, K. M. (1998). The influence of applicant and interviewer characteristics on the use of impression management. *Journal of Applied Psychology, 28*, 1649–1669.

DeGroot, T., & Gooty, J. (2009). Can nonverbal cues be used to make meaningful personality attributions in employment interviews? *Journal of Business and Psychology, 24*, 179–192.

DePaulo, B. M. (1992). Nonverbal behavior and self-presentation. *Psychological Bulletin, 111*, 203–243. doi: 10.1037/0033-2909.111.2.203.

Dipboye, R. L. (1994). Structured and unstructured interviews: Beyond the job-fit model. In G. R. Ferris (Ed.), *Research in personnel and human resources management* (Vol. 12). Greenwich, CT: JAI Press.

Dixon, J. A., & Foster, D. H. (1998). Gender, social context, and backchannel responses. *The Journal of Social Psychology, 138*, 134–136.

Dunn, W. S., Mount, M. K., Barrick, M. R., & Ones, D. S. (1995). Relative importance of personality and general mental ability in managers' judgments of applicant qualifications. *Journal of Applied Psychology, 80*, 500–509. doi: 10.1037/0021-9010.80.4.500.

Edinger, J. A., & Patterson, M. L. (1983). Nonverbal involvement and social control. *Psychological Bulletin, 93*, 30–56.

Forbes, R. J., & Jackson, P. R. (1980). Non-verbal behaviour and the outcome of selection interviews. *Journal of Occupational Psychology, 53*, 65–72.

Frauendorfer, D., & Schmid Mast, M. (2014a). *Can recruiters accurately predict applicants' job performance based on thin-slices of applicant job interview behavior? Yes, they can!* Manuscript in preparation.

Frauendorfer, D., & Schmid Mast, M. (2014b). *The relation between applicant nonverbal behavior and recruiter hiring decision: A meta-analysis*. Manuscript in preparation.

Frauendorfer, D., Schmid Mast, M., Nguyen, L. S., & Gatica-Perez, D. (2014a). *Predicting job performance based on automatically sensed and extracted applicant nonverbal interview behavior*. Manuscript in preparation.

Frauendorfer, D., Schmid Mast, M., Nguyen, L. S., & Gatica-Perez, D. (2014b). *The role of the applicant's nonverbal behvior in the job interview: A lens model approach*. Manuscript in preparation.

Frauendorfer, D., Schmid Mast, M., Nguyen, L. S., & Gatica-Perez, D. (2014). Nonverbal social sensing: Unobstrusive recording and extracting of nonverbal behavior in social interactions illustrated with a research example. *Journal of Nonverbal Behavior, 38*(2), 231–245.

Fugita, S. S., Wexley, K. N., & Hillery, J. M. (1974). Black-white differences in nonverbal behavior in an interview setting. *Journal of Applied Social Psychology, 4*(4), 343–350.

Furnham, A. (2008). HR professionals' beliefs about, and knowledge of, assessment techniques and psychometric tests. *International Journal of Selection and Assessment, 16*, 300–305. doi: 10.1111/j.1468-2389.2008.00436.x.

Gatewood, R. D., Feild, H. S., & Barrick, M. R. (2011). *Human resource selection*. Mason, OH: South-Western Cengage Learning.

Gatica-Perez, D., Guillaume, L., Odobez, J.-M., & McCowan, I. (2007). Audio-visual tracking of multiple speakers in meetings. *IEEE Trans. on Audio, Speech, and Language Processing, 15*, 601–616.

Gifford, R. (2006). Personality and nonverbal behavior: A complex conundrum. In V. Manusov & M. L. Patterson (Eds.), *The sage handbook of nonverbal communication*. Thousand Oaks, CA: Sage Publications, Inc.

Gifford, R. (2011). The role of nonverbal communication in interpersonal relations. In L. M. Horowitz & S. Strack (Eds.), *Handbook of interpersonal psychology: Theory, research, assessment, and therapeutic interventions* (pp. 171–190). NY: Wiley.

Gifford, R., Ng, C. F., & Wilkinson, M. (1985). Nonverbal cues in the employment interview: Links between applicant qualities and interviewer judgments. *Journal of Applied Psychology, 70*(4), 729–736. doi: 10.1037/0021-9010.70.4.729

Gilmore, D. C., & Ferris, G. R. (1989). The effects of applicant impression management tactics on interviewer judgments. *Journal of Management, 15*, 557–564. doi: 10.1177/014920638901500405.

Gilmore, D. C., Stevens, C. K., Harrell-Cook, G., & Ferris, G. R. (1999). Impression management tactics. In R. W. Eder & M. M. Harris (Eds.), *The employment interview handbook* (pp. 321–336). Thousand Oakds, CA: Sage.

Glueck, W. (1973). Recruiters and executives: How do they affect job choice? *Journal of College Placement, 34*, 77–78.

Goldberg, S., & Rosenthal, R. (1986). Self-touching behavior in the job interview: Antecedents and consequences. *Journal of Nonverbal Behavior, 10*, 65–80.

Goltz, S. M., & Giannantonio, C. M. (1995). Recruiter friendliness and attraction to the job: The mediating role of interferences about the organization. *Journal of Vocational Behavior, 46*, 109–118.

Guerrero, L. K. (2005). Observer ratings of nonverbal involvement and immediacy. In V. Manusov (Ed.), *The sourcebook of nonverbal measures*. Mahwah, NJ: Lawrence Erlbaum Associates, Inc. Publishers.

Guion, R. M., & Highhouse, S. (2006). *Essentials of personnel assessment and selection*. Mahwah, NJ: Lawrence Erlbaum Associates.

Hall, J. A. (1984). *Nonverbal sex differences: Communication accuracy and expressive style*. Baltimore: Johns Hopkins University Press.

Hall, J. A., & Carter, J. D. (2000). Gender differences in nonverbal communication of emotion. In A. H. Fischer (Ed.), *Gender and emotion: Social psychological perspectives*. The Edinburgh Building, Cambridge: Cambridge University Press.

Hall, J. A., Coats, E. J., & LeBeau, L. S. (2005). Nonverbal behavior and the vertical dimension of social relations: A meta-analysis. *Psychological Bulletin, 131*, 898–924.

Harn, T. J., & Thornton, G. C. (1985). Recruiter counselling behaviours and applicant impressions. *Journal of Occupational Psychology, 58*(1), 57–65. doi: 10.1111/j.2044-8325.1985.tb00180.x.

Harris, M. M. (1989). Reconsidering the employment interview: A review of recent literature and suggestions for future research. *Personnel Psychology, 42*(4), 691–726.

Imada, A. S., & Hakel, M. D. (1977). Influence of nonverbal communication and rater proximity on impressions and decisions in simulated employment interviews. *Journal of Applied Psychology, 62*, 295–300.

Janz, T. (1982). Initial comparisons of patterned behavior description interviews versus unstructured interviews. *Journal of Applied Psychology, 67*, 577–580. doi: 10.1037/0021-9010.67.5.577.

Kanki, B. G. (1985). Participant differences and interactive strategies. In S. F. Dunca & D. W. Fiske (Eds.), *Interaction structure and strategy*. New York: Cambridge University Press.

Keenan, A. (1976). Effects of the nonverbal behavior of interviewers on candidates' performance. *Journal of Occupational Psychology, 49*, 171–176.

Keenan, A., & Wedderburn, A. A. I. (1975). Effects of the nonverbal behavior of interviewers on candidates' impressions. *Journal of Occupational Psychology, 48*, 129–132.

Kenny, D. A. (1994). *Interpersonal perception: A social relations analysis*. New York: Guilford.

Kleinke, C. L., Staneski, R. A., & Berger, D. E. (1975). Evaluation of an interviewer as a function of interviewer gaze, reinforcement of subject gaze, and interviewer attractiveness. *Journal of Personality and Social Psychology, 31*(1), 115–122. doi: 10.1037/h0076244.

Kristof-Brown, A. L. (2000). Perceived applicant fit: Distinguishing between recruiter's perception of person-job and person-organization fit. *Personnel Psychology, 53*(3), 643–671.

Kristof-Brown, A. L., Barrick, M. R., & Franke, M. (2002). Applicant impression management: Dispositional influences and consequences for recruiter perceptions of fit and similarity. *Journal of Management, 28*, 27–46.

Krumhuber, E., Manstead, A., Cosker, D., Marshall, D., & Rosin, P. (2009). Effects of dynamic attributes of smiles in human and synthetic faces: A simulated job interview setting. *Journal of Nonverbal Behavior, 33*(1), 1–15. doi: 10.1007/s10919-008-0056-8.

Latu, I. M., Schmid Mast, M., & Stewart, T. L. (2013, January). *Implicit behavioral confirmation in job interviews: Male recruiters' implicit gender stereotypes (but not attitudes) decrease performance self-evaluations of female applicants*. Paper presented at the Annual meeting of the Society for Personality and Social Psychology, New Orleans, LA.

Leigh, T. W., & Summers, J. O. (2002). An initial evaluation of industrial buyers' impressions of salespersons' nonverbal cues. *Journal of Personal Selling & Sales Management, 22*, 41–53.

Levashina, J., & Campion, J. E. (2006). A model of faking likelihood in the employment interview. *International Journal of Selection and Assessment, 14*, 299–316.

Levashina, J., & Campion, M. A. (2007). Measuring faking in the employment interview: Development and validation of an interview faking behavior scale. *Journal of applied psychology, 92*, 1638–1656.

Levine, S. P., & Feldman, R. S. (2002). Women and men's nonverbal behavior and self-monitoring in a job interview setting. *Applied H.R.M. Research, 7*(1), 1–14.

Liden, R. C., Martin, C. L., & Parsons, C. K. (1993). Interviewer and applicant behaviors in employment interviews. *The Academy of Management Journal, 36*(2), 372–386.

Marcus, B. (2006). Relationships between faking, validity, and decision criteria in personnel selection. *Psychology Science, 48,* 226–246.

McComb, K. B., & Jablin, F. M. (1984). Verbal correlates of interviewer empathic listening and employment interview outcomes. *Communication Monographs, 51,* 353–371.

McDaniel, M. A., Whetzel, D. L., Schmidt, F. L., & Maurer, S. D. (1994). The validity of employment interviews: A comprehensive review and meta-analysis. *Journal of Applied Psychology, 79,* 599–616. doi: 10.1037/0021-9010.79.4.599.

McGovern, T. V., & Tinsley, H. E. A. (1978). Interviewer evaluations of interviewee nonverbal behavior. *Journal of Vocational Behavior, 13,* 163–171. doi: 10.1016/0001-8791(78)90041-6.

Motowidlo, S. J., Carter, G. W., Dunnette, M. D., Tippins, N., Werner, S., Burnett, J. R., & Vaughan, M. J. (1992). Studies of the structured behavioral interview. *Journal of Applied Psychology, 77,* 571–587. doi: 10.1037/0021-9010.77.5.571.

Murphy, N. A. (2005). Using thin slices for behavioral coding. *Journal of Nonverbal Behavior, 29*(4), 235–246.

Murphy, N. A., Hall, J., & Colvin, C. R. (2003). Accurate intelligence assessment in social interactions: Mediators and gender effects. *Journal of Personality, 71,* 465–493.

Ng, E. S. W., & Sears, G. J. (2010). The effect of adverse impact in selection practices on organizational diversity: A field study. *The International Journal of Human Resource Management, 21,* 1454–1471.

Nicholls, M. A. M., & Visser, D. (2010). Validation of a test battery for the selection of call centre operators in a communications company. *South African Journal of Psychology, 39,* 19–31.

Parsons, C. K., & Liden, R. C. (1984). Interviewer perceptions of applicant qualifications: A multivariate field study of demographic characteristics and nonverbal cues. *Journal of Applied Psychology, 69,* 557–568. doi: 10.1037/0021-9010.69.4.557.

Peeters, H., & Lievens, F. (2006). Verbal and nonverbal impression management tactics in behavior description and situational interviews. *International Journal of Selection and Assessment, 14,* 206–222.

Pelligrini, R. J., Hicks, R. A., & Gordon, L. (1970). The effect of an approval-seeking induction on eye-contact in dyads. *British Journal of Social and Clinical Psychology, 9,* 373–374.

Peterson, R. T. (2005). An examination of the relative effectiveness of training in nonverbal communication: Personal selling implications. *Journal of Marketing Education, 27,* 143–150. doi: 10.1177/0273475305276627.

Powell, G. N. (1984). Effects of job attributes and recruiting practices on applicant decisions: A comparison. *Personnel Psychology, 37,* 721–732. doi: 10.1111/j.1744-6570.1984.tb00536.x.

Prickett, T., Gada-Jain, N., & Bernieri, F. J. (2000, May). *First impression formation in a job interview: The first 20-seconds.* Paper presented at the annual meeting of the Midwestern Psychological Associaton Chicago, IL.

Reis, H. T., & Charles, M. J. (2000). *Handbook of research methods in social and personality psychology.* The Edinburgh Building, Cambridge: Cambridge University Press.

Roulin, N., Bangerter, A., & Levashina, J. (2014). Interviewers' perceptions of impression management in employment interviews. *Journal of Managerial Psychology, 29*(2), 141–163.

Ruben, M., Hall, J., & Schmid Mast, M. (2012, January). *Smiling in a job interview: When less is more.* Paper presented at the Annual Meeting of the Society of Personality and Social Psychology, San Diego, CA.

Rynes, S. L., & Miller, H. E. (1983). Recruiter and job influences on candidates for employment. *Journal of Applied Psychology, 68,* 147–154.

Salgado, J. F., Viswesvaran, C., & Ones, D. S. (2001). Predictors used for pesonnel selection: An overview of constructs, methods, and techniques. In N. Anderson, D. S. Ones, H. K. Sinangil, & C. Viswesvaran (Eds.), *Handbook of industrial, work, and organizational psychology* (Vol. 1). Thousands Oaks, CA: Sage.

Schlenker, B. R. (1980). *Impression management: The self-concept, social identity, and interpersonal relations.* Monterey, CA: Brooks/Cole.

Schmid Mast, M., Bangerter, A., Bulliard, C., & Aerni, G. (2011). How accurate are recruiters' first impressions of applicants in employment interviews? *International Journal of Selection and Assessment, 19,* 198–208.

Schmid Mast, M., Frauendorfer, D., & Sutter, C. (2014). *To Add or not to Add a Photograph? Accuracy of Personality Judgments from Resumes with and without Photographs.* Manuscript submitted for publication.

Schmidt, F. L., & Hunter, J. E. (1998). The validity and utility of selection methods in personnel psychology: Practical and theoretical implications of 85 years of research findings. *Psychological Bulletin, 124,* 262–274. doi: 10.1037/0033-2909.124.2.262.

Sigelman, C. K., & Davis, P. J. (1978). Making good impressions in job interviews: Verbal and nonverbal predictors. *Education and Training of the Mentally Retarded, 13,* 71–76.

Sigelman, C. K., Elias, S. F., & Danker-Brown, P. (1980). Interview behaviors of mentally retarded adults as predictors of employability. *Journal of Applied Psychology, 65,* 67–73.

Snyder, M., & Swann, W. B. (1978). Behavioral confirmation in social interaction: From social perception to social reality. *Journal of Experimental Social Psychology, 14,* 148–162.

Sommers, M. S., Greeno, D. W., & Boag, D. (1989). The role of non-verbal communication in service provision and representation. *The Service Industrial Journal, 9*(4), 162–173.

Staneski, R. A., Kleinke, C. L., & Meeker, F. B. (1977). Effects of integration, touch, and use of name on evaluation of job applicants and interviewers. *Social Behavior and Personality, 5,* 13–19.

Sterrett, J. H. (1978). The job interview: Body language and perceptions of potential effectiveness. *Journal of Applied Psychology, 63,* 388–390.

Stevens, C. K., & Kristof, A. L. (1995). Making the right impression: A field study of applicant impression management during job interviews. *Journal of Applied Psychology, 80,* 587–606. doi: 10.1037/0021-9010.80.5.587.

Taute, H. A., Heiser, R. S., & McArthur, D. N. (2011). The effect of nonverbal signals on student role-play evaluations. *Journal of Marketing Education, 33,* 28–40. doi: 10.1177/0273475310389153.

Tessler, R., & Sushelsky, L. (1978). Effects of eye contact and social status on perception of a job applicant in an employment interviewing situation. *Journal of Vocational Behavior, 13,* 338–347.

Tews, M. J., Stafford, K., & Tracey, J. B. (2011). What matters most? The perceived importance of ability and personality for hiring decisions. *Human Resources Management, 52,* 94–101.

Tsai, W.-C., Chen, C.-C., & Chiu, S.-F. (2005). Exploring boundaries of the effects of applicant impression management tactics in job interviews. *Journal of Management, 31,* 108–125.

Turban, D. B. (1992). Influences of campus recruiting on applicant attraction to firms. *The Academy of Management Journal, 35*(4), 739.

Turban, D. B., Forret, M. L., & Hendrickson, C. L. (1998). Applicant attraction to firms: Influences of organization reputation, job and organizational attributes, and recruiter behaviors. *Journal of Vocational Behavior, 52,* 24–44. doi: http://dx.doi.org/10.1006/jvbe.1996.1555.

Van Vianen, A. E. M., & Van Schie, E. C. M. (1995). Assessment of male and female behavior in the employment interview. *Journal of Community and Applied Social Psychology, 5,* 243–257.

Washburn, P. V., & Hakel, M. D. (1973). Visual cues and verbal content as influences on impressions formed after simulated employment interviews. *Journal of Applied Psychology, 58,* 137–141.

Webster, E. C. (1964). *Decision making in the employment interview.* Montreal: Eagle.

Wood, J. A. (2006). NLP revisited: Nonverbal communications and signals of trustworthiness. *Journal of Personal Selling & Sales Management, 26,* 197–204. doi: 10.2753/pss0885-3134260206.

Woodzicka, J., & LaFrance, M. (2005). The effects of subtle sexual harassment on women's performance in a job interview. *Sex Roles, 53,* 67–77. doi: 10.1007/s11199-005-4279-4.

Word, C. O., Zanna, M. P., & Cooper, J. (1974). The nonverbal mediation of self-fulfilling prophecies in interracial interaction. *Journal of Experimental Social Psychology, 10,* 109–120.

11

Nonverbal Communication in Interaction: Psychology and Literature

Fernando Poyatos

> Havill's face had been not unpleasant until this
> moment, when he smiled; whereupon there instantly
> gleamed over him a phase of meanness, remaining
> until the smile died away. It might have been an
> accident; it might have been otherwise.
>
> (T. Hardy, *A Laodicean*)

The need for a realistic approach to interaction

When about 40 years ago I began to ponder the complexity of interaction – face-to-face and with the environment – I realized researchers tended to neglect a great number of instances as merely "incidental," "contextual" or "marginal," and thus identified at most a series of interactive facts in a cause-effect sequence that dismissed what "did not happen," even more what "would or would have not happened" (had an activity or non-activity taken place), let alone what "had not happened yet" or "was not even going to happen." I always conceived of *interaction* as:

> The conscious or unconscious exchange of behavioral or nonbehavioral, sensible and intelligible signs from the whole arsenal of somatic and extrasomatic systems (independently of whether they are activities or non-activities or did or will happen at all) and the rest of the surrounding cultural systems, as they all act as sign emitting components (and as potential elicitors of further emissions) which determine the specific characteristics of the exchange.

I was simultaneously discovering the wealth of virtually inexhaustible illustrative data offered by creative literature, particularly the novel, only one aspect of the unsuspected fruitfulness hidden in interdisciplinary research within the social sciences (Poyatos, 2002a). Here, joining psychology and literature – as I did dealing only with kinesics (Poyatos, 2002b) – I will outline a number of methodological avenues for the study of: personal and extrapersonal components of interaction, both face-to-face and with the environment; their sensory perception and how the physiopsychological synesthesial associations operate also as components; how sensible and intelligible components can function independently or in double or multiple clusters; the qualifiers of interactive activities and non-activities; and how components are associated to preceding, simultaneous or succeeding ones. Since, as will be seen, most of the instances of personal encounters are non-conversational, the last part will be specifically devoted to outlining the structure of conversation.

The components of interaction

We cannot have a complete image of a given interactive situation and analyze *what* exactly happens – to later determine *how* and *why* things happen the way they do – without first identifying *all* the components of that situation, instead of hastily deciding that any one of them plays no interactive function. Otherwise, we would perceive "gaps" that do not exist, for we find nonverbal signs (e.g., a co-interactant's distracted look) with specific functions, without which we will inevitably fail to perceive a series of interrelationships – not only between verbal and nonverbal elements (even within speech itself), but among the latter – which contain important sign clusters and messages and in turn elicit other activities or non-activities, showing the manifold interdisciplinary perspective we can develop through this model. For instance: the ontogenetic development of the language-paralanguage-kinesics structure (*vs.* the study of language development only, and not necessarily independently of other systems like proxemics or the conceptualization and frequency of chemical and dermal reactions, varying personally and cross-culturally), since all three repertoires clearly develop morphologically as well as functionally (any imbalance betraying different developmental abnormalities); a sociopsychological and cross-cultural study of the conceptualization and interactive functions of interactive silences; the many sociopsychological implications of the use of "body-adaptors" and "object-adaptors," like various types of furniture (actually body-adaptors if anatomically designed); the effect on interpersonal interactions of the intelligible components of encounters, according to age, personality, and cultural background; the deeper relationships between the built environment (urban design, architectural spaces, and volumes) and interpersonal and person-environment interaction; and many more.

The first basic differentiation is between two fundamental categories of interaction components: *internal* (active or passive elements that can be exchanged among the participants, or have a direct relationship with the exchange, as with language, perfume, or social status) and *external* (behavioral or non-behavioral activities, and static elements, which cannot be part of that mutual personal exchange, but occur in the periphery of the encounter proper).

Internal components

A. Sensible Bodily Personal Components, produced by somatic activities or non-activities and comprising three groups:

Personal sensible behavioral activities:

(a) The *basic triple structure of speech*: *verbal language* (i.e., variable lexico-morphologico-syntactical sign structures with their basic prosodic features), *paralanguage* (voice modifiers, voice types and independent word-like utterances like voice registers, voice types, throat-clearings, moans, momentary silences, etc.), and *kinesics* (movements and positions of eyes, face, trunk, and extremities, perceived visually, audiovisually, tactually, and kinesthetically). Even when hidden from view, kinesics is linked to the person's other verbal and nonverbal behaviors: "She clenched her hands and felt the hard little coins she was holding" (V. Woolf, *The Years*);

(b) *Proxemics* (conceptualization and conscious or unconscious behavioral structuring of interpersonal and person-environment space), resulting: from kinesic activities and conditioned (perhaps covertly) by room size, room density and furniture layout, the latter exerting a positive "sociopetal" effect (attracting toward the center); or from the opposite, a negative "sociofugal" effect (Sommer, 1969); and from exterior urban design, often including physical contact: "I [Laura] held her away from me in astonishment [...] 'Don't be angry with me, Mariam,' she said, mistaking my silence./ I only answered by drawing her close to me again. I was afraid of crying if I spoke" (W. Collins, *Woman in White*);

(c) *Body sounds beyond language and paralanguage,* of social or clinical significance, thus overlapping the nonbehavioral type of sounds, such as intestinal rumbling (perhaps embarrassing), bronchial whizzing (provoked by a cat or by anxiety, both as components of that interaction), or produced externally as four kinds of behavior: visual-audible *self-adaptors*: "'Wall, you can marry Latch,' rejoined Keetch, vigorously slapping his leg" (Z. Grey, *The Lost Wagon Train*); visual-audible *alter-adaptors* (e.g., slapping someone, involving two semiotic levels: the action and its humiliating sound; affectionate or deceitful back-slapping): "'[...] Cheer up, man,' he continued, giving Lord Lowborough a thump on the back" (A. Brontë, *The Tennant of Wildfell Hall*); visual-audible *body-adaptors*, involving food, drinks, masticatories (chewing gum, betel, kola, and associated behaviors), and clothes (the swishing of a long dress): "The silk of her dress rustled sharply [...] she was standing only one step above him [on the stairs], very close" (A. Huxley, *Eyeless in Gaza*); audible-audible *single and object-mediated object-adaptors* (e.g., door-knocking), and the objects themselves: "Holmes [...], as minute followed minute without result [...]. He gnawed his lip, drummed his fingers upon the table, and showed every other symptom of acute impatience" (A. Conan Doyle, *A Study in Scarlet*), "She heard a trampling of feet in the hall, a rasping of chairs" (W. Faulkner, *Sanctuary*).

Personal sensible nonbehavioral activities, uncontrollable bodily reactions (often reflexes) that are perceived olfactorily, visually, dermally and even gustatorily, at times with central functions as conveyors of messages of social or clinical value.

(a) *Chemical reactions* like physiological sweat due to room temperature, different from emotional sweat (e.g., the "palmar sweat" during interviews or interrogations); silent tear-shedding, or blended with accompanying language, paralanguage or kinesics (e.g., with visible signs of self-control); pathological odors like those of organic failure, tissue deterioration, the schizophrenic's crisis perceived by some therapists, and even imminent death: "Suddenly his throat contracted, the tears came into his eyes, the muscles of his chest tightened in spasm after violent spasm" (A. Huxley, *Eyeless in Gaza*). Personal odors – perhaps combined with artificial ones – are susceptible of intimate interaction through time (hence their chronemic aspect), as happens with the deeply felt smell of a garment that evokes its deceased or absent owner. There are also many negative interpretations (intentional or not, but interactive) of natural or artificial body odors due to racism, class prejudices and even moral status (e.g., "cheap perfume");

(b) *Dermal reactions*, mainly reddening, emotional blushing (both perceivable also by dermal contact in an intimate proxemic situation), blanching, paling and goose flesh: "At her first words the colour had rushed to his forehead; but as she continued she saw his face compose itself and his blood subside" (E. Wharton, *The Reef*). Blushing may trigger a second and deeper blushing, or provoke its attempted masking by feigning a different emotion (cf. Ekman, 1981): "She flushed slightly, and then, conscious of an embarrassment new and strange to her, blushed rosy red" (Z. Grey, *The Last Trail*);

(c) *Thermal reactions*, mainly rises and falls in body temperature – from crowding or in social or clinical situations acting as interactive signals – usually accompanied by another physiological activity: "I heard her [Laura's] breath quickening – I felt her hand growing cold" (W. Collins, *The Woman in White*).

Personal sensible behavioral non-activities, which can be as important as what is being expressed verbally or through gestures and postures, individually or combined with other components. There are two types:

(a) *Silence and stillness* (Poyatos, 2002c): "Again there ensued a silence, except for Nels' cough, and tapping of his pipe upon the table, while Madge sat there, strung and tense, her heart bursting" (Z. Grey, *Majestic Ranch*);

(b) *Static bodily characteristics* of shape, size, consistency, weight, strength (perceived tactually and kinesthetically, consciously or not), color of skin, hair and eyes, and specifically facial features, can play relevant roles: "He still held her hand [...] A sense of his strength came with the warm pressure, and comforted her" (Z. Grey, *The Last Trail*), "His [Roy Kear's] slight corpulence only added to his dignity. It gave weight to his observations" (W. Somerset Maugham, *Cakes and Ale*).

Since the speaking or silent face is the main channel of communication, one must distinguish four kinds of facial features (Poyatos, 2002a): *permanent*, that is, position, size and shape of brows, eyelids and eyelashes, nose, cheeks, mouth, forehead, chin, and mandible, to which can be added the long-term presence of a beard or moustache, conspicuous sideburns, or hairdo: "with fat little squirrel cheeks and a mouth perpetually primed in contemptuous judgement [...] in all ways smug and insufferable" (E. L. Doctorow, *World's Fair*); *changing*, with time, aging, work, suffering, hardships, or motor habits, such as wrinkles, folds, blotches, etc., usually intellectually evaluated components of an interaction: "His neck was ridged with muscles acquired from a life-long habit of stiffening his jaw and pushing it forward" (H. MacLennan, *Two Solitudes*); *dynamic*, perceived positively or negatively as part of speech, but based solely on their static state (e.g., in a portrait), crucial in first encounters (e.g., in a job interview): "His [Reginald Portway's] mobile, handsome features took on a look of understanding compassion, then changed to lively interest" (E. Wilson, *Anglo-Saxon Attitudes*); *artificial*, enhancing or de-emphasizing natural features: "Wearing the vermilion mark of marriage at the central parting of her hair, as a woman must, she would gain freedom, freedom to live her own way" (B. Bhattacharya, *He Who Rides a Tiger*).

B. Sensible Body-Related Personal Components, operating in inter-action as static elements or as behavioral manifestations when they become part (or rather, conditioners) of our kinesic activities, at which point they are communicating at two mutually complementary sign levels: by their own characteristics and by the associated behavior.

Body-adaptors, substances and objects most intimately related to the body which, consciously or unconsciously, can influence our co-inter-actants negatively or positively:

(a) *nutritional products* like food and drink, through which we, con-sciously or not, manifest our social status through good or bad man-ners, as well as emotional state, mood, etc.: "At least he had fairly good manners; he did not wolf or gulp or gobble or crunch or talk with his mouth full" (K. A. Porter, *Ship of Fools*);

(b) *pseudonutritional products and smoking tobacco*, the former mainly masticatories like tobacco, chewing-gum, Indian betel or African kola, whose use reflects personal, social and cultural characteristics: "His mouth had opened in a kind of grin, the teeth red with the juice of betel leaf" (B. Bhattacharya, *He Who Rides a Tiger*), "He [Waythorn] opened his cigar case and held it out to his visitor [his wife's first husband], and Haskett's acceptance seemed to mark a fresh stage in their intercourse. The spring evening was chilly, and Waythorn invited his guest to draw up a chair to the fire [...] The two were enclosed in the intimacy of their blended cigar-smoke" (E. Wharton, *The Other Two*);

(c) *clothes and accessories*, historically determining behaviors and com-municating esthetic preferences, mood, intentional social functions (tightness of a dress, hat-tipping), pathological self-neglect, etc., some producing interactive sounds rarely heard today, as in this early twentieth-century example: "The rustle of her pretty skirt was like music to him" (T. Dreiser, *Sister Carrie*);

(d) *jewelry*, which, as with clothes, may consciously condition our behaving with, and thinking of, our co-interactors who wear it, blending with our verbal and nonverbal delivery: "Mr. Waterbrook, pursing up his mouth, and playing with his watch-chain, in a comfortable, prosperous sort of way" (C. Dickens, *David Copperfield*);

(e) *perfume, cosmetics, paint and tattoos, and other body markings*, often powerful interaction components: "Only the observant might have noticed lines of strain and weariness in her face which cosmetics and an effort of will power had not obscured entirely" (A. Hailey, *Hotel*);

(f) *artifactual body-adaptors* like culturally differentiated eating, drinking and smoking utensils (e.g., fork and knife, chopsticks, a water pipe, a toothpick, a cigarette holder, eyeglasses, a walking stick, an umbrella, walkers) not only become "artifactual kinesics" and may characterize a person's image (e.g., Chaplin's hat and stick, Churchill's cigar), but above all reveal attitudes and states which can consciously or unconsciously influence our co-interactors' thoughts and behaviors (e.g., if irritated by our using some of these objects as conversational props): "Elvira stubbed out her cigarette angrily on a plate. 'I think all that's rather awful really'" (E. Wilson, *Anglo-Saxon Attitudes*).

Object-adaptors, artifacts which we can manipulate as kinesic behaviors and may have a bearing on the interaction as added signs and messages (thus additional information) that can also affect the exchange: writing with a pen, a pipe used as a conversational prop, a hat tipped, the bread crumb or lint that seems to occupy us in a tense situation, ledges and steps on which we sit, etc.: (a) *anatomical furniture*. How we behave in relation to a chair, sofa, cushion or bed (e.g., sitting on its edge, with feet on it, slouching, tensely clasping it) discloses much about the person and even his or her attitude toward us: "'Sit down!' said Mr. Jordan, irritably pointing Mrs. Morel to horse-hair chair. She sat on the edge in an uncertain fashion" (D. H. Lawrence, *Sons and Lovers*); (b) *tools and work artifacts*, handled also attitudinally while interacting or even as a lingering effect of a previous encounter: "As the woman departed, he [Frank] resumed his scrubbing, but without the same angry violence" (E. Wilson, *Anglo-Saxon Attitudes*); (c) *other object-adaptors*, flicking real or imaginary lint or tapping on a table or counter: "The scratching of Eleanor's pen irritated him" (V. Woolf, *The Years*).

Environmental components, eliciting peculiar postures and movements: "Temple [walking in the sand] struggling and lurching on her high heels" (W. Faulkner, *Sanctuary*).

C. Personal Intelligible Components, traditionally neglected by researchers, although they operate in the interaction, either uninterruptedly (as if through the behaviors and nonbehaviors, activities and non-activities we are perceiving) or intermittently.

Mental activities and the next category, non-activities, constitute the deepest and most hidden realm of an interpersonal or person-environment interaction, sometimes just imagined but still decisive components of the interaction. For instance, I may react verbally or nonverbally upon realizing quite unequivocally that another person (by his/her words, paralanguage or how he/she keeps me standing instead of motioning me to a chair) regards me as an inferior, or not too bright after making a regretted blunder; but even if I am mistaken in thinking that that person thinks that way of me, I react as I do, something to consider in our social and professional encounters, since at times our interlocutor may behave the way he does precisely because he is imagining that we are thinking what actually we do not. Thus, something that has not happened at all becomes most real in our mind and a component of our interaction. On the other hand, that anxiety, for instance, might be elicited by the conviction of a real inferiority in front of someone who, however, is not thinking what we believe he is: "What was he thinking? Had she made a fool of herself? Her voice faltered, the blood rose to her cheeks, she looked down at her plate; and for the next few minutes he would get nothing but short mumbled answers to his questions, nothing but the most perfunctory of nervous laughs" (A. Huxley, *Eyeless in Gaza*).

Non-activities, "thought of" through the same mental reactions elicited by our cointeractant's real or nonexisting thoughts, and represented by factors we rightly or wrongly associate with that person (e.g., true or apparent personality traits, socioeconomic and socioeducational status, moral values), nevertheless unconsciously or subtly consciously condition our verbal and nonverbal behaviors (choice of vocabulary, paralanguage and kinesics, even the very topics we may want to discuss): "It was one of those irritating smiles that seem to say: 'My friend, what can you know of suffering?' There was something very patronizing and superior about it and intolerably snobbish" (N. West, *The Day of the Locust*).

External components

D. Sensible Artifactual and Environmental Components, not exchanged in the interpersonal encounter, with specific interactive values and stimuli for behavioral and attitudinal exchanges.

Contextual or interfering activities occurring (not always perceived) in the periphery of the encounter or only contextual to the interpersonal interaction and without any concrete bearing on it, produced or generated:

(a) *by a behavior*: "There would be the swift, slight 'cluck' of her needle, the sharp 'pop' of his lips as he let out the smoke, the warmth, the sizzle on the bars as he spat in the fire" (D. H. Lawrence, *Sons and Lovers*);
(b) *by mechanical artifacts*: "On the train…too excited to sleep, listening to the rumble of the wheels over the rails, the clatter of crossings, the faraway spooky wails of the locomotive" (J. Dos Passos, *The Big Money*);
(c) *by the natural environment* (including animals): "the rain fell gently, persistently, making a little chuckling and burbling noise in the gutters" (V. Woolf, *The Years*).

Contextual or interfering non-activities, related to factors like age, interactional fluency, attention rate, psychological configuration, socioeducational status, or the nature of the encounter:

(a) *objectual environment's non-activities* eliciting our judgement and first-impression forming, particularly in a home: furniture, rugs, lamps, original art or reproductions, reading material (type of books, newspapers and magazine subscriptions, etc.), heirlooms, photos and diplomas in a doctor's office (whose waiting-room decor may even anticipate his fee), or a lavishly set dinner table that intimidates lower-status guests and affects their verbal and nonverbal behaviors and attitudes: "The room was propitious to meditation. The red-veiled lamp, the corners of shadow, the splashes of firelight on the curves of old full-bodied wardrobes and cabinets, gave it an air of intimacy increased by its faded hangings, its slightly frayed and threadbare rugs" (E. Wharton, *The Reef*);
(b) the *built environment*, included also in the above example, can act as a contextual or interfering element and encourage, intimidate, sooth, etc., and thus predispose us, consciously or unconsciously, to certain attitudes toward those with whom we are interacting,

as with some domestic architectural spaces whose influence on our daily life is ignored by insensitive architects, or the associated elements of color ("discreet," "gaudy," "unnerving"), lighting (conducive to intimate verbal and nonverbal interaction, or the opposite), temperature (causing physiopsychological well-being or discomfort), music, etc.: "she allowed the dark to fall upon them, refraining from lighting the lamp. The dark discreet room, their isolation, the music that still vibrated in their ears united them" (J. Joyce, *Dubliners*);

(c) the *natural environment*, as with an open landscape that inspires freedom (or agoraphobia), natural sounds, sight and sounds of animals: "The whole empty world seemed haunted. Rustlings of the sage, seepings of the sand, gusts of the wind, the night, the loneliness" (Z. Grey, *The U. P. Trail*);

(d) a blending of *environmental and personal components*: "On that walk ... the twittering of chaffinches ..., the perfume of weeds being already burned, the turn of her neck, the fascination of those dark eyes ...], the lure of her whole figure, made a deeper impression than the remarks they exchanged. Unconsciously he held himself straighter, walked with a more elastic step" (J. Galsworthy, *In Chancery*). In addition, *light effects* influence our perception of whatever surrounds us: "The group [...] about the tea-table. The lamps and the fire crossed their gleams on silver and porcelain, on the bright haze of Eiffe's hair and on the whiteness of Anna's forehead, as she leaned back in her chair behind the tea-urn" (E. Wharton, *The Reef*).

Neutral function and effective function of interaction components

Interaction components play two different functions:

(a) a *neutral function*: "a thick drunken voice [...] Then the door slammed./ They listened./ [...] They could hear heavy footsteps lurching up the stairs in the next house. Then the door slammed" (V. Woolf, *The Years*)

(b) *effective function*, truly affecting our encounter consciously or unconsciously: "the dismal wailing of babies at night, the thumping of feet [...] hoarse shoutings [...] the rattling of wheels on the cobbles [...] the screams of the child and the roars of the mother" (S. Crane, *Maggie: A Girl of the Streets*).

Sensory channels, time, vision, and synesthesia

Besides sensory perception (Poyatos, 2002c) and intellectual perception of interaction components, we must acknowledge three basic dimensions:

(a) *chronemic* dimension of auditive, visual, tactile and kinesthetic types of perception, as part of a process of intellectualization, since a look, a handshake, an aggressive door-slam or a silence, depending on their intensity and importance, remains consciously or unconsciously in the receiver's mind after happening, while other components are already operating in the interactive continuum between the two ends of the encounter, emission and reception: "'Just what I supposed,' said Tom. 'Quite natural!' and, in his great satisfaction, he took a long sip out of his wine-glass" (C. Dickens, *Martin Chuzzlewit*).

(b) the *visual perception* of interaction components, using mostly "macular vision" (covering 12°–15° horizontally and 3° vertically) to explore someone's face, and "peripheral vision" (90° on each side of the sagittal plane: 180° and 150° vertically) to "be aware" of people's bodies or the environment, with a bearing on our interaction: "His [Sir Percival's] attentive face relaxed a little. But I saw one of his feet, softly, quietly, incessantly beating on the carpet under the table, and I felt that he was secretly as anxious as ever" (W. Collins, *The Woman in White*)

(c) the phenomenon of *synesthesia* in our perception of people and environment (Poyatos, 2002c), as with the softness of an upholstery contrasting with the general "roughness" of a rustic person, and all sorts of indirect synesthesial associations, as in this example: "He tipped the keg, and the slap and gurgle of water told of the quantity" (Z. Grey, *The Thundering Herd*).

The intellectual evaluation of sensible signs

Often sensibly perceived signs undergo a process of intellectual evaluation with sociopsychological and linguistic implications. For instance, in a man-woman interaction, simultaneously to the mutual perception of their respective sensible signs as they are emitted (words, voice timbre, gestures, postures, perfume, shaving lotion, clothes, physique), they are also being mutually "thought of" and "evaluated" by each of the two, as if he, for instance, were saying with the silent language of the mind: "You are talking to me, telling me ___ with a voice of___ characteristics, and with those gestures, activating those facial features of yours (which I really like), while letting me be aware (even though I don't look directly) of your figure and your posture, and while I smell the fragrance of that perfume; I like the sound of your voice as you talk to me, I'm attracted by the way you accompany your voice with hands and eyes, and by the way those facial features move as they say *that* right now; I see all those things as perfectly befitting your whole self, and become even more aware of it through that perfume that envelops your voice, eyes, face, hands, as you tell me what you are telling me. Yes, it is all those things together that make me like you...". Added to those direct sensations are the synesthesial ones; and, beyond those internal personal components of the encounter, it is the mutual orientation of the twosome, the characteristics of the place (in semi-darkness and with soft music, in silence and with faraway sounds, or with rain softly drum-ming on the window panes), and perhaps the satisfaction derived from the physicopsychological effects of shared food and drink:

> It caused her a slight pang to discover that his thoughts could wan-der at such a moment; then, with a flush of joy she perceived the reason. In some undefinable way she had become aware, without turning her head, that he was steeped in the sense of her nearness, absorbed in contemplating the details of her face and dress; and the discovery made the words throng to her lips. She felt herself speak with ease, authority, conviction. She said to herself: "He doesn't care what I say – it's enough that I say it – even if it's stupid he'll like me better for it ... " [...] and for the first time she felt in her veins the security and lightness of happy love. (E. Wharton, *The Reef*)

Free and bound and momentary and permanent interactive components

Interactive component can be *free* and *bound* in their mutual relation, whether personal or environmental, but can be also related to any of the intelligible components (e.g., the fragrance of a perfume plus social status) and appear in clusters: "She [...] turned her eyes upon me with a dawning smile, most sweetly melancholy, and a look of timid though keen enquiry that made my cheeks tingle with inexpressible emotions" (A. Brontë, *The Tenant of Wildfell Hall*); a binding can be so momentary and flitting as to go unnoticed: "At the word Father, I saw his former trouble come into his face. He subdued it, as before, and it was gone in an instant; but it had been there, and it had come so swiftly upon my words" (C. Dickens, *Bleak House*).

Momentary components are of a very short duration (e.g., a word, a sigh, a crossing of legs), while *permanent components* cover the whole encounter or a good part of it (e.g., a person's voice timbre, pallor, sensual lips, gum-chewing): "Mr George, smoking not quite as placidly as before, for since the entrance of Judy he has been in some measure disturbed by a fascination [...] which obliges him to look at her" (C. Dickens, *Bleak House*); but they can be *variable*: "suddenly her cheeks became a rosy read [...] noting her countenance, he [Havill] allowed his glance to stray into the street" (T. Hardy, *A Laodicean*), or *invariable*: "a carpet [...] so thick and soft that it felt like piles of velvet under my feet" (W. Collins, *The Woman in White*).

Qualifying features of interactive components: Location, intensity, duration

Besides the components of an interaction, we must acknowledge three qualifying features:

(a) *Location*, the position of any somatic, extrasomatic, or environmental activity or non-activity between beginning and end of the encounter, either strictly *temporal* (where it happens) or *functional* (where it affects the interaction, not necessarily the same point), the latter being instantaneous (e.g., noticing a person's threadbare sleeve), more lasting (e.g., eyes on the brink of tears during a conversation), or spanning the whole interaction with people or with the environment (e.g., a scar on someone's face, the fragrance of a forest).

(b) *Intensity*, or degree of "occurrence" of the component's main characteristic (e.g., a tensely articulated statement, deep blushing, the duration of a posture, violent or gentle door-knocking): "he said, with a smile of the most provoking self-sufficiency – 'you don't hate me, you know?'" (A. Brontë, *The Tenant of Wildfell Hall*), perhaps with a *lingering effect* beyond its actual occurrence, affecting the participants' behaviors and determine its truly effective duration.

(c) *Duration*, the exact temporal length, affecting the peripheral behaviors and the whole encounter (e.g., meaningful word drawling, length of a telephone ringing), considering the elements present during the interaction (e.g., furniture, lighting, perfume) and their truly *effective duration*, the one that truly matters, without neglecting the possible *intermittent effect* (e.g., change in facial muscle tonus under the effect of a recurrent memory or recent verbal insult).

Internal co-structurations of components with preceding, simultaneous, and succeeding components

This is the most intricate and deepest feature of an interaction, involving not only the mutual relationships of the speaker's behavioral or non-behavioral activities or non-activities (preceding, simultaneous to, or succeeding a given interaction component), but those between them and the co-interactors', and even between those interpersonal elements and the external components, affecting each other in three possible ways.

A *posteriori co-structuration*, most frequent, as when a man's "I love you!" is elicited by her immediately preceding long, silent look (the much-too-often-sought cause-effect sequence in research), although it could have been elicited by her words before that, depending always on location, duration, and, above all, intensity of the affecting behavior or nonbehavior, as with the silence in: "Mr Pinch was just then looking thoughtfully at the bars [of the fireplace]. But on his companion pausing in this place [while talking], he started, and said 'Oh! of course,' and composed himself to listen again" (C. Dickens, *Martin Chuzzlewit*).

On the other hand, his intense "I love you!" leads to her present intent look, but it could have been triggered by his immediately previous behavior, or the one before, and so on. But her immediately preceding behavior or non-activity (e.g., an averted tearful look) could have been an added, or the sole, stimulus for his own look, as could have any of her preceding ones. In other words, the space or time slot for his present behavior could have been filled with a different component, or he might have said what he would not have said otherwise. What is more, it could be the *cumulative stimulus* of his or her activities or non-activities that finally causes the verbal or nonverbal expression (including silence) in the last example; or even the *lingering effect* of their previous behaviors or non-behaviors, or both (e.g. their embrace a while earlier) acting above and "through" the more recent components to still affect the present one, as with the effect that a shout has on one of Dickens's famous characters, subtly running through the following sequence of activities:

[after a man at a window unexpectedly shouts for him and his daughters to leave his property] Mr Pecksniff put on his hat, and walked with great deliberation and in profound silence [*effect of the shout*] to the fly, gazing at the clouds as he went, with great interest [*the effect continues*]. After helping his daughters and Mrs Todgers into the conveyance, he stood looking at it for some moments, as if he were not quite certain whether it was a carriage or a temple [*the effect continues*] (C. Dickens, *Martin Chuzzlewit*).

On a behavioral level, the effective duration and location of, for instance, a woman's beautiful facial static signs may have elicited my look, or it could have been her perfume or her dress. A personal behavioral or nonbehavioral activity may have been elicited by the cumulative effect of, for instance, alcohol, an intimate proxemic relationship, or the real or imagined thoughts of the other person, as when we think that someone is thinking that we look ridiculous, when he or she is not thinking that at all, yet our believing it triggers in us a verbal or nonverbal reaction of some sort. Finally, that cumulative effect and a momentary component may together elicit a behavior, for instance: the intimate interpersonal distance, her perfume, and an unexpected thunderbolt leads to a couple's embrace. But a controllable cumulative effect can be manipulated to elicit the desired behavior. Naturally, a posteriori co-structuration may prove even harder to identify if we look only for sensible components and not also for the possible effects of mental activities or synesthesial associations – perfectly effective, but very difficult to verify, since they lie hidden at even deeper levels. In addition, a reaction may be triggered by a component from way back when it is combined with a stimulus similar to the present one. But on occasion, the most important stimulus is that of positive or negative remembrance: "'But you did too many unpleasant things to too many pictures I cared about [...] ' A forgotten hatred came back to his voice. 'And the worst of it is [...] '" (N. Mailer, *The Deer Park*).

Finally, the perception of any type of signs at a given time can suddenly provide us with special information regarding previous signs we had not totally, or correctly, decoded, and this discovery will make us re-interpret them a posteriori: "Her astonishing quickness of perception, detected a change in my voice, or my manner, when I put that question, which warned her that I had been speaking all along with some ulterior object in view. She stopped, and taking her arm out of mine, looked me searchingly in the face" (W. Collins, *The Moonstone*).

Simultaneous co-structuration. One person's blushing, for instance, may be eliciting in another's hesitating paralanguage, gestures, and even postures. But there are two levels here: the realization of, for instance, language-paralanguage-kinesics, or laughter-paralanguage, as logically-bound elements that just occur in fixed clusters; and the truly simultaneous effect of one component on another, which is what "simultaneous" means in this case: "as the meaning of his words shaped itself in her [Anna's] mind he [Darrow] saw a curious inner light dawn through her set look" (E. Wharton, *The Reef*); "She spoke with girlish shyness, which increased as he stared at her" (Z. Grey, *The Last Trail*).

A priori co-structuration, finally, is the most ignored aspect of interpersonal or intrapersonal co-structuration as well as of person-environment interaction, due precisely to the almost exclusive attention given to the cause-effect pattern, as if something that has not yet occurred, or that might never occur, could not play a specific interactive function at the present moment (in fact, it can include succeeding extrapersonal components, or a foreseen or feared interfering activity): "'She's coming!' she thought with a little catch of her breath, laying down the pen" (V. Woolf, *The Years*).

But the most interesting form of this a priori relationship is what can be called *advanced hidden feedback*, that is, when something that has not yet happened affects not only the person who will do it, but another one as well (manipulative or positive functions may crucially affect the development): "Waythorn felt himself reddening in anticipation of the other's smile" (E. Wharton, *The Other Two*). It could happen, for instance, in a business meeting with relation to something that has not been said yet but could be crucial; but also because of its positive functions, according to our ability to observe and our sensitiveness: "He saw Webley opening his mouth to speak and made haste to anticipate what he imagined was going to be his objection" (A. Huxley, *Point Counter Point*).

The structural analysis of conversation and its literary illustrations

Many years ago I built a comprehensive structural model for the study of the many types of behaviors involved in a conversational encounter that would contain not only those that were being analyzed again and again, but all that actually happened, or could happen, which I realized depended largely on nonverbal elements. Thus, gratefully adopting the basic conversational units defined by Duncan (1972) as "turns" (i.e., speaker's state and auditor's state), I strived to fathom much further the true nature of conversation, which disclosed an unsuspected number of central or less central behaviors, and so I understood conversation as:

> a series of spontaneous verbal and nonverbal exchanges between at least two participants (who observe but also break certain rules) in an irregular flow of speaker-actor's and auditor-viewer's turns, and of some permissible simultaneous activities, acoustic and visual pauses and negative and positive behaviors.

However, I saw the need to broaden the concept of conversation to include not only a one-to-one or many-to-many exchange, but also one-to-many encounters (in a classroom, a political campaign speech, or a congress or parliament address). Further, I tried to define the *configuration* of each encounter, subject to the proxemic relationship and mutual orientation among the participants, for we should distinguish, as did Kendon (1970, 1973), between *focused interaction* (an ordinary conversation) and *unfocused interaction* (e.g., a barber and a client who reads a magazine). Besides, there are within a conversation certain obvious *interactional axes* that can keep changing and alternating, as established by the orientation and gaze between speaker and auditor or auditors and, therefore, *axial and nonaxial participants* (cf. Kendon, 1973), whether the speaker excludes some of them at times by not orienting himself toward them and looking at them: "She addressed the explanation to her sister, to the exclusion of Margaret, who, nevertheless, listened with a smiling face and a resolutely polite air of being a party to the conversation" (D. Howells, *A Hazard of New Fortunes*), or because they exclude themselves partially (by not paying much attention, as evinced by gaze and head or body orientation) or totally (e.g., listening or speaking to another participant, even making him his listener, looking somewhere although posture and orientation may still identify a previous listener status): "'And what will you have, Kay, it's your birthday. You choose what you like.' Gerald looked at his leggy daughter with affection. But Kay looked at her mother" (E. Wilson, *Anglo-Saxon Attitudes*). But it is also possible to momentarily keep a simultaneous *double axis*, one just visual and the other verbal, with two interactants: "he went on, and once again he seemed to wink at Gerald as he addressed Lionel Stokesay" (E. Wilson, *Anglo-Saxon Attitudes*). Another interesting phenomenon is that of *mirroring behaviors*, particularly when the behavior that consciously or unconsciously serves as a model is the one of the higher-status participant (e.g., crossing or uncrossing the legs when the other person does it).

In spite of the editors' generosity, I must refer readers to my complete model (Poyatos, 2002d) and just identify the various categories of conversational behaviors, but not all the behaviors contained in each one, nor the possible interactive functions played by bodily signs (paralinguistic, kinesic, chemical, dermal, etc.) and environmental signs (interfering noise, temperature, etc.).

Speaker's and auditor's basic behaviors

Turn pre-opening: "She [Eliza] had a curious trick of pursing her lips reflectively before she spoke" (T. Wolfe, *Look Homeward, Angel*)

Turn opening: "[The Judge] cleared his throat, took a sip of water, broke the nib of a quill against the desk, and, folding his bony hands before him, began" (J. Galsworthy, *A Man of Property*).

Speaker-auditor turn-change behaviors

Turn closing: "Lyman [...] was shaking with fury [after an aggressive tirade at a meeting] [...] / 'Ruffians,' he shouted from the threshold, 'ruffians, bullies [...] '/ He went out slamming the door [truly closing his turn then]" (F. Norris, *The Octopus*).

Turn relinquishing: "'You think they'll acquit him that fast?' asked Jem./ Atticus opened his mouth to answer, but shut it and left us" (H. Lee, *To Kill a Mockingbird*).

Turn holding: "The Squire had delivered his speech in a coughing and interrupted manner, but with no pause long enough for Godfrey to make it a pretext for taking up the word again. He felt his father meant to ward off any request for money" (G. Eliot, *Silas Marner*).

Turn suppressing: "'It's very kind of you, but – '/ My uncle was going to refuse, but Driffield interrupted him./ 'I'll see he doesn't get up to any [...] '" (W. Somerset Maugham, *Cakes and Ale*).

Reciprocal behaviors between listener and speaker

Feedback by the listener is actually a whole series of activities travelling over the various somatic channels and the only permissible and in fact desirable kind of activity simultaneous to the speaker's. It must be intermittent in order to prove that one is actually listening, agrees or disagrees, likes it or dislikes it, as a running commentary on which may depend the encounter's success or failure, for instance: "'So you're leaving us, eh?' he said./ 'Yes, sir. I guess I am.'/ He [while Holden tells him about his academic failure] started going into this nodding routine" (J. D. Salinger, *Catcher in the Rye*).

Prompting behaviors: "he broke off, admonished by the nudge of an adjoining foot and the smile that encircled the room" (E. Wharton, *The House of Mirth*).

Speaker's secondary behaviors

A speaker who is already acting as such, may or may not display certain behaviors that serve to comment on his or her listeners' behaviors, and to gradually announce the conclusion of his turn or his intention to resume it when it has temporarily ceased.

Turn pre-opening: "[After being asked to 'tell the story'] 'There's a lot for you to learn in it,' McLeod observed. [After a long sentence still another preopener] He drew smoke from his cigarette and began to talk" (N. Mailer, *Barbary Shore*).

Self-correction: "'He can say things – things that might be unp—might be disagreeable to you: say them publicly [...] '" (E. Wharton, *The Age of Innocence*).

Interlistener behaviors

Interlistener feedback: "' [...] I often said it to him,' he [Sir Edgar] chuckled grimly./ Theo Roberts whispered to Jaspers, 'I'd like to have heard that'" (E. Wilson, *Anglo-Saxon Attitudes*).

Coinciding activities: Simultaneous behaviors and crossed conversations

A conversation does not occur in an unrealistically fluent and smooth succession of behaviors, for there are situations in which at least two participants become engaged in the same activity at the same time, whether of the same or different type. There are either *simultaneous* activities, of the same or different type, or *symmetrical*, that is, truly coinciding identical activities, while *multiple* refers to the co-occurrence of two or more participants.

Simultaneous turns, a cause for intercultural clash between, for instance, the average Anglo-Saxon and Latin or Arab speaker (but not between the latter two, who have the same tendency to simultaneous floor-holding behaviors), characterized by syntactical disorder and word repetition:

DOOLITTLE	*exclaiming*	Bly me! it's Eliza!
HIGGINS	*simul-*	What's that? This!
PICKERING	*taneously*	By Jove!

Overlapping behaviors, seen as a cultural characteristic in direct proportion to the familiarity or emotional freightage of the encounter and, naturally, the participants' personalities. Quite typically and with a frequency generally not perceived, they happen: (a) when the next speaker starts his turn (perhaps only to reply to a question) before the first speaker has totally finished speaking: "'What on earth are the children...'/ Inge answered his unfinished question. 'I have told them that Dollie's drunk,' she said" (A. Wilson, *Anglo-Saxon Attitudes*); (b) when, at the beginning of the listener's future turn, he, without asking, starts making short remarks that break up the speaker's discourse and coincide with his words: "'I am sorry, but I shall have to protest—'/ [...]:/ 'Go to the devil!'/ 'It is as much to your interest as to ours that the safety of the public—'/ 'You heard what I said. Go to the devil!'/ 'That all may show obstinacy, Mr. Annixter, but—'"/ [...] / "You," he vociferated, "I'll tell you what you are. You're a – a – a *pip*!/ '—may show obstinacy,' pursued Mr. Behrman, bent upon finishing the phrase, 'but it don't show common sense'" (F. Norris, *The Octopus*). But the new speaker's verbal behavior may also overlap the former's nonverbal behavior (not necessarily his words): "'Don't deny it! Don't deny it!' – this apropos of a protesting movement on the part of Eugene's head – 'I know all!'" (T. Dreiser, *The Genius*).

Acoustic and visual pauses or breaks

These (which I treated more in depth when studying silence in Poyatos, 2002d) should be studied in depth as to: the possible coincidence of silence and stillness; the coincidence of the acoustic pause's onset with the slowdown of movement, and then how both resume at its offset; the co-structuration of a paralinguistic-kinesic pause with the immediately preceding, simultaneous, and succeeding activities; the intensity of pauses (determined by their duration and the co-structuration just mentioned); how a pause, which is not at all a semiotic vacuum, can be filled with activities others than sound and movement (tears, blushing, emotional sweat, etc.); how a pause can be only paralinguistic or kinesic, one of the systems still operating while the other one ceases to, but still communicates either by its very absence or precisely through the meaningful characteristics of silence, stillness, or both; and the conversational functions of each occurrence of a single (silence) or twofold (silence and stillness) pause. Here I shall identify only a few of the more than 40 I have studied, some of which have a conscious interactive function, while others are uncontrolled and happen when some interactive activity fails, which allows us to distinguish attitudinal pauses from uncontrolled ones.

Absent-participation pause is not produced simply by total lack of participation, that is, because nobody tries to say anything, some having perhaps changed from listeners to mere withdrawn auditors, and, depending on their duration (one of the qualifiers of silence), cause those typical tense: "Miss Fairlie seemed to feel the oppression of the long pauses in the conversation, and looked appealingly to her sister to fill them up–' (Collins, *The Woman in White*).

Pre-statement, very carefully utilized by the expert speaker when preceding important words as an emphatic preparation with a possible expectancy effect on the listener or listeners, may be combined with gesture or even the manipulation of an object: "When Dr. Mortimer had finished reading [...] he pushed his spectacles up on his forehead and stared across at Mr. Sherlock Holmes" (A. Conan Doyle, *The Hound of the Baskervilles*), "'I love you, darling,' he would say out of a silence and kiss her" (N. Mailer, *The Deer Park*).

Transitional pause may happen between different topics (or just turns), but also due to psychological variables and according to the socioeducational status of the interlocutors, involving, among other behaviors, different types of laughter, tongue clicks, audible ingression, throat-clearings, postural shift, hand-rubbing, hair-preening, adjusting a trouser-crease, busying oneself with a drink, a pipe or cigarette, flicking imaginary lint, fidgeting with a necklace, or non-behaviors, such as blushing caused by the previous topic: "The arrival of the second bottle seemed a signal for her [Elvira] to relax. She lit a cigarette, turned sideways in her chair and crossed her legs" (E. Wilson, *Anglo-Saxon Attitudes*).

Pre-response pause, between the question and its reply, while the other person gets ready for it (not out of hesitancy): "'What makes you think that?'/ Mark drew up a chair and sat down before answering" (A. Huxley, *Eyeless in Gaza*).

Hesitation pause, due to a break in one's train of thought, not daring say anything, or out of insecurity, or caused by the listener or listeners' disturbing feedback, differently manifested according to sex, personality and other factors ("And, uuh—," "Er – yes – yes," stammering, broken speech, clearing the throat, coughing, sniffling, breaking eye contact during the pause, touching the nose or the lower lip with the forefinger, staring vaguely at the floor or ceiling, touching the eyebrows with thumb and forefinger, tensely crossed arms and looking down): "'I could not accommodate myself to his ways very often – not out of the least reference to myself, you understand, but because—' he stammered here, and was rather at a loss" (C. Dickens, *Martin Chuzzlewit*), As with any of the other speaker's behaviors, the listener can always take advantage of it to cut in and open his own turn with no preambles, or to prompt the speaker: " 'I thought all – all middle-aged people liked my father and mother.'/ He had been about to call me old [...] so I made a face when I saw him hesitating, which drove him into 'middle-aged'" (S. Butler, *The Way of All Flesh*).

Elliptical pause, either because words that are unnecessary to be understood beyond doubt are never said: "'Did *she* see anything in the boy—?'/ 'That wasn't right? She never told me.'" (H. James, *The Turn of the Screw*).

Self-overlapping pause, triggered by interrupting the expression of a thought to verbalize another one that replaces it or modifies it: "'No, no – How can we tell that it isn't all a false report? It's highly im—'/ 'Oh, I'm sure it isn't'" (A. Brontë, *The Tenant of Wildfell Hall*).

Feedback pause, a silent reaction under the effect of what has been said or done by the speaker: "'[I]t is hopeless to expect people who are accustomed to the European courts to trouble themselves about our little republican distinctions [...] ' Mr. van der Luyden paused, but no one spoke. 'Yes – it seems [...] '" (E. Wharton, *The Age of Innocence*).

Thinking pause, usually interrupting eye contact with our interlocutor, while frowning, crossing arms, grabbing or scratching the chin, stroking the beard, fidgeting with something, lighting a cigarette to give oneself time to think, etc.: "A long pause succeeded [...] Mr Pecksniff toyed abstractedly with his eye-glass, and kept his eyes shut, that he might ruminate the better" (C. Dickens, *Martin Chuzzlewit*).

Somatic-function pause, allowing the speaker to carry out or cope with usually brief bodily activities like nose-blowing, scratching, spitting, postural shift, hand-rubbing, hair-preening, sneezing, yawning (handled differently cross-culturally), and even to uncontrollably express physical discomfort and pain; either truly random behaviors (Poyatos, 2002c, pp. 195–198) or with intentional positive or negative (manipulative) interactive functions: "'I figured out that would be your reaction,' he [Munshin] said, and he leaned forward in his chair. What would you say Charley, if I tell you that I think you owe me something?'" (N. Mailer, *The Deer Park*).

External-task pause, possibly, although not very obviously, very important interactively: puffing at a pipe or blowing out smoke, picking up a cup, swallowing food, changing eyeglasses, pulling up a chair for more intimacy: "Mr. Bounderby stayed her [Mrs. Sparsit, who had offered to leave the room], by holding a mouthful of chop in suspension before swallowing it, and putting out his left hand. Then, withdrawing his hand and swallowing his mouthful of chop, he said [...] " (C. Dickens, *Hard Times*); "He stood by the window, making much of clipping and lighting a cigar, and he did not look at her while he grumbled" (S. Lewis, *Dodsworth*); "So he had recourse to the usual means of gaining time for such cases made and provided; he said 'ahem,' and coughed several times, took out his pocket-handkerchief, and began to wipe his glasses" (H. Beecher Stowe, *Uncle Tom's Cabin*).

Manipulative pause, not only to influence someone negatively, but to take advantage of a situation: "McQueen took his time answering: a deliberately measured pause, to break the natural flow of feeling between himself and Athanase" (H. MacLennan, *Two Solitudes*).

External-interference pause, when there is a communicative gap because someone or something distracts our attention: "' [...] You go to parties to—'/ Here the dance music crashed out [...] Lady Pargiter stopped in the middle of her sentence. She sighed [...]/ 'What's that they are playing?' she murmured" (V. Woolf, *The Years*).

Emotional pause, when strongly affected by an emotion, after which break we may react verbally or nonverbally: "'But I shall never speak to you again.'/ For a few seconds they looked at one another in silence. Anthony had gone very pale. Close-lipped and crookedly [...], her eyes [Mary's] were bright with malicious laughter" (A. Huxley, *Eyeless in Gaza*).

Conclusion

Although this outline has turned out to be, as expected, the proverbial tip of the iceberg, I hope it will at least have accomplished its dual purpose, namely, to emphasize how natural observation can greatly assist even the researcher before and after experimental work, and the great value of the creative writer's incisive, reality-based observations of whatever behaviors or non-behavioral activities or non-activities may have a bearing on interactions, both interpersonal and with the environment.

References

Duncan, S., Jr. (1972). Some signals and rules for taking speaking turns in conversation. *Journal of Personality and Social Psychology, 23*(2), 283–292.

Ekman, P. (1981). Mistakes when deceiving. *Annals of the New York Academy of Sciences, 364,* 269–278.

Kendon, A. (1970). Movement coordination in social interaction. *Acta Psychologica,* (32), 1–25.

Kendon, A. (1973). The role of visible behavior in the organization of face-to-face interaction. In M. von Cranach & I. Vine (Eds.), *Social communication and movement: Studies of interaction and expression in man and chimpanzee* (pp. 29–74). London, New York: Academic Press.

Poyatos, F. (2002a). Anthropology/Psychology/Sociology. In P. Gossin (Ed.), *Encyclopedia of literature and sciences* (pp. 13–20). Westport, London: Greenwood Press.

Poyatos, F. (2002b). The nature, morphology and functions of gestures, manners and postures as documented by creative literature. *Gesture, 2*(1), 99–117.

Poyatos, F. (2002c). *Nonverbal communication across disciplines, vol. I: Culture, communication, interaction, language.* Amsterdam, Philadelphia: John Benjamins.

Poyatos, F. (2002d). *Nonverbal communication across disciplines, vol. II: Paralanguage, kinesics, silence, personal and environmental interaction.* Amsterdam, Philadelphia: John Benjamins.

Sommer, R. (1969). *Personal space: The behavioral basis of design.* Englewood Cliffs: Prentice-Hall.

12

Nonverbal Behavior Online: A Focus on Interactions with and via Artificial Agents and Avatars

Dennis Küster, Eva Krumhuber, and Arvid Kappas

If someone picks up a book on nonverbal behavior, the reader is likely to expect topics relating to the emotions, intentions, or beliefs of people in interaction. Often readers are particularly keen to learn whether it is possible to detect deception from bodily or facial cues. Interest in skills not only addresses the decoding of nonverbal messages, but also whether and how one might improve one's own nonverbal behavior in interaction to achieve certain goals, such as in a business context, a job talk, or in a relationship. These are indeed topics that are generally well covered in current handbooks on nonverbal behavior (see Hall & Knapp, 2013) and interpersonal communication (e.g., Smith & Wilson, 2009). In contrast, new emerging forms of online behavior are still relatively young among communication research foci (Walther & Ramirez, 2010). This is, however, bound to change as Internet research and more traditional perspectives on nonverbal communication become increasingly integrated (see, e.g., Joinson et al., 2009).

To a large extent, staple questions of research on nonverbal behavior have been related to face-to-face communication, where two interaction partners are in the same room (co-presence), facing each other, and engaged in real-time interaction. In fact, arguably, much of the research on nonverbal communication in the last decades has focused either on the study of dyads (or much more rarely triads and small groups) in interaction in a shared space (Hall & Knapp, 2013). In addition, there is much research where participants might be acting out affective states, while being filmed or recorded to understand patterns of nonverbal behavior associated with specific emotions, or intentions (e.g., Bänziger & Scherer, 2007; Busso et al., 2008; Bänziger et al., 2009). Similarly, there are many studies where participants will look at pictures, watch videos, listen to recordings, and have to indicate what they perceive to be the intention, or the underlying affective state of the individual they are currently looking at, or listening to. In such encoding or decoding studies, the actual physical co-presence has been dropped based on the attempt to create a necessary degree of experimental control. Instead, both encoders and decoders are asked, explicitly or implicitly, to imagine communicating with someone in a real situation.

Of course, breaking the complex real-time dynamics of interaction by decoupling encoding and decoding in controlled laboratory conditions creates all kinds of problems with regard to an inhibition of the multiple dynamic feedback loops that characterize interaction and co-regulation processes in real time (see Kappas & Descôteaux, 2003; Kappas, 2013). But in addition, direct communication is transformed into a mediated process with everything that entails, without reflecting on the differences between mediated and non-mediated communication. To account for the artificiality of such imposed mediation, occasionally the rationale is explicitly placed in the context of mediated communication. For example, in an early application, Hess et al., 1988, framed a decoding task in the context of a video phone – this explained why the encoder was looking into the camera and talking, as if the decoder in the study was the actual interaction partner (see also, Kappas & Krämer, 2011a). At the time, a video phone was something subjects would have heard about, but not had the chance to experience first-hand. At that time, mediated communication would have been associated with writing and reading letters as asynchronous mediated communications, or using the telephone, as a synchronous medium with reduced band-width (audio only). In other words, synchronous mediated face-to-face communication would have been somewhere between science fiction and fancy technology for a privileged few.

How times have changed. At this point, a large percentage of the earth's population is using computer-mediated communication (CMC) on a day-to-day basis, with some geographical regions having almost complete coverage (see http://www.internetworldstats.com/). Here, the gamut ranges from email, participation in forums and blogs, to more synchronous text-based media, such as chat systems (see Bargh & McKenna, 2004). In the last few years, there has been more development on including visuals in CMC, from static avatars, to dynamic avatars, immersive virtual interactions, and particularly face-to-face communication via the Internet in the guise of popular systems such as Skype or Google+ Hangouts (see Kappas & Krämer, 2011b). Despite the fact that many of the readers of this chapter will spend considerable time every day using different forms of CMC, systematic research on nonverbal communication in this context is to be found in dedicated texts or journals on Cyberpsychology, Mediapsychology, or CMC, but not as a regular part of nonverbal communication (NVC) research, and only rarely included in textbooks on NVC. The term CMC is anachronistically used for text-only mediated communication, despite the fact that this has changed a long time ago. Given the rapid changes in the last couple of decades on the one hand, and the pervasiveness of Internet and related mediated communication (e.g., via hand-held devices that do not technically use the Internet) it is time to pull this topic into the canon of issues to be studied in classical NVC. In this chapter we will introduce some relevant research and point out how there is relevance in "classical" NVC research to understanding Internet communication. Similarly, we will try to emphasize that the world of NVC is larger now than in the 1970s when many of the methods and theories that dominate this type of research originated.

Early research on CMC was dominated by a focus on the lack of nonverbal information in text-based communication. CMC was seen as suffering from a deficit that would render felicitous communication difficult (e.g., Short et al., 1976; Kiesler et al., 1984; Siegel et al., 1986; Sproull & Kiesler, 1986; Kiesler & Sproull, 1992; Kiesler, 1997). Similarly, using the Internet was seen as something with negative social consequences (e.g., Kraut et al., 1998) and users of early social media were seen as potentially socially challenged (see Philippot & Douilliez, 2011). This has changed. Firstly, it has become clear that the change in bandwidth from non-mediated, face-to-face communication to various forms of CMC leads to changes in behavior to compensate for this (e.g., Walther, 1992, 2011; Burgoon & Walther, 2013). Similarly, as Internet usage is constantly reaching new levels, it is moot to discuss that Internet users are motivated due to their experiencing social challenges. Instead, the second generation question here has become: What are the effects of various Internet communication processes in the long run as a function of personality differences?

In the following sections we will address some recent developments in computer-mediated-communication, but also other aspects of interactions between humans and artificial systems as they relate to NVC. Specifically, we will discuss general aspects of the function, application, and design of artificial systems and psychological aspects of interacting with them.

Function, application and design of artificial systems

There have been rapid advances in technology with the aim of enriching communication between human and computer. Besides improving the technical aspects on an engineering level, many efforts have been targeted towards the social domain. This has led to the emergence of virtual characters, autonomous agents, and robots that act as a social layer of mediation with the computer. Such characters are meant to assist the user with specific tasks and are used in a variety of applications (for an overview see Dehn & van Mulken, 2000; Fong et al., 2002; Krämer et al., 2011). These concern public applications in e-commerce, customer service, and information kiosks in which many users interact with the agent over a relatively short period of time. Alternatively, these also involve private or individual applications for entertainment, education, or therapy. Here, the user likely interacts with a few characters, but the conversations are aimed towards more long-term relationships (Hüttenrauch & Severinson-Eklundh, 2002; Hegel et al., 2007; Eimler et al., 2010). Whether embodied in the form of virtual agents or physical agents in the form of robots, the anthropomorphic representation renders a computer system more approachable (Sproull et al., 1996). Instead of a "black box" displaying printed text on the screen, the interaction becomes social, thereby allowing for the system to be an immediate source of communication.

In order for this new form of human-computer interaction to be effective, trustworthiness plays a crucial role (see Donath, 2007). Only if the user feels comfortable with its visual representation, will s/he assign tasks to it (e.g., sorting emails, collecting information from the World Wide Web). As shown by Van Mulken, André, and Müller (1999) people form distinct impressions of trustworthiness when interacting with computer-based systems. Such responses usually arise quickly and automatically on first encounter. Similarly as in human-human interaction (e.g., Willis & Todorov, 2006), people are sensitive to the social characteristics, features, and behaviors of the technology. The *Media Equation Theory* by Nass and colleagues (Nass et al., 1994; Reeves & Nass, 1996; Nass & Moon, 2000) argues that computers and robots are commonly treated as social actors as if they were human beings. That is, they are endowed with personality and character traits just as human partners are. People therefore apply conventional social schemas and heuristics in their interactions with technological artifacts, particularly when there is limited information available. This is done, for example, by using social rules to explain their behavior or by applying norms of reciprocity and politeness (Nass et al., 1994; Nass et al., 1997; Krämer, 2005). Given that machines reflect the intentions of their producers, this tendency does not seem to be counter-intuitive. However, on the grounds of these human-based attribution processes, such dispositions to respond socially can be difficult to avoid. That is, even when people know that their assumptions may not be valid in the context of human-computer interaction, they use the same strategies for assessing machine behavior (Nass et al., 1994). To evoke appropriate impressions as intended by its developer, the design of artificial systems therefore plays an important role.

Design specifications are relevant for developing effective systems. Depending on the social and instrumental goals the technology needs to fulfill, the guidelines may differ. These concern physical aspects, but also behavioral features such as verbal and nonverbal cues. They can have dramatic effects on perceivers' judgment and their relationship with the system (Goetz et al., 2003; Bethel & Murphy, 2006; Komatsu & Yamada, 2007). Acceptance by the user is therefore crucial in choosing specific representations and behaviors. As such, the agent or robot should make users feel comfortable and gain their trust and cooperation. This is not so much a question of technicality, but more of the socio-affective processes in interaction. Unfortunately, most computer characters have not been designed with psychological knowledge in mind. Rather they are the product of design ideas that are intended to be unique (Zimmerman et al., 2005). Hence, principled understanding to make informed design choices is lacking. In the next chapter, we will review empirical research on how the design of computer characters' visual form and their resemblance to human appearance shapes perceivers' attributions.

Appearance and human-likeness

The appearance of an artificial system can make its function more explicit and aid the user in forming impressions in the initial exposure. By choosing a certain design, the developer can specify what type of character s/he wants the system to embody and the exact role it should perform (Robins et al., 2004). Adding a computer system with a visual form therefore contributes to social perceptions as to the character's propensities and capabilities. Depending on the appearance the application may seem more or less appropriate. In work by Hegel and colleagues (Hegel et al., 2007; Lohse et al., 2007; Hegel et al., 2009), users suggested different application areas as a function of the appearance of robots. While animal-looking robots (e.g., Aibo or iCat) were well liked, they were expected to serve mainly as pets, toys or companions. This is because animal likeness is considered to be a feature of toy applications and hence applicable for private use. As a result, zoomorphic design may be useful in implicitly showing the functional limitations of a system. A dog may be able to fulfill certain tasks (e.g., guard duty, catching balls), but its ability to understand human language and communication skills are rather limited (Fong et al., 2002). The form and structure of the technology consequently frames assumptions as to its perceived intelligence as well as social role. This in turn serves as a guide in interaction with the technology and sets the stage for social expectations.

Based on a classification of robot appearances Von der Pütten and Krämer (2012) found that users rated them differently with respect to six dimensions: likeability, threat, submissiveness, familiarity, humanlike, and mechanical. The mechanic form acts as another cue to the system's propensities. In a study by Kiesler and Goetz (2002), adding hardware to a robot caused participants to create more favorable impressions of its power. Thus, the additional physical features contributed to its mechanical perception. Such visual form, which is guided largely by operational objectives, can be useful in the context of functional requirements (Fong et al., 2002). In view of this, research has demonstrated that machine-like robots are proposed largely for the service domain, such as security, cleaning, and assistance (Hegel et al., 2007; Lohse et al., 2007). These robots were also suggested for public applications that require a more serious behavior as compared to animal-like robots.

In gaining acceptance by the user, the visual form and structure of an artificial system should be consistent with the specific task or behavior it performs. In this sense, its appearance needs to elicit the correct estimation of the character's abilities. For example, an agent being used as a museum tour guide needs to look differently compared to when being employed for military purposes. Because the task the agent performs critically shapes users' perceptions, the external features of a system must mirror its interior. This is not so much a question of liking, but of a match between the appearance and its implied function or application. Kiesler and colleagues (Kiesler & Goetz, 2002; Goetz et al., 2003), for example, showed that people complied more with a playful robot when the task was entertaining (i.e., jellybean task). However, for areas that were rather taxing in nature such as an exercise task, a more authoritative robot was efficient for interaction. An animal-like robot/agent may therefore not be undesirable for any given role or task, but given its perceived playfulness it will be potentially more suitable for the personal, domestic domain. In a similar vein, a mechanical form of an artificial system might be a better match for tasks that are not so much social in nature. This is supported by evidence showing that mechanical-looking robots tend to be treated in a less socially interactive way (Hinds et al., 2004).

To enable engaging human-computer interaction in socially intense situations, it has been suggested that a human-like appearance may be advantageous (Breazeal, 2002; Appel et al., 2012). This is because a humanoid form indicates human qualities that evoke perceptions of lifelikeness in the system. By varying the degree of human-likeness in robots and agents (from mechanical- to human-looking), research has revealed that people prefer computer characters with more human-like appearance and this is particularly the case for tasks requiring social skills (e.g., Goetz et al., 2003; Zimmerman et al., 2005; Walters et al., 2008). Because a human-looking form represents human-like behavior, anthropomorphic representations have been shown to make the computer appear more intelligent, engaging and capable of higher agency than those with non-human visual forms (King & Ohya, 1996; Koda & Maes, 1996). This in turn eases social interaction, as conventional schemas and norms from transactions with people in the real world can be applied (Breazeal & Scassellati, 1999). In this sense, people don't need to follow new rules, e.g. of spatial or language use, but can employ those they know from human interaction. Sproull and colleagues (1996), for example, showed that people presented themselves more positively and were more aroused when the interface was a talking face compared to a text-display. As the interface becomes more human-like, users of computerized systems may therefore apply similar impression-formation and management techniques to those that would be expected in human-to-human dialogue.

Additionally, a humanoid form allows for a more complex and richer set of attributions concerning the system's abilities. In several studies it was demonstrated that the agents' human-likeness significantly influenced cooperation rates in a social dilemma task (Parise et al., 1996, 1999). Specifically, participants were found to keep their promises and cooperate more with agents that resembled a person rather than a dog or cartoon dog. Despite the fact that the dog-like computer agents were well liked, the humanoid representation made participants feel more similar to the agents, thereby increasing their sense of shared social identity (Parise et al., 1996). Such conception of the self as a member of the same social group can also have an effect on people's willingness and ability to take the perspective of and share emotions with others. If people identify themselves more with human representations, they may be more motivated to engage in empathic behavior. This was found in a study by Riek, Rabinowitch, Chakrabarti, and Robinson (2009) in which people empathized more strongly with human-like robots that were shown to be maltreated by humans. In particular, participants felt more sorry for the protagonist if it was human-looking rather than mechanical. Furthermore, there is variation in people's sense of responsibility as a function of the degree of human-likeness of the system. When carrying out a joint task, participants took to a lower extent credit and responsibility for successfully completing the task when they collaborated with a human-like robot than a mechanical one (Hinds et al., 2004). This is an indicator that they relied more on and shared responsibility with their humanoid partner. Together these findings suggest that a human appearance proves beneficial in the attribution of cognitive and social qualities. Hence, computerized systems should profit from human-like representations by rendering the interaction more intuitive and socially engaging.

Uncanny valley and theory of mind

Considering this personification process, designers have attempted to increase the humanness of agents and robots by adding human-typical attributes. This was inspired by ideas that a higher number of human characteristics would engender a more human-like representation, including human traits and values (DiSalvio et al., 2002; Powers & Kiesler, 2006). In this sense, people should feel more familiar and natural in contact with the system if it closely resembles humans. With increasingly powerful graphics algorithms, technology has in turn aimed towards high realism with life-like appearance and behavior. The ultimate goal of such efforts consists in the creation of artificial humans that are indistinguishable from real humans (Borshukov & Lewis, 2005; Ishiguro & Nishio, 2007; Plantec, 2008; Alexander et al., 2010). However, at the same time this also means that the more human-like an agent/robot looks, the higher will be people's expectations of what the system can do. Specifically, people might expect that lifelike characters are capable of behaving and understanding natural language exactly like a human being. Anthropomorphic representations with high fidelity may in turn be endangered to violate the expectations of the user. As such, if the system becomes too close to realism, thereby looking highly human-like, the appearance may be more advanced than its actual state. Given that approaches are still limited with regard to the quality of simulated behavior and the type of realism to be achieved, humanoid characters may be therefore subject to the "uncanny valley" (UV) effect (Mori, 1970, 2012).

The phenomenon of the UV was first described by the roboticist Mashiro Mori at the Tokyo Institute of Technology. Mori was interested in the relationship between the human-likeness of an artificial entity and people's affinity to it. By considering a number of artifacts ranging from non-human (industrial robot) to human (prosthetic hands, corpse) he argued that realism and affinity may not be linearly related to each other. Instead he proposed that with increasing human-likeness, the once-positive emotional response of people falls sharply, leading to a dramatic decrease in acceptance. That is, although human-likeness results in increased familiarity and affinity there may be a certain point (around 85% human-likeness) after which characters appear too human and are perceived as uncanny or emotionally unsettling (MacDorman et al., 2009; Gray & Wegner, 2012). As such, the original positive evaluation reverses and elicits a sense of unease that is due to a mismatch between their appearance and performance. This drop in which any sense of affinity is lost was termed by Mori as "bukimi no tani" and became later popularized as "uncanny valley" (see Pollick, 2009 for a historical discussion of the term). Often cited examples of uncanny valley phenomena are found in the public entertainment domain. For example, many viewers found characters in the animated films *The Polar Express* and *The Final Fantasy: The Spirits Within* to be disturbing and off-putting (Levi, 2004; Plantec, 2007; Geller, 2008). Similar experiences are reported for characters in video games as well as robots that blur the line between humans and machines (e.g., Gouskos, 2006; Ishiguro, 2006; Pollick, 2009).While the UV is widely accepted there have been few scientific explorations of this phenomenon (MacDorman & Ishiguro, 2006; Seyama & Nagayama, 2007; Steckenfinger & Ghazanfar, 2009; MacDorman et al., 2009; Saygin et al., 2012), with evidence partly unable to replicate the exact shape of Mori's diagram (see e.g. Bartneck et al., 2009; Tinwell & Grimshaw, 2009).

This is complicated by the fact that various aspects moderate how uncanny something is perceived as being. One of the most crucial components is motion which – according to Mori – steepens the slope of the UV by increasing the peaks and valleys (Mori, 2012). Given that most characters do not remain still, movement may therefore contribute to a mismatch between perceived realism and its actual ability. For example, when an android robot is seen in its static form it may achieve a human-like appearance. However, as soon as it is moving, imperfections of its creation can cause sensations of eeriness and unpleasantness. Thus, motion might add to negative responses that are amplified by the character's behavior (Pollick, 2009). In recent research we found that motion significantly moderated people's perceptions of characters varying in their degree of humanness. Interestingly, the effects of human movement (i.e., bowing, waving) were most evident in how non-human characters (i.e., object-like and animal-like agents) were judged (Krumhuber et al., 2012). These findings suggested that not only the presence, but also the type of motion and how closely it resembles human-like behavior plays a role.

Furthermore, subtle differences in the dynamics of facial responses or head movements of computer generated human-like characters can have profound effects with regard to the genuineness of the expression and the overall trustworthiness. In several studies, we have demonstrated that smile expressions are judged differently depending on their dynamic trajectory such as onset, apex and offset duration. Specifically, smiles that unfolded quickly (short onset) and disappeared abruptly (short offset) made the sender appear less authentic and believable in terms of the expressed emotion (Krumhuber & Kappas, 2005; Krumhuber et al., 2007). This also led to lower ratings of personal dispositions (i.e., trustworthiness, attractiveness, flirtatiousness) and less trusting decisions in social situations such as an economic trust game and a simulated job interview (Krumhuber et al., 2007; Krumhuber et al., 2009). Dynamic parameters therefore seem to be crucial in maintaining believability and may even exceed static parameters such as appearance in importance (Grammer et al., 1997).

To avoid feelings of repulsion or eeriness on the part of the viewer, researchers have consequently focused on examining specific features. These included facial features including proportions as well as textural detail and resolution (Green et al., 2008; see Tinwell et al., 2011 for an overview). Powers and Kiesler (2006), for example, recommended a short chin length for robots to evoke perceptions of human-likeness and sociability. Others suggested that the eyes are vital for impressions regarding lifelikeness and to avoid facial "creepiness" (Geller 2008; Looser & Wheatley, 2010). In a study by Tinwell et al. (2011) lack of expressivity in the upper face (i.e., forehead area) was found to increase perceptions of uncanniness of virtual characters. These authors also argued that it is important to consider the type of emotional expression, with survival-related emotions such as fear, sadness, surprise and disgust being more likely to exaggerate the UV in highly human-like characters.

Unless the agent/robot is structurally and functionally similar to humans and capable of human-like behavior, it may be therefore wise to avoid perfect human resemblance. This is because human realism provokes viewers to see human mind in an artificial entity (Gray & Wegner, 2012). According to Gray and colleagues (Gray et al., 2007), mental experience is one of the key essentials of humankind and reserved only for humans. In studying people's attributions of mind to various types of characters (e.g., baby, frog, adult man, dead woman, god), humans were found to be judged as significantly more able to feel and more able to sense than robots and machines. The experience of mind with complex emotions is therefore seen as fundamental to humans and lacking in artificial entities. Further evidence comes from research showing that people rarely ascribe moral rights and privileges to machines (Friedman et al., 2003). Phenomena like the UV may accordingly be due to some inconsistency in perceiving mental experience in an otherwise unfeeling human without conscious experience (Gray & Wegner, 2012).

To circumvent any pitfalls, design guidelines have in turn proposed a mix of human- and machine-like attributes to achieve a balance of illusion and functionality (Fong et al., 2002). This includes on the one hand some "robot-ness" to make the mechanical component of the artificial system evident and to prevent the user from forming wrong expectations about its mental and emotional abilities. On the other hand, a certain amount of "human-ness" is maintained to facilitate human-like interaction and to make it socially engaging (DiSalvio et al., 2002). In line with these recommendations, efforts have been targeted towards the implementation of cartoon-like humanoid characters that avoid the UV (see Hanson, 2006). Such anthropomorphic representations of lower extent do not deny the technology in the system, while providing an intuitive and human-like interface (Kiesler & Goetz, 2002).

Avatars and nonverbal self-presentation on the Internet

As can be seen from the literature reviewed above, cartoon-like representations such as simple 2D avatars have found a place as a tool to study human-robot interaction and the UV. Yet why exactly should idealized avatars avoid the UV whereas more realistic virtual embodiments often do not? In other words, is there something special about idealized avatars that more realistic forms of virtual representations might be lacking? We argue that 2D avatars may indeed offer a number of features that make them interesting for the study of nonverbal behavior on the Internet across a fairly wide range of contexts.

Perhaps one of the main reasons why simple avatars may avoid the UV is because it should be easier to remove all the uncanny flaws from them in comparison to very realistic humanoid robots (see Hanson, 2006).Yet this is probably not the whole story. For example, we might also be more ready to accept certain flaws on a cartoon-like character that would be perceived as extremely creepy on a human or otherwise flawless android. For example, a sickly green skin tone could be expected to elicit a strong sense of the uncanny if it was encountered in an android – whereas it might look just a little bit silly on a cartoon-like character. Yet there are also social factors that should be considered, such as when and how people typically use avatars. Cartoonlike avatars are frequently found and studied in the context of casual applications or games (e.g., Ducheneaut et al., 2009; Trepte et al., 2009; Seung, 2010; Merola & Peña, 2010; Poncin & Garnier, 2012) where, due to market constraints, considerable design effort can be expected to have gone into providing users with a wide and enjoyable range of customization options to personalize their avatar. This implies that most of us will associate avatars with relatively relaxed and fun creative activities that are open to experimentation. From a social psychological perspective, this creates a very interesting case because it means that avatars allow the user room for self-expression, including a possible idealization of the self (e.g., Seung, 2010) or the body (e.g., Villani et al., 2012).

Avatars are a form of visual online self-representation that can be abstract, cartoonish, or somewhat anthropomorphic but do not depend on photos (Walther & Ramirez, 2010). In addition to being a creative form of self-expression on the Internet, avatars offer a number of possibilities for the study of nonverbal behavior that would be difficult to realize with other tools. For social psychologists, this primarily implies that avatars can be easily and consistently manipulated without becoming too difficult for participants to accept. For example, Lee and colleagues (2014) recently studied how we conform with gender stereotypes when participants were given a cartoon-like avatar with randomly-assigned gender. The study authors pretended to give participants a choice between six avatars that was, however, controlled by the computer to result in the desired random assignment of avatar gender. The avatar was then inserted into a virtual triad in which the participant was set up to be the only female (male). With this design, Lee and colleagues (2014) could demonstrate stereotype-consistent differences on an arithmetic task, in which participants who were assigned a male avatar outperformed those who were assigned a female avatar – irrespective of their actual gender. Note that participants in this study seemed to have little difficulty identifying with the avatar of the opposite gender, or at least they showed no indication of having stumbled over this discrepancy with their gender identity in real life. This is an important point because this type of manipulation would almost certainly not have worked if the researchers had, for example, used photographs of fake subjects. A photograph, in this design, would virtually have shouted "not me!" whereas the avatar likely allowed participants to slip into another gender role almost naturally. Methodologically, the intentional lack of detail in simple avatars makes it easier to control a large range of potential confounds (e.g., ethnicity, attractiveness) while facilitating acceptance.

With 2D or 3D avatars, experimenters can create conditions with pre-assigned avatars that only differ in respect to one critical variable, e.g., race (Vang & Fox, 2014), or gender (Lee, 2004, 2005). Another recent example for this was a study by Yoon and Vargas (2014), who showed that avatars can be used to promote pro- or antisocial behaviors in everyday life. In a set of two experiments, they assigned participants to play a simple game with either a heroic (Superman) or villainous (Voldemort) avatar, and could show that this manipulation was sufficient to influence the amount of pleasant (chocolate) vs. unpleasant (chili sauce) food these participants would be willing to give to fictional future participants in an ostensible taste test. However, while the potential uses of pre-assigned avatars for social psychological research are intriguing, other research has started to focus on the avatars themselves, and what they may reveal about a user's personality.

User-generated avatars can be studied on the basis of what is created and shown "in the wild," i.e., the Internet (e.g., Bessière et al., 2007; Duchenaut et al., 2009; Martey & Consavalo, 2011). Alternatively, participants can be asked about an avatar that they *might* create without actually having to create it (e.g., Trepte et al., 2009). Finally, avatars can be investigated in the context of laboratory studies in which a sample of participants is asked to create an avatar of themselves for a particular application or game (e.g. Seung, 2010; Sung et al., 2011; Poncin & Garnier, 2012; Villani et al., 2012). Each of these three basic approaches has its individual strengths and weaknesses.

To start with the first approach, a clear advantage of collecting extant avatars from the Internet is that a large and varied corpus of cases can be collected at minimal cost. For example, Ducheneaut and colleagues (2009) investigated avatar personalization for three different worlds (*World of Warcraft, Second Life, Maple Story*) by asking participants to upload the screenshot of their avatar and to fill out a questionnaire about the character-creation interface and customization features, as well as questions instructing participants to compare themselves to their avatar. On the downside, this approach is limited by sampling biases as well as technical differences between the tools used to create avatars across different contexts. However, it can be used to study important factors that have been identified in game-related research, such as gender, age, and personality (see Lee et al., 2009). For example, Duchenaut and colleagues (2009) found that the distribution of age and gender varied substantially across different virtual worlds, while a common trend suggested that men wanted to stand out more whereas women tended to idealize more.

The second type of approach relates to quasi-experimental research, such as when participants are asked about what features they would choose for their avatar in a particular game or scenario. For example, Trepte and colleagues (2011) gave participants descriptions of five existing computer games, and instructed them to imagine an avatar that would optimally match the requirements of each game. The experimenters then asked a second sample of subjects to choose attributes that they would prefer to have for an avatar that they would like to play the game with. Trepte and colleagues (2011) found that participants aimed to identify with and chose an avatar of their own sex, while whereas both male and female participants nevertheless chose pretested masculine (e.g., analytical, forceful) or feminine (e.g., warm, beautiful) attributes for their avatars according to the requirements of the game. A clear advantage of this approach is that idealized avatars can be compared on the same set of dimensions even if a particular game or application does not technically support this feature or dimension to be manipulated. However, a limitation is that the "creation" process remains at a purely imaginative level, which limits conclusions about the impact of the actual design process or changes that users might intuitively make in response to seeing an actual avatar rather than describing an ideal. It is further limited to features that participants can reliably verbalize, and likely more susceptible to experimental demand effects than if the same tool could be used for the creation of avatars across different online contexts.

Finally, avatars can be studied by asking participants to create actual avatars for one or more online contexts. For example, Poncin and Garnier (2012) instructed a large sample of 286 participants to create avatars for *Second Life*. They observed that participants who identified strongly with their avatar also experienced higher immersion and satisfaction with the game. Further, women appeared to represent themselves as they really were, or with some degree of idealization, whereas men appeared to create generally more fanciful and imaginary characters (Poncin & Garnier, 2012).

In an extension of this approach, groups of participants can further be asked to create an avatar for more than one online context. This type of design can, for example, be used to investigate the effects of different online contexts on the type and perceived personality traits of avatars (e.g., Sung et al., 2011), or the effect of the avatar-creation task itself can be used as an experimental manipulation to prime a particular type of self-concept – comparable to the use of assigned avatars (cf., e.g., Yoon & Vargas, 2014). An example of such a between-subjects design with different online contexts is a study by Vasalou and Joinson (2009) in which separate groups of participants used a single avatar creation tool (Yahoo! Avatars) across different online settings. The researchers instructed participants to create an avatar either for blogging, dating, or gaming – and because they selected a single tool to fit more than one online context, Vasalou and Joinson (2009) could compare the same set of avatar attributes without the need to resort to the imagination of a hypothetical avatar (cf., Trepte et al., 2011). The outcome of this study was a set of interesting differences that suggested that different online contexts may indeed facilitate the expression of different traits (see also Sung et al., 2011). For example, avatars created for dating were indeed made to look more attractive than avatars created for gaming, which were, in turn, made to look more intellectual. A clear advantage of this approach is that it allows a high level of standardization in a way that renders the resulting avatars directly comparable. However, it is nevertheless limited in the degree to which one particular avatar creation tool is equally suited to different online contexts or games. Thus, while one and the same tool might be appropriate for different casual uses on the Internet, commercial games are usually more closely tied to the specific avatar-generation engine that was created for the needs of one particular game. Finally, whenever user-created avatars are to be compared across online contexts, differences in experience and familiarity of participants with these contexts need to be considered.

From the perspective of psychological research, differences in familiarity with diverging online context may warrant further attention. This can even be positive because it means that the Internet still holds the potential for the typical student to step outside his or her familiar comfort zone and present him or herself in a largely unfamiliar and emotionally or intellectually challenging environment, even if it is just a mouse click away. We used this fact in a recent study (Vujović et al., 2011) in which the same 68 students were asked to create an avatar of themselves that was to be used either for Facebook, an online dating website, or a political discussion forum (see Figure 12.1 for examples). For the avatar creation, we followed an earlier study by Vasalou and Joinson (2009), and asked participants to use the Yahoo! Avatars website to create their visual alter ego. Comparably to Vasalou and Joinson (2009), certain differences between online contexts could be observed when we later asked participants about their avatars. Primarily, participants identified slightly more strongly with their avatar if they had created it for Facebook rather than a political discussion forum. Yet what conclusions might be drawn about personality and online self-presentation when participants are asked to take a step outside their usual comfort zone and create an avatar of themselves for an online dating website?

This question can, for example, be addressed by showing the output of an avatar-creation task to subjects who are unfamiliar with the creator of the avatar. In a follow-up study to our avatar creation experiment, an independent sample of 289 online participants evaluated the personality expressed by a randomly chosen avatar using the Five-Item Personality Inventory (Gosling et al., 2003). We then correlated these personality judgments with the self-report obtained with the S5 personality questionnaire (Konstabel et al., 2011) from the participants in

Figure 12.1 Examples of the avatars created for the Facebook (left), dating (middle), and discussion forum (right) conditions. Participants created these avatars using Yahoo! Avatars

the original sample. As might be expected given this form of avatar-mediated self-presentation of personality with a minimal personality measure, most of the Big Five personality dimensions did not show substantial correlations. The exception, was Openness, which observers guessed correctly at an above-chance level ($r = .27$; $p < .05$), in particular for avatars that were created in the Dating condition ($r = .42$). This suggests that, in the future, more reliable personality measures and creative self-presentation tasks may have a higher predictive value as regards the self-described offline personality of the individual who created some type of nonverbal online self-presentation. At the same time it suggests that, just as in everyday life, personally more challenging situations, such as online dating for someone who has never tried it, may be more diagnostic for online judgments of someone's personality. Furthermore, while this chapter is focused on nonverbal behavior on the Internet, we should keep in mind that the Internet is still an environment where verbal information plays an important role. Therefore, instead of focusing on nonverbal behavior exclusively, we should aim to integrate also verbal and text-based information into our analyses of nonverbal online behavior.

The recent avatar-creation study that we have already mentioned could again serve as an example here. In this study, in addition to specific differences between the avatars as such, we were interested in how the different types of social affordances associated with online dating and political discussions might shape how participants can access self-relevant knowledge in associative memory. In order to test the relative accessibility of true and actual self-concepts (e.g., Higgins, 1987) elicited by the different avatar conditions, we adapted a reaction-time task that was originally designed by Markus (1977) and later modified by Bargh and colleagues (2002). Bargh and colleagues (2002) compared the accessibility of the true-self concept and the actual self after participants had interacted with another participant either face-to-face or in an Internet chat room. Before this interaction, all participants were asked to list a number of the traits that they believed they actually possessed and were able to express (*actual self*), as well as those (*true self*) traits and characteristics that they "would like to but are not usually able to express" (p. 37). While the participants were engaged in the interaction, these words were unobtrusively hidden in a version of the "Me/Not-Me" response task (Markus, 1977), in which participants have to respond as quickly as possible to a larger set of words and decide if these words are self-descriptive by pressing a button. When participants performed

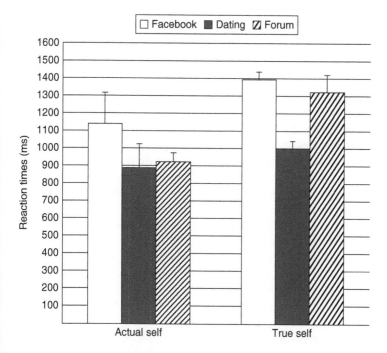

Figure 12.2 Response times to words generated by participants about their actual and true selves per condition

Note: Facebook: N= 23; Dating: N = 21; Forum: N = 23.

This figure uses means and standard errors (*SEM*) for ease of presentation. All statistical tests were run non-parametrically on log-transformed data.

this task soon after completion of their face-to-face or online interaction, Bargh and colleagues (2002) observed that participants were faster to respond to traits of their actual self, as well as a significant interaction between self-concept and interaction mode in which the true self was relatively more accessible after the online interaction. After, in our study, participants had created avatars for Facebook, a discussion forum, or a dating website, we observed the same type of main effect between actual and true selves, and overall similar reaction times. We further found a significant effect for the type of online context, such as that having created an avatar for the online dating condition resulted in significantly shorter reaction times for the true-self traits generated by participants (see Figures 12.1 and 12.2).

Outlook: on the diversity of online contexts, and the persons behind the screen

Perhaps one of the most exciting questions about nonverbal communication on the Internet is how certain types of online behaviors relate to offline behaviors face-to-face (Kappas & Krämer, 2011b). This question, however, is not limited simply to comparisons between online and offline behaviors. Rather, we should be aware that personality and individual differences shape the way that people use the Internet, and that the Internet is a much more complex and diverse environment than many psychologists used to believe (Amichai-Hamburger, 2002, 2007). For psychologists, the Internet has previously often been perceived intuitively as a single entity (Amichai-Hamburger, 2002), and this perception has led many psychologists to focus on stereotypical questions, such as whether Internet use is harmful or not (Amichai-Hamburger, 2002; Kraut et al., 1998; Kraut et al., 2002). Yet once we realize that the Internet today allows for much more diverse types of online interactions, and that personality differences are likely to play an important role in how we use some services on the Internet while ignoring others, the question of how online behavior relates to a face-to-face situation may need to be partially rephrased. For example, in 2002, McKenna and colleagues (McKenna et al., 2002) suggested that the relative anonymity of interactions on the Internet greatly reduces the risks of intimate self-disclosures. Today, however, most people are familiar with "nonymous" (Zhao et al., 2008) social networking sites such as Facebook in which people interact online using their real names. Can we, for example, still expect today that users will feel more comfortable in anonymous online contexts than in nonymous contexts?

The rapid development of the Internet over the past decade has greatly increased the diversity of environments for online communication, and this may change the focus of future research from direct online vs. offline comparisons to the study of differences between online environments and how they relate to the person behind the screen. For example, a number of recent studies have investigated to what extent different online environments may elicit changes in self-presentation (e.g., Whitty, 2008; Vasalou & Joinson, 2009; Boyle & Johnson, 2010; Mazur & Kozarian, 2010; Guadagno et al., 2012), including potential differences between contexts in which everyone knows everyone else by their real name or not (Zhao et al., 2008). In the example of avatars that we have discussed in the previous section, this implies that the avatars should ideally reflect the personalities of a representative sample of people. On first glance, this issue appears almost trivial, given that the Internet now reaches already more than a third of the world's population (see Broadband Commission for Digital Development, 2012). However, large scale Internet access does not yet equate with a broad and diversified familiarity and experience. Thus, when we aim to compare specific online contexts, it will be relevant to know to what extent participants have had experience with a particular service or setting at the time – in particular since the Internet is likely to continue to change at a rapid pace.

An example of the relevance of individual differences in research on online behavior are certain types of heated discussions and online insults that sometimes make headlines in the popular media. The issue here is not that there is no scientific basis to study online discussions. In fact, some scientific research has begun to emerge on this question (e.g., Chmiel et al., 2011). Chmiel and colleagues (2011) observed clusters of negative online discussions on political forums (BBC) that appeared to fuel and sustain e-communities. Yet what is less clear is the extent to which such online environments can indeed polarize random casual readers in the same way, or if only a certain type of person is attracted to this kind of online communication in the first place. Some initial evidence appears to suggest the latter. When we (Kappas et al., 2012) recently asked a sample of 51 student dyads to discuss a set of emotional topics in an online discussion chat, we observed that these discussions were indeed emotional and activating for our student sample. However, while we further found some effects for factors such as anonymity and gender, the differences in respect to disclosure and language style were generally more subtle than we had expected. Unfortunately, we found no clear pattern emerged for trait-like differences that might explain why some people appear to lean toward such extreme emotional outbursts in anonymous political discussion forums. Possibly, our sample of students was simply not similar enough to the angry disputants in online discussion forums.

The study of emotional online discussions is furthermore an example of a case in which the verbal behavior alone might not be sufficient to explain the psychological mechanisms of interest. Why, for example, do only a relatively small number of people participate in online discussions whereas others people might never even have looked at a political discussion before? Clearly, inter-individual differences in interests, personality, and self-presentation should play an important role here – and this again leads us to emphasize that we should not assume that everyone is using the Internet and online communication in quite the same way.

Further research is still needed to identify systematic inter-individual differences that might help to explain why some people appear to present themselves very differently online vs. offline. Thus, while we have argued at the beginning of this chapter that certain uses of the Internet such as Skype or Facebook have become very commonplace for young people, this does not mean that all young people will have explored all kinds of online communication tools to the extent that the mass media might sometimes aim to make us believe. There are almost certainly still-more specialized online communication contexts that most young people have never experienced first hand, or in which they might be more sensitive in how they present themselves. Political online discussions are one example that we have already mentioned – whereas a contrasting example is the case of online dating.

While few of us might be surprised to hear that involvement in political discussions may not be any more popular online than offline, online dating appears to be quite consistent with what we would expect young people to do on the Internet. Online dating is regularly depicted in widely recognized media such as the *New York Times* as a place where young people meet to date "at hyperspeed" (St. John, 2002), and that is used by millions of Americans (Rosenbloom, 2011). Likewise, already in 2006, Ellison, Heino, and Gibbs argued that online dating had evolved from a marginalized activity into the social mainstream. It is therefore tempting to assume that everyone, and in particular young people, will be familiar and comfortable with these kinds of settings. However, recent large-scale survey data (Smith & Duggan, 2013) presents a somewhat more frugal picture. Overall, about one in ten Americans (USA) say that they have engaged in some form of online dating via an online dating site or mobile application, with the largest percentage found for the age groups between 25 and 44 years, where up to 17% admit to having used an online dating website. As this Pew study (Smith & Duggan, 2013) with more than 2,000 participants found, online dating is now perceived more positively by Americans than a few years ago. For example, a majority (56%) now agrees that "online dating is a good way to meet people," whereas only a minority (23%) still agree with the view that "people who use online dating sites are desperate" (Smith & Duggan, 2013, p. 54). Nevertheless, at least for the somewhat younger age group of most student samples, online dating can still be expected to be an activity that the majority of students may have little actual personal experience with.

While we have argued that the increasing diversity of the Internet allows researchers to ask new questions about nonverbal online and offline behavior, it is important to note that the Internet is psychologically perhaps even more diverse than the number of different services might suggest. Thus, while services such as Facebook, Skype, or Twitter may have greatly reshaped the Internet over the past decade, the extent to which even young people are comfortable with different services is clearly not uniform. When we recently asked a sample of 68 young students (M age = 19.7 years, SD = 1.8, 42 female) at a highly international university about their familiarity with different types of online environments such as Facebook, online dating websites, and discussion forums, we expected them to be more or less familiar with all three types of environments, even if Facebook could be expected to be most popular. What we found instead in this anonymous survey was, however, an extremely one-sided distribution. Thus, while all except one of the 68 students said that they had a Facebook account, only two of these same 68 admitted to have an account on an online dating website – and out of the remaining 66 students, only five indicated that they would consider online dating in the future. Further, only nine participants (12.7%) indicated having an account for a discussion forum. When asked if they had at least occasionally read a post on a political discussion forum on a 7-point Likert scale there was somewhat more agreement (M = 3.8, SD = 1.9). However, overall, our participants' comfort-zone with different types of online communication environments appeared to be quite sharply focused on Facebook, which participants in this sample reported to use very frequently (M = 6.0 on a 7-point Likert scale). Does this data imply then that research aiming at comparisons between different online contexts will have to wait until everyone is as familiar with, e.g., Twitter, as with Facebook? Probably not – particularly since this may never happen. Instead, researchers may either aim to obtain participant samples with sufficient prior experience – or the apparent differences in familiarity may rather be integrated into the study.

Communication between humans over the Internet, or between humans and artificial agents is clearly related to offline interaction between humans, but there are many features that require adaptation of research methods, and possibly of theories as well, to a certain degree. For this, much research is needed in the immediate future. The fact that the technologies involved are rapidly evolving poses an additional challenge. The present chapter is an attempt to highlight some of the relevant findings and identify some of the questions that should be investigated if we want to have a better grasp of technology-based and technology-enhanced communication. This is relevant to identifying potential problems for the communicators, but also facilitating the development of better systems, where better might mean anything between effective, entertaining, and ethical.

References

Alexander, O., Rogers, M., Lambeth, W., Chiang, J.-Y., Ma, W.-C., Wang, C.-C., & Debevec, P. (2010). The Digital Emily Project: Achieving a photorealistic digital actor. *IEEE Computer Graphics, 30*, 20–31.

Amichai-Hamburger, Y. (2002). Internet and personality. *Computers in Human Behavior, 18*, 1–10.

Amichai-Hamburger, Y. (2007). Personality, individual differences and Internet use. In A. N. Joinson, K. Y. A. McKenna, T. Postmes & U-D. Reips (Eds). *The Oxford handbook of Internet psychology* (pp. 187–204). Oxford: Oxford University Press.

Appel, J., von der Pütten, A., Krämer, N. C., & Gratch, J. (2012). Does humanity matter? Analyzing the importance of social cues and perceived agency of a computer system for the emergence of social reactions during human-computer interaction. *Advances in Human-Computer Interaction, 2012*, 1–10.

Bänziger, T., Grandjean, D., & Scherer, K. R. (2009). Emotion recognition from expressions in face, voice, and body: The multimodal emotion recognition test (MERT). *Emotion, 9*, 691–704.

Bänziger, T. & Scherer, K. R. (2007). Using actor portrayals to systematically study multimodal emotion expression: The GEMEP corpus. In A. Paiva, R. Prada, & R. W. Picard (Eds), *Affective Computing and Intelligent Interaction: Proceedings of the 2nd International Conference on Affective Computing and Intelligent Interaction.* Berlin: Springer-Verlag (LNCS 4738, pp. 476–487).

Bargh, J. A. & McKenna, K. Y. (2004). The Internet and social life. *Annual Review of Psychology, 55*, 573–590.

Bargh, J. A., McKenna, K. Y. A., & Fitzsimons, G. M. (2002). Can you see the real me? Activation and expression of the "true self" on the Internet. *Journal of Social Issues, 58*, 33–48.

Bartneck, C., Kanda, T., Ishiguro, H., & Hagita, N. (2009). My robotic doppelganger – A critical look at the Uncanny Valley theory. In *Proceedings of the 18th IEEE International Symposium on Robot and Human Interactive Communication (RO-MAN 2009)* (vol. 1, pp. 1–8). Toyama, Japan: IEEE Press.

Bessière, K. M. A., Seay, A. F., & Kiesler, S. (2007). The ideal elf: Identity exploration in World of Warcraft. *Cyberpsychology & Behavior, 10*, 530–535.

Bethel, C. L. & Murphy, R. R. (2006). Affective expression in appearance-constrained robots. In *Proceedings of the 1st ACM SIGCHI/SIGART conference on human-robot interaction* (pp. 327–328). New York, NY: ACM.

Borshukov, G. & Lewis, J. P. (2005). Realistic human face rendering for 'The Matrix Reloaded'. In *ACM SIGGRAPH 2003 Sketches & Applications* (p. 1). New York, NY: ACM.

Boyle, K. & Johnson, T. J. (2010). MySpace is your space? Examining self-presentation of MySpace users. *Computers in Human Behavior, 26*, 1392–1399.

Breazeal, C. L. (2002). *Designing social robots.* Cambridge, MA: MIT Press.

Breazeal, C. & Scasselatti, B. (1999). How to build robots that make friends and influence people. In *Proceedings of the 1999 IEEE/RSJ International Conference on*

Intelligent Robots and Systems (IROS '99) (vol. 2, pp. 858–863). Kyongju, Korea: IEEE.

Broadband Commission for Digital Development. (2012). *The state of broadband 2012: Achieving digital inclusion for all.* Retrieved from http://www.broadband commission.org/documents/bb-annualreport2012.pdf.

Burgoon, J. K. & Walther, J. B. (2013). Media and computer mediation. In J.A. Hall, & M.L. Knapp (Eds), *Nonverbal Communication. Handbooks of Communication Science Vol. 2.* (pp. 731–770). Berlin, Germany: Walter de Gruyter GmbH.

Busso, C., Bulut, M., Lee, C.-C., Kazemzadeh, A., Mower, E., Kim, S., ... Narayanan, S. S. (2008). IEMOCAP: Interactive emotional dyadic motion capture database. *Language Resources & Evaluation, 42,* 335–359.

Chmiel, A., Sienkiewicz, J., Thelwall, M., Paltoglou, G., Buckley, K., Kappas, A., & Hołyst, J. A. (2011). Collective emotions online and their influence on community life. *PLoS ONE, 6,* e22207. doi:10.1371/journal.pone.0022207.

Dehn, D. M. & van Mulken, S. (2000). The impact of animated interface agents: A review of empirical research. *International Journal of Human-Computer Studies, 52,* 1–22.

DiSalvio, C, F., Gemperle, F., Forlizzi, J., & Kiesler, S. (2002). All robots are not created equal: The design and perception of humanoid robot heads. In *Proceedings of the 4th Conference on Designing Interactive Systems: Processes, practices, methods, and techniques (DIS '02)* (pp. 321–326). New York, NY: ACM.

Donath, J. (2007). Virtually trustworthy. *Science, 317,* 53–54.

Ducheneaut N., Wen, M.-H. D., Yee, N., & Wadley, G. (2009). Body and mind: A study of avatar personalization in three virtual worlds. In *Proceedings of the SIGCHI Conference on Human Factors in Computing Systems (CHI '09)* (pp. 1151–1160). New York, NY: ACM.

Eimler, S. C., Krämer, N. C., & von der Pütten, A. M. (2010). Prerequisites for human-agent and human-robot interaction: Towards an integrated theory. In R. Trappl (Ed.), *Cybernetics & Systems 2010 – Proceedings of the Twentieth European meeting on Cybernetics and Systems Research (EMCSR 2010)* (pp. 541–546). Vienna, Austria: Austrian Society for Cybernetic Studies.

Ellison, N., Heino, R., & Gibbs, J. (2006). Managing impressions online: Self-presentation processes in the online dating environment. *Journal of Computer-Mediated Communication, 11,* 415–441.

Fong, T. W., Nourbakhsh, I., & Dautenhahn, K. (2002). A survey of socially interactive robots: Concepts, design, and applications. *Robotics and Autonomous Systems, 42,* 142–166.

Friedman, B., Kahn, P. H., Jr., & Hagman, J. (2003). Hardware companions? – What online AIBO discussion forums reveal about the human-robotic relationship. In *Proceedings of the SIGCHI Conference on Human Factors in Computing Systems (CHI'03)* (pp. 273–280). New York, NY: ACM.

Geller, T. (2008). Overcoming the uncanny valley. *IEEE Computer Graphics and Applications, 28,* 11–17.

Goetz, J., Kiesler, S., & Powers, A. (2003). Matching robot appearance and behavior to tasks to improve human-robot cooperation. In *Proceedings of the 12th IEEE International Workshop on Robot and Human Interactive Communication (RO-MAN'03)* (pp. 55–60). doi:10.1109/ROMAN.2003.1251796.

Gosling, S. D., Rentfrow, P. J., & Swann, W. B., Jr. (2003). A very brief measure of the Big-Five personality domains. *Journal of Research in Personality, 37,* 504–528.

Gouskos, C. (2006). The depths of the Uncanny Valley. Retrieved from http://www.gamespot.com/features/the-depths-of-the-uncanny-valley-6153667/.

Grammer, K., Filova, V., & Fiedler, M. (1997). The communication paradox and possible solutions: Towards a radical empiricism. In A. Schmitt, K. Atzwanger, K. Grammer & K. Schaefer (Eds), *New aspects of human ethology* (pp. 91–120). New York, USA: Plenum Press.

Gray, H. M., Gray, K., & Wegner, D. M. (2007). Dimensions of mind perception. *Science, 315,* 619.

Gray, K. & Wegner, D. M. (2012). Feeling robots and human zombies: Mind perception and the uncanny valley. *Cognition, 125,* 125–130.

Green, R. D., MacDorman, K. F., Ho, C.-C., & Vasudevan, S. K. (2008). Sensitivity to the proportions of faces that vary in human likeness. *Computers in Human Behavior, 24,* 2456–2474.

Guadagno, R. E., Okdie, B. M., & Kruse, S. A. (2012). Dating deception: Gender, online dating, and exaggerated self-presentation. *Computers in Human Behavior, 28,* 642–647.

Hall, J. A., & Knapp, M. L. (Eds). (2013). *Nonverbal Communication.* Berlin & New York: de Gruyter/Mouton.

Hanson, D. (2006). Exploring the aesthetic range for humanoid robots. In *Proceedings of the ICCS/ CogSci-2006 long symposium: Toward social mechanisms of android science* (pp. 16–20). Vancouver, Canada: Cognitive Science Society.

Hegel, F., Lohse, M., Swadzba, A., Wachsmuth, S., Rohlfing, K., &Wrede, B. (2007). Classes of application for social robots: A user study. In *Proceedings of the 16th IEEE International Symposium on Robot & Human Interactive Communication (RO-MAN'07)* (pp. 938–943). doi:10.1109/ROMAN.2007.4415218.

Hegel, F., Lohse, M., & Wrede, B. (2009). Effects of visual appearance on the attribution of applications in social robotics. In *Proceedings of the 18th IEEE International Symposium on Robot and Human Interactive Communication (RO-MAN'09)* (pp. 64–71). doi:10.1109/ROMAN.2009.5326340.

Hess, U., Kappas, A., & Scherer, K. R. (1988). Multichannel communication of emotion: Synthetic signal production. In K. R. Scherer (Ed.) *Facets of emotion: Recent research* (pp. 161–182). Hillsdale, NJ: Lawrence Erlbaum Associates.

Higgins, T. E. (1987). Self-Discrepancy: A theory relating self and affect. *Psychological Review, 94,* 319–340.

Hinds, P. J., Roberts, T. L., & Jones, H. (2004). Whose job is it anyway? A study of human-robot interaction in a collaborative task. *Human-Computer Interaction, 19,* 151–181.

Hüttenrauch, H. & Severinson-Eklundh, K. (2002). Fetch and carry with CERO: Observations from a long term study with a service robot. In *Proceedings of the 11th IEEE International Workshop on Robot and Human Interactive Communication (RO-MAN'02)* (pp. 158–163). doi:10.1109/ROMAN.2002.1045615.

Ishiguro, H. (2006). Android science: Conscious and subconscious recognition. *Connection Science, 18,* 319–332.

Ishiguro, H., & Nishio, S. (2007). Building artificial humans to understand humans. *Journal of Artificial Organs, 10,* 133–142.

Joinson, A., McKenna, K., Postmes, T., & Reips, U.-D. (Eds). (2009). *Oxford handbook of Internet Psychology.* New York: Oxford University Press.

Kappas, A. (2013). Social regulation of emotion: Messy layers. *Frontiers in Psychology, 4*(51). doi:10.3389/fpsyg.2013.00051.

Kappas, A. & Descôteaux, J. (2003). Of butterflies and roaring thunder: Nonverbal communication in interaction and regulation of emotion. In P. Philippot, E.J. Coats & R.S. Feldman (Eds), *Nonverbal behavior in clinical settings* (pp. 45–74). New York: Oxford University Press.

Kappas, A. & Krämer, N. C. (Eds). (2011a). Introduction: Electronically mediated face-to-face communication: Issues, questions and challenges. In A. Kappas & N.C. Krämer (Eds) *Face-to-face communication over the Internet. Emotions in a web of culture, language and technology* (pp. 1–13). Cambridge: Cambridge University Press.

Kappas, A. & Krämer, N. C. (Eds). (2011b). *Face-to-face communication over the Internet. Emotions in a web of culture, language and technology.* Cambridge: Cambridge University Press.

Kappas, A., Küster, D., Theunis, M., & Tsankova, E. (2012, September). *Cyberemotions: An analysis of synchronous computer mediated communication and dyadic interaction.* Poster presented at the 52nd Annual Meeting of the Society for Psychophysiological Research, New Orleans, Louisiana.

Kiesler, S. (1997). *Culture of the Internet.* Mahwah, NJ: Lawrence Erlbaum Associates.

Kiesler, S., & Goetz, J. (2002). Mental models and cooperation with robotic assistants. In *Proceedings of the Conference on Human Factors in Computing Systems (CHI'02)* (pp. 576–577). New York, NY: ACM.

Kiesler, S., Siegel, J, & McGuire, T.W. (1984). Social psychological aspects of computer-mediated communication. *American Psychologist, 39,* 1123–1134.

Kiesler, S., & Sproull, L. (1992). Group decision making and communication technology. *Organizational Behavior and Human Decision Processes, 52,* 96–123.

King, W. J. & Ohya, J. (1996). The representation of agents: Anthropomorphism, agency, and intelligence. In *Conference Companion on Human Factors in Computing Systems (CHI'96)* (pp. 289–290). New York, USA: ACM.

Koda, T. & Maes, P. (1996). Agents with faces: The effects of personification of agents. In *Proceedings of the 5th IEEE International Workshop on Robot and Human Communication (RO-MAN'96)* (pp. 189–194). doi:10.1109/ROMAN. 1996.568812.

Komatsu, T. & Yamada, S. (2007). Effects of robotic agents' appearances on users' interpretation of the agents' attitudes: Towards an expansion of "uncanny valley" assumption. In *Proceedings of the 16th IEEE International Symposium on Robot and Human Interactive Communication (RO-MAN'07)* (pp. 380–385). Jeju, South Korea: IEEE Press.

Konstabel, K., Lönnqvist, J.-E., Walkowitz, G., Konstabel, K.,& Verkasalo, M. (2011). The Short Five (S5): Measuring personality traits using comprehensive single items. *European Journal of Personality, 26*(1), 13–29.

Krämer, N. C. (2005). Social communicative effects of a virtual program guide. In T. Panayiotopoulos (Ed.), *Intelligent virtualagents* (pp. 442–543). Hamburg: Springer.

Krämer, N. C., Eimler, S., von der Pütten, A. & Payr, S. (2011). "Theory of companions" What can theoretical models contribute to applications and understanding of human-robot interaction? *Applied Artificial Intelligence, 25,* 503–529.

Kraut, R., Kiesler, S., Boneva, B., Cummings, J., Helgeson, V., & Crawford, A. (2002). Internet paradox revisited. *Journal of Social Issues, 58,* 49–74.

Kraut, R., Patterson, M., Landmark, V., Kiesler, S., Mukophadhyay, T., & Scherlis, W. (1998). Internet paradox: A social technology that reduces social involvement and psychological well-being? *American Psychologist, 53,* 1017–1031.

Krumhuber, E., Hall, M., Hodgson, J., & Kappas, A. (2012). Designing interface agents: Beyond realism, resolution, and the uncanny valley. In D. Reichardt (Ed.), *Proceedings of the 6th Workshop on Emotion and Computing – Current Research and Future Impact* (pp. 18–25). Saarbrücken, Germany.

Krumhuber, E., & Kappas, A. (2005). Moving smiles: The role of dynamic components for the perception of the genuineness of smiles. *Journal of Nonverbal Behavior, 29,* 3–24.

Krumhuber, E., Manstead, A. S. R, Cosker, D., Marshall, D., & Rosin, P. L. (2009). Effects of dynamic attributes of smiles in human and synthetic faces: A simulated job interview setting. *Journal of Nonverbal Behavior, 33,* 1–15.

Krumhuber, E., Manstead, A. S. R, Cosker, D., Marshall, D., Rosin, P. L., & Kappas, A. (2007). Facial dynamics as indicators of trustworthiness and cooperative behavior. *Emotion, 7,* 730–735.

Krumhuber, E., Manstead, A. S. R, & Kappas, A. (2007). Temporal aspects of facial displays in person and expression perception. The effects of smile dynamics, head-tilt and gender. *Journal of Nonverbal Behavior, 31,* 39–56.

Lee, E.-J. (2004). Effects of gendered character representation on person perception and informational social influence in computer-mediated communication. *Computers in Human Behavior, 20,* 779–799.

Lee, E.-J. (2005). Effects of the agent's sex and self-confidence on informational social influence in computer-mediated communication: Quantitative versus verbal presentation. *Communication Research, 32,* 29–58.

Lee, J.-E. R., Nass, C. I., & Bailenson, J. N. (2014). Does the mask govern the mind? Effects of arbitrary gender representation on quantitative task performance in avatar-represented virtual groups. *Cyberpsychology, Behavior, and Social Networking, 17*(4), 248–254.

Lee, K. M., Peng, W., & Park, N. (2009). Effects of computer/video games and beyond. In J. Bryant & M. B. Oliver (Eds), *Media effects: Advances in theory and research* (3rd ed., pp. 551–566).

Levi, S. (2004). Why Tom Hanks is less than human: While sensors cannot capture how humans act, humans can give life to digital characters. *Newsweek, 650,* 305–306.

Lohse, M., Hegel, F., Swadzba, A., Rohlfing, K., Wachsmuth, S., & Wrede, B. (2007). What can I do for you? Appearance and application of robots. In *Proceedings of the 4th International Artificial Intelligence and Simulation of Behaviour Conference (AISB'07)* (pp. 121–126). Newcastle, UK: Society for the for the Study of Artificial Intelligence and Simulation of Behavior.

Looser, C. E. & Wheatley, T. (2010). The tipping point of animacy: How, when, and where we perceive life in a face. *Psychological Science, 21,* 1854–1862.

MacDorman, K. F., Green, R. D., Ho, C.-C., & Koch, C. T. (2009). Too real for comfort? Uncanny responses to computer generated faces. *Computers in Human Behavior, 25,* 695–710.

MacDorman, K. F. & Ishiguro, H. (2006). The uncanny advantage of using androids in cognitive and social science research. *Interaction Studies, 7,* 297–337.

Markus, H. (1977). Self-schemata and processing information about the self. *Journal of Personality and Social Psychology, 35,* 63–78.

Martey, R. M. & Consavalo, M. (2011). Performing the looking-glass self: Avatar appearance and group identity in Second Life. *Popular Communication, 9,* 165–180.

Mazur, E. & Kozarian, L. (2010). Self-Presentation and interaction in blogs of adolescents and young emerging adults. *Journal of Adolescent Research, 25,* 124–144.

McKenna, K. Y. A., Green, A. S., & Gleason, M. E. J. (2002). Relationship formation on the Internet: What's the big attraction? *Journal of Social Issues, 58,* 9–31.

Merola, N., & Peña, J. (2010). The effects of avatar appearance in virtual worlds. *Journal of Virtual Worlds Research, 5,* 3–12.

Mori, M. (1970). Bukimi No Tani. The Uncanny Valley (K. F. MacDorman & T. Minato, Trans.). *Energy, 7*(4), 33–35.

Mori, M. (2012). The Uncanny Valley (K. F. MacDorman & N. Kageki, Trans.). *IEEE Robotics and Automation Magazine, 19,* 98–100.

Nass, C. & Moon, Y. (2000). Machines and mindlessness: Social responses to computers. *Journal of Social Issues, 56,* 81–103.

Nass, C., Steuer, J., Henriksen, L., & Dryer, D. C. (1994). Machines, social attributions, and ethopoeia: Performance assessments of computers subsequent to "self- "or "other"- evaluations. *International Journal of Human-Computer Studies, 40,* 543–559.

Nass, C. I., Moon, Y., Morkes, J., Kim, E., & Fogg, B. J. (1997). Computers are social actors: A review of current research. In B. Friedman (Ed.), *Human values and the design of computer technology* (pp. 137–162). Cambridge, MA: CSLI Publications.

Parise, S., Kiesler, S., Sproull, L., & Waters, K. (1996). My partner is a real dog: Cooperation with social agents. In *Proceedings of the 1996 ACM Conference on Computer Supported Cooperative Work (CSCW'96)* (pp. 399–408). New York, NY: ACM.

Parise, S., Kiesler, S., Sproull, L., & Waters, K. (1999). Cooperating with life-like interface agents. *Computers in Human Behavior, 15,* 123–142.

Philippot, P. & Douilliez, C. (2011). Impact of social anxiety on the processing of emotional information in video-mediated interaction. In A. Kappas & N.C. Krämer (Eds) *Face-to-face communication over the Internet. Emotions in a web of culture, language and technology* (pp. 127–143). Cambridge: Cambridge University Press.

Plantec, P. (2007). Crossing the great Uncanny Valley. Retrieved from http://www.awn.com/articles/production/crossing-great-uncanny-valley.

Plantec, P. (2008). The digital eye: Image metrics attempts to leap the Uncanny Valley. Retrieved from http://www.awn.com/articles/technology/digital-eye-image-metrics-attempts-leap-uncanny-valley.

Pollick, F. (2009). In search of the Uncanny Valley. In P. Daras & O. M. Ibarra (Eds.), *UC Media 2009. Lecture notes of the institute for computer sciences, social informatics and telecommunications engineering* (pp. 69–78). Venice, Italy: Springer.

Poncin, I., & Garnier, M. (2012). Avatar identification on a 3D commercial website: Gender issues. *Journal of Virtual Worlds Research, 5,* 1–20.

Powers, A., & Kiesler, S. (2006). The advisor robot: Tracing people's mental model from a robot's physical attributes. In *Proceedings of the 1st ACM SIGCHI/SIGART Conference on Human-Robot Interaction (HRI'06)* (pp. 218–225). New York, NY: ACM.

Reeves, B. & Nass, C. (1996). *The media equation: How people treat computers, television, and new media like real people and places.* New York, NY: Cambridge University Press.

Riek, L. D., Rabinowitch, T.-C., Chakrabarti, B., & Robinson, P. (2009). Empathizing with robots: Fellow feeling along the anthropomorphic spectrum. In *Proceedings of the 3rd International Conference on Affective Computing and Intelligent Interaction and Workshops (ACII 2009)* (pp. 1–9). Amsterdam, The Netherlands: IEEE Press.

Robins, B., Dautenhan, K., Boekhorst, R., & Billard, A. (2004). Robots as assistive technology – does appearance matter? *Proceedings of the 13th IEEE International Workshop on Robot and Human Interactive Communication* (RO-MAN) (pp. 277 – 282). Kurashiki, Okayama, Japan.

Rosenbloom, S. (2011, November 12). Love, lies and what they learned. *The New York Times.* Retrieved from http://www.nytimes.com

Saygin, A. P., Chaminade, T., Ishiguro, H., Driver, J., & Frith, C. (2012). The thing that should not be: predictive coding and the uncanny valley in perceiving human and humanoid robot actions. *Scan, 7,* 413–422.

Seung, A. A. J. (2010). "I feel more connected to the physically ideal mini me than the mirror-image mini me": Theoretical implications of the "malleable self" for speculations on the effects of avatar creation on avatar-self connection in Wii. *Cyberpsychology, Behavior, and Social Networking, 13,* 567–570.

Seyama, J. & Nagayama, R. (2007). The uncanny valley: Effect of realism on the impression of artificial human faces. *Presence: Teleoperators and Virtual Environments, 16,* 337–351.

Short, J.A., Williams, E., & Christie, B. (1976). *The Social Psychology of Telecommunications.* New York, NY: John Wiley & Sons.

Siegel, J., Dubrovsky, V., Kiesler, S., & McGuire, T.W. (1986). Group processes in computer-mediated communication. *Organizational Behavior and Human Decision Processes, 37,* 157–187.

Smith, A., & Duggan, M. (2013, October 21). *Online dating & relationships.* Retrieved from Pew Internet & American Life Project website: http://pewinternet.org/Reports/2013/Online-Dating.aspx.

Smith, S. W., & Wilson, S. R. (2009). *New directions in interpersonal communication research.* London: Sage Publications.

Sproull, L., & Kiesler, S. (1986). Reducing social context cues: Electronic mail in organizational communication. *Management Science, 32,* 1492–1512.

Sproull, L., Subramani, M., Kiesler, S., Walker, J. H., & Waters, K. (1996). When the interface is a face. *Human-Computer Interaction, 11,* 97–124.

St. John, W. (2002, April 12). Young, single and dating at hyperspeed. *The New York Times.* Retrieved from http://www.nytimes.com.

Steckenfinger, S. A. & Ghazanfar, A. A. (2009). Monkey visual behavior falls into the uncanny valley. *Proceedings of the National Academy of Science USA, 106,* 18362–18366.

Sung, Y., Moon, J. H., Kang, M., & Lin, J.-S. (2011). Actual self vs. avatar self: The effect of online social situation on self-expression. *Journal of Virtual Worlds Research, 4,* 3–21.

Tinwell, A. & Grimshaw, M. (2009). Bridging the uncanny: An impossible traverse? In *Proceedings of the 13th International MindTrek Conference: Everyday Life in the Ubiquitous Era (pp. 66–73).* New York, NY: ACM.

Tinwell, A., Grimshaw, M., Nabi, D. A., & Williams, A. (2011). Facial expression of emotion and perception of the Uncanny Valley in virtual characters. *Computers in Human Behavior, 27*, 741–749.

Trepte, S., Reinecke, L., & Behr, K. (2009). Creating virtual alter egos or superheroines? Gamers' strategies of avatar creation in terms of gender and sex. *International Journal of Gaming and Computer-Mediated Simulations, 1*, 52–76.

Trepte, S., Reinecke, L., & Behr, K.-M. (2011). Playing myself or playing to win? Gamers' strategies ofavatar creation in terms of gender and sex. In R. E. Ferdig (Ed.), *Discoveries in gaming and computer-mediated simulations: New interdisciplinary applications* (pp. 329–352). Hershey, PA:IGI Global.

Vang, M. H. & Fox, J. (2014). Race in virtual environments: Competitive versus cooperative games with black or white avatars. *Cyberpsychology, Behavior, and Social Networking, 17*(4), 235–240.

Van Mulken, S., Andre, E., & Müller, J. (1999). An empirical study on the trustworthiness of life-like interface agents. In H.-J. Bullinger & J. Ziegler (Eds), *Human computer interaction* (pp. 152–156). Mahwah, New Jersey: Lawrence Erlbaum Associates.

Vasalou, A. & Joinson, A. N. (2009). Me, myself and I: The role of interactional context on self-presentation through avatars. *Computers in Human Behavior, 25*, 510–520.

Villani, D., Gatti, E., Confalonieri, E., & Riva, G. (2012). Am I my avatar? A tool to investigate virtual body image representation in adolescence. *Cyberpsychology, Behavior, and Social Networking, 15*, 435–440.

Von der Pütten, A., & Krämer, N. (2012). A survey on robot appearances. In *Proceedings of the 7th annual ACM/IEEE International Conference on Human-Robot Interaction* (pp. 267–268). New York, NY: ACM.

Vujović, L., Tsankova, E., Kappas, A., & Küster, D. (2011, August). *Avatars in a "nonymous" vs. anonymous online setting.* Poster presented at the 7th Conference of the Media Psychology Division of the Deutsche Gesellschaft für Psychologie, Bremen, Germany.

Walters, M. L., Syrdal, D. S., Dautenhahn, K., Boekhorst, R. T., & Koay, K. L. (2008). Avoiding the Uncanny Valley – Robot appearance, personality and consistency of behavior in an attention-seeking home scenario for a robot companion. *Journal of Autonomous Robots, 24*, 159–178.

Walther, J. B. (1992). Interpersonal effects in computer-mediated interaction: A relational perspective. *Communication Research, 19*, 52–90.

Walther, J. B. (2011). Visual cues in computer-mediated communication: Sometimes less is more. In A. Kappas & N.C. Krämer (Eds) *Face-to-face communication over the Internet. Emotions in a web of culture, language and technology* (pp. 17–38). Cambridge: Cambridge University Press.

Walther, J. B., & Ramirez, A., Jr. (2010). New technologies and new directions in online relating. In S. W. Smith & S. R. Wilson (Eds), *New directions in interpersonal communication research* (264–284). London: Sage Publications.

Whitty, M. T. (2008). Revealing the 'real' me, searching for the 'actual' you: Presentations of self on an internet dating site. *Computers in Human Behavior, 24*, 1707–1723.

Willis, J. & Todorov, A. (2006). First impressions: Making up your mind after a 100-ms exposure to a face. *Psychological Science, 17*, 592–598.

Yoon, G. & Vargas, P. T. (2014). Know thy avatar: The unintended effect of virtual-self representation on behavior. *Psychological Science*. Advance online publication. doi: 10.1177/0956797613519271

Zhao, S., Grasmuck, S., & Martin, J. (2008). Identity construction on Facebook: Digital empowerment in anchored relationships. *Computers in Human Behavior, 24*, 1816–1836.

Zimmerman, J., Ayoob, E., Forlizzi, J., & McQuaid, M. (2005). Putting a face on embodied interface agents. In S. Wensveen (Ed.), *Proceedings of Designing Pleasurable Products and Interfaces Conference* (pp. 233–248). Eindhoven, The Netherlands: Eindhoven Technical University Press.

Author Index

Subject Index

age differences, 122
Duchenne smile, of, 114–130
face, 2, 32–49, 53
identity, 32, 35
peripheral nerves, 9
personal identity nodes, 43
personal sensible behavioral
    non-activities, 252
  silence and stillness, 252
  static bodily characteristics, 252
personal sensible nonbehavioral
    activities, 251–252
  chemical reactions, 251
  dermal reactions, 252
  thermal reactions, 252
personality, 3, 37, 41, 50, 97, 98, 99,
    190, 209, 212, 214, 215, 216, 220,
    225, 226, 227, 228, 230, 231, 232,
    233, 234, 235, 238, 239, 240, 250,
    255, 274, 275, 284, 285, 286, 287,
    288, 290, 291
  agreeableness, 120, 209, 229, 230,
    233
  conscientiousness, 121, 209, 215,
    226, 228, 229, 230, 232
  extraversion, 226, 228, 229, 230,
    232, 233
  neuroticism, 145, 198, 207, 209,
    215, 229, 230, 232
  openness to experience, 230
  self-monitoring, 226
pharyngeal arches, 14–15, 73
pharynx, *see also* pharyngeal arches,
    14, 15, 19
phenotypic markers, 47
pheromones, 2, 4, 32, 44, 48, 56, 173,
    177, 178, 179, 188
  androstadienone, 177, 179
  gonadotropin releasing hormaone
    (GnRH), 177
  primer, 178
physiological arousal, 47, 174, 179
pi statistic, 101
pitch, *see* fundamental frequency
Pleasure-Arousability-Dominance
    (PAD) Temperament Model,
    207–212
Pleasure-Arousal-Dominance (PAD)
    Emotion Model, 199–207

Point Counter Point, 263
politeness, 187–188, 276
political campaigns, 198–216
  age-based affinities, 211
  gender-based affinities, 211–212
  political candidates, 5, 212
  voter temperament, 209–211
  voter turnout, 198, 214
political participation, 198, 214, 216
positive and negative affect scale
    (PANAS), 201
positron emission tomography (PET),
    32, 47, 54
post-traumatic stress disorder (PTSD),
    141, 143
postural change, 229
postures, 4, 9, 10, 14, 38, 52, 74, 75,
    76, 173, 191, 252, 255, 258, 262
  crouch, 21, 71, 72, 73, 77, 85
poverty, 199, 205
pre-statement, *see also* pauses, 268
prosody, 20, 50, 93
prosopagnosia, 33
proto-languages, 51
proxemics, 165, 249
psychopathology, 213
PTSD, *see* post traumatic stress
    disorder

R
race, 42, 99, 157, 191, 192, 225, 227,
    238, 240, 284
  black, 157, 208, 227, 236
  white, 157, 208, 227, 236, 237
receptors, 10, 45
  5–hydroxytryptamine (5–HT), 45
  postsynaptic, 45
  sex steroid, 45
reciprocity, 5, 162, 188, 189, 190, 193,
    276
Reef, The, 252, 256, 257, 259, 263
reflexes
  muscular stretch, 72
  spinal cord, 72, 73, 74
  startle, 10
  subcortical, 2, 27
  tactile-withdrawal, 12, 21, 72
regional cerebral blood flow (rCBF), 32
relational demise, 169

Printed and bound by CPI Group (UK) Ltd, Croydon, CR0 4YY